1001
One Pot, Casseroles,
Soups & Stews

1001
One Pot, Casseroles,
Soups & Stews

This edition published in 2012
LOVE FOOD is an imprint of Parragon Books Ltd

Parragon
Queen Street House
4 Queen Street
Bath BA1 1HE, UK

www.parragon.com/lovefood

ISBN: 978-1-4454-5778-9
Printed in China

Created and produced by Ivy Contract
New recipes by Judith Wills

Notes for the Reader
This book uses both metric and imperial measurements. Follow the same
units of measurement throughout; do not mix metric and imperial. All spoon
measurements are level: teaspoons are assumed to be 5 ml, and tablespoons are
assumed to be 15 ml. Unless otherwise stated, milk is assumed to be full fat, eggs
and individual vegetables are medium, and pepper is freshly ground black pepper.

The times given are an approximate guide only. Preparation times differ according
to the techniques used by different people and the cooking times may also vary
from those given. Optional ingredients, variations or serving suggestions have not
been included in the calculations.

Recipes using raw or very lightly cooked eggs should be avoided by infants, the
elderly, pregnant women, convalescents and anyone suffering from an illness.
Pregnant and breastfeeding women are advised to avoid eating peanuts and peanut
products. Sufferers from nut allergies should be aware that some of the ready-
made ingredients used in the recipes in this book may contain nuts. Always check
the packaging before use.

Vegetarians should be aware that some of the ready-made ingredients used in the
recipes in this book may contain animal products. Always check the packaging
before use.

Contents

Introduction 6

Soups 10

Meat and Poultry 52

Fish and Seafood 148

Rice and Pasta 190

Vegetarian 236

Desserts 284

Index 300

Introduction

Making cooking more simple

You don't need a lot of equipment – or several hobs, or a great deal of expertise – to produce delicious and satisfying meals, snacks and desserts at home. For many meals, all you really need is one pot to cook up a delightful meal which doesn't take too much hovering over, or time spent in the kitchen. There are many ways that one-pot cooking can help today's busy cooks.

It can save time

Most of the recipes in this book can be cooked in just one pot. Cooking your meal in fewer pans means you have less to keep your eye on and many of the meals can be left to look after themselves in the oven or on the hob until they are ready to eat.

This style of cooking is usually simple so it can also save on preparation time. Sometimes one-pot cooking itself can be very quick indeed – for example, stir-frying takes only minutes.

It can save money

If you are using the oven, you can cook other dishes, such as a dessert or bread, at the same time to reduce your energy bills. One-pot cooking can also mean slow cooking, which means that cheaper cuts of meat, such as mince or stewing steak, or cheap items such as dried pulses and grains, can be used.

It is easy

The method is adaptable and forgiving so that, in most cases, you don't need to be all that exact with your quantities or timings. And if one ingredient isn't available or you simply don't like it, you can easily swap it for another. Most of the recipes in this book are easy to follow with no complicated instructions.

It is tasty and good for you

One-pot suppers, cooked with their own liquid or sauce, herbs or spices, and vegetables, meat, etc., all in one pot, means that the flavour is contained and retained – nothing is wasted, and

the cooking liquid is rich in taste and full of vitamins, minerals and healthy antioxidants, which are often thrown away with the cooking water!

The equipment you will need:

Good quality pots

If cooking for a family, you will need a large casserole pot. The ideal one is flameproof, so that you can put it on the hob as well as using it in the oven. Otherwise, you will need separate pans for hob and oven if, for example, you want to brown your meat on the hob before adding it to a casserole. An additional small- to medium-sized pot is also a good idea, which is ideal for side vegetables or when there are only two of you for a meal.

Good quality saucepans

Heavy-based saucepans are a wise purchase as they will last longer and help prevent burning. You will need saucepans in several sizes so it is best to buy a complete set.

Good quality frying pans

You will use these all the time – so a small one (for cooking when you are on your own, for example), a medium one (for example, for omelettes or cooking for two) and a large one (for family cooking) are ideal. Try to buy pans with handles not made of metal so that they won't be too hot to pick up.

Ovenproof dishes/gratin dishes

You will need a set of shallow ovenproof dishes – for gratins, vegetable dishes, puddings – and one or two deeper ones, for crumbles and pies.

Utensils

You'll find you use spoons of all sizes, for measuring and stirring and transferring. A soup ladle is important and you will need good quality sharp knives in two or three different sizes for the preparation of vegetables, meat and so on. Spatulas, both with and without slots, are essential.

Other equipment

Oven gloves are vital, as are baking trays, a chopping board for meat and another for vegetables, and a grater. If you buy only one piece of electric equipment choose a blender, which can be used for puréeing soups and vegetables and also for chopping breadcrumbs; some come with a small goblet ideal for chopping herbs.

The ingredients you will need most often

While the recipes in this book cover a wide spectrum of world cuisines, tastes, and different types of food and meal occasion, there are certain items that tend to crop up again and again, and if you have a well-stocked larder and freezer you will find it much easier to rustle up a really tasty pot of food. Here is a blueprint list of items to consider:

Larder

Pasta – a small selection of different shapes (for example, macaroni for soups and bakes, spaghetti for serving with a sauce, and lasagne sheets for lasagne).

Rice – buy good quality rice, which is easier to cook well. The basic is a long-grain rice such as basmati, but you may also consider brown rice which has a nutty flavour, jasmine rice for Thai dishes, and paella/risotto rice for those dishes. For an easy oven dessert you might like pudding rice.

Couscous – the instant variety is a boon for serving with stews and casseroles when they contain no starch element (for example, no potatoes or pasta in the pan).

Other grains – your cooking will be more interesting if you try some of the less usual grains, such as bulgar wheat, pearl and pot barley and spelt, in your recipes; they are all easy to cook.

Pulses – use dried pulses if you don't mind the overnight soaking required in most cases, or canned otherwise. Examples of some often-used pulses include red, green and brown lentils, kidney beans, cannellini beans, chick peas and borlotti beans.

Flours – go for plain white flour (you can always add baking powder if necessary for making sponges, etc.) for thickening stews and making sauces, and wholemeal flour for a nutty flavour in a cobbler topping or pastry.

Spices – essential for many of the recipes in this book, spices add so much flavour to one-pot cooking. Either buy whole spices and grind them yourself as necesssary, or buy small amounts of ready-ground spices, as they don't tend to keep well for more than a few months. Put them in opaque containers away from light and heat.

Herbs – again, these are essential in the kitchen. Buy them dried in small amounts and don't keep them in glass jars in the hot, light kitchen – they will deteriorate rapidly! Use fresh herbs when you can, which normally have the most flavour and a better colour.

Oils and vinegars – the basics are olive oil and groundnut (peanut) oil, the latter being especially good for Asian-inspired dishes. Red, white and balsamic vinegars all have different uses and are a sensible addition to your larder.

The techniques you will use

Most one-pot recipes are suitable for novice cooks so there is little to worry about as you will not need to know or use any complicated or expert techniques.

Casseroles and stews – and often, soups – usually involve softening and/or browning vegetables and sometimes meat and poultry too, and then adding liquid and flavourings and allowing your meal to cook for a fairly long time, usually at a low to medium heat. Casseroles are ideal in winter, and when you want inexpensive food that will take care of itself. Some of the best are those that include protein (meat, lentils, etc.), vegetables and carbohydrate (potatoes, pasta, etc.) all in the one pan. Otherwise, you can serve the meal with a side salad and/or bread.

Stir fries are at the other end of the spectrum. You prepare everything for your stir fry before you begin cooking, usually thinly slicing vegetables, meat, etc., so that they cook quickly; lay everything out in the order you will need it to make life easy and then cook, stirring constantly, over high heat. Stir fries are ideal for when you want a meal in a hurry and don't want to use the oven.

Some dishes involve other techniques such as making a sauce in a frying pan to go with pasta or rice – or making a stock for a soup.

Many basic items such as stocks, sauces and soups will freeze – so if you have large enough pans and plenty of freezerproof containers it is wise to make double the quantities or even more, and freeze the surplus.

Canned vegetables and fruits – canned tomatoes are essential and are used in many dishes, while canned sweetcorn is also a good stand-by. Some fruits can well – pineapple, mandarin oranges, pears and prunes are good when you can't get fresh.

Purées, pastes and pestos – you will certainly need tomato purée, while other very good storecupboard stand-bys include sun-dried tomato paste, olive paste (tapenade), ready-to-use garlic purée and ready-to-use chopped ginger. Don't forget some ready-made basil pesto, too.

Sauces – soy sauce, Worcestershire sauce and fish sauce all add flavour to casseroles and stir-fries. And you will need a range of stock cubes.

Canned fish – tuna, mackerel, anchovies and sardines are all useful to have in the storecupboard.

Freezer

Use your freezer in two ways – to store items that you are going to use in your cooking, and to freeze meals that you have cooked in quantity to use another time. Your freezer can save you a lot of money. Items to freeze fresh to use later include:

Vegetables – most need peeling, chopping and blanching in boiling water for two minutes before freezing in bags.

Fruits – larger fruits need preparing, chopping and bagging, while others such as berries can be frozen as they are, on open trays, and then bagged.

Meats and poultry – chop if necessary, then bag and label clearly, taking care the bag is strong and well sealed to prevent freezer burn.

Fish – make sure the fish is suitable to freeze (fish that has been frozen and thawed before purchase cannot be refrozen – ask the fishmonger), and then proceed as for meats.

Bread – a few different types of bread (for example white, wholemeal, rye, ciabatta, French and small rolls) are very handy additions to the freezer. Bag, seal, label and freeze, and use within three months.

You can also freeze butter, cream, soft and hard cheeses, double cream, crème fraîche and even milk.

Fridge

The fridge is the place to store fresh fruit (even bananas, contrary to what you may have heard), salad leaves, green leafy vegetables such as spinach and cabbage, and dairy produce that you are currently using. Don't keep too much of anything in the fridge – produce will tend to deteriorate and you want to avoid throwing food away. Eggs can be stored at room temperature if you like.

Recipes

Vegetable stock

Makes approx. 1 litre/1¾ pints
2 onions
2 carrots
2 leeks
3 sticks celery
1 bouquet garni
1 tbsp black peppercorns
1 tsp salt

Peel and chop all the vegetables and put into a large saucepan with the remaining ingredients. Add water to cover.
　Bring to simmer and cook for 1½ hours. Strain.

Chicken stock

While raw chicken makes the best stock (ask your butcher to remove the breast and leg meat for another dish), you can make a very passable one using a leftover roast chicken carcass.

Makes approx. 1 litre/1¾ pint
1 chicken carcass
2 carrots
2 onions
2 sticks celery
1 leek
4 whole garlic cloves
1 tbsp black peppercorns
1 bouquet garni
1 tsp salt

Put carcass in a large saucepan and add cold water to cover. Add chopped carrots, onions, celery and leek with the remaining ingredients.
　Bring to a boil and skim off the surface scum. Turn down heat and simmer for 40 minutes. Strain. Will keep in a lidded container in the fridge for 1–2 days, or freeze.

Beef/lamb stock

While raw bones make the best stock, you can also use leftover bones and meat from a roast.

Makes approx. 1 litre/1¾ pint
approx. 1.3 kg (3 lb) meat bones
2 onions
2 carrots
4 sticks celery
1 bouquet garni
1 tbsp black peppercorns
1 tsp salt

Put the meat bones in a large saucepan and add cold water to cover. Bring to a simmer, skim off any scum and cook for 1 hour. Peel and chop vegetables and add to the pan with the remaining ingredients and simmer for a further 1½ hours. Strain.

Fish stock

When you buy whole fish, use the bones and trimmings to make stock. White fish is preferable to oily fish.

Makes approx. 600 ml/1 pint
approx. 550 g (1lb 4oz)
   trimmings from white fish
2 sticks celery
1 onion
1 carrot
½ tsp salt
1 tsp whole black peppercorns
1 small bay leaf
several sprigs of parsley

Put the fish trimmings in a saucepan and add cold water to cover. Add peeled, chopped vegetables and the remaining ingredients. Bring to a simmer, skim off any scum that forms, then cook for 20 minutes.
   Strain through a fine sieve (beware of any tiny bones). Use within 24 hours or freeze.

Béchamel sauce

This is a basic white sauce recipe to which you can add cheese, parsley, or onions.

Makes 400 ml/14 fl oz
25 g (1 oz) butter
1 tbsp plain flour
350 ml (12 fl oz) warm milk
salt and pepper

Melt the butter in a pan over a low heat. Add the flour and stir with a wooden spoon. Turn the heat up a little and continue stirring for 2 minutes.
   Turn the heat to medium. Add 50 ml of the milk and stir thoroughly until you have a smooth paste. Gradually add the remaining milk, stirring, until you have a smooth white sauce. Season.

Tomato sauce

Makes approx. 500 ml/18 fl oz
1 tbsp olive oil
1 small onion, chopped
2–3 garlic cloves, crushed
1 celery stick, finely chopped
1 bay leaf
450 g/1lb ripe tomatoes, peeled
   and chopped
1 tbsp tomato purée
few fresh oregano sprigs
pepper

Heat the oil in a heavy-bottom saucepan. Add the onion, garlic, celery, and bay leaf, and gently sauté, stirring frequently, for 5 minutes. Pour in the tomatoes and the tomato purée. Season with pepper to taste and add the oregano. Bring to a boil, then reduce the heat, cover, and simmer, stirring occasionally, for 20–25 minutes, until the tomatoes have completely collapsed. Discard the bay leaf and the oregano. Transfer to a food processor and process until a chunky purée forms. Taste and adjust the seasoning, if necessary.

Basic pasta dough

Serves 3–4
200 g/7oz white bread flour
1 tsp salt
1 tbsp olive oil
2 eggs, lightly beaten

Lightly dust a counter with flour. Sift the flour and salt into a mound and make a well in the centre. Add the oil and beaten eggs and work to form a stiff dough. If necessary, add 2–3 tablespoons of water to make the dough pliable. Knead the dough vigorously for 8–10 minutes until smooth, firm and soft. Wrap the dough in a plastic bag and leave to rest in the refrigerator for 30 minutes.
   Divide the dough into 2 equal pieces. Cover a counter with a clean cloth or dish towel and dust it liberally with flour. Place one portion of the dough on the floured cloth and roll it out as thinly and evenly as possible, stretching the dough gently until the pattern of the weave shows through. Alternatively, use a pasta machine to roll the dough.

Basic risotto

Serves 4
1 tbsp olive oil
3 tbsp butter
1 small onion, finely chopped
450 g/1 lb arborio rice
2 litres/3 ½ pints stock or water,
   simmering
55 g/2 oz freshly grated
   Parmesan cheese
pepper

Heat the oil with 2 tablespoons of the butter over a low heat until melted. Stir in the onion and cook gently until soft and golden. Add the rice and mix to coat in the oil and butter. Cook and stir for 2–3 minutes, or until the grains are translucent. Gradually add the stock, a ladle at a time. Stir constantly and add more liquid as the rice absorbs it. Increase the heat and cook for 20 minutes, or until all the liquid is absorbed. Season.
   Remove from the heat and add the Parmesan cheese and the remaining butter. Serve, garnished with Parmesan cheese shavings.

Soups

1 Potato & pesto soup

2 tbsp olive oil
3 rashers rindless, smoked bacon, finely chopped
25 g/1 oz butter
450 g/1 lb floury potatoes, chopped
450 g/1 lb onions, finely chopped
600 ml/1 pint chicken stock
600 ml/1 pint milk
100 g/3½ oz dried conchigliette
150 ml/5 fl oz double cream
2 tbsp chopped fresh parsley
2 tbsp pesto
salt and pepper
freshly grated Parmesan cheese, to serve

Heat the oil in a large saucepan and cook the bacon over a medium heat for 4 minutes. Add the butter, potatoes and onions and cook for 12 minutes, stirring constantly. Add the stock and milk, bring to the boil and simmer for 5 minutes. Add the conchigliette and simmer for a further 3–4 minutes. Blend in the cream and simmer for 5 minutes. Add the parsley, salt and pepper to taste and pesto. Transfer the soup to individual serving bowls and serve with Parmesan cheese.

 ## 2 Potato, chicken & red pesto soup

Replace the bacon with 100 g/3½ oz cooked chopped chicken, added to the pan with the stock; replace the pesto with 2 tablespoons of red pepper pesto.

3 Beef & bean soup

2 tbsp vegetable oil
1 large onion, finely chopped
2 garlic cloves, finely chopped
1 green pepper, deseeded and sliced
2 carrots, sliced
400 g/14 oz canned black-eyed beans
225 g/8 oz fresh beef mince
1 tsp each ground cumin, chilli powder and paprika
¼ cabbage, sliced
225 g/8 oz tomatoes, peeled and chopped
600 ml/1 pint beef stock
salt and pepper

Heat the oil in a large saucepan over a medium heat. Add the onion and garlic and cook, stirring frequently, for 3 minutes, or until softened. Add the green pepper and carrots and cook for a further 5 minutes. Meanwhile, drain the beans, reserving the liquid from the can. Place two thirds of the beans, reserving the remainder, in a food processor or blender with the bean liquid and process until smooth. Add the beef to the saucepan and cook, stirring constantly, until well browned. Add the spices and cook, stirring, for 2 minutes. Add the cabbage, tomatoes, stock and puréed beans and season to taste. Bring to the boil, then reduce the heat, cover and simmer for 15 minutes, or until the vegetables are tender. Stir in the reserved beans, cover and simmer for a further 5 minutes. Ladle into warmed soup bowls and serve.

 ## 4 Beef & red lentil soup

Replace the black-eyed beans with 400 g/14 oz canned red lentils.

BEEF STOCK

550 g/1 lb 4 oz boneless beef shin or
    stewing steak, cut into large cubes
750 g/1 lb 10 oz veal, beef or pork bones
2 onions, quartered
2.5 litres/4¹/₂ pints water
4 garlic cloves, sliced
2 carrots, sliced
1 large leek, sliced
1 celery stick, cut into 5-cm/2.5-inch pieces
1 bay leaf

4–5 sprigs of fresh thyme,
    or ¹/₄ tsp dried thyme
salt and pepper

200 g/7 oz celeriac, peeled and finely diced
2 large carrots, finely diced
2 tsp chopped fresh marjoram leaves
2 tsp chopped fresh parsley
2 plum tomatoes, skinned,
    deseeded and diced
salt and pepper

Preheat the oven to 190°C/375°F/Gas Mark 5. To make the stock, trim as much fat as possible from the beef and put in a large roasting tin with the bones and onions. Roast in a preheated oven for 30–40 minutes until browned, turning once or twice. Transfer the ingredients to a large flameproof casserole and discard the fat.

Add the water (it should cover by at least 5 cm/2 inches) and bring to the boil. Skim off any foam that rises to the surface. Reduce the heat and add the garlic, carrots, leek, celery, bay leaf, thyme and a pinch of salt. Simmer very gently, uncovered, for 4 hours, skimming occasionally. Do not stir. If the ingredients emerge from the liquid, then top up with more water.

Gently ladle the stock through a muslin-lined sieve into a large container and remove as much fat as possible. Save the meat for another purpose, if wished, and discard the bones and vegetables. (There should be about 2 litres/3¹/₂ pints of stock.)

Boil the stock very gently until it is reduced to 1.5 litres/2³/₄ pints, or if the stock already has concentrated flavour, measure out that amount and save the rest for another purpose. Taste the stock and adjust the seasoning if necessary.

Bring a saucepan of salted water to the boil and drop in the celeriac and carrots. Reduce the heat, cover and boil gently for about 15 minutes until tender. Drain. Add the marjoram and parsley to the boiling beef stock. Divide the cooked vegetables and diced tomatoes among warmed bowls, ladle over the boiling stock and serve.

3 tbsp olive oil
500 g/1 lb 2 oz boneless stewing beef, cut into 2.5-cm/1-inch pieces
150 ml/5 fl oz red wine
1 onion, finely chopped
1 green pepper, deseeded and finely chopped
1 small fresh red chilli, deseeded and finely chopped
2 garlic cloves, finely chopped
1 carrot, finely chopped
¼ tsp ground coriander
¼ tsp ground cumin
⅛ tsp ground cinnamon
¼ tsp dried oregano
1 bay leaf
grated rind of ½ orange
400 g/14 oz canned chopped tomatoes
1.2 litres/2 pints beef stock
50 g/1¾ oz long-grain white rice
25 g/1 oz raisins
15 g/½ oz plain chocolate, melted
chopped fresh coriander, to garnish

Heat half the oil in a large frying pan over a medium–high heat.

Add the meat in one layer and cook until well browned, turning to colour all sides. Remove the pan from the heat and pour in the wine.

Heat the remaining oil in a large saucepan over a medium heat.

Add the onion, cover and cook for about 3 minutes, stirring occasionally, until just softened. Add the green pepper, chilli, garlic and carrot, and continue cooking, covered, for 3 minutes.

Add the coriander, cumin, cinnamon, oregano, bay leaf and orange rind. Stir in the tomatoes and stock, along with the beef and wine. Bring almost to the boil and when the mixture begins to bubble, reduce the heat to low. Cover and simmer gently, stirring occasionally, for about 1 hour until the meat is tender.

Stir in the rice, raisins and chocolate, and continue cooking, stirring occasionally, for about 30 minutes until the rice is tender.

Ladle into warmed bowls and garnish with coriander.

7 *Mexican-style beef & bean soup*

Omit the rice and add 150 g/5 oz canned, drained red kidney beans to the pot with the raisins and chocolate.

8 *Mexican-style chicken soup*

Replace the beef with 8 skinless chicken thigh fillets, cooking only lightly in the pan until barely golden. Replace the red wine with white wine and the beef stock with chicken stock.

9 *Spicy beef & noodle soup* SERVES 4

1 litre/1¾ pints beef stock
150 ml/5 fl oz vegetable or groundnut oil
85 g/3 oz rice vermicelli noodles
2 shallots, thinly sliced
2 garlic cloves, crushed
2.5-cm/1-inch piece fresh ginger, thinly sliced
225-g/8-oz piece fillet steak, cut into thin strips
2 tbsp green curry paste
2 tbsp Thai soy sauce
1 tbsp fish sauce
chopped fresh coriander, to garnish

Pour the stock into a large saucepan and bring to the boil. Meanwhile, heat the oil in a wok or large frying pan. Add a third of the noodles and fry for 10–20 seconds, until they have puffed up. Lift out with tongs, drain on kitchen paper and set aside. Discard all but 2 tablespoons of the oil.

Add the shallots, garlic and ginger to the wok or frying pan and stir-fry for 1 minute. Add the steak and curry paste and stir-fry for a further 3–4 minutes, until tender.

Add the steak mixture, the uncooked noodles, soy sauce and fish sauce to the saucepan of stock and simmer for 2–3 minutes, until the noodles have swelled. Serve hot, garnished with the chopped coriander and the reserved crispy noodles.

10 *Spicy turkey & noodle soup*

When making the soup use chicken stock rather than beef stock; use 225 g/ 8 oz turkey breast fillets, cut into strips, instead of the steak.

11 Chicken & potato soup with bacon

1 tbsp butter
2 garlic cloves, chopped
1 onion, sliced
250 g/9 oz smoked lean back
    bacon, chopped
2 large leeks, sliced
2 tbsp plain flour

1 litre/1¾ pints chicken stock
800 g/1 lb 12 oz potatoes, chopped
200 g/7 oz skinless chicken breast, chopped
4 tbsp double cream
salt and pepper
grilled bacon and sprigs of fresh flat-leaf
    parsley, to garnish

Melt the butter in a large saucepan over a medium heat. Add the garlic and onion and cook, stirring, for 3 minutes, until slightly softened. Add the chopped bacon and leeks and cook for a further 3 minutes, stirring.

In a bowl, mix the flour with enough stock to make a smooth paste, then stir it into the pan. Cook, stirring, for 2 minutes. Pour in the remaining stock, then add the potatoes and chicken. Season with salt and pepper. Bring to the boil, then lower the heat and simmer for 25 minutes, until the chicken and potatoes are tender and cooked through. Stir in the cream and cook for a further 2 minutes, then remove from the heat and ladle into serving bowls. Garnish with the grilled bacon and flat-leaf parsley, and serve immediately.

12 Bean & potato soup with bacon

Omit the chicken breasts. Add 250 g/9 oz shelled weight broad beans, fresh or frozen, defrosted, at the same time as the potatoes.

13 Chicken & potato soup with croûtons

Omit the bacon garnish. Toast 2 slices of bread, drizzle with olive oil then rub with a peeled clove of garlic. Cut into small cubes and toss over the soup.

14 Chicken noodle soup

2 skinless chicken breasts
1.2 litres/2 pints water or chicken stock
3 carrots, peeled and sliced into
    5-mm/¼-inch slices

85 g/3 oz vermicelli
    (or other thin noodles)
salt and pepper
fresh tarragon leaves, to garnish

Place the chicken breasts in a large saucepan, add the water and bring to a simmer. Cook for 25–30 minutes. Skim any foam from the surface if necessary. Remove the chicken breasts from the stock and keep warm. Continue to simmer the stock, add the carrots and vermicelli and cook for 4–5 minutes. Thinly shred the chicken breasts and place in warmed serving dishes. Season the soup to taste with salt and pepper and pour over the chicken. Serve immediately, garnished with the tarragon.

15 Pork noodle soup

Replace the chicken breasts with 250 g/9 oz leftover roast pork. Omit the first step and simply simmer the stock with the carrots and vermicelli, adding the thinly sliced pork for the last minute to warm through.

25 g/1 oz butter
1 small onion, finely chopped
1 leek, thinly sliced
4 skinless, boneless chicken thighs, diced
25 g/1 oz long-grain rice

850 ml/1½ pints chicken stock
1 tbsp chopped fresh flat-leaf parsley
salt and pepper
fresh parsley sprigs, to garnish
bread, to serve

Melt the butter in a large heavy-based saucepan. Add the onion and leek and cook over a low heat, stirring occasionally, for 5 minutes, or until softened. Add the chicken and cook over a medium heat for 2 minutes.

Add the rice and cook, stirring constantly, for 1 minute, or until the grains are coated with butter. Pour in the stock, bring to the boil, reduce the heat and simmer gently for 20 minutes, or until the chicken and rice are tender.

Stir in the chopped parsley and season the soup to taste with salt and pepper.

Ladle into warmed bowls, garnish with parsley sprigs and serve immediately with bread.

17 *Chicken & barley soup*

Replace the rice with 25 g/1 oz pearl barley.

---

1 tbsp olive oil
1 tbsp butter
3 boneless, skinless chicken breasts, cubed
2 small leeks, green part included,
    thinly sliced
1 small butternut squash, cut into
    2-cm/¾-inch cubes
1 small green chilli (optional), deseeded
    and very finely chopped

400 g/14 oz canned chickpeas,
    drained and rinsed
¼ tsp ground cumin
1 litre/1¾ pints chicken stock
115 g/4 oz baby spinach,
    coarsely chopped
salt and pepper
warm crusty bread, to serve

19 *Chicken, squash & broccoli soup*

Replace the spinach with 115 g/4 oz broccoli, cut into small florets.
Add the broccoli to the soup after the stock has simmered for 10 minutes.

20 *Chicken, sweet potato & spinach soup*

Replace the squash with 300 g/10½ oz sweet potato, peeled and cut into 2-cm/¾-inch cubes.

Heat the oil and butter in a large saucepan over a medium–low heat. Add the chicken, leeks, squash and chilli, if using. Cover and cook for 5 minutes, stirring occasionally, until the vegetables are beginning to soften. Add the chickpeas, cumin, salt and pepper. Pour in the stock.

Bring to the boil, then simmer over a low heat for 20 minutes, or until the squash is tender. Stir in the spinach. Cook for a few more minutes until the spinach is just wilted, and serve with warm crusty bread while piping hot.

21 Cock-a-leekie soup

2 tbsp olive oil
2 onions, roughly chopped
2 carrots, roughly chopped
5 leeks, 2 roughly chopped,
    3 thinly sliced

1 chicken, weighing 1.3 kg/3 lb
2 bay leaves
6 prunes, sliced
salt and pepper
sprigs of fresh parsley, to garnish

Heat the oil in a large saucepan over a medium heat, then add the onions, carrots and the 2 roughly chopped leeks. Sauté for 3–4 minutes until just golden brown. Wipe the chicken inside and out and remove any excess skin and fat. Place the chicken in the saucepan with the cooked vegetables and add the bay leaves. Pour in enough cold water to just cover and season well with salt and pepper. Bring to the boil, reduce the heat, then cover and simmer for 1–1½ hours. From time to time, skim off any foam that forms.

Remove the chicken from the stock, remove and discard the skin, then remove all the meat. Cut the meat into neat pieces.

Strain the stock through a colander, discard the vegetables and bay leaves and return the stock to the rinsed-out saucepan. Expect to have 1.2–1.4 litres/2–2½ pints of stock. If you have time, it is a good idea to allow the stock to cool so that the fat may be removed. If not, blot the fat off the surface with pieces of kitchen paper. Heat the stock to simmering point, add the sliced leeks and prunes to the saucepan and heat for about 1 minute.

Return the chicken to the pan and heat through. Serve immediately in warmed deep dishes. Garnish with the parsley.

22 With rice

Some traditional Scottish recipes for Cock-a-leekie include rice as well. Add 25 g/1 oz rice to the pan for the last 30 minutes of cooking time. Other recipes do not include the prunes – omit these if preferred.

23 Cream of chicken soup

3 tbsp butter
4 shallots, chopped
1 leek, sliced
450 g/1 lb skinless chicken breasts,
    chopped
600 ml/1 pint chicken stock
1 tbsp chopped fresh parsley
1 tbsp chopped fresh thyme, plus extra
    sprigs to garnish
175 ml/6 fl oz double cream
salt and pepper

Melt the butter in a saucepan over a medium heat. Add the shallots and cook, stirring, for 3 minutes, until softened. Add the leek and cook for a further 5 minutes, stirring. Add the chicken, stock and herbs, and season. Bring to the boil, then simmer for 25 minutes, until the chicken is cooked through. Remove from the heat and leave to cool for 10 minutes.

Transfer the soup to a food processor or blender and process until smooth (you may need to do this in batches). Return the soup to the rinsed-out pan and warm over a low heat for 5 minutes.

Stir in the cream and cook for a further 2 minutes, then remove from the heat and ladle into serving bowls. Garnish with sprigs of thyme and serve immediately.

24 Lower-fat cream of chicken soup

Omit the double cream but replace half the chicken stock with semi-skimmed milk. The soup will still taste smooth and creamy.

115 g/4 oz dried vermicelli noodles
1.2 litres/2 pints chicken or
vegetable stock
1 lemon grass stalk, crushed
1-cm/½-inch piece fresh ginger,
peeled and very finely chopped
2 fresh kaffir lime leaves, thinly sliced
1 fresh red chilli, or to taste, deseeded
and thinly sliced
2 skinless, boneless chicken breasts,
thinly sliced
200 ml/7 fl oz coconut cream
2–3 tbsp nam pla (Thai fish sauce)
1–2 tbsp fresh lime juice
55 g/2 oz beansprouts
4 spring onions, green part only,
finely sliced
fresh coriander leaves, to garnish

Soak the dried noodles in a large bowl with enough lukewarm water to cover for 20 minutes, until soft. Or, cook according to the packet instructions. Drain well and set aside.

Meanwhile, bring the stock to the boil in a large saucepan over a high heat. Lower the heat, add the lemon grass, ginger, lime leaves and chilli and simmer gently for 5 minutes. Add the chicken and continue simmering for a further 3 minutes, or until cooked.

Stir in the coconut cream, nam pla and 1 tablespoon of lime juice and continue simmering for 3 minutes. Add the beansprouts and spring onions and simmer for a further 1 minute.

Taste and gradually add extra nam pla or lime juice, if needed. Remove and discard the lemon grass stalk.

Divide the vermicelli noodles between 4 bowls. Bring the soup back to the boil, then add to each bowl. The heat of the soup will warm the noodles. To garnish, sprinkle with coriander leaves.

100 g/3½ oz Yunnan ham or
ordinary ham, chopped
2 dried Chinese mushrooms, soaked
in warm water for 20 minutes
85 g/3 oz fresh or canned bamboo
shoots, rinsed (if using fresh shoots,
boil in water first for 30 minutes)
1 whole chicken
1 tbsp slivered spring onion
8 slices fresh ginger
225 g/8 oz lean pork, chopped
2 tsp Shaoxing rice wine
3 litres/5¼ pints water
2 tsp salt
300 g/10½ oz Chinese cabbage,
cut into large chunks

Blanch the ham in a large saucepan of boiling water for 30 seconds.

Skim the surface, then remove the ham and set aside. Squeeze out any excess water from the mushrooms, then finely slice and discard any tough stems. Chop the bamboo shoots into small cubes. Stuff the chicken with the spring onion and ginger. Put the chicken and all the ingredients except the cabbage in a casserole. Bring to the boil, then lower the heat and simmer, covered, for 1 hour. Add the cabbage and simmer for a further 3 minutes. Remove the chicken skin before serving, then place chunks of chicken meat in individual bowls, adding pieces of vegetable and the other meats, and pour the soup on top.

27 *Whole chicken & mushroom soup*

Omit the ham. Slice or tear 300 g/10½ oz mixed oriental mushrooms – e.g. shiitake, white and yellow oyster mushrooms, enoki – and add to the soup for the last 15 minutes of cooking time.

2 tsp butter
1 large leek, thinly sliced
2 shallots, finely chopped
125 ml/4 fl oz dry cider
300 ml/10 fl oz fish stock
250 g/9 oz potatoes, diced
1 bay leaf

4 tbsp plain flour
200 ml/7 fl oz milk
200 ml/7 fl oz double cream
55 g/2 oz fresh sorrel leaves
350 g/12 oz skinless monkfish or cod
    fillet, cut into 2.5-cm/1-inch pieces
salt and pepper

Melt the butter in a large saucepan over a medium–low heat. Add the leek and shallots and cook for about 5 minutes, stirring frequently, until they start to soften. Add the cider and bring to the boil.

Stir in the stock, potatoes and bay leaf with a large pinch of salt (unless the stock is salty) and bring back to the boil. Reduce the heat, cover and cook gently for 10 minutes. Put the flour in a small bowl and very slowly whisk in a few tablespoons of the milk to make a thick paste. Stir in a little more milk to make a smooth liquid.

Adjust the heat so the soup bubbles gently. Stir in the flour mixture and cook, stirring frequently, for 5 minutes. Add the remaining milk and half the cream. Continue cooking for about 10 minutes until the potatoes are tender.

Chop the sorrel finely and combine with the remaining cream. (If using a food processor, add the sorrel and chop, then add the cream and process briefly.)

Stir the sorrel cream into the soup and add the fish. Continue cooking, stirring occasionally, for about 3 minutes, until the monkfish stiffens or the cod just begins to flake. Taste the soup and adjust the seasoning, if needed. Ladle the soup into warmed bowls and serve.

29 *Mixed Breton soup with wine*

Replace the cider with dry white French wine. Replace the sorrel with 25 g/ 1 oz chopped fresh parsley. Use two varieties of white fish – choose from hake, haddock, bass, halibut or cod – and mackerel fillet, in the proportion of 3:1. Mackerel fillets are used in many traditional soups made in Brittany.

30 *Duck with spring onion soup* SERVES 2

2 duck breasts, skin on
2 tbsp red curry paste
2 tbsp vegetable or groundnut oil
bunch of spring onions, chopped
2 garlic cloves, crushed
5-cm/2-inch piece fresh ginger, grated
2 carrots, thinly sliced

1 red pepper, deseeded and cut into strips
1 litre/1¾ pints chicken stock
2 tbsp sweet chilli sauce
3–4 tbsp Thai soy sauce
400 g/14 oz canned straw
    mushrooms, drained

Slash the skin of the duck 3–4 times with a sharp knife and rub in the curry paste. Cook the duck breasts, skin-side down, in a wok or frying pan over a high heat for 2–3 minutes. Turn over, reduce the heat and cook for a further 3–4 minutes, until cooked through. Lift out and slice thickly. Set aside and keep warm. Meanwhile, heat the oil in a wok or large frying pan and stir-fry half the spring onions, the garlic, ginger, carrots and red pepper for 2–3 minutes. Pour in the stock and add the chilli sauce, soy sauce and mushrooms. Bring to the boil and simmer for 4–5 minutes. Ladle the soup into warmed bowls, top with the duck slices and garnish with the remaining spring onions. Serve immediately.

31 *Chicken with spring onion soup*

Replace the duck breasts with chicken breast fillets, skin-on. You can also use guinea fowl breasts in this recipe.

3 tbsp vegetable oil
1 tsp cumin seeds, crushed
1 tsp dried thyme or oregano
1 onion, diced
½ green pepper, deseeded and diced
1 sweet potato, diced
2–3 fresh green chillies,
    deseeded and very finely chopped
1 garlic clove, very finely chopped

1 litre/1¾ pints chicken stock
400 g/14 oz red snapper
    fillets, skinned and cut into chunks
25 g/1 oz frozen peas
25 g/1 oz frozen sweetcorn
125 ml/4 fl oz single cream
salt and pepper
3 tbsp chopped fresh coriander, to
    garnish

Heat the oil with the cumin seeds and thyme in a large saucepan over a medium heat. Add the onion, green pepper, sweet potato, chillies and garlic and cook, stirring constantly, for 1 minute. Reduce the heat to medium–low, cover and cook for 10 minutes, or until beginning to soften. Pour in the stock and season generously with salt and pepper. Bring to the boil, then reduce the heat to low-medium, cover and simmer for 20 minutes. Add the snapper, peas, sweetcorn and cream. Cook over a low heat, uncovered and without boiling, for 7–10 minutes until the fish is just cooked. Serve immediately, garnished with chopped coriander.

33 *Caribbean red fish chowder*

Replace the onion with red onion; green pepper and chilli with red pepper and chilli. Add 1 teaspoon of sweet ground paprika to the pan before pouring in the stock – stir for a few seconds. Omit the peas and increase amount of sweetcorn to 50 g/2 oz.

4 tsp butter
1 large onion, finely chopped
1 small carrot, finely diced
3 tbsp plain flour
300 ml/10 fl oz fish stock
200 ml/7 fl oz water
450 g/1 lb potatoes, diced

125 g/4½ oz cooked or defrosted
    frozen sweetcorn
450 ml/16 fl oz full-fat milk
280 g/10 oz canned clams,
    drained and rinsed
salt and pepper
chopped fresh parsley, to garnish

Melt the butter in a large saucepan over a medium–low heat. Add the onion and carrot and cook for 3–4 minutes, stirring frequently, until the onion is softened. Stir in the flour and continue cooking for 2 minutes.

Slowly add about half the stock and stir well, scraping the bottom of the pan to mix in the flour. Pour in the remaining stock and the water and bring to the boil, stirring.

Add the potatoes, sweetcorn and milk and stir to combine.

Reduce the heat and simmer gently, partially covered, for about 20 minutes, stirring occasionally, until all the vegetables are tender.

Chop the clams, if large. Stir in the clams and continue cooking for about 5 minutes until heated through. Taste and adjust the seasoning, if needed.

Ladle the soup into bowls and serve, sprinkled with parsley and black pepper to taste.

35 *Smoked cod chowder*

Replace the clams with 250 g/9 oz smoked cod fillet, cut into bite-sized pieces; add to the pan for the last 5 minutes of cooking time.

36 Genoese fish soup

25 g/1 oz butter
1 onion, chopped
1 garlic clove, finely chopped
55 g/2 oz rindless streaky bacon, diced
2 celery sticks, chopped
400 g/14 oz canned chopped tomatoes
150 ml/5 fl oz dry white wine

300 ml/10 fl oz fish stock
4 fresh basil leaves, torn
2 tbsp chopped fresh flat-leaf parsley
450 g/1 lb white fish fillets, such as cod
    or monkfish, skinned and chopped
115 g/4 oz cooked peeled prawns
salt and pepper

Melt the butter in a large heavy-based saucepan. Add the onion and garlic and cook over a low heat, stirring occasionally, for 5 minutes, or until softened.

Add the streaky bacon and celery and cook, stirring frequently, for a further 2 minutes. Add the tomatoes, wine, stock, basil and 1 tablespoon of the parsley. Season to taste with salt and pepper. Bring to the boil, then reduce the heat and simmer for 10 minutes.

Add the fish and cook for 5 minutes, or until it is opaque. Add the prawns and heat through gently for 3 minutes. Ladle into warmed serving bowls, garnish with the remaining chopped parsley and serve immediately.

37 Genoese seafood soup

Omit the white fish and replace with 300 g/10½ oz of seafood from a choice of squid, mussels, clams and scallops. Increase prawns to 200 g/7 oz. Reduce fish cooking time to 3–4 minutes and taste soup before adding salt.

38 Fishermen's soup

900 g/2 lb fillets of mixed white fish, such
    as cod, flounder, halibut, monkfish,
    sea bass and whiting, and peeled
    prawns
150 ml/5 fl oz olive oil
2 large onions, sliced
2 celery stalks, thinly sliced
2 garlic cloves, chopped

150 ml/5 fl oz white wine
4 canned tomatoes, chopped
pared rind of 1 orange
1 tsp chopped fresh thyme
2 tbsp chopped fresh parsley
2 bay leaves
salt and pepper
lemon wedges, to serve

Cut the fish into fairly large portions, discarding any skin. Heat the oil in a saucepan, add the onion, celery and garlic and fry for 5 minutes or until softened. Add the fish and prawns to the pan, then add the wine, tomatoes, orange rind, herbs, salt and pepper, and enough cold water to cover. Bring to the boil, then simmer, uncovered, for 15 minutes. Serve the soup hot, with lemon wedges.

39 Fishermen's soup with squid & mussels

Use mixed seafood – prawns, squid and mussels – instead of just prawns, and replace one third of the white fish with salmon fillet.

450 g/1 lb cooked lobster
40 g/1½ oz butter
1 small carrot, grated
1 celery stick, finely chopped
1 leek, finely chopped
1 small onion, finely chopped
2 shallots, finely chopped
3 tbsp brandy or Cognac

50 ml/2 fl oz dry white wine
1.2 litres/2 pints water
1 tbsp tomato purée
125 ml/4 fl oz whipping cream, or to taste
6 tbsp plain flour
salt and pepper
snipped fresh chives, to garnish

Pull off the lobster tail. With the legs up, cut the body in half lengthways. Scoop out the tomalley (the soft pale greenish-grey part) and, if it is a female, the roe (the solid red-orange part). Reserve these, covered and refrigerated. Remove the meat and cut into bite-sized pieces; cover and refrigerate. Chop the shell into large pieces.

Melt half the butter in a large saucepan over a medium heat and add the lobster shell pieces. Fry until brown bits begin to stick on the bottom of the pan. Add the carrot, celery, leek, onion and shallots. Cook, stirring, for 1½–2 minutes (do not allow to burn). Add the brandy and wine and bubble for 1 minute. Pour over the water, add the tomato purée, a large pinch of salt and bring to the boil. Reduce the heat, simmer for 30 minutes and strain the stock, discarding the solids.

Melt the remaining butter in a small saucepan and add the tomalley and roe, if any. Add the cream, whisk to mix well, remove from the heat and set aside.

Put the flour in a small mixing bowl and very slowly whisk in 2–3 tablespoons of cold water. Stir in a little of the hot stock mixture to make a smooth liquid.

Bring the remaining lobster stock to the boil and whisk in the flour mixture. Boil gently for 4–5 minutes until the soup thickens, stirring frequently. Press the tomalley, roe and cream mixture through a sieve into the soup. Reduce the heat and add the reserved lobster meat. Simmer gently until heated through.

Taste the soup and adjust the seasoning, adding more cream if wished. Ladle into warmed bowls, sprinkle with chives and serve.

41 Salmon & leek soup

SERVES 4

1 tbsp olive oil
1 large onion, finely chopped
3 large leeks, including green parts, thinly sliced
1 potato, finely diced
450 ml/16 fl oz fish stock
700 ml/1¼ pints water

1 bay leaf
300 g/10½ oz skinless salmon fillet, cut into 1-cm/½-inch cubes
80 ml/3 fl oz double cream
fresh lemon juice (optional)
salt and pepper
sprigs of fresh chervil or parsley, to garnish

Heat the oil in a heavy-based saucepan over a medium heat.

Add the onion and leeks and cook for about 3 minutes until they begin to soften. Add the potato, stock, water and bay leaf with a large pinch of salt. Bring to the boil, reduce the heat, cover and cook gently for about 25 minutes until the vegetables are tender. Remove the bay leaf.

Allow the soup to cool slightly, then transfer about half of it to a food processor or blender and process until smooth. (If using a food processor, strain off the cooking liquid and reserve. Purée half the soup solids with enough cooking liquid to moisten them, then combine with the liquid that is remaining.)

Return the puréed soup to the saucepan and stir to blend. Reheat gently over a medium–low heat.

Season the salmon with salt and pepper and add to the soup. Continue cooking for about 5 minutes, stirring occasionally, until the fish is tender and starts to break up.

Stir in the cream, taste and adjust the seasoning, adding a little lemon juice, if using. Ladle into warmed bowls, garnish with chervil or parsley and serve.

42 Crab & leek soup

Replace the salmon with 150 g/5½ oz dark crab meat and 150 g/5½ oz white crab meat (fresh, frozen or canned). Stir the dark crab meat into the soup before reheating. Scatter white crab meat over the soup to serve.

43 Seared scallops in garlic broth

SERVES 4

1 large garlic bulb (about 100 g/3½ oz), separated into unpeeled cloves
1 celery stick, chopped
1 carrot, chopped
1 onion, chopped
10 peppercorns

5–6 parsley stems
1.2 litres/2 pints water
225 g/8 oz large sea scallops
1 tbsp oil
salt and pepper
fresh coriander leaves, to garnish

Combine the garlic cloves, celery, carrot, onion, peppercorns, parsley stems and water in a saucepan with a good pinch of salt. Bring to the boil, reduce the heat and simmer, partially covered, for 30–45 minutes. Strain the stock into a clean saucepan. Taste and adjust the seasoning, and keep hot. If using sea scallops, slice in half horizontally to form 2 thinner rounds from each. (If the scallops are very large, slice them into 3 rounds.) Sprinkle with salt and pepper.

Heat the oil in a frying pan over a medium–high heat and cook the scallops on one side for 1–2 minutes, until lightly browned and the flesh becomes opaque.

Divide the scallops between 4 warmed shallow bowls, arranging them browned-side up. Ladle the soup over the scallops, then float a few coriander leaves on top. Serve immediately.

44 Seared monkfish in garlic broth

Replace the scallops with 400 g/14 oz monkfish fillet. Cut into small bite-sized cubes and stir-fry in the oil in the frying pan over medium–high heat for 3–4 minutes until cooked through (don't overcook or it will toughen). Divide between dishes, then ladle over the soup.

Squid, chorizo & tomato soup

450 g/1 lb cleaned squid
150 g/5½ oz lean chorizo, peeled and
 very finely diced
1 onion, finely chopped
1 celery stick, thinly sliced
1 carrot, thinly sliced
2 garlic cloves, finely chopped or crushed
400 g/14 oz canned chopped tomatoes

1.2 litres/2 pints fish stock
½ tsp ground cumin
pinch of saffron
1 bay leaf
chilli purée (optional)
salt and pepper
chopped fresh parsley, to garnish

Cut off the squid tentacles and cut into bite-sized pieces. Slice the bodies into rings. Place a large saucepan over a medium–low heat and add the chorizo. Cook for 5–10 minutes, stirring frequently, until it renders most of its fat. Remove and drain on paper towels.

Pour off all the fat from the pan and add the onion, celery, carrot and garlic. Cover and cook for 3–4 minutes, until the onion is slightly softened. Stir in the tomatoes, fish stock, cumin, saffron, bay leaf and chorizo. Add the squid to the soup. Bring almost to the boil, reduce the heat, cover and cook gently for 40–45 minutes, or until the squid and carrot are tender, stirring occasionally. Taste the soup and stir in a little chilli purée for a spicier flavour, if using. Season with salt and pepper. Ladle into warmed bowls, sprinkle with parsley and serve.

46 *Chorizo, pepper & prawn soup*

Omit the squid. Replace the carrot with 2 red peppers, deseeded and chopped – add to pan with the onion and celery. To serve, garnish each soup dish with 25 g/1 oz cooked prawns.

Thai-style seafood soup

1.2 litres/2 pints fish stock
1 lemon grass stalk, split lengthways
pared rind of ½ lime, or 1 lime leaf
2.5-cm/1-inch piece fresh
 ginger, sliced
¼ tsp chilli purée, or to taste

200 g/7 oz large or medium
 raw prawns, peeled
4–6 spring onions, sliced
250 g/9 oz scallops
2 tbsp fresh coriander leaves
salt
finely sliced red chillies, to garnish

Put the stock in a saucepan with the lemon grass, lime rind, ginger and chilli purée. Bring just to the boil, reduce the heat, cover and simmer for 10–15 minutes.

Cut the prawns almost in half lengthways, keeping the tail intact. Strain the stock, return to the saucepan and bring to a simmer.

Add the spring onion and cook for 2–3 minutes. Taste and season with salt, if needed, and stir in a little more chilli purée if wished.

Add the scallops and prawns and poach for about 1 minute until they turn opaque and the prawns curl. Stir in the fresh coriander leaves, ladle the soup into warmed bowls, dividing the shellfish evenly, and garnish with chillies.

48 *Thai-style seafood soup with tilapia*

Replace the scallops with 250 g/9 oz tilapia fillets, cut into approximately 12 slices. Add to the pan after the spring onions have cooked and simmer gently for 2–3 minutes before adding the prawns.

Asian lamb soup

150 g/5½ oz lean tender lamb, such as neck fillet or leg steak
2 garlic cloves, very finely chopped
2 tbsp soy sauce
1.2 litres/2 pints chicken stock
1 tbsp grated fresh ginger
5-cm/2-inch piece lemon grass, sliced into very thin rounds
¼ tsp chilli purée, or to taste
6–8 cherry tomatoes, quartered
4 spring onions, finely sliced
50 g/1¾ oz beansprouts, snapped in half
2 tbsp fresh coriander leaves
1 tsp olive oil

Trim all visible fat from the lamb and slice the meat thinly. Cut the slices into bite-sized pieces. Spread the meat in one layer on a plate and sprinkle over the garlic and 1 tablespoon of the soy sauce. Leave to marinate, covered, for at least 10 minutes or up to 1 hour.

Put the stock in a saucepan with the ginger, lemon grass, remaining soy sauce and the chilli purée. Bring just to the boil, reduce the heat, cover and simmer for 10–15 minutes. When ready to serve the soup, drop the tomatoes, spring onions, beansprouts and fresh coriander leaves into the simmering stock. Heat the oil in a frying pan and add the lamb with its marinade. Stir-fry the lamb just until it is no longer red and divide between warmed bowls. Ladle over the hot stock and serve immediately.

50 Asian beef soup

Replace the lamb with 150 g/5½ oz fillet of beef, sliced, and replace the stock with 1.2 litres/2 pints beef stock.

Classic lamb, chickpea & lentil soup

2–3 tbsp olive or argan oil
2 onions, chopped
2 celery sticks, diced
2 small carrots, peeled and diced
2–3 garlic cloves, peeled and lightly crushed but kept whole
1 tbsp cumin seeds
450 g/1 lb lean lamb, cut into bite-sized cubes
2–3 tsp ground turmeric
2 tsp paprika
2 tsp ground cinnamon
2 tsp granulated sugar
2 bay leaves
2 tbsp tomato purée
1 litre/1¾ pints lamb or chicken stock
400 g/14 oz canned chopped tomatoes, drained
400 g/14 oz canned chickpeas, drained and rinsed
100 g/3½ oz brown or green lentils, thoroughly rinsed
1 small bunch of fresh flat-leaf parsley, roughly chopped
1 small bunch of fresh coriander, roughly chopped
salt and pepper
1 lemon, cut into quarters, to serve

Heat the oil in a deep, heavy-based saucepan, add the onions, celery and carrots and cook over a medium heat for 2–3 minutes, stirring frequently, until the onions begin to colour. Add the garlic, cumin seeds and lamb and cook, stirring, until the lamb is lightly browned all over. Add the spices, sugar and bay leaves and stir in the tomato purée.

Pour in the stock and bring to the boil. Reduce the heat, cover and simmer for 1 hour, or until the meat is tender. Add the tomatoes, chickpeas and lentils and simmer gently for a further 30 minutes, or until the lentils are soft and the soup is almost as thick as a stew. Discard the bay leaves. Season to taste with salt and pepper and toss in most of the parsley and coriander. Garnish with the remaining parsley and coriander and serve the soup piping hot with lemon wedges for squeezing over.

2 aubergines	HARISSA
3 tbsp olive oil	2 red peppers, roasted, peeled, deseeded
6 lamb shanks	and chopped
1 small onion, chopped	½ tsp coriander seeds, dry-fried
400 ml/14 fl oz chicken stock	25 g/1 oz fresh red chillies, chopped
2 litres/3½ pints water	2 garlic cloves, chopped
400 g/14 oz sweet potato, cut into chunks	2 tsp caraway seeds
5-cm/2-inch piece cinnamon stick	olive oil
1 tsp ground cumin	salt
2 tbsp chopped fresh coriander	

Preheat the oven to 200°C/400°F/Gas Mark 6. Prick the aubergines, place on a baking sheet and bake for 1 hour. When cool, peel and chop. Heat the oil in a saucepan. Add the lamb and cook until browned. Add the onion, stock and water. Bring to the boil. Reduce the heat and simmer for 1 hour. For the harissa, process the peppers, coriander seeds, chillies, garlic and caraway seeds in a food processor or blender. With the motor running, add enough oil to make a paste. Add salt to taste, then spoon into a jar. Cover with oil, seal and chill. Remove the shanks from the stock, cut off the meat and chop. Add the sweet potato, cinnamon and cumin to the stock, bring to the boil, cover and simmer for 20 minutes. Discard the cinnamon stick and process the mixture in a food processor with the aubergine. Return to the saucepan, add the lamb and coriander and heat until hot. Serve with the harissa.

53 *Quick Middle Eastern soup*

For a quicker, chunkier version, use 400 g/14 oz leftover roast lamb instead of the lamb shanks – roughly chop, stir-fry with the finely chopped onion over medium heat for a few minutes, then add stock and water, bring to simmer and cook for 20 minutes. Add sweet potato, cinnamon and cumin to the pan, simmer for 20 minutes, remove cinnamon. Add aubergine and harissa, stir for a minute. Serve garnished with coriander leaf.

Lamb, barley & turnip soup

700 g/1 lb 9 oz neck of lamb
1.7 litres/3 pints water
55 g/2 oz pearl barley
2 onions, chopped
1 garlic clove, finely chopped
3 small turnips, cut into small dice

3 carrots, peeled and finely sliced
2 celery sticks, sliced
2 leeks, sliced
salt and pepper
2 tbsp chopped fresh parsley, to garnish

Cut the meat into small pieces, removing as much fat as possible. Put into a large saucepan and cover with the water. Bring to the boil over a medium heat and skim off any foam that appears. Add the pearl barley, reduce the heat and cook gently, covered, for 1 hour.

Add the prepared vegetables and season well with salt and pepper. Continue to cook for a further hour. Remove from the heat and allow to cool slightly.

Remove the meat from the saucepan using a slotted spoon and strip the meat from the bones. Discard the bones and any remaining fat or gristle. Place the meat back in the saucepan and leave to cool thoroughly, then refrigerate overnight.

Scrape the solidified fat off the surface of the soup. Reheat, season with salt and pepper to taste and serve piping hot, garnished with the parsley scattered over the top.

55 Lamb & orzo soup

Orzo is a tiny grain-shaped wheat pasta ideal for adding substance and thickening to soups and often cooked in Greece with lamb. Omit the barley and add 50 g/2 oz orzo to the soup when reheated – cook for 10 minutes before serving.

56 Sausage & red cabbage soup

2 tbsp olive oil
1 garlic clove, chopped
1 large onion, chopped
1 large leek, sliced
2 tbsp cornflour
1 litre/1¾ pints vegetable stock
450 g/1 lb potatoes, sliced

200 g/7 oz skinless sausages, sliced
150 g/5½ oz red cabbage, chopped
200 g/7 oz canned black-eyed beans, drained
125 ml/4 fl oz double cream
salt and pepper
ground paprika, to garnish

Heat the oil in a large saucepan. Add the garlic and onion and cook over a medium heat, stirring, for 3 minutes, until slightly softened. Add the leek and cook for a further 3 minutes, stirring.

In a bowl, mix the cornflour with enough stock to make a smooth paste, then stir it into the pan. Cook, stirring, for 2 minutes. Stir in the remaining stock, then add the potatoes and sausages. Season with salt and pepper. Bring to the boil, then lower the heat and simmer for 25 minutes.

Add the red cabbage and beans and cook for 10 minutes, then stir in the cream and cook for a further 5 minutes. Remove from the heat and ladle into serving bowls. Garnish with ground paprika and serve immediately.

57 Spiced meatball & red cabbage soup

Use 300 g/10½ oz skinless sausages or pork sausage meat. In a bowl, combine beaten sausage meat with 1 teaspoon of ground paprika, ½ teaspoon of ground caraway seeds, salt and black pepper. Form into 16 balls, brown on all sides in the oil, remove and reserve. Use 1 tablespoon of cornflour only to thicken the stock, 200 g/7 oz potatoes, cut into 1-cm/½-inch cubes, 200 g/7 oz red cabbage and 100 ml/3½ fl oz sour cream instead of the double cream. Return the meatballs to the pot with the potatoes.

1 tbsp vegetable oil
500 g/1 lb 2 oz lean neck of lamb
1 large onion, sliced
2 carrots, sliced
2 leeks, sliced

1 litre/1¾ pints vegetable stock
1 bay leaf
sprigs of fresh parsley
55 g/2 oz pearl barley
salt and pepper

Heat the vegetable oil in a large heavy-based saucepan and add the pieces of lamb, turning them to seal and brown on both sides. Lift the lamb out of the pan and set aside until required. Add the onion, carrots and leeks to the saucepan and cook gently for about 3 minutes.

Return the lamb to the saucepan and add the vegetable stock, bay leaf, parsley and pearl barley. Bring the mixture to the boil, then reduce the heat. Cover and simmer for 1½–2 hours.

Discard the parsley sprigs. Lift the pieces of lamb from the broth and allow them to cool slightly.

Remove the bones and any fat and chop the meat. Return the lamb to the broth and reheat gently. Season to taste with salt and pepper. It is best to prepare this soup a day ahead, then leave it to cool, cover and refrigerate overnight. When ready to serve, remove and discard the layer of fat from the surface and reheat the soup gently. Ladle into warmed bowls and serve immediately.

59 *Thick Scotch broth*

For a more substantial soup, add 1 small chopped swede or turnip with the carrots and add 85 g/3 oz split peas to the pan with the stock.

1–2 tbsp olive oil
450 g/1 lb lean boneless lamb, such as shoulder or neck fillet, trimmed of fat and cut into 1-cm/½-inch cubes
1 onion, finely chopped
2–3 garlic cloves, crushed
1.2 litres/2 pints water
400 g/14 oz canned chopped tomatoes
1 bay leaf
½ tsp dried thyme
½ tsp dried oregano
⅛ tsp ground cinnamon
¼ tsp ground cumin
¼ tsp ground turmeric
1 tsp harissa, or more to taste
400 g/14 oz canned chickpeas, drained and rinsed
1 carrot, diced
1 potato, diced
1 courgette, quartered lengthways and sliced
100 g/3½ oz fresh or defrosted frozen green peas
sprigs of fresh mint or coriander, to garnish

Heat 1 tablespoon of the oil in a large saucepan or cast-iron casserole over a medium–high heat. Add the lamb, in batches if necessary to avoid crowding the pan, and cook until evenly browned on all sides, adding a little more oil if needed.

Remove the meat with a slotted spoon when browned. Reduce the heat and add the onion and garlic to the pan. Cook, stirring frequently, for 1–2 minutes. Add the water and return all the meat to the pan. Bring just to the boil and skim off any foam that rises to the surface. Reduce the heat and stir in the tomatoes, bay leaf, thyme, oregano, cinnamon, cumin, turmeric and harissa.

Simmer for about 1 hour, or until the meat is very tender. Discard the bay leaf. Stir in the chickpeas, carrot and potato and simmer for 15 minutes. Add the courgette and peas and continue simmering for 15–20 minutes, or until all the vegetables are tender.

Taste and add more harissa, if desired. Ladle the soup into warmed bowls and garnish with mint or coriander.

61 *Spicy lamb soup with cannellini beans*

Replace the chickpeas with 400 g/14 oz canned cannellini beans.

2 tbsp butter
2 garlic cloves, chopped
1 large onion, sliced
250 g/9 oz smoked lean back bacon,
    chopped
2 large leeks, trimmed and sliced
2 tbsp plain flour

1 litre/1¾ pints vegetable stock
450 g/1 lb potatoes, chopped
100 ml/3½ fl oz double cream
300 g/10½ oz grated Cheddar cheese,
    plus extra to garnish
salt and pepper

Melt the butter in a large saucepan over a medium heat. Add the garlic and onion and cook, stirring, for 3 minutes, until slightly softened. Add the chopped bacon and leeks and cook for a further 3 minutes, stirring.

In a bowl, mix the flour with enough stock to make a smooth paste, then stir it into the pan. Cook, stirring, for 2 minutes. Pour in the remaining stock, then add the potatoes. Season with salt and pepper. Bring the soup to the boil, then lower the heat and simmer gently for 25 minutes, until the potatoes are tender and cooked through. Stir in the cream and cook for 5 minutes, then gradually stir in the cheese until melted. Remove from the heat and ladle into serving bowls. Garnish with grated Cheddar cheese and serve immediately.

63 *Blue cheese & bacon soup*

Use 150 g/5½ oz Cheddar and 150 g/5½ oz soft blue cheese, such as St Agur or Dolcelatte.

64 *Cheese, sweet potato & bacon soup*

Replace the potatoes with the same weight of sweet potatoes. Use only 150 g/5½ oz Cheddar and garnish with 25 g/1 oz grated Parmesan to serve.

2 tbsp olive oil
2 garlic cloves, chopped
2 red onions, chopped
1 red pepper, deseeded and chopped
2 tbsp cornflour
1 litre/1³/₄ pints vegetable stock
450 g/1 lb potatoes, peeled,
   halved and sliced

150 g/5¹/₂ oz chorizo, sliced
2 courgettes, trimmed and sliced
200 g/7 oz canned red kidney
   beans, drained
125 ml/4 fl oz double cream
salt and pepper
thick slices of fresh bread, to serve

Heat the oil in a large saucepan. Add the garlic and onions and cook over a medium heat, stirring, for 3 minutes, until slightly softened. Add the red pepper and cook for a further 3 minutes, stirring. In a bowl, mix the cornflour with enough stock to make a smooth paste and stir it into the pan. Cook, stirring, for 2 minutes.

Stir in the remaining stock, then add the potatoes and season with salt and pepper. Bring to the boil, then lower the heat and simmer for 25 minutes, until the vegetables are tender.

Add the chorizo, courgettes and kidney beans to the pan. Cook for 10 minutes, then stir in the cream and cook for a further 5 minutes. Remove from the heat and ladle into serving bowls. Serve with slices of fresh bread.

66 *Chorizo, sweetcorn & kidney bean soup*

Omit the potatoes and add 100 g/3¹/₂ oz sweetcorn instead. Omit the double cream and add 200 ml/7 fl oz chopped tomatoes with the stock.

1 tbsp chilli oil
1 garlic clove, chopped
3 spring onions, sliced
1 red pepper, deseeded and finely sliced
2 tbsp cornflour
1 litre/1³/₄ pints vegetable stock
1 tbsp soy sauce
2 tbsp rice wine or dry sherry
150 g/5¹/₂ oz pork fillet, sliced

1 tbsp finely chopped lemon grass
1 small red chilli, deseeded
   and finely chopped
1 tbsp grated fresh ginger
115 g/4 oz fine egg noodles
200 g/7 oz canned water chestnuts,
   drained and sliced
salt and pepper

Heat the oil in a large saucepan. Add the garlic and spring onions and cook over a medium heat, stirring, for 3 minutes, until slightly softened. Add the red pepper and cook for a further 5 minutes, stirring. In a bowl, mix the cornflour with enough of the stock to make a smooth paste, then stir it into the pan. Cook, stirring, for 2 minutes. Stir in the remaining stock and the soy sauce and rice wine, then add the pork, lemon grass, chilli and ginger.

Season with salt and pepper. Bring to the boil, then lower the heat and simmer for 25 minutes.

Bring a separate saucepan of water to the boil, add the noodles and cook for 3 minutes. Remove from the heat, drain, then add the noodles to the soup along with the water chestnuts. Cook for a further 2 minutes, then remove from the heat and ladle into serving bowls.

68 *Chicken & vegetable broth*

Use 1 tablespoon of cornflour only. Use 300 g/10½ oz sliced chicken breast fillet instead of the pork. Omit water chestnuts. Use rice noodles instead of the egg noodles – add the dry noodles to the pot and cook for 3 minutes or according to pack instructions.

2 tsp olive oil
500 g/1 lb 2 oz fresh lean pork mince
1 onion, finely chopped
1 celery stick, finely chopped
1 red pepper, deseeded and
    finely chopped
2–3 garlic cloves, finely chopped
3 tbsp tomato purée
400 g/14 oz canned chopped tomatoes

450 ml/16 fl oz chicken or meat stock
1/8 tsp ground coriander
1/8 tsp ground cumin
1/4 tsp dried oregano
1 tsp mild chilli powder, or to taste
salt and pepper
fresh coriander leaves, to garnish
soured cream, to serve

Add the tomato purée, tomatoes and the stock. Add the coriander, cumin, oregano and chilli powder. Stir in the ingredients to combine well.

Bring just to the boil, reduce the heat to low, cover and simmer for 30–40 minutes until all the vegetables are very tender. Taste and adjust the seasoning, adding more chilli powder if you like it hotter.

Ladle the soup into warmed bowls and sprinkle with coriander. Top each serving with a spoonful of soured cream and serve.

Heat the oil in a large saucepan over a medium–high heat. Add the pork, season with salt and pepper, and cook until no longer pink, stirring frequently. Reduce the heat to medium and add the onion, celery, red pepper and garlic. Cover and continue cooking for 5 minutes, stirring occasionally, until the onion is softened.

70 *Beef chilli soup*

Use beef mince instead of the pork and use beef stock.

Split pea & ham soup

SERVES 6–8

500 g/1 lb 2 oz split green peas
1 tbsp olive oil
1 large onion, finely chopped
1 large carrot, finely chopped
1 celery stick, finely chopped
1 litre/1¾ pints chicken or vegetable stock
1 litre/1¾ pints water
225 g/8 oz lean smoked ham, finely diced
¼ tsp dried thyme
¼ tsp dried marjoram
1 bay leaf
salt and pepper

Rinse the peas under cold running water. Put in a saucepan and cover generously with water. Bring to the boil and boil for 3 minutes, skimming off the foam from the surface. Drain the peas.

Heat the oil in a large saucepan over a medium heat. Add the onion and cook for 3–4 minutes, stirring occasionally, until just softened.

Add the carrot and celery and continue cooking for 2 minutes. Add the peas, pour over the stock and water and stir to combine. Bring just to the boil and stir the ham into the soup. Add the thyme, marjoram and bay leaf. Reduce the heat, cover and cook gently for 1–1½ hours, until the ingredients are very soft.

Remove the bay leaf. Taste and adjust the seasoning. Ladle into warmed soup bowls and serve.

Turkey & lentil soup

SERVES 4

1 tbsp olive oil
1 garlic clove, chopped
1 large onion, chopped
200 g/7 oz mushrooms, sliced
1 red pepper, deseeded and chopped
6 tomatoes, skinned, deseeded and chopped
1.2 litres/2 pints chicken stock
150 ml/5 fl oz red wine
85 g/3 oz cauliflower florets
1 carrot, peeled and chopped
200 g/7 oz red lentils
350 g/12 oz cooked turkey meat, chopped
1 courgette, trimmed and chopped
salt and pepper
1 tbsp shredded fresh basil
basil leaves, to garnish

Heat the oil in a large saucepan. Add the garlic and onion and cook over a medium heat, stirring, for 3 minutes, until slightly softened. Add the mushrooms, red pepper and tomatoes and cook for a further 5 minutes, stirring. Pour in the stock and red wine, then add the cauliflower, carrot and red lentils. Season with salt and pepper. Bring to the boil, then lower the heat and simmer for 25 minutes, until the vegetables are tender and cooked through. Add the turkey and courgette to the pan and cook for 10 minutes.

Stir in the shredded basil and cook for a further 5 minutes, then remove from the heat and ladle into serving bowls. Garnish with basil leaves.

2 litres/3½ pints chicken stock
2 tsp salt
½ tsp white pepper
2 tbsp finely chopped spring onion,
to serve
1 tbsp chopped fresh coriander leaves,
to serve

WONTONS
175 g/6 oz minced pork, not too lean
225 g/8 oz raw prawns, peeled,
deveined and chopped
½ tsp finely chopped fresh ginger
1 tbsp light soy sauce
1 tbsp Shaoxing rice wine
2 tsp finely chopped spring onion
pinch of sugar
pinch of white pepper
dash of sesame oil
30 square wonton wrappers
1 egg white, lightly beaten

For the wonton filling, mix together the pork, prawns, ginger, soy sauce, rice wine, spring onion, sugar, pepper and sesame oil, and stir well until the texture is thick and pasty. Set aside for at least 20 minutes.

To make the wontons, place a teaspoon of the filling at the centre of a wrapper. Brush the edges with a little egg white. Bring the opposite points towards each other and press the edges together, creating a flower-like shape. Repeat with the remaining wrappers and filling. To make the soup, bring the stock to the boil and add the salt and the pepper (omit the salt if using a stock that is already salty). Boil the wontons in the stock for about 5 minutes until the wrappers begin to wrinkle around the filling. To serve, put the spring onion in individual bowls, spoon in the wontons and soup and top with the coriander.

74 *Crab wonton soup*

Replace the pork with 175 g/6 oz white crab meat and mix with the prawns and remaining ingredients; use fish stock instead of chicken stock.

75 *Chicken wonton soup*

Replace the pork with 200 g/7 oz minced chicken and add 100 g/3½ oz shredded Chinese cabbage to the other ingredients.

Asparagus soup

1 bunch asparagus, about 350 g/12 oz, or
    2 packs fine asparagus, about
    150 g/5¹/₂ oz each
700 ml/1¹/₄ pints vegetable stock
55 g/2 oz butter or margarine
1 onion, chopped

3 tbsp plain flour
¹/₄ tsp ground coriander
1 tbsp lemon juice
450 ml/16 fl oz milk
4–6 tbsp double or single cream
salt and pepper

Wash and trim the asparagus, discarding the woody part of the stem. Cut the remainder into short lengths, reserving a few tips for garnish. Fine asparagus does not need to be trimmed. Cook the tips in the minimum of boiling salted water for 5–10 minutes. Drain and set aside.

Put the asparagus in a saucepan with the stock, bring to the boil, cover and simmer for about 20 minutes, until soft. Drain and reserve the stock.

Melt the butter or margarine in a saucepan. Add the onion and cook over a low heat until soft, but only barely coloured. Stir in the flour and cook for 1 minute, then gradually whisk in the reserved stock and bring to the boil. Simmer for 2–3 minutes, until thickened, then stir in the cooked asparagus, coriander, lemon juice and salt and pepper to taste. Simmer for 10 minutes. Remove from the heat and allow to cool a little. Transfer to a food processor or blender and process until smooth. Pour into a clean pan, add the milk and reserved asparagus tips and bring to the boil. Simmer for 2 minutes. Stir in the cream, reheat gently and serve.

77 *Purple sprouting broccoli soup*

Replace the asparagus with 350 g/12 oz purple sprouting broccoli, which has a fine flavour and will result in a deep green soup with a hint of purple.

78 *Celery & Stilton soup*

2 tbsp butter
1 onion, finely chopped
4 large celery sticks, finely chopped
1 large carrot, finely chopped
1 litre/1³/₄ pints chicken or vegetable stock
3–4 thyme sprigs

1 bay leaf
125 ml/4 fl oz double cream
150 g/5¹/₂ oz Stilton cheese, crumbled
freshly grated nutmeg
salt and pepper
celery leaves, to garnish

Melt the butter in a large saucepan over a medium–low heat. Add the onion and cook for 3–4 minutes, stirring frequently, until just softened. Add the celery and carrot and continue cooking for 3 minutes. Season lightly with salt and pepper.

Add the stock, thyme and bay leaf and bring to the boil. Reduce the heat, cover and simmer gently for about 25 minutes, stirring occasionally, until the vegetables are very tender. Allow the soup to cool slightly and remove the thyme and bay leaf.

Transfer the soup to a food processor or blender and process until smooth, working in batches, if necessary. (If using a food processor, strain off the cooking liquid and reserve. Purée the soup solids with enough cooking liquid to moisten them, then combine with the remaining liquid.) Return the puréed soup to the rinsed-out saucepan and stir in the cream. Simmer over a low heat for 5 minutes.

Add the Stilton slowly, stirring constantly, until smooth. (Do not allow the soup to boil.) Taste and adjust the seasoning, adding salt, if needed, plenty of pepper, and nutmeg to taste.

Ladle into warmed bowls, garnish with celery leaves and serve immediately.

79 *Broccoli & Stilton soup*

Omit the celery. Add 300 g/10½ oz broccoli florets to the pan for the last 10 minutes of simmering time.

80 Chunky minestrone

2 tbsp olive oil
2 garlic cloves, chopped
2 red onions, chopped
75 g/2³/₄ oz Parma ham, sliced
1 red pepper, deseeded and chopped
1 orange pepper, deseeded and chopped
400 g/14 oz canned chopped tomatoes
1 litre/1³/₄ pints vegetable stock
1 celery stick, trimmed and sliced
400 g/14 oz canned borlotti beans

100 g/3½ oz green leafy cabbage,
    shredded
75 g/2³/₄ oz frozen peas, defrosted
1 tbsp chopped fresh parsley
75 g/2³/₄ oz dried vermicelli
salt and pepper
freshly grated Parmesan cheese,
    to garnish
fresh crusty bread, to serve

Heat the oil in a large saucepan. Add the garlic, onions and Parma ham and cook over a medium heat, stirring, for 3 minutes, until slightly softened. Add the red and orange peppers and the tomatoes and cook for a further 2 minutes, stirring. Stir in the stock, then add the celery. Drain and add the borlotti beans along with the cabbage, peas and parsley. Season with salt and pepper. Bring to the boil, then lower the heat and simmer for 30 minutes.

Add the vermicelli to the pan. Cook for a further 10–12 minutes, or according to the instructions on the packet. Remove from the heat and ladle into bowls. Garnish with freshly grated Parmesan and serve with fresh crusty bread.

81 Green chunky minestrone

Replace the red and orange peppers with green peppers; replace the vermicelli with ditalini, pastina, elbow macaroni or other small pasta shapes and replace the borlotti beans with flageolet beans for a minestrone with a natural, green look and larger chunks of pasta.

82 Creamy potato, onion & cheese soup

3 tbsp butter
1 small onion, finely chopped
6 spring onions, green part included,
    finely chopped
4 potatoes, cut into chunks
700 ml/1¼ pints chicken stock
150 ml/5 fl oz milk

150 ml/5 fl oz whipping cream
2 tbsp chopped fresh flat-leaf parsley
75 g/2³/₄ oz coarsely grated
    Cheddar cheese
salt and pepper
fresh flat-leaf parsley leaves, to garnish
fried garlic croûtons, to serve (optional)

Heat the butter in a large saucepan over a medium heat. Add the onion, spring onions and potatoes. Cover and cook for 5–7 minutes, or until the onions are just tender.

Add the stock. Bring to the boil, then cover and simmer over a medium–low heat for 15–20 minutes, or until the potatoes are tender. Remove from the heat.

Mash the potatoes and season to taste with salt and pepper. Stir in the milk, cream and chopped parsley. Reheat gently. Ladle into bowls and sprinkle with the cheese and parsley leaves. Serve with garlic croûtons, if desired.

83 Lower-fat potato, onion & cheese soup

Use 2 tablespoons of butter. Use 300 ml/10½ fl oz milk instead of milk and cream. Add 100 g/3½ oz ricotta cheese to the potato when mashing. Sprinkle finished soup with 1 tablespoon of freshly grated Parmesan per bowl.

Easy gazpacho

1 small cucumber, peeled and
chopped
2 red peppers, deseeded and chopped
2 green peppers, deseeded and
chopped
2 garlic cloves, roughly chopped
1 fresh basil sprig
600 ml/1 pint passata
1 tbsp extra virgin olive oil
1 tbsp red wine vinegar
1 tbsp balsamic vinegar
300 ml/10 fl oz vegetable stock
2 tbsp lemon juice
salt and pepper

TO SERVE
2 tbsp diced, peeled cucumber
2 tbsp finely chopped red onion
2 tbsp finely chopped red pepper
2 tbsp finely chopped green pepper
ice cubes
4 fresh basil sprigs
fresh crusty bread

Put the cucumber, peppers, garlic and basil in a food processor and process for 1½ minutes. Add the passata, olive oil and both kinds of vinegar and process again until smooth.

Pour in the vegetable stock and lemon juice and stir. Transfer the mixture to a large bowl. Season to taste with salt and pepper. Cover with clingfilm and leave to chill in the refrigerator for at least 2 hours.

To serve, prepare the cucumber, onion and peppers, then place in small serving dishes or arrange decoratively on a plate. Place ice cubes in 4 large soup bowls. Stir the soup and ladle it into the bowls. Garnish with the basil sprigs and serve with the prepared vegetables and chunks of fresh crusty bread.

Mulligatawny soup

55 g/2 oz butter
2 onions, chopped
1 small turnip, cut into small dice
2 carrots, finely sliced
1 Cox's apple, cored, peeled and chopped
2 tbsp mild curry powder
1.2 litres/2 pints chicken stock

juice of ½ lemon
175 g/6 oz cold cooked chicken, cut into
small pieces
2 tbsp chopped fresh coriander, plus
extra to garnish
salt and pepper
55 g/2 oz cooked rice, to serve

Melt the butter in a large saucepan over a medium heat, add the onions and sauté gently until soft but not brown. Add the turnip, carrots and apple and continue to cook for a further 3–4 minutes.

Stir in the curry powder until the vegetables are well coated, then pour in the stock. Bring to the boil, cover and simmer for about 45 minutes. Season well with salt and pepper to taste and add the lemon juice. Transfer the

soup to a food processor or blender. Process until smooth and return to the rinsed-out saucepan. Add the chicken and coriander to the saucepan and heat through.

Place a spoonful of rice in each serving bowl and pour the soup over the top. Garnish with coriander and serve.

Vegetarian mulligatawny soup

Omit the chicken and use vegetable stock. Add 150 g/5½ oz red lentils (dry weight) to the pot with the stock. When soup is blended, add a little more water if necessary as the lentils will absorb some of the liquid in the soup.

French onion soup

675 g/1 lb 8 oz onions
3 tbsp olive oil
4 garlic cloves, 3 chopped and 1 peeled
    but kept whole
1 tsp sugar
2 tsp chopped fresh thyme

2 tbsp plain flour
125 ml/4 fl oz dry white wine
2 litres/3½ pints vegetable stock
6 slices of French bread
300 g/10½ oz Gruyère cheese, grated
fresh thyme sprigs, to garnish

Thinly slice the onions. Heat the olive oil in a large heavy-based saucepan, then add the onions and cook, stirring occasionally, for 10 minutes, until they are just beginning to brown. Stir in the chopped garlic, sugar and thyme, then reduce the heat and cook, stirring occasionally, for 30 minutes, or until the onions are golden brown.

Sprinkle in the flour and cook, stirring for 1–2 minutes. Stir in the wine. Gradually stir in the stock and bring to the boil, skimming off any foam that rises to the surface, then reduce the heat and simmer for 45 minutes. Meanwhile, preheat the grill to medium. Toast the bread on both sides under the grill. Rub the toast with the garlic clove.

Ladle the soup into 6 flameproof bowls set on a baking sheet. Float a piece of toast in each bowl and divide the grated cheese among them.

Place under the preheated grill for 2–3 minutes, or until the cheese has just melted. Garnish with thyme and serve.

88 *English onion soup*

Replace olive oil with corn oil. Add 2 chopped leeks to the pan with the sliced onions. Replace thyme with 2 teaspoons of fresh chopped sage. Omit wine, use 2 litres/3½ pints beef stock. Top the toasts with grated Cheddar cheese, instead of Gruyère, and add a dash of Worcestershire sauce.

89 *Garlic & chickpea soup*

8 tbsp olive oil
12 garlic cloves, very finely chopped
350 g/12 oz chickpeas, soaked overnight
    in cold water and drained
2.5 litres/4½ pints water
1 tsp ground cumin
1 tsp ground coriander

2 carrots, very finely chopped
2 onions, very finely chopped
6 celery sticks, very finely chopped
juice of 1 lemon
salt and pepper
4 tbsp chopped fresh coriander, to
    garnish

Heat half the oil in a large heavy-based saucepan. Add the garlic and cook over a low heat, stirring frequently, for 2 minutes. Add the chickpeas to the saucepan with the water, cumin and ground coriander. Bring to the boil, then reduce the heat and simmer for 2½ hours, or until tender.

Meanwhile, heat the remaining oil in a separate saucepan. Add the carrots, onions and celery, cover and cook over a medium–low heat, stirring occasionally, for 20 minutes. Stir the vegetable mixture into the saucepan of chickpeas. Transfer about half the soup to a food processor or blender and process until smooth. Return the purée to the saucepan, add about half the lemon juice and stir. Taste and add more lemon juice as required. Season to taste with salt and pepper. Ladle into warmed bowls, sprinkle with the fresh coriander and serve.

90 *Garlic, chickpea & red pepper soup*

Halve and deseed 3 red peppers, brush with olive oil and grill or bake until skins begin to blacken. Place in plastic bag for a few minutes, then remove and peel off skin. Omit carrots from recipe. Add peeled peppers to the food processor or blender with the half of the soup to be blended.

Green vegetable soup with basil pesto

SERVES 6

1 tbsp olive oil
1 onion, finely chopped
1 large leek, split and thinly sliced
1 celery stick, thinly sliced
1 carrot, quartered and thinly sliced
1 garlic clove, finely chopped
1.4 litres/2¹/₂ pints water
1 potato, diced
1 parsnip, finely diced
1 small kohlrabi or turnip, diced
150 g/5¹/₂ oz French beans,
    cut into small pieces
150 g/5¹/₂ oz fresh or frozen peas

2 small courgettes, quartered and sliced
400 g/14 oz canned flageolet beans,
    rinsed and drained
100 g/3¹/₂ oz fresh spinach leaves,
    finely shredded
salt and pepper

PESTO
1 large garlic clove, very finely chopped
15 g/¹/₂ oz fresh basil leaves
4 tbsp extra virgin olive oil
85 g/3 oz freshly grated Parmesan cheese

Heat the oil in a large saucepan. Cook the onion and leek over a low heat, stirring occasionally, for 5 minutes. Add the celery, carrot and garlic, cover and cook for a further 5 minutes. Add the water, potato, parsnip, kohlrabi and French beans. Bring to the boil, then reduce the heat, cover and simmer for 5 minutes. Add the peas, courgettes and flageolet beans and season to taste with salt and pepper. Cover and simmer for 25 minutes, or until all the vegetables are tender.

Meanwhile, make the pesto. Put all the ingredients in a food processor and process until smooth, scraping down the sides as necessary.

Alternatively, pound together using a pestle and mortar. Add the spinach to the soup and simmer for 5 minutes. Stir in a spoonful of the pesto.

Ladle the soup into bowls and hand round the remaining pesto separately.

Spinach soup with basil pesto

Omit carrot, parsnip, kohlrabi and flageolets. Increase spinach to 600 g/ 1 lb 5 oz. Follow rest of recipe as it is but blend half of it in a food processor or blender after the spinach has simmered and before stirring in the pesto.

Indian potato & pea soup

SERVES 4

2 tbsp vegetable oil
225 g/8 oz floury potatoes, diced
1 large onion, chopped
2 garlic cloves, crushed
1 tsp garam masala
1 tsp ground coriander
1 tsp ground cumin

850 ml/1¹/₂ pints vegetable stock
1 fresh red chilli, deseeded and chopped
100 g/3¹/₂ oz frozen peas
4 tbsp natural yogurt
salt and pepper
chopped fresh coriander, to garnish

Heat the vegetable oil in a large saucepan. Add the potatoes, onion and garlic and sauté over a low heat, stirring constantly, for about 5 minutes. Add the garam masala, ground coriander and cumin and cook, stirring constantly, for 1 minute.

Stir in the vegetable stock and red chilli and bring the mixture to the boil. Reduce the heat, cover the pan and simmer for 20 minutes, until the potatoes begin to break down. Add the peas and cook for a further 5 minutes. Stir in the yogurt and season to taste with salt and pepper. Pour into warmed soup bowls, garnish with chopped fresh coriander and serve immediately.

With cauliflower

Add 200 g/7 oz small cauliflower florets to the soup with the stock. Stir 1 tablespoon of thick natural yogurt into each bowl before serving.

95 Hearty lentil & vegetable soup

2 tbsp vegetable oil
3 leeks, green part included, finely sliced
3 carrots, diced
2 celery sticks, quartered lengthways and diced
115 g/4 oz brown or green lentils
75 g/2¾ oz long-grain rice
1 litre/1¾ pints chicken stock
2 corn cobs, quartered
4 tbsp chopped fresh chives
salt and pepper
soured cream, to serve

Heat the oil in a large saucepan over medium heat. Add the leeks, carrots and celery. Cover and cook for 5–7 minutes, or until just tender. Stir in the lentils and rice.

Pour in the stock. Bring to the boil, then cover and simmer over a medium–low heat for 20 minutes. Add the corn cobs. Simmer for 10 minutes more, or until the lentils and rice are tender. Season with salt and pepper. Stir in the chives.

Ladle into individual bowls, top with a spoonful of soured cream and serve immediately.

96 Hearty lentil & butternut squash soup

Peel, chop and add 200 g/7 oz butternut squash to the pan with the leeks, carrots and celery. Omit the rice and corn cobs and increase lentils to 200 g/7 oz.

97 Hearty bean & pasta soup

4 tbsp olive oil
1 onion, finely chopped
1 celery stick, chopped
1 carrot, peeled and diced
1 bay leaf
1.2 litres/2 pints low-salt vegetable stock
400 g/14 oz canned chopped tomatoes
175 g/6 oz dried pasta shapes, such as farfalle, shells or twists

400 g/14 oz canned cannellini beans, drained and rinsed
200 g/7 oz spinach or chard, thick stalks removed and shredded
salt and pepper
40 g/1½ oz Parmesan cheese, finely grated, to serve

Heat the olive oil in a large heavy-based saucepan. Add the onion, celery and carrot and cook over a medium heat for 8–10 minutes, stirring occasionally, until the vegetables have softened. Add the bay leaf, stock and tomatoes, then bring to the boil.

Reduce the heat, cover and simmer for 15 minutes, or until the vegetables are just tender. Add the pasta and beans, then bring the soup back to the boil and cook for 10 minutes, or until the pasta is just tender. Stir occasionally to prevent the pasta sticking to the bottom of the pan and burning. Season to taste, add the spinach and cook for a further 2 minutes, or until tender. Serve the soup in warmed bowls, sprinkled with Parmesan cheese.

98 Hearty French bean & pasta soup

Add 175g/6 oz French beans, halved, and 150 g/5½ oz broccoli florets to the soup with the stock. Omit the spinach/chard.

3 strips of rind and juice of 1 lime
2 garlic cloves, peeled
2 slices fresh ginger
1 litre/1¾ pints chicken stock
1 tbsp vegetable oil
150 g/5½ oz firm tofu
(drained weight), cubed
200 g/7 oz dried fine egg noodles
100 g/3½ oz shiitake
mushrooms, sliced
1 fresh red chilli, deseeded and sliced
4 spring onions, sliced
1 tsp soy sauce
1 tsp Chinese rice wine
1 tsp sesame oil
chopped fresh coriander, to garnish

Put the lime rind, garlic and ginger into a large saucepan with the stock and bring to the boil. Reduce the heat and simmer for 5 minutes. Remove the lime rind, garlic and ginger with a slotted spoon and discard.

Meanwhile, heat the vegetable oil in a large frying pan over a high heat, add the tofu and cook, turning frequently, until golden.

Remove from the pan and drain on kitchen paper. Add the noodles, mushrooms and chilli to the stock and simmer for 3 minutes. Add the tofu, spring onions, soy sauce, lime juice, rice wine and sesame oil and briefly heat through. Divide the soup among 4 warmed bowls, scatter the coriander over and serve immediately.

100 *Hot & sour soup with chicken*

Use 200 g/7 oz skinless chicken breast fillet, thinly sliced, instead of the tofu. Soak 1 x 50 g/2 oz pack dried Chinese mushrooms in a little warm water for 15 minutes and add them – and their soaking water – to pan with the noodles and fresh mushrooms. Increase the simmering time to 5 minutes.

101 *Kidney bean, pumpkin & tomato soup* SERVES 4–6

250 g/9 oz dried kidney beans
1 tbsp olive oil
2 onions, finely chopped
4 garlic cloves, finely chopped
1 celery stick, thinly sliced
1 carrot, halved and thinly sliced
1.2 litres/2 pints water
2 tsp tomato purée
⅛ tsp dried thyme

⅛ tsp dried oregano
1 bay leaf
⅛ tsp ground cumin
400 g/14 oz canned chopped tomatoes
250 g/9 oz peeled pumpkin flesh, diced
¼ tsp chilli purée, or to taste
salt and pepper
fresh coriander leaves, to garnish

Pick over the beans, cover generously with cold water and leave to soak for 6 hours or overnight.

Drain the beans, put in a saucepan and add enough cold water to cover by 5 cm/2 inches. Bring to the boil and boil for 10 minutes. Drain and rinse well.

Heat the oil in a large saucepan over a medium heat. Add the onions, cover and cook for 3–4 minutes, until they are just softened, stirring occasionally. Add the garlic, celery and carrot, and continue cooking for a further 2 minutes.

Add the water, drained beans, tomato purée and herbs and cumin. When the mixture begins to bubble, reduce the heat to low. Cover and simmer gently for 1 hour, stirring occasionally.

Stir in the tomatoes, pumpkin and chilli purée and continue simmering for a further hour, or until the beans and pumpkin are tender, stirring from time to time. Season to taste with salt and pepper and stir in a little more chilli purée, if liked. Ladle the soup into bowls, garnish with coriander and serve.

102 *Cannellini, pumpkin & tomato soup*

Omit kidney beans. Add 400 g/14 oz canned cannellini beans to the pot with the water. When tomatoes and pumpkin, etc., are added, cook for 30 minutes only. Cool a little then blend the soup in food processor or blender. Reheat gently to serve.

103 Leek & potato soup

55 g/2 oz butter
1 onion, chopped
3 leeks, sliced
225 g/8 oz potatoes,
cut into 2-cm/³/₄-inch cubes
850 ml/1½ pints vegetable stock
salt and pepper
2 tbsp snipped fresh chives,
to garnish
150 ml/5 fl oz single cream,
to serve (optional)

Melt the butter in a large saucepan over a medium heat, add the onion, leeks and potatoes and sauté gently for 2–3 minutes, until soft. Pour in the stock, bring to the boil, then reduce the heat and simmer, covered, for 15 minutes.

Transfer the mixture to a food processor or blender and process until smooth. Return to the saucepan and season with salt and pepper to taste. Serve in warmed bowls, swirled with the cream, if using, and garnished with chives.

104 Onion & potato soup

If you have no leeks, use 3 onions instead of 1 and make the soup in the same way.

105 Miso soup

1 litre/1³/₄ pints water
2 tsp dashi granules
175 g/6 oz silken tofu, drained and
cut into small cubes
4 shiitake mushrooms, finely sliced
4 tbsp miso paste
2 spring onions, chopped

Put the water in a large pan with the dashi granules and bring to the boil. Add the tofu and mushrooms, reduce the heat, and let simmer for 3 minutes.

Stir in the miso paste and let simmer gently, stirring, until it has fully dissolved.

Add the spring onions and serve immediately. If you leave the soup, the miso will settle, so give the soup a thorough stir before serving to recombine the miso.

106 Miso soup with chicken & noodles

Omit the tofu. Add 150 g/5½ oz (dry weight) egg thread noodles and 1 chicken breast, thinly sliced, to the soup with the mushrooms and simmer for 5 minutes.

107 With asparagus

Add 6 asparagus spears, sliced on the diagonal, to the soup at the same time as the tofu and mushrooms.

108 Mushroom & ginger soup

15 g/½ oz dried Chinese mushrooms or 125 g/4½ oz field or chestnut mushrooms
1 litre/1¾ pints hot vegetable stock
125 g/4½ oz thread egg noodles
2 tsp sunflower oil
3 garlic cloves, crushed

2.5-cm/1-inch piece fresh ginger, finely shredded
½ tsp mushroom ketchup
1 tsp light soy sauce
125 g/4½ oz beansprouts
fresh coriander sprigs, to garnish

Soak the Chinese mushrooms (if using) for at least 30 minutes in 300 ml/10 fl oz of the hot stock. Drain the mushrooms and reserve the stock. Remove the stalks of the mushrooms and discard. Slice the caps and reserve. Cook the noodles for 2–3 minutes in boiling water, then drain and rinse. Reserve until required.

Heat the sunflower oil in a preheated wok or large heavy-based frying pan over a high heat.

Add the garlic and ginger, stir and add the mushrooms. Stir over a high heat for 2 minutes.

Add the remaining vegetable stock with the reserved stock and bring to the boil. Add the mushroom ketchup and soy sauce. Stir in the beansprouts and cook until tender.

Place some noodles in each soup bowl and ladle the soup on top. Garnish with fresh coriander sprigs and serve immediately.

109 With bamboo shoots & water chestnuts

Add 125 g/4 oz canned, drained and sliced bamboo shoots and 85 g/3 oz sliced water chestnuts to the pan with the mushrooms and other ingredients to be stir-fried. Omit the egg thread noodles.

110 Mushroom & noodle soup

½ cucumber
2 tbsp vegetable oil
2 spring onions, finely chopped
1 garlic clove, cut into thin strips
125 g/4½ oz flat or open-cap mushrooms, thinly sliced
600 ml/1 pint water
25 g/1 oz Chinese rice noodles
¾ tsp salt
1 tbsp soy sauce

Halve the cucumber lengthways and scoop out the seeds using a teaspoon, then slice the flesh thinly.

Heat the oil in a large preheated wok. Add the spring onions and garlic and stir-fry for 30 seconds. Add the mushrooms and stir-fry for 2–3 minutes.

Stir in the water. Break the noodles into short lengths and add to the soup. Bring to the boil, stirring. Add the cucumber slices, salt and soy sauce and simmer for 2–3 minutes. Ladle the soup into warmed bowls.

111 Mushroom & vegetable soup

Omit the noodles. Use vegetable stock instead of water. Add 85 g/3 oz each of carrot, celery and green pepper, cut into thin strips, when you stir-fry. Simmer for 3 minutes before adding the cucumber slices.

2 tsp olive oil
1 large onion, chopped
1 large leek, sliced
2 carrots, thinly sliced
800 g/1 lb 12 oz parsnips, sliced
4 tbsp grated fresh ginger

2–3 garlic cloves, finely chopped
grated rind of ½ orange
1.4 litres/2½ pints water
225 ml/8 fl oz orange juice
salt and pepper
snipped chives, to garnish

Heat the olive oil in a large saucepan over a medium heat. Add the onion and leek and cook for about 5 minutes, stirring occasionally, until softened.

Add the carrots, parsnips, ginger, garlic, grated orange rind, water and a large pinch of salt. Reduce the heat, cover and simmer for about 40 minutes, stirring occasionally, until the vegetables are very soft. Allow the soup to cool slightly, then transfer to a food processor or blender and process until smooth, working in batches if necessary.

(If using a food processor, strain off the cooking liquid and reserve. Purée the soup solids with enough cooking liquid to moisten them, then combine with the remaining liquid.) Return the soup to the rinsed-out saucepan and stir in the orange juice. Add a little water or more orange juice, if you prefer a thinner consistency. Taste and adjust the seasoning if necessary. Simmer for about 10 minutes to heat through. Ladle into warm bowls, garnish with chives and serve.

113 *Curried parsnip soup*

Fry 1 large chopped onion with 2 cloves garlic in 1 tablespoon of butter over a medium–low heat for 5 minutes, adding 2 teaspoons of mild curry paste or powder for the last minute. Add 800 g/1 lb 12 oz parsnips and 1 large chopped potato to the pan with 1.4 litres/2½ pints chicken stock; simmer, covered, for 40 minutes. Cool, blend, reheat and adjust seasoning. Stir in 100 ml/3½ fl oz single cream, and garnish with chives.

Roasted garlic & potato soup

1 large garlic bulb with large cloves,
  peeled (about 100 g/3½ oz)
2 tsp olive oil, plus extra for brushing
2 large leeks, thinly sliced
1 large onion, finely chopped
500 g/1 lb 2 oz potatoes, diced
1.2 litres/2 pints chicken or
  vegetable stock

1 bay leaf
150 ml/5 fl oz single cream
freshly grated nutmeg
fresh lemon juice (optional)
salt and pepper
snipped fresh chives and a sprinkle
  of paprika, to garnish

Preheat the oven to 180°C/350°F/ Gas Mark 4. Put the garlic cloves in an ovenproof dish, lightly brush with oil and bake for about 20 minutes, until golden.

Heat the oil in a large saucepan over a medium heat. Add the leeks and onion, cover and cook for about 3 minutes, stirring frequently, until they begin to soften. Add the potatoes, roasted garlic, stock and bay leaf. Season with salt (unless the stock is salty already) and pepper. Bring to the boil, reduce the heat, cover and cook gently for about 30 minutes, until the vegetables are tender.

Remove the bay leaf. Allow the soup to cool slightly, then transfer to a blender or food processor and process until smooth, working in batches if necessary. (If using a food processor, strain off the cooking liquid and reserve. Process the soup solids with enough cooking liquid to moisten them, then combine with the remaining liquid.) Return the soup to the saucepan and stir in half the cream and a generous grating of nutmeg. Taste and adjust the seasoning, if necessary, adding a few drops of lemon juice, if using.

Reheat over a low heat. Ladle into warmed soup bowls, swirl in remaining cream, garnish with chives and paprika and serve.

115 *Roasted garlic & sweet potato soup*

Replace the potatoes with sweet potatoes; reduce the simmering time to 25 minutes.

Roasted Mediterranean vegetable soup

3 tbsp olive oil
700 g/1 lb 9 oz ripe tomatoes,
  skinned, cored and halved
3 large yellow peppers, deseeded
  and halved
3 courgettes, halved lengthways
1 small aubergine, halved lengthways
4 garlic cloves, halved
2 onions, cut into eighths
pinch of dried thyme
1 litre/1¾ pints chicken, vegetable
  or meat stock
125 ml/4 fl oz single cream
salt and pepper
shredded basil leaves, to garnish

Preheat the oven to 190°C/375°F/ Gas Mark 5. Brush a large shallow baking dish with olive oil. Laying them cut-side down, arrange the tomatoes, peppers, courgettes and aubergine in one layer (use two dishes, if necessary). Tuck the garlic cloves and onion pieces into the gaps and drizzle the vegetables with the remaining olive oil. Season lightly with salt and pepper and sprinkle with the thyme. Place in the preheated oven and bake, uncovered, for 30–35 minutes, or until soft and browned around the edges. Leave to cool, then scrape out the aubergine flesh and remove the skin from the peppers.

Working in batches, put the aubergine and pepper flesh, together with the tomatoes, courgettes, garlic and onion, into a food processor and chop to the consistency of salsa or pickle; do not purée. Alternatively, place in a bowl and chop together with a knife. Combine the stock and chopped vegetable mixture in a saucepan and simmer over a medium heat for 20–30 minutes, until all the vegetables are tender and the flavours have completely blended. Stir in the cream and simmer over a low heat for about 5 minutes, stirring occasionally until hot. Taste and adjust the seasoning, if necessary. Ladle the soup into warmed bowls, garnish with basil and serve.

117 *With fennel & cheese garnish*

Make the soup as above but omit the cream. While the soup is cooking, very thinly slice 1 small bulb of Florence fennel and stir-fry in a little olive oil over high heat until golden and lightly crispy. Reserve. When the soup is ready, sprinkle on the fennel to garnish and grate a little Parmesan cheese over, using a fine grater.

---

1 sweet potato, about 350 g/12 oz
1 acorn squash
4 shallots
2 tbsp olive oil
5–6 garlic cloves, unpeeled

850 ml/1½ pints chicken stock
125 ml/4 fl oz single cream
salt and pepper
snipped chives, to garnish

Preheat the oven to 190°C/375°F/Gas Mark 5. Cut the sweet potato, squash and shallots in half lengthways, through to the stem end. Scoop the seeds out of the squash. Brush the cut sides with the oil.

Put the vegetables, cut-side down, in a shallow roasting tin. Add the garlic cloves. Roast in the preheated oven for about 40 minutes, until tender and light brown.

When cool, scoop the flesh from the potato and squash halves and put in a saucepan with the shallots. Remove the garlic peel and add the soft insides to the other vegetables. Add the stock and a pinch of salt. Bring just to the boil, reduce the heat and simmer, partially covered, for about 30 minutes, stirring occasionally, until the vegetables are very tender. Allow the soup to cool slightly, then transfer to a food processor or blender and process until smooth, working in batches, if necessary. (If using a food processor, strain off the cooking liquid and reserve. Process the soup solids with enough cooking liquid to moisten them, then combine with the remaining liquid.)

Return the soup to the rinsed-out saucepan and stir in the cream. Season to taste with salt and pepper, then simmer for 5–10 minutes until completely heated through. Ladle into warmed serving bowls, garnish with pepper and snipped chives and serve.

119 *With herbs*

Stir 2 teaspoons each of chopped fresh rosemary, sage and oregano leaves and 1 tablespoon of extra oil into the tray of vegetables and garlic halfway through roasting, making sure they are thoroughly mixed in, to prevent burning. Leave them in when you prepare the vegetables for simmering.

120 *Spiced pumpkin soup*

2 tbsp olive oil
1 onion, chopped
1 garlic clove, chopped
1 tbsp chopped fresh ginger
1 small red chilli, deseeded and finely chopped
2 tbsp chopped fresh coriander

1 bay leaf
1 kg/2 lb 4 oz pumpkin, peeled, deseeded and diced
600 ml/1 pint vegetable stock
salt and pepper
single cream, to garnish

Heat the oil in a saucepan over a medium heat. Add the onion and garlic and cook, stirring, for about 4 minutes, until slightly softened. Add the ginger, chilli, coriander, bay leaf and pumpkin and cook for another 3 minutes. Pour in the stock and bring to the boil. Using a slotted spoon, skim any foam from the surface. Reduce the heat and simmer gently, stirring occasionally, for about 25 minutes, or until the pumpkin is tender. Remove from the heat, take out the bay leaf and leave to cool a little. Transfer the soup to a food processor or blender and process until smooth (you may have to do this in batches).

Return the mixture to the rinsed-out pan and season to taste with salt and pepper. Reheat gently, stirring. Remove from the heat, pour into 4 warmed soup bowls, garnish each one with a swirl of cream and serve.

121 *Spiced carrot & swede soup*

Use the same recipe as above but replace the pumpkin with half carrot and half swede, both peeled and chopped.

122 *Spicy courgette soup with rice & lime*

2 tbsp vegetable oil
4 garlic cloves, thinly sliced
1–2 tbsp mild red chilli powder
1/4–1/2 tsp ground cumin
1.5 litres/2³/4 pints chicken, vegetable or beef stock
2 courgettes, cut into bite-sized chunks
4 tbsp long-grain rice
salt and pepper
fresh oregano sprigs, to garnish
lime wedges, to serve

Heat the oil in a heavy-based saucepan. Add the garlic and cook for 2 minutes, or until softened. Add the chilli powder and cumin and cook over a medium–low heat for 1 minute. Stir in the stock, courgettes and rice, then cook over a medium–high heat for 10 minutes, or until the courgettes are just tender and the rice is cooked through. Season the soup to taste with salt and pepper.

Ladle into soup bowls, garnish with oregano sprigs and serve with lime wedges.

123 *Spicy squash & pinto bean soup*

Instead of rice, use rice-shaped pasta, such as orzo or seme di melone, or very thin pasta known as fideo. Use yellow summer squash instead of the courgettes and add cooked pinto beans in place of the rice. Diced tomatoes also make a tasty addition.

350 g/12 oz dried haricot beans
1 tbsp olive oil
1 large onion, finely chopped
1 large leek (white part only), thinly sliced
3 garlic cloves, finely chopped
2 celery sticks, finely chopped
2 small carrots, finely chopped
1 small fennel bulb, finely chopped
2 litres/3½ pints water

¼ tsp dried thyme
¼ tsp dried marjoram
salt and pepper

TAPENADE
1 garlic clove
1 small bunch fresh flat-leaf parsley, stems removed
240 g/8½ oz almond-stuffed green olives
5 tbsp olive oil

Pick over the beans, cover generously with cold water and leave to soak for 6 hours or overnight. Drain the beans, put in a saucepan and add cold water to cover by 5 cm/2 inches. Bring to the boil and boil for 10 minutes. Drain and rinse well.

Heat the oil in a large heavy-based saucepan over a medium heat. Add the onion and leek, cover and cook for 3–4 minutes, stirring occasionally, until just softened. Add the garlic, celery, carrots and fennel, and continue cooking for 2 minutes. Add the water, drained beans and the herbs. When the mixture begins to bubble, reduce the heat to low. Cover and simmer gently, stirring occasionally, for about 1½ hours, until the beans are tender. Meanwhile make the tapenade. Put the garlic, parsley and drained olives in a food processor or blender with the olive oil. Blend to a purée and scrape into a small serving bowl.

Allow the soup to cool slightly, then transfer to a food procesor or blender and process until smooth, working in batches if necessary. (If using a food processor, strain off the cooking liquid and reserve. Purée the soup solids with enough cooking liquid to moisten them, then combine with the remaining liquid.) Return the puréed soup to the saucepan and thin with a little water, if necessary. Season with salt and pepper to taste, and heat through. Ladle into warmed bowls and serve, stirring a generous teaspoon of the tapenade into each serving.

125 *White bean soup with red pepper pesto*

Replace the olive tapenade with a pesto. Drain 1 jar skinned red peppers, chop and put into a food processor or blender. Add 2 cloves peeled garlic, 1 level tablespoon of sun-dried tomato purée, 2 black olives (stoned), salt, pepper and 1 tablespoon of olive oil. Blend briefly (so not too smooth) adding a little more oil as necessary.

Vegetable & noodle soup

2 tbsp vegetable or groundnut oil	400 ml/14 fl oz coconut milk
1 onion, sliced	3–4 tbsp Thai soy sauce
2 garlic cloves, finely chopped	2 tbsp Thai red curry paste
1 large carrot, cut into thin sticks	55 g/2 oz wide rice noodles
1 courgette, cut into thin sticks	115 g/4 oz mung or soy bean sprouts
115 g/4 oz broccoli, cut into florets	4 tbsp chopped fresh coriander
1 litre/1¾ pints vegetable stock	

Heat the oil in a wok or large frying pan and stir-fry the onion and garlic for 2–3 minutes.

Add the carrot, courgette and broccoli and stir-fry for 3–4 minutes, until just tender.

Pour in the stock and coconut milk and bring to the boil. Add the soy sauce, curry paste and noodles and simmer gently for 2–3 minutes, until the noodles have swelled. Stir in the bean sprouts and coriander and serve immediately.

127 *French bean, mangetout & noodle soup*

Replace the courgette and broccoli with the same weights of fresh French beans and mangetout.

128 *Red pepper, cabbage & noodle soup*

Replace the courgette and broccoli with the same weights of thinly sliced red pepper and shredded Chinese cabbage.

129 *Chilled garlic soup*

500 g/1 lb 2 oz day-old country-style	4–5 tbsp sherry vinegar
white bread, crusts removed and torn	300 g/10½ oz ground almonds
5 large garlic cloves, halved	1.2 litres/2 pints water, chilled
125 ml/4 fl oz extra virgin olive oil, plus	salt and white pepper
a little extra for drizzling	seedless white grapes, to garnish

Put the bread in a bowl with just enough cold water to cover and leave to soak for 15 minutes. Squeeze the bread dry and transfer it to a food processor. Add the garlic, oil, sherry vinegar to taste, and the ground almonds to the food processor with 250 ml/9 fl oz of the water and process until blended. With the motor running, slowly pour in the remaining water until a smooth soup forms. Taste and add extra sherry vinegar if necessary. Cover and chill for at least 4 hours.

To serve, stir well and adjust the seasoning if necessary. Ladle into bowls and float grapes on top with a drizzle of olive oil.

130 *Chilled garlic soup with dry sherry*

Replace the sherry vinegar with 4 tablespoons of dry sherry.

Tomato broth with angel hair pasta SERVES 4

500 g/1 lb 2 oz ripe tomatoes,
  peeled and halved
8 garlic cloves, peeled but left whole
1 Spanish onion, chopped
½ tsp saffron threads, lightly crushed
1 tsp sugar
1 bouquet garni

5-cm/2-inch strip thinly pared
  lemon rind
600 ml/1 pint vegetable or chicken stock
2 tbsp extra virgin olive oil
280 g/10 oz dried angel hair pasta
salt and pepper

Put the tomatoes, garlic cloves, onion, saffron, sugar, bouquet garni and lemon rind into a large heavy-based saucepan. Pour in the stock and bring to the boil, then lower the heat, cover and simmer, stirring occasionally, for 25–30 minutes, until the tomatoes have disintegrated.

Remove the pan from the heat and leave to cool slightly. Remove and discard the garlic cloves, bouquet garni and lemon rind. Ladle the tomato mixture into a food processor or blender and process to a purée. Return the purée to the rinsed-out pan and season to taste with salt and pepper. Stir in the oil and bring to the boil. Add the pasta, bring back to the boil and cook for 2–4 minutes, until tender but still firm to the bite.

Taste and adjust the seasoning, if necessary. Ladle the broth and pasta into warmed soup bowls and serve immediately.

132 *Tomato broth with rose harissa*

Omit saffron and bouquet garni. Add 1 level tablespoon of rose harissa paste to the soup for the last few minutes of cooking.

133 *Tomato soup* SERVES 4

55 g/2 oz butter
1 small onion, finely chopped
450 g/1 lb tomatoes, coarsely chopped
1 bay leaf

3 tbsp plain flour
600 ml/1 pint milk
salt and pepper
sprigs of fresh basil, to garnish

Melt half the butter in a large saucepan. Add the onion and cook over a low heat, stirring occasionally, for 5–6 minutes until softened.

Add the tomatoes and bay leaf and cook, stirring occasionally, for 15 minutes, or until pulpy. Meanwhile, melt the remaining butter in another saucepan. Add the flour and cook, stirring constantly, for 1 minute.

Remove the pan from the heat and gradually stir in the milk. Return to the heat, season with salt and pepper and bring to the boil, stirring constantly. Continue to cook, stirring, until smooth and thickened.

When the tomatoes are pulpy, remove the pan from the heat. Discard the bay leaf and pour the tomato mixture into a blender or food processor. Process until smooth, then push through a sieve into a clean saucepan. Bring the tomato mixture to the boil, then gradually stir it into the milk mixture. Season to taste with salt and pepper. Ladle into warmed bowls, garnish with basil and serve immediately.

134 *Roast tomato soup*

Use 600 g/1 lb 5 oz tomatoes. Halve, toss with 1 tablespoon of light olive oil and put on baking tray. Roast at 190°C/375°F/Gas Mark 5 for 20 minutes, basting halfway through. Use only 15 g/½ oz butter to fry the onions, reducing total amount of butter in the recipe to 40 g/1½ oz. Add the roast tomatoes to the soup directly before blending.

25 g/1 oz butter
1 onion, chopped
2 tsp chopped fresh tarragon, plus
extra to garnish
450 g/1 lb potatoes, peeled and grated
1.7 litres/3 pints vegetable stock
700 g/1 lb 9 oz broccoli, cut into
small florets
175 g/6 oz Cheddar cheese
1 tbsp chopped fresh parsley
salt and pepper

Melt the butter in a large, heavy-based saucepan. Add the onion and cook, stirring occasionally, for 5 minutes, until soft. Add the chopped fresh tarragon to the saucepan with the potatoes, season to taste and mix well. Pour in just enough of the stock to cover and bring to the boil. Reduce the heat, cover and simmer for 10 minutes.

Meanwhile, bring the remaining stock to the boil in another saucepan. Add the broccoli and cook for 6–8 minutes, until just tender.

Remove both saucepans from the heat, leave to cool slightly, then ladle the contents of both into a blender or food processor. Process until smooth, then pour the mixture into a clean saucepan.

Grate the cheese, stir into the pan with the parsley and heat gently to warm through, but do not allow the soup to boil. Check the seasoning and add more salt and pepper if necessary. Ladle into warmed soup bowls, garnish with tarragon and serve immediately.

Watercress soup

2 bunches of watercress (approx. 200 g/7 oz), thoroughly cleaned
40 g/1½ oz butter
2 onions, chopped
225 g/8 oz potatoes, peeled and roughly chopped
1.2 litres/2 pints vegetable stock or water
salt and pepper
125 ml/4 fl oz crème fraîche
whole nutmeg, for grating (optional)

Remove the leaves from the stalks of the watercress and keep on one side. Roughly chop the stalks.

Melt the butter in a large saucepan over a medium heat, add the onion and cook for 4–5 minutes until soft. Do not brown. Add the potato to the saucepan and mix well with the onion. Add the watercress stalks and the stock.

Bring to the boil, then reduce the heat, cover and simmer for 15–20 minutes until the potato is soft. Add the watercress leaves and stir in to heat through. Remove from the heat and use a hand-held stick blender to process the soup until smooth.

Alternatively, liquidize the soup in a blender and return to the rinsed-out saucepan. Reheat and season with salt and pepper to taste.

Serve in warm bowls with the crème fraîche spooned on top and a good grating of nutmeg, if using.

137 Creamy watercress soup

Replace half the vegetable stock with milk. Omit the crème fraîche but stir in 25 ml/1 fl oz single cream.

Mushroom & sherry soup

4 tbsp butter
2 garlic cloves, chopped
3 onions, sliced
450 g/1 lb mixed white and chestnut mushrooms, sliced
100 g/3½ oz fresh ceps or porcini mushrooms, sliced
3 tbsp chopped fresh parsley, plus extra to garnish
500 ml/18 fl oz vegetable stock
3 tbsp plain flour
125 ml/4 fl oz milk
2 tbsp sherry
125 ml/4 fl oz soured cream
salt and pepper

Melt the butter in a large saucepan over a low heat. Add the garlic and onions and cook, stirring, for 3 minutes, until slightly softened. Add the mushrooms and cook for a further 5 minutes, stirring. Add the chopped parsley, pour in the stock and season with salt and pepper. Bring to the boil, then reduce the heat, cover the pan and simmer for 20 minutes.

Put the flour into a bowl, mix in enough milk to make a smooth paste, then stir it into the soup. Cook, stirring, for 5 minutes.

Stir in the remaining milk and the sherry and cook for a further 5 minutes. Remove from the heat and stir in the soured cream. Return the pan to the heat and warm gently. Remove from the heat and ladle into serving bowls. Garnish with chopped fresh parsley and serve immediately.

139 With croûtons

Make the soup extra special for a supper party. Toast 4 slices of French bread on both sides, spread each slice with mushroom pâté and cut into bite-sized pieces. Carefully place on soup just before serving.

Meat and Poultry

140 Braised veal in red wine

4 tbsp plain flour
900 g/2 lb stewing veal or beef, cubed
4 tbsp olive oil
350 g/12 oz whole pickling onions, peeled
2 garlic cloves, finely chopped
350 g/12 oz carrots, sliced
300 ml/10 fl oz dry red wine
150 ml/5 fl oz beef or chicken stock
400 g/14 oz canned chopped tomatoes

pared rind of 1 lemon
1 bay leaf
1 tbsp chopped fresh flat-leaf parsley
1 tbsp chopped fresh basil
1 tsp chopped fresh thyme
salt and pepper
chopped fresh basil and thyme leaves,
    to garnish

Preheat the oven to 180°C/350°F/Gas Mark 4. Put the flour and pepper in a polythene bag, add the meat and shake well to coat each piece. Heat the oil in a large flameproof casserole. Add the meat and fry, in batches, for 5–10 minutes, stirring constantly, until browned on all sides. Remove with a slotted spoon and set aside.

Add the whole onions, garlic and carrots to the casserole and fry for 5 minutes or until beginning to soften. Return the meat to the casserole.

Pour in the wine, stirring in any glazed bits from the bottom, then add the stock, the tomatoes, lemon rind, bay leaf, parsley, basil, thyme and season to taste with salt and pepper. Bring to the boil, then cover the casserole and place in the oven.

Cook for about 2 hours or until the meat is tender. Garnish with the chopped fresh herbs and serve hot.

141 Braised pork in red wine

This recipe works very well using the same amount of pork fillet instead of veal or beef. You can also use stewing venison. For a richer finish, add 200 g/7 oz sliced mushrooms to the pan with the vegetables.

142 Thick beef & baby onion casserole

2 tbsp olive oil
450 g/1 lb baby onions, peeled
    and left whole
2 garlic cloves, peeled and halved
900 g/2 lb stewing beef, cubed
½ tsp ground cinnamon
1 tsp ground cloves
1 tsp ground cumin

2 tbsp tomato purée
1 bottle full-bodied red wine
grated rind and juice of 1 orange
1 bay leaf
salt and pepper
chopped fresh flat-leaf parsley, to garnish
boiled or mashed potatoes, to serve

Preheat the oven to 150°C/300°F/Gas Mark 2. Heat the oil in a large flameproof casserole. Add the whole onions and the garlic and fry for about 5 minutes or until softened and beginning to brown.

Add the beef to the casserole and fry for about 5 minutes, stirring frequently, until browned on all sides.

Stir the cinnamon, cloves, cumin, tomato purée, salt and pepper into the casserole. Pour in the wine, stirring in any glazed bits from the bottom, then add the grated orange rind and juice and the bay leaf. Bring to the boil, then cover the casserole.

Cook in the oven for about 1¼ hours. Remove the lid and cook the casserole for another hour, stirring once or twice during this time, until the meat is tender.

Garnish with chopped fresh parsley and serve hot, with boiled or mashed potatoes.

143 Thick lamb & baby onion casserole

This recipe works well using lamb instead of the beef – use 900 g/2 lb neck of lamb, cut into slices. Replace the orange zest and juice with the same amount of lemon zest and juice, and add 1 teaspoon of chopped fresh rosemary.

Brittany chicken casserole

500 g/1 lb 2 oz dried beans, such as flageolets, soaked overnight and drained
25 g/1 oz butter
2 tbsp olive oil
3 rindless bacon rashers, chopped
900 g/2 lb chicken pieces
1 tbsp plain flour
300 ml/10 fl oz cider
150 ml/5 fl oz chicken stock
14 shallots
2 tbsp clear honey, warmed
225 g/8 oz cooked beetroot, chopped
salt and pepper

Preheat the oven to 160°C/325°F/Gas Mark 3. Cook the beans in boiling water for 25 minutes, then drain thoroughly. Heat the butter and oil in a large flameproof casserole. Add the bacon and chicken and cook for 5 minutes. Sprinkle with the flour, then add the cider and stock, stirring constantly to avoid lumps forming. Season to taste with salt and pepper and bring to the boil. Add the drained beans, then cover the casserole tightly and bake in the centre of the oven for 2 hours, or until the chicken is very tender.

About 15 minutes before the end of the cooking time, uncover the casserole. Gently cook the shallots and honey together in a frying pan for 5 minutes, turning the shallots frequently until golden. Add the shallots and beetroot to the casserole and return to the oven for the last 15 minutes of the cooking time. Serve hot.

145 *Brittany chicken casserole with leeks*

If you are not so keen on beetroot in a casserole or feel like a change, omit and add instead 2 chopped leeks and 1 chopped carrot to the pan with the bacon and chicken, adding a little more oil if the pan is too dry.

146 *Chicken casserole with a herb crust*

4 whole chicken legs, dusted in flour
1 tbsp olive oil
1 tbsp butter
1 onion, chopped
3 cloves garlic, sliced
4 parsnips, peeled and cut into large chunks
150 ml/5 fl oz dry white wine
850 ml/1½ pints chicken stock
3 leeks, white parts only, sliced
85 g/3 oz prunes, halved (optional)
1 tbsp English mustard
1 bouquet garni
100 g/3½ oz fresh breadcrumbs
85 g/3 oz Caerphilly cheese, crumbled
50 g/2 oz mixed chopped tarragon and flat-leaf parsley
salt and pepper

Preheat the oven to 180°C/350°F/Gas Mark 4. Fry the chicken in a casserole with the olive oil and butter, until golden brown. Remove with a slotted spoon and keep warm.

Add the onion, garlic and parsnips to the casserole and cook for 20 minutes or until the mixture is golden brown. Add the wine, stock, leeks, prunes (if using), English mustard and bouquet garni and season with salt and pepper.

Add the chicken to the casserole, cover with a lid and cook in the oven for 1 hour. Meanwhile mix together the breadcrumbs, cheese and herbs.

Remove the casserole from the oven and increase the heat to 200°C/400°F/Gas Mark 6. Remove the lid of the casserole and sprinkle over the crust mixture. Return to the oven for 10 minutes, uncovered, until the crust starts to brown slightly. Remove from the oven and serve.

147 *Rabbit casserole with a herb crust*

The recipe above works very well with rabbit instead of chicken. You will need 2 average-sized rabbits, as 1 rabbit will serve 2 people. Chop each rabbit into 4 pieces, discarding the rib section, which contains little meat.

148 Chicken, beans & spinach with olives

2 tbsp olive oil

600 g/1 lb 5 oz skinless, boneless chicken breasts, cut into chunks

1 small onion, finely chopped

2 celery sticks, diced

3 large garlic cloves, finely chopped

2 tsp chopped fresh rosemary

¼ tsp dried chilli flakes

400 g/14 oz canned chopped tomatoes

400 g/14 oz canned cannellini beans, drained and rinsed

250 ml/9 fl oz chicken stock

350 g/12 oz baby spinach leaves, chopped

salt and pepper

8–10 stoned black olives, sliced, to garnish

Heat the oil in a casserole over a medium–high heat. Add the chicken and cook until lightly browned all over. Reduce the heat to medium.

Add the onion and celery and cook, stirring frequently, for about 5 minutes, or until softened. Stir in the garlic, rosemary and chilli flakes and cook, stirring, for 1 minute. Stir in the tomatoes, beans and stock. Season to taste with salt and pepper. Bring to the boil, then reduce the heat and simmer over a medium–low heat, stirring occasionally, for 20 minutes. Stir in the spinach leaves and cook for 3 minutes, or until just wilted. Garnish with the sliced olives and serve immediately.

149 Chicken, beans & chard with olives

Instead of the spinach you could add chard to the dish (simmer in the pot for 4 minutes before serving), or curly kale (simmer for 5 minutes).

150 Chicken, pumpkin & chorizo casserole

2.25 kg/5 lb chicken, cut into 8 pieces and dusted in flour

3 tbsp olive oil

200 g/7 oz fresh chorizo sausages, roughly sliced

small bunch of sage leaves

1 onion, chopped

6 garlic cloves, sliced

2 sticks celery, sliced

1 small pumpkin/butternut squash, peeled and roughly chopped

200 ml/7 fl oz dry sherry

600 ml/1 pint chicken stock

400 g/14 oz canned chopped tomatoes

2 bay leaves

salt and pepper

1 tbsp chopped fresh flat-leaf parsley

Preheat the oven to 180°C/350°F/Gas Mark 4. Fry the chicken in the olive oil in a casserole with the chorizo and sage leaves, until golden brown. Remove with a slotted spoon and reserve. You may need to do this in two batches. Add the onion, garlic, celery and pumpkin to the casserole and cook for 20 minutes or until the mixture is golden brown.

Add the sherry, chicken stock, tomatoes and bay leaves, and season with salt and pepper. Return the reserved chicken, chorizo and sage to the casserole dish. Cover with a lid and cook in the oven for 1 hour.

Remove from the oven, stir in the chopped parsley and serve.

151 Chicken, pepper & chorizo casserole

Chorizo and sweet pepper go very well together – omit the pumpkin from the recipe and instead add two large, deseeded and sliced red peppers to the pot with the onion.

152 Chicken, tomato & onion casserole

1½ tbsp unsalted butter
2 tbsp olive oil
1.8 kg/4 lb skinned chicken drumsticks
2 red onions, sliced
2 garlic cloves, finely chopped
400 g/14 oz canned chopped tomatoes

2 tbsp chopped flat-leaf parsley,
    plus extra to garnish
6 fresh basil leaves, torn
1 tbsp sun-dried tomato purée
150 ml/5 fl oz full-bodied red wine
225 g/8 oz mushrooms, sliced
salt and pepper

Preheat the oven to 160°C/325°F/Gas Mark 3. Heat the butter with the olive oil in a large ovenproof casserole. Add the chicken drumsticks and cook, turning frequently, for 5–10 minutes, or until golden all over and sealed. Using a slotted spoon, transfer the drumsticks to a plate.

Add the onions and garlic to the casserole and cook over low heat, stirring occasionally, for 10 minutes, or until golden. Add the tomatoes, the parsley, basil, tomato purée and wine, and season to taste with salt and pepper.

Bring to the boil, then return the chicken drumsticks to the casserole, pushing them down under the liquid. Cover and cook in the oven for 50 minutes.

Add the mushrooms and cook for a further 10 minutes, or until the chicken drumsticks are tender and the juices run clear when a skewer is inserted into the thickest part of the meat. Serve immediately, garnished with chopped parsley.

153 Chicken, tomato & aubergine casserole

Use aubergine in the casserole instead of mushrooms – both have a great, meaty texture and flavour. Thinly slice 1 medium aubergine, brush slices with a little olive oil and, after browning the chicken, fry in the pan for 2 minutes each side to brown and soften slightly; remove with slotted spatula and reserve. You may need to add more oil before the onions and garlic go in if the pan is dry. Then continue with the recipe, returning the aubergine slices to the pan for the last 30 minutes of cooking time.

154 Chicken with garlic

4 tbsp plain flour
Spanish paprika, either hot or smoked
    sweet, to taste
salt and pepper
1 large chicken, about 1.75 kg/3 lb 12 oz,
    cut into 8 pieces, rinsed and patted dry
4–6 tbsp olive oil
24 large garlic cloves, peeled and halved

450 ml/¾ pint chicken stock
4 tbsp dry white wine, such as white Rioja
2 sprigs of fresh flat-leaf parsley,
    1 bay leaf and 1 sprig of fresh
    thyme, tied together
fresh flat-leaf parsley and thyme leaves,
    to garnish

Sift the flour on to a large plate and season with paprika and salt and pepper to taste. Coat the chicken pieces with the flour on both sides, shaking off the excess.

Heat 4 tablespoons of the oil in a large, deep frying pan or flameproof casserole over a medium heat. Add the garlic and fry, stirring frequently, for about 2 minutes to flavour the oil. Remove with a slotted spoon and set aside to drain on kitchen paper.

Add as many chicken pieces, skin-side down, as will fit in a single layer. Work in batches if necessary, to avoid over-crowding the casserole, adding a little extra oil if necessary. Fry for 5 minutes until the skin is golden brown. Turn over and fry for 5 minutes longer. Pour off any excess oil. Return the garlic and chicken to the frying pan and add the stock, wine and herbs. Bring to the boil, then reduce the heat, cover and

simmer for 20–25 minutes until the chicken is cooked through and tender and the garlic is very soft.

Transfer the chicken pieces to a serving platter and keep warm. Bring the cooking liquid to the boil, with the garlic and herbs, and boil until reduced to about 300 ml/½ pint. Remove and discard the cooked herbs. Taste and adjust the seasoning, if necessary. Spoon the sauce and the garlic cloves over the chicken pieces. Garnish with fresh parsley and thyme, and serve.

155 With mushrooms

Add 200 g/7 oz sliced closed cup mushrooms to the pan when the last batch of chicken has finished frying – stir in the surplus oil until lightly golden and tender, then continue with recipe.

Rich Mediterranean chicken casserole

8 boneless chicken thighs
2 tbsp olive oil
1 red onion, sliced
2 garlic cloves, crushed
1 large red pepper, deseeded and
    thickly sliced
thinly pared rind and juice of
    1 small orange
125 ml/4 fl oz chicken stock

400 g/14 oz canned chopped tomatoes
25 g/1 oz sun-dried tomatoes,
    thinly sliced
1 tbsp chopped fresh thyme
50 g/1¾ oz stoned black olives
salt and pepper
orange rind and fresh thyme sprigs, to
    garnish
fresh crusty bread, to serve

Dry-fry the chicken in a large heavy-based or non-stick frying pan over a fairly high heat, turning occasionally, until golden brown. Using a slotted spoon, drain off any excess fat from the chicken and transfer to a large, flameproof casserole.

Heat the oil in the frying pan. Add the onion, garlic and pepper and fry over a medium heat for 3–4 minutes. Transfer to the casserole. Add the orange rind and juice, stock, tomatoes and sun-dried tomatoes and stir.

Bring to the boil, then cover the casserole and simmer very gently over a low heat for 1 hour, stirring occasionally, until the chicken is tender.

Add the chopped thyme and black olives, then season to taste with salt and pepper.

Sprinkle orange rind and thyme sprigs over the casserole to garnish, and serve with fresh crusty bread.

157 *With a herb mix*

When you have time, make up a herb mix as follows: 1 teaspoon each of dried oregano, dried thyme, dried basil, dried rosemary, and ½ teaspoon each of dried sage and dried fennel seed. Increase quantities if you like (in same proportions). Add 3 teaspoons of this mix to the casserole during the last minute of onion/garlic frying time – omit fresh thyme.

Xinjiang lamb casserole

1–2 tbsp vegetable or groundnut oil
400 g/14 oz lamb or mutton, cut into
    bite-sized cubes
1 onion, roughly chopped
1 green pepper, roughly chopped
1 carrot, roughly chopped

1 turnip, roughly chopped
2 tomatoes, roughly chopped
2.5-cm/1-inch piece of fresh ginger,
    finely sliced
300 ml/10 fl oz water
1 tsp salt

In a preheated wok or deep saucepan, heat the oil and stir-fry the lamb for 1–2 minutes, or until the meat is sealed on all sides.

Transfer the meat to a large casserole and add all the other ingredients. Bring to the boil, then cover and simmer over a low heat for 35 minutes.

159 *Xinjiang lamb with lemon grass*

Replace the turnip with 1 medium kohlrabi, sliced. Use 1 stalk fresh or dried, crushed lemon grass instead of the ginger and use lamb stock instead of the water.

2 tbsp plain flour
4 skinless, boneless chicken breasts,
cut into bite-sized chunks
2 tbsp butter
2 tbsp olive oil
1 large leek, trimmed and sliced
2 spring onions, trimmed and
chopped
1 garlic clove, crushed
2 carrots, peeled and chopped
1 orange pepper, deseeded
and chopped
1 tbsp tomato purée
½ tsp ground turmeric
200 ml/7 fl oz white wine
200 ml/7 fl oz chicken stock
1 bay leaf
salt and pepper

COBBLER TOPPING
175 g/6 oz self-raising flour,
plus extra for dusting
2 level tsp baking powder
½ tsp ground turmeric
salt
3 tbsp butter
4–5 tbsp milk

Preheat the oven to 180°C/350°F/Gas Mark 4. Put the flour in a bowl, season with salt and pepper, then add the chicken chunks and toss in the flour to coat. Melt the butter with the oil in a large flameproof casserole, add the chicken and cook, stirring, until the chicken is golden all over. Lift out with a slotted spoon, transfer to a plate and set aside.

Add the leek, spring onions and garlic to the casserole and cook over a medium heat, stirring, for 2 minutes until softened. Add the carrots and orange pepper to the pan and cook for another 2 minutes, then stir in the remaining seasoned flour, the tomato purée and the turmeric. Pour in the wine and stock, bring to the boil, then reduce the heat and cook over a low heat, stirring, until thickened. Return the chicken to the pan, add the bay leaf, cover, then bake in the preheated oven for 30 minutes.

Meanwhile, to make the cobbler topping, sift the flour, baking powder, turmeric and a pinch of salt into a large mixing bowl. Rub in the butter until the mixture resembles fine breadcrumbs, then stir in enough of the milk to make a smooth dough. Transfer to a clean,

lightly floured board, knead lightly, then roll out to a thickness of about 1 cm/½ inch. Cut out rounds using a 5-cm/2-inch biscuit cutter.

Remove the casserole from the oven, remove and discard the bay leaf, and adjust the seasoning. Arrange the dough rounds over the top, then return to the oven and bake for another 30 minutes, or until the cobbler topping has risen and is lightly golden. Remove from the oven and serve hot.

161 *Golden chicken crumble*

If you haven't time to make a cobbler topping, make a delicious savoury crumble to sprinkle over the top – combine 85 g/3 oz softened butter with 125 g/4 oz wholemeal flour, ½ teaspoon of turmeric powder, ½ teaspoon of mustard powder, 2 teaspoons of mixed herbs, 40 g/1½ oz rolled oats and 50 g/2 oz grated Cheddar. Bake for 25 minutes.

1 duck, weighing 2.25 kg/5 lb
225 g/8 oz small brown lentils
1 tbsp virgin olive oil
2 onions
2 celery sticks
2 tbsp brandy or grappa
150 ml/5 fl oz dry white wine
1 tsp cornflour
salt and pepper

STOCK
wings, backbone and neck
from the duckling
1 celery stick
1 garlic clove
6 peppercorns, lightly crushed
1 bay leaf
5 fresh flat-leaf parsley sprigs
1 onion
1 clove
large pinch of salt

Cut the duck into joints. Cut off the wings. Fold back the skin at the neck end and cut out the wishbone with a small, sharp knife. Using poultry shears or heavy kitchen scissors, cut the breast in half along the breastbone, from the tail end to the neck. Cut along each side of the backbone to separate the 2 halves. Remove the backbone. Cut each portion in half diagonally.

To make the stock, put the wings, backbone and neck, if available, in a large saucepan and add the celery, garlic, peppercorns, bay leaf and parsley. Stick the onion with the clove and add to the saucepan with the salt. Add cold water to cover and bring to the boil. Skim off any foam that rises to the surface, then reduce the heat and simmer very gently for 2 hours. Strain into a clean saucepan and boil until reduced and concentrated. Reserve the stock, keeping 150 ml/5 fl oz separate from the rest.

Rinse the lentils and place in a saucepan. Add the oil and cold water to cover. Halve 1 of the onions and add to the saucepan with 1 celery stick. Bring to the boil, then simmer for 15 minutes, or until the lentils have softened. Drain and set aside. Meanwhile, add the duck pieces, skin-side down, to a frying pan and cook for 10 minutes. Transfer to an ovenproof casserole and drain off any excess fat. Finely chop the

remaining onion and celery and add to the frying pan. Cook over a low heat, stirring occasionally, for 5 minutes, until softened. Using a slotted spoon, transfer the vegetables to the casserole.

Cook the casserole over medium heat, add the brandy and ignite. When the flames have died down, add the wine and reserved stock less 2 tablespoons. Bring to the boil, add the lentils, salt and pepper. Cover and simmer over low heat for 40 minutes, or until the lentils and duck are tender.

In a bowl, blend the cornflour to a smooth paste with 2 tablespoons of the remaining reserved stock. Stir the paste into the casserole and cook, stirring constantly, for 5 minutes, or until thickened. Add salt to taste and adjust the seasoning, if necessary. Serve immediately.

163 *Duck with lentils & orange juice*

If you have no wine or prefer not to use it, the casserole is very tasty if you substitute orange juice for the wine. You can also use cannellini beans instead of the lentils for a creamy result.

164 Pheasant & chestnut casserole

1 tbsp olive oil
2 tbsp butter
1 large, prepared pheasant, jointed
175 g/6 oz lardons or streaky
    bacon, cut into strips
225 g/8 oz vacuum-packed chestnuts
2 onions, peeled and finely sliced
1 garlic clove, peeled and chopped

2 tbsp plain flour
425 ml/15 fl oz game or vegetable stock
150 ml/5 fl oz red wine
zest and juice of 1 orange
2 tbsp redcurrant jelly
salt and pepper
1 whole orange, sliced, to garnish
small bunch fresh watercress, to garnish

Melt the oil and butter in a large frying pan. Add the pheasant joints and cook over a high heat for 4–5 minutes until brown. Use a slotted spoon to remove the pheasant from the pan and place in the casserole dish.

Add the bacon to the pan and cook over a medium heat for about 2–3 minutes until crisp and golden, then transfer to the casserole dish. Preheat the oven to 180°C/350°F/Gas Mark 4. Gently fry the chestnuts over a low heat for 3–4 minutes until lightly browned, then transfer to the casserole. Add the onions and garlic to the pan and sauté over a medium heat for 2–3 minutes until soft and brown.

Stir in the flour and mix well to prevent any lumps. Add the stock, a little at a time, and gradually mix with the onions, scrape up the sediment and bring to the boil. Pour in the wine. Pour the contents of the frying pan over the pheasant. Add the orange zest and juice and the redcurrant jelly.

Season well, cover and cook in the centre of the preheated oven for 1½ –2 hours until the pheasant is tender. Turn the joints in the sauce halfway through. Remove from the oven, then check the seasoning and adjust if necessary. Serve garnished with slices of orange and watercress.

165 Chicken & chestnut casserole

The casserole also works if you use 1 smallish chicken or 1 guinea fowl instead of the pheasant. If you can't find any ready-prepared chestnuts, use 200 g/7oz chopped celery. Add to the pan with the onions and garlic.

166 Braised lamb shanks with cannellini beans

250 g/9 oz dried cannellini beans,
    soaked overnight
2 tbsp sunflower or maize oil
1 large onion, thinly sliced
4 carrots, chopped
2 celery sticks, thinly sliced
1 garlic clove, chopped
4 large lamb shanks

400 g/14 oz canned chopped tomatoes
300 ml/10 fl oz red wine
finely pared zest and juice of 1 orange
2 bay leaves
3 rosemary sprigs
about 200 ml/7 fl oz water
salt and pepper
chopped fresh parsley, to garnish

Preheat the oven to 160°C/325°F/Gas Mark 3. Drain the soaked beans and rinse under cold running water. Put in a large saucepan of cold water, bring to the boil and skim off any foam, then boil rapidly for 10 minutes. Drain and reserve.

Meanwhile, heat the oil in a large flameproof casserole, add the onion and fry for 5 minutes, or until softened. Add the carrots and celery and fry for a further 5 minutes, or until beginning to soften and the onion is beginning to brown. Add the garlic and fry for a further 1 minute. Push the vegetables to the sides of the casserole.

Add the lamb shanks to the casserole and fry for about 5 minutes, or until browned on all sides. Add the beans to the casserole with the tomatoes, wine and orange zest and juice and stir together. Add the bay leaves and rosemary. Pour in the water so that the liquid comes halfway up the shanks. Season with pepper but do not add salt as this will stop the beans softening.

Bring to the boil, then cover the casserole and cook in the oven for about 1 hour. Turn the shanks over in the stock then continue cooking for 1½ hours until the lamb and beans are tender.

Remove the bay leaves, then taste and add salt and pepper if necessary. Serve hot, garnished with chopped parsley.

167 Braised lamb with cannellini beans

You can use other cuts of lamb for this casserole – if using 800 g/1 lb 12 oz cubed leg or neck, use only enough liquid just to cover the solid pan contents and reduce cooking time by 10–15 minutes. Or you can use a shoulder of lamb, in which case follow the basic recipe.

Cinnamon lamb casserole

2 tbsp plain flour

1 kg/2 lb 4 oz lean boneless lamb, cubed

2 tbsp olive oil

2 large onions, sliced

1 garlic clove, finely chopped

300 ml/10 fl oz full-bodied red wine

2 tbsp red wine vinegar

400 g/14 oz canned chopped tomatoes

55 g/2 oz seedless raisins

1 tbsp ground cinnamon

pinch of sugar

1 bay leaf

salt and pepper

paprika, to garnish

TOPPING

150 ml/5 fl oz natural Greek yogurt

2 garlic cloves, crushed

salt and pepper

Season the flour with salt and pepper to taste then put it with the lamb in a polythene bag, hold the top closed and shake until the lamb cubes are lightly coated all over. Remove the lamb from the bag, shake off any excess flour and set aside. Heat the oil in a large flameproof casserole and cook the onions and garlic, stirring frequently, for 5 minutes, or until softened. Add the lamb and cook over a high heat, stirring frequently, for 5 minutes, or until browned on all sides and sealed.

Stir the wine, vinegar and tomatoes into the casserole, scraping any sediment from the base of the casserole, and bring to the boil. Reduce the heat and add the raisins, cinnamon, sugar and bay leaf. Season to taste with salt and pepper. Cover and simmer gently for 2 hours, or until the lamb is tender.

Meanwhile, make the topping. Put the yogurt into a small serving bowl, stir in the garlic and season to taste with salt and pepper. Cover and chill in the refrigerator until required.

Discard the bay leaf and serve hot, topped with a spoonful of the garlicky yogurt and dusted with a little paprika.

169 *Light cinnamon lamb casserole*

Make a slightly lighter but equally delicious casserole by replacing the red wine with dry white wine, the red wine vinegar with white wine vinegar and the raisins with sultanas.

170 *Fruity lamb casserole*

450 g/1 lb lean lamb, trimmed and cut into 2.5-cm/1-inch cubes

1 tsp ground cinnamon

1 tsp ground coriander

1 tsp ground cumin

2 tsp olive oil

1 red onion, finely chopped

1 garlic clove, crushed

400 g/14 oz canned chopped tomatoes

2 tbsp tomato purée

125 g/4½ oz ready-to-eat dried apricots

1 tsp caster sugar

300 ml/10 fl oz vegetable stock

salt and pepper

1 small bunch of fresh coriander, to garnish

rice or steamed couscous, to serve

Preheat the oven to 180°C/350°F/Gas Mark 4. Place the lamb in a mixing bowl and add the cinnamon, coriander, cumin and oil. Mix thoroughly to coat the lamb in the spices.

Place a non-stick frying pan over a high heat for a few seconds until hot, then add the spiced lamb, reduce the heat and cook for 4–5 minutes, stirring, until browned all over. Remove the lamb using a slotted spoon and transfer to a large ovenproof casserole.

Add the onion, garlic, tomatoes and tomato purée to the frying pan and cook, stirring occasionally, for 5 minutes. Season to taste with salt and pepper. Stir in the dried apricots and sugar, add the stock and bring to the boil.

Spoon the sauce over the lamb and mix well. Cover and cook in the oven for 1 hour, removing the lid of the casserole for the last 10 minutes. Roughly chop the coriander and sprinkle over the casserole to garnish. Serve immediately with rice or steamed couscous.

171 *With fresh mint*

Add 2 tablespoons of chopped fresh mint to the casserole with the coriander leaf to give it a fresh zing.

Lamb, garlic & bean casserole

2 tbsp olive oil, plus extra for drizzling
900 g/2 lb boneless lamb, cut into 4-cm/
    1½ -inch cubes
2 onions, finely chopped
1 tbsp chopped fresh rosemary
12 large garlic cloves, peeled
    and left whole
2–3 anchovy fillets, roughly chopped

2 tbsp plain flour
½ tsp pepper
600 ml/1 pint chicken or lamb stock
225 g/8 oz dried cannellini or haricot beans,
    soaked overnight and drained
salt
115 g/4 oz stale, coarse breadcrumbs
chopped fresh flat-leaf parsley, to garnish

Preheat the oven to 150°C/300°F/Gas Mark 2. Heat half the oil in a flameproof casserole. When very hot, cook the lamb, in batches, until evenly browned. Remove with a slotted spoon and transfer to a plate.

Cook the onions and rosemary in the remaining oil in the casserole, stirring, for 5–7 minutes, or until golden brown. Reduce the heat, stir in the garlic and anchovies and cook for 1 minute. Return the meat and any juices to the casserole. Sprinkle with the flour and stir well. Season with the pepper. Pour in the stock, stirring constantly, and add the drained beans. Bring to the boil, cover tightly and cook in the oven for 2 hours, or until soft. Remove from the oven. Season to taste with salt.

Preheat the grill to high. Spread the breadcrumbs over the lamb and beans. Drizzle a little oil over the top. Place under the grill for a few minutes, or until the crumbs are golden brown. Sprinkle with parsley and serve immediately.

173 *With zesty breadcrumb topping*

Make a lemon breadcrumb topping by adding 1–2 teaspoons of lemon zest to the breadcrumbs with a very finely-chopped clove of garlic and 2 tablespoons of chopped parsley. Then you can omit the parsley garnish.

174 *Mediterranean lamb with apricots & pistachios*

pinch of saffron threads
2 tbsp boiling water
450 g/1 lb lean boneless lamb,
    such as leg steaks
1½ tbsp plain flour
1 tsp ground coriander
½ tsp ground cumin
½ tsp ground allspice
1 tbsp olive oil
1 onion, chopped
2–3 garlic cloves, chopped
450 ml/16 fl oz lamb or chicken stock
1 cinnamon stick, bruised
85 g/3 oz ready-to-eat dried apricots,
    roughly chopped
175 g/6 oz courgettes, sliced
115 g/4 oz cherry tomatoes
1 tbsp chopped fresh coriander
salt and pepper
2 tbsp roughly chopped pistachio
    nuts, to garnish
couscous, to serve

Put the saffron threads in a heatproof jug with the water and leave for at least 10 minutes to infuse. Trim off any fat or gristle from the lamb and cut into 2.5-cm/1-inch chunks. Mix the flour and spices together, then toss the lamb in the spiced flour until well coated and reserve any remaining spiced flour.

Heat the oil in a large heavy-based saucepan and cook the onion and garlic, stirring frequently, for 5 minutes, or until softened.

Add the lamb and cook over a high heat, stirring frequently, for 3 minutes, or until browned on all sides and sealed. Sprinkle in the reserved spiced flour and cook, stirring constantly, for 2 minutes, then remove from the heat.

Gradually stir in the stock and the saffron and its soaking liquid, then return to the heat and bring to the boil, stirring. Add the cinnamon stick and apricots. Reduce the heat, cover and simmer, stirring occasionally, for 1 hour.

Add the courgettes and tomatoes and cook for a further 15 minutes. Discard the cinnamon stick. Stir in the fresh coriander and season to taste with salt and pepper. Serve sprinkled with the pistachio nuts, accompanied by couscous.

175 *Mediterranean lamb with aubergine*

Try replacing the courgettes with sliced aubergine, cooked in the same way.

4 lamb leg steaks
4 tsp ground coriander
1 tbsp ground cumin
1 small butternut squash
1 tbsp olive oil
1 onion, chopped
600 ml/1 pint chicken stock

2 tbsp chopped fresh ginger
100 g/3½ oz ready-to-eat dried apricots
2 tbsp clear honey
finely grated rind and juice of 1 lemon
200 g/7 oz couscous
salt and pepper
3 tbsp chopped fresh mint, to garnish

half the stock, then bring to the boil. Add the ginger, dried apricots, honey and lemon juice and season to taste with salt and pepper. Cover and cook over a medium heat for about 20 minutes, stirring occasionally.

Meanwhile, bring the remaining stock to the boil in a small saucepan, then stir in the couscous and lemon rind with salt and pepper to taste. Remove from the heat, cover and leave to stand for 5 minutes. Serve the lamb with the couscous, sprinkled with fresh mint.

Sprinkle the lamb steaks with the ground coriander and cumin. Peel and deseed the squash and cut into bite-sized chunks.

Heat the oil in a flameproof casserole. Add the lamb and cook over a high heat for 2–3 minutes, turning once. Stir in the squash, onion and

177 *With preserved lemon*

Add 4 slices preserved lemon (available in jars from the supermarket), chopped, to the pot with the lemon juice. They give a unique flavour.

Braised pork with garlic & herbs

1 boned and rolled leg of pork, weighing
    1.5 kg/3 lb 5 oz
12 garlic cloves, peeled
2 fresh rosemary sprigs
2 fresh sage leaves
4 black peppercorns, lightly crushed
125 ml/4 fl oz dry white wine
25 g/1 oz butter, diced
salt and pepper
200 g/7 oz runner beans, trimmed, to serve

Preheat the oven to 160°C/325°F/Gas Mark 3. Place the pork, garlic, herbs, peppercorns, pinch of salt and water to cover in a flameproof casserole dish.

Cover and bring to the boil, skimming the cooking liquid occasionally to remove any foam that rises to the surface. Transfer to the oven. Turning the pork occasionally, cook for 3 hours or until very tender. Long, slow cooking not only makes the meat deliciously tender, but infuses it with flavour.

Remove the pork. Strain the stock into a large jug. Rinse the casserole dish, add a ladleful of stock and bring to the boil.

Add the pork and cook over a medium heat until the liquid has almost evaporated. Continue adding the stock, a ladleful at a time, turning the pork occasionally, until 2 ladlefuls remain. Transfer the pork to a carving dish.

Add the wine to the casserole dish, bring to the boil and cook for 1 minute. Add the remaining stock and boil until reduced by half. Whisk in the butter, a piece at a time, then season to taste with salt and pepper. Serve with the carved pork and the runner beans.

179 *Braised pork chops with garlic & herbs*

Use 6 large trimmed pork chops instead of the joint – follow the recipe until transferring to the oven – cook for 1 hour or until chops are tender, remove from the pot with slotted spatula and keep warm, put the pot on hob and reduce liquid by half. Whisk in butter and season to serve.

Chorizo, chilli & chickpea casserole

2 tbsp olive oil
1 onion, sliced
1 large yellow pepper, deseeded and
    sliced
1 garlic clove, crushed
1 tsp chilli flakes
225 g/8 oz chorizo sausage
400 g/14 oz canned chopped tomatoes
400 g/14 oz canned chickpeas, drained
200 g/7 oz basmati rice
handful of rocket leaves
salt and pepper
4 tbsp roughly chopped fresh basil,
    to garnish

Heat the oil in a flameproof casserole and fry the onion over a medium heat, stirring occasionally, for 5 minutes. Add the yellow pepper, garlic and chilli flakes and cook for 2 minutes, stirring. Chop the chorizo into bite-sized chunks and stir into the casserole. Add the tomatoes and chickpeas with salt and pepper to taste. Bring to the boil, cover and simmer for 10 minutes. Meanwhile, cook the rice in a saucepan of lightly salted boiling water for 10–12 minutes, until tender. Drain. Stir the rocket into the casserole. Serve with the rice, garnished with basil.

181 *Chorizo, chilli & potato casserole*

Omit the chickpeas and add 500 g/1 lb 2 oz waxy potatoes, peeled, cooked and sliced into rounds, along with the tomatoes.

85 g/3 oz plain flour
1.3 kg/3 lb lean pork fillet, cut into
5-mm/¼-inch thick slices
4 tbsp sunflower oil
2 onions, thinly sliced
2 garlic cloves, finely
chopped
400 g/14 oz canned chopped tomatoes
350 ml/12 fl oz dry white wine
1 tbsp torn fresh basil leaves
2 tbsp chopped fresh parsley, plus
extra sprigs to garnish
salt and pepper
fresh crusty bread, to serve

Spread the flour out on a plate and season to taste with salt and pepper. Toss the pork slices in the flour to coat, shaking off any excess. Heat the oil in a flameproof casserole over a medium heat. Add the pork slices and cook until browned all over. Using a slotted spoon, transfer the pork to a plate.

Add the onions to the casserole and cook over a low heat, stirring occasionally, for 10 minutes, or until golden brown. Add the garlic and cook, stirring, for 2 minutes, then add the tomatoes, the wine and basil leaves and season to taste with salt and pepper. Cook, stirring frequently, for 3 minutes.

Return the pork to the casserole, cover and simmer gently for 1 hour, or until the meat is tender. Stir in the chopped parsley. Serve immediately with fresh crusty bread and garnished with parsley sprigs.

183 *Herby lamb or chicken casserole*

You can replace the pork with lamb fillet or skinned, boned, chicken thigh fillets, diced. Try 1 tablespoon of dried Herbes de Provence instead of the fresh basil and parsley, and for a change, serve with steamed new potatoes.

675 g/1 lb 8 oz waxy potatoes, cubed
25 g/1 oz butter
8 large herb sausages
4 smoked bacon rashers
1 onion, quartered
1 courgette, sliced
150 ml/¼ pint dry white wine
300 ml/½ pint vegetable stock
1 tsp Worcestershire sauce
2 tbsp chopped mixed fresh herbs
salt and pepper
chopped fresh herbs, to garnish

Bring a large saucepan of lightly salted water to the boil, add the cubed potatoes and cook for 10 minutes, or until soft. Drain thoroughly and set aside.

Meanwhile, melt the butter in a large frying pan. Add the herb sausages and cook for 5 minutes, turning them frequently to make sure that they brown evenly on all sides.

Add the bacon rashers, onion, courgette and cooked potatoes to the pan. Cook for a further 10 minutes, stirring, and turning the sausages frequently.

Stir in the white wine, stock, Worcestershire sauce and chopped mixed herbs. Season to taste with salt and pepper and cook the mixture over a gentle heat for 10 minutes.

Transfer the potato and sausage pan-fry to warmed serving plates, garnish with chopped fresh herbs and serve at once.

185 *Potato, butterbean & sausage pan-fry*

Replace the courgette with 100 g/3½ oz sliced French beans, and add 125 g/4 oz canned, drained butterbeans to the pan with the wine and stock.

Sausage & bean casserole

8 Italian sausages
3 tbsp olive oil
1 large onion, chopped
2 garlic cloves, chopped
1 green pepper, deseeded
    and sliced

225 g/8 oz fresh tomatoes, skinned and
    chopped or 400 g/14 oz canned
    tomatoes, chopped
2 tbsp sun-dried tomato purée
400 g/14 oz canned cannellini beans
mashed potatoes or rice, to serve

Prick the sausages all over with a fork. Heat 2 tablespoons of the oil in a large, heavy frying pan. Add the sausages and cook over a low heat, turning frequently, for 10–15 minutes, until evenly browned and cooked through. Remove them from the frying pan and keep warm. Drain off the oil and wipe out the pan with kitchen paper.

Heat the remaining oil in the frying pan. Add the onion, garlic and pepper to the frying pan and cook for 5 minutes, stirring occasionally, or until softened.

Add the tomatoes to the frying pan and leave the mixture to simmer for about 5 minutes, stirring occasionally, or until slightly reduced and thickened.

Stir the sun-dried tomato purée, cannellini beans and Italian sausages into the mixture in the frying pan. Cook for 4–5 minutes or until the mixture is piping hot.

Add 4–5 tablespoons of water, if the mixture becomes too dry during cooking.

Transfer the Italian sausage and bean casserole to serving plates and serve with mashed potatoes or cooked rice.

187 Sausage, bean & pasta bake

Cook the casserole as above, adding an extra 3 tablespoons of water at the end, then transfer to a large shallow ovenproof dish. Stir in 400 g/14 oz cooked pasta shapes. Top with 3 tablespoons of breadcrumbs mixed with 3 tablespoons of grated Parmesan cheese and place under grill until golden.

Venison casserole

3 tbsp olive oil
1 kg/2 lb 4 oz casserole venison,
    cut into 3-cm/1¼-inch cubes
2 onions, finely sliced
2 garlic cloves, chopped
2 tbsp plain flour
350 ml/12 fl oz beef or vegetable stock
125 ml/4 fl oz port or red wine
2 tbsp redcurrant jelly
6 crushed juniper berries
pinch of ground cinnamon
whole nutmeg, for grating
175 g/6 oz vacuum-packed chestnuts
    (optional)
salt and pepper
mashed potatoes, to serve

Preheat the oven to 150°C/300°F/ Gas Mark 2.

Heat the oil in a large frying pan and brown the cubes of venison over a high heat. You may need to fry the meat in 2 or 3 batches – do not overcrowd the frying pan. Remove the venison using a slotted spoon and place in a large casserole dish.

Add the onion and garlic to the frying pan and fry until golden, then add to the meat. Sprinkle the meat in the casserole dish with the flour and turn to coat evenly.

Gradually add the stock to the frying pan, stir well and scrape up the sediment, then bring to the boil. Add to the casserole dish and stir well, ensuring that the meat is just covered.

Add the port, redcurrant jelly, juniper berries, cinnamon, a small grating of nutmeg and the chestnuts, if using. Season well with the salt and pepper, cover and cook gently in the centre of the oven for 2–2½ hours. Remove from the oven and season with more salt and pepper, if necessary. Serve immediately, piping hot, with the mashed potatoes.

This casserole is best made the day before to allow the flavours to develop. Reheat gently before serving. Ensure you cool the casserole as quickly as possible and then store in the refrigerator or a cool larder overnight.

189 Venison & mushroom casserole

Omit the chestnuts and add 350 g/12 oz sliced chestnut mushrooms to the pan at the same time as the port.

Balti beef curry

2 tbsp ghee or vegetable oil
1 onion, thinly sliced
1 garlic clove, finely chopped
3-cm/1¼-inch piece fresh
    ginger, grated
2 fresh red chillies, deseeded and
    finely chopped
450 g/1 lb rump steak, cut into thin strips
1 green pepper, deseeded and thinly sliced

1 yellow pepper, deseeded
    and thinly sliced
1 tsp ground cumin
1 tbsp garam masala
4 tomatoes, chopped
2 tbsp lemon juice
1 tbsp water
salt
chopped fresh coriander, to garnish

Heat 1 tablespoon of the ghee in a preheated wok or large heavy-based frying pan. Add the onion and cook over a low heat, stirring occasionally, for 8–10 minutes, or until golden. Increase the heat to medium, add the garlic, ginger, chillies and steak and cook, stirring occasionally, for 5 minutes, or until the steak is browned all over. Remove with a slotted spoon, reserve and keep warm. Add the remaining ghee to the wok, add the peppers and cook over a medium heat, stirring occasionally, for 4 minutes, or until softened. Stir in the cumin and garam masala and cook, stirring, for 1 minute.

Add the tomatoes, lemon juice and water, season to taste with salt and simmer, stirring constantly, for 3 minutes. Return the steak mixture to the wok and heat through. Transfer to a warmed serving dish, garnish with coriander and serve immediately.

191 *Balti beef curry with aubergine*

Replace the green and yellow peppers with 1 thinly sliced aubergine and 1 thinly sliced courgette.

192 Beef korma with almonds

300 ml/10 fl oz vegetable oil
3 onions, finely chopped
1 kg/2 lb 4 oz lean beef, cubed
1½ tsp garam masala
1½ tsp ground coriander
1½ tsp finely chopped fresh ginger
1½ tsp crushed fresh garlic
1 tsp salt
150 ml/5 floz natural yogurt
2 whole cloves
3 green cardamom pods
4 black peppercorns
600 ml/1 pint water
chapatis, to serve

TO GARNISH
chopped blanched almonds
sliced fresh green chillies
chopped fresh coriander

Heat the oil in a heavy-based frying pan. Add the onions and stir-fry for 8–10 minutes, until golden. Remove half of the onions and reserve. Add the meat to the remaining onions in the frying pan and stir-fry for 5 minutes. Remove the pan from the heat. Mix the garam masala, ground coriander, ginger, garlic, salt and yogurt together in a large bowl. Gradually add the meat to the yogurt and spice mixture and mix to coat the meat on all sides. Place the meat mixture in the frying pan, return to the heat, and stir-fry for 5–7 minutes, or until the mixture is nearly brown.

Add the cloves, cardamom pods and peppercorns. Add the water, reduce the heat, cover and simmer for 45–60 minutes. If the water has evaporated, but the meat is still not tender enough, add another 300 ml/10 fl oz water and cook for a further 10–15 minutes, stirring occasionally.

Transfer to serving dishes and garnish with the reserved onions, chopped almonds, chillies and fresh coriander.

Serve with chapatis.

193 Chicken korma with almonds

Replace the beef with 800 g/1¾ lb chicken fillet, sliced, and add 140 g/5 oz French beans to the pot with the water. Reduce cooking time to 25 minutes.

194 Coconut beef curry

1 tbsp ground coriander
1 tbsp ground cumin
3 tbsp Mussaman curry paste
150 ml/5 fl oz water
75 g/2¾ oz creamed coconut
450 g/1 lb beef fillet, cut into strips
400 ml/14 fl oz coconut milk

50 g/1¾ oz unsalted peanuts, finely chopped
2 tbsp fish sauce
1 tsp soft light brown sugar or palm sugar
4 kaffir lime leaves
fresh coriander sprigs, to garnish
cooked rice, to serve

Combine the coriander, cumin and curry paste in a bowl. Pour the water into a saucepan, add the creamed coconut and heat until it has dissolved.

Add the curry paste mixture and simmer for 1 minute. Add the beef and simmer for 6–8 minutes, then add the coconut milk, peanuts, fish sauce and sugar. Simmer gently for 15–20 minutes, until the meat is tender.

Add the lime leaves and simmer for 1–2 minutes. Garnish with coriander sprigs and serve with cooked rice.

195 Fragrant coconut beef curry

Add 1 teaspoon of galangal or finely chopped fresh ginger to the pan with the curry paste, and 1 tablespoon of chopped fresh lemon grass with the lime leaves.

Meatballs in creamy cashew nut sauce

125 g/4½ oz raw cashew nuts
150 ml/5 fl oz boiling water
450 g/1 lb fresh lean lamb mince
1 tbsp thick set natural yogurt
1 medium egg, beaten
1½ tsp ground cardamom
½ tsp ground nutmeg
½ tsp pepper
½ tsp dried mint
½ tsp salt, or to taste
300 ml/10 fl oz water
2.5-cm/1-inch piece cinnamon stick
5 green cardamom pods
5 cloves
2 bay leaves
3 tbsp sunflower or olive oil
1 onion, finely chopped
2 tsp garlic purée
1 tsp ground ginger
1 tsp ground fennel seeds
½ tsp ground turmeric
½ –1 tsp chilli powder
150 ml/5 fl oz double cream
1 tbsp crushed pistachio nuts,
to garnish
Indian bread or cooked rice,
to serve

Soak the cashew nuts in the boiling water for 20 minutes. Put the lamb mince in a mixing bowl and add the yogurt, egg, cardamom, nutmeg, pepper, mint and salt. Knead the mince until it is smooth and velvety. Alternatively, put the ingredients in a food processor and process until fine. Chill the mixture for 30–40 minutes, then divide it into quarters.

Make five balls (koftas) out of each quarter and compress so that they are firm, rolling them between your palms to make them smooth and neat.

Bring the 300 ml/10 fl oz water to the boil in a large shallow pan and add all the whole spices and the bay leaves. Arrange the meatballs in a single layer in the spiced liquid, reduce the heat to medium, cover the pan and cook for 12–15 minutes. Remove the meatballs, cover and keep hot. Strain the spiced stock and set aside.

Wipe out the pan and add the oil. Place over a medium heat and add the onion and garlic purée. Cook until the mixture begins to brown and add the ground ginger, ground fennel seeds, turmeric and chilli powder. Stir-fry for 2–3 minutes, then add the strained stock and meatballs. Bring to the boil, reduce the heat to low, cover and simmer for 10–12 minutes.

Meanwhile, purée the cashew nuts in a blender and add to the meatball mixture along with the cream. Simmer for a further 5–6 minutes, then remove from the heat.

Garnish with crushed pistachio nuts and serve with Indian bread or cooked rice.

Balti chicken

3 tbsp ghee or vegetable oil
2 large onions, sliced
3 tomatoes, sliced
½ tsp kalonji seeds
4 black peppercorns
2 cardamom pods
1 cinnamon stick
1 tsp chilli powder
1 tsp garam masala
1 tsp garlic pureé
1 tsp ginger pureé
700 g/1 lb 9 oz skinless, boneless
chicken breasts or thighs, diced
50 ml/2 fl oz chicken stock or water
2 tbsp natural yogurt
2 tbsp chopped fresh coriander,
plus extra to garnish
2 fresh green chillies, deseeded and
finely chopped
2 tbsp lime juice
salt

Heat the ghee in a large heavy-based frying pan. Add the onions and cook over a low heat, stirring occasionally, for 10 minutes, or until golden.

Add the sliced tomatoes, kalonji seeds, peppercorns, cardamoms, cinnamon stick, chilli powder, garam masala, garlic purée and ginger purée, and season with salt to taste. Cook, stirring constantly, for 5 minutes. Add the chicken and cook, stirring constantly, for 5 minutes, or until well coated in the spice paste. Stir in the stock or water and yogurt. Cover and simmer, stirring occasionally, for 10 minutes.

Stir in the chopped coriander, chillies and lime juice. Transfer to a warmed serving dish, sprinkle with more chopped coriander and serve immediately.

198 *Balti chicken with broccoli & peas*

Add 200 g/7 oz broccoli divided into very small florets, and 85 g/3 oz small peas to the pan, plus 50 ml/2 fl oz chicken stock, when the chicken has finished its initial cooking. Increase simmering time to 12 minutes.

199 *Balti chicken with spinach & baby corn*

Add 150 g/5 oz baby spinach leaves and 85 g/3 oz sliced baby corn to the pan as above.

200 *Chicken dopiaza*

700 g/1 lb 9 oz skinless, boneless chicken
breasts or thighs
juice of ½ lemon
1 tsp salt, or to taste
5 tbsp sunflower or olive oil
2 large onions, roughly chopped
5 large garlic cloves, roughly chopped
2.5-cm/1-inch piece fresh ginger,
roughly chopped
2 tbsp natural yogurt
2.5-cm/1-inch piece cinnamon
stick, halved
4 green cardamom pods, bruised

4 cloves
½–2 tsp black peppercorns
½ tsp ground turmeric
1½–2 tsp chilli powder
1 tsp ground coriander
4 tbsp passata
150 ml/5 fl oz warm water
½ tsp granulated sugar
8 shallots, halved
1 tsp garam masala
2 tbsp chopped fresh coriander leaves
1 tomato, chopped

Cut the chicken into 2.5-cm/1-inch cubes and put in a non-metallic bowl.

Add the lemon juice and half the salt and rub well into the chicken. Cover and leave to marinate in the refrigerator for 20 minutes.

Heat 1 tablespoon of the oil in a small saucepan over a medium heat, add the onions, garlic and ginger and cook, stirring frequently, for 4–5 minutes. Remove from the heat and leave to cool slightly. Transfer the ingredients to a blender or food processor, add the yogurt and blend to a purée.

Heat 3 tablespoons of the remaining oil in a medium heavy-based saucepan over a low heat, add the cinnamon stick, cardamom pods, cloves and peppercorns and cook, stirring, for 25–30 seconds. Add the puréed ingredients, increase the heat to medium and cook, stirring frequently, for 5 minutes. Add the turmeric, chilli powder and ground coriander and cook, stirring, for 2 minutes.

Add the passata and cook, stirring, for 3 minutes. Increase the heat, then add the marinated chicken and cook, stirring, until it changes colour. Add the warm water, the remaining salt and the sugar. Bring to the boil, then reduce the heat to low, cover and cook for 10 minutes. Remove the lid and cook, uncovered, for a further 10 minutes, or until the sauce has thickened.

Meanwhile, heat the remaining 1 tablespoon of the oil in a small saucepan, add the shallots and stir-fry until browned and separated. Add the garam masala and cook, stirring, for 30 seconds. Stir the shallot mixture into the curry and simmer for 2 minutes.

Stir in the fresh coriander and chopped tomato and remove from the heat. Serve immediately.

25 g/1 oz coriander leaves and stalks,
   roughly chopped
25 g/1 oz fresh spinach, roughly chopped
2.5-cm/1-inch piece fresh ginger,
   roughly chopped
3 garlic cloves, roughly chopped
2–3 fresh green chillies, roughly chopped
15 g/½ oz fresh mint leaves
1½ tbsp lemon juice
85 g/3 oz thick set natural yogurt

4 tbsp sunflower or olive oil
1 large onion, finely chopped
700 g/1 lb 9 oz skinless chicken thighs
   or breasts, cut into 2.5-cm/1-inch cubes
1 tsp ground turmeric
½ tsp sugar
salt
1 small tomato, deseeded and cut into
   julienne strips, to garnish
cooked basmati rice, to serve

Place the coriander, spinach, ginger, garlic, chillies, mint, lemon juice and ½ teaspoon of salt in a food processor or blender and process to a smooth purée. Add a little water, if necessary, to facilitate the blade movement in the blender. Remove and set aside.

Whisk the yogurt until smooth (this is important as the yogurt will curdle otherwise) and set aside.

Heat the oil in a medium saucepan. Cook the onion for 5–6 minutes, stirring regularly, until soft. Add the chicken and stir-fry over a medium–high heat for 2–3 minutes, until the meat turns opaque. Add the turmeric, sugar and salt to taste and stir-fry for a further 2 minutes, then reduce the heat to medium and add half the yogurt. Cook for 1 minute and add the remaining yogurt, then continue cooking over a medium heat until the yogurt resembles a thick batter and the oil is visible.

Add the puréed ingredients and cook for 4–5 minutes, stirring constantly. Remove from the heat and garnish with the strips of tomato. Serve with basmati rice.

202 *Chicken in basil & coriander sauce*

Replace the mint with 15 g/½ oz fresh basil leaves and use another 15 g/½ oz leaves to garnish the finished dish.

203 *Lamb in mint & coriander sauce*

Replace the chicken with 700 g/1 lb 9 oz lamb leg fillet, cubed.

Chicken jalfrezi

½ tsp cumin seeds
½ tsp coriander seeds
1 tsp mustard oil
3 tbsp vegetable oil
1 large onion, finely chopped
3 garlic cloves, crushed
1 tbsp tomato purée
2 tomatoes, peeled and chopped
1 tsp ground turmeric

½ tsp chilli powder
½ tsp garam masala
1 tsp red wine vinegar
1 small red pepper, deseeded and chopped
125 g/4½ oz frozen broad beans
500 g/1 lb 2 oz cooked chicken, chopped
salt
sprigs of fresh coriander, to garnish
freshly cooked rice, to serve

Grind the cumin and coriander seeds in a mortar with a pestle, then reserve. Heat the mustard oil in a large heavy-based frying pan over a high heat for 1 minute, or until it begins to smoke. Add the vegetable oil, reduce the heat and add the onion and garlic. Cook for 10 minutes, or until golden.

Add the tomato purée, tomatoes, turmeric, chilli powder, garam masala, vinegar and reserved ground cumin and coriander seeds to the frying pan. Stir the mixture until fragrant.

Add the red pepper and broad beans and stir for a further 2 minutes, or until the pepper is softened. Stir in the chicken, and season to taste with salt.

Simmer the curry gently for 6–8 minutes, or until the chicken is heated through and the beans are tender. Transfer to warmed serving bowls, garnish with sprigs of coriander and serve with freshly cooked rice.

205 Lamb jalfrezi

Although a jalfrezi – a hot dish with peppers and tomatoes – is most often made with chicken, it is also made with lamb. Add 500 g/1 lb 2 oz raw lamb steaks, each cut into 3 pieces, to the pan towards the end of onion cooking time. Increase simmering time to 10 minutes.

Chicken pasanda

4 cardamom pods
6 black peppercorns
½ cinnamon stick
½ tsp cumin seeds
2 tsp garam masala
1 tsp chilli powder
1 tsp grated fresh ginger
1 garlic clove, very finely chopped
4 tbsp thick natural yogurt
pinch of salt
675 g/1 lb 8 oz skinless, boneless chicken, diced
5 tbsp groundnut oil
2 onions, finely chopped
3 fresh green chillies, deseeded and chopped
2 tbsp chopped fresh coriander
125 ml/4 fl oz single cream
fresh coriander sprigs, to garnish

Place the cardamom pods in a non-metallic dish with the peppercorns, cinnamon, cumin, garam masala, chilli powder, ginger, garlic, yogurt and salt. Add the chicken pieces and stir well to coat. Cover and leave to marinate in the refrigerator for 2–3 hours.

Heat the oil in a preheated wok or karahi. Add the onions and cook over a low heat, stirring occasionally, for 5 minutes, or until softened, then add the chicken pieces and marinade and cook over a medium heat, stirring, for 15 minutes, or until the chicken is cooked through.

Stir in the fresh chillies and coriander and pour in the cream. Heat through gently, but do not let it boil. Garnish with fresh coriander and serve immediately.

Creamy chicken tikka

700 g/1 lb 9 oz skinless, boneless chicken
   breasts, cut into 2.5-cm/1-inch cubes
2 tbsp lemon juice
½ tsp salt, or to taste
125 g/4½ oz whole milk natural yogurt,
   strained, or Greek-style yogurt
3 tbsp double cream
25 g/1 oz mild Cheddar cheese, grated
1 tbsp garlic purée
1 tbsp ginger purée

½–1 tsp chilli powder
½ tsp ground turmeric
½ tsp granulated sugar
1 tbsp gram flour, sifted
1 tsp garam masala
2 tbsp sunflower or olive oil, plus 2 tbsp
   for brushing
3 tbsp melted butter or olive oil
salad and chutney, to serve

Put the chicken in a non-metallic bowl and add the lemon juice and salt. Rub well into the chicken. Cover and leave to marinate in the refrigerator for 20–30 minutes.

Put the yogurt in a separate non-metallic bowl and beat with a fork until smooth. Add all the remaining ingredients, except the melted butter. Beat well until the ingredients are fully incorporated. Add the chicken and mix thoroughly until fully coated with the marinade. Cover and leave to marinate in the refrigerator for 4–6 hours, or overnight. Return to room temperature before cooking.

Preheat the grill to high. Brush 6 metal skewers generously with the remaining 2 tablespoons of oil and thread on the chicken cubes. Brush over any remaining marinade. Place the prepared skewers in a grill pan and grill about 7.5 cm/3 inches below the heat source for 4–5 minutes.

Brush generously with the melted butter and cook for a further 1–2 minutes. Turn over and cook for 3–4 minutes, basting frequently with the remaining melted butter.

Balance the skewers over a large saucepan or frying pan and leave to rest for 5–6 minutes before sliding the chicken cubes off the skewers with a knife. Serve with salad and chutney.

208 *Lower-fat creamy chicken tikka*

For a lower fat version that is still creamy, omit the cream and cheese and replace the yogurt with 200 ml/7 fl oz half-fat Greek yogurt.

Fiery chicken vindaloo

1 tsp ground cumin
1 tsp ground cinnamon
2 tsp mustard powder
1½ tsp ground coriander
1 tsp cayenne pepper
5 tbsp red wine vinegar
1 tsp brown sugar
150 ml/5 fl oz vegetable oil
8 garlic cloves, crushed
3 red onions, sliced

4 skinless chicken breasts, cut into
   bite-sized chunks
2 small red chillies, deseeded and chopped
450 g/1 lb potatoes, peeled and cut into
   chunks
800 g/1 lb 12 oz canned chopped tomatoes
1 tbsp tomato purée
a few drops of red food colouring
salt and pepper
freshly cooked rice, to serve

red food colouring. Stir in the spice mixture, season generously with salt and pepper and bring to the boil. Lower the heat, cover the pan and simmer, stirring occasionally, for 1 hour.

Arrange the rice on a large serving platter. Remove the pan from the heat, spoon the chicken mixture over the rice and serve immediately.

Put the cumin, cinnamon, mustard, ground coriander and cayenne pepper into a bowl. Add the vinegar and sugar and mix well.

Heat the oil in a large frying pan. Add the garlic and onions and cook, stirring, over a medium heat for 5 minutes. Add the chicken and cook for a further 3 minutes, then add the chillies, potatoes, chopped tomatoes and tomato purée, and a few drops of

210 *Hot chicken vindaloo*

For a slightly less fiery vindaloo, replace the cayenne pepper with mild paprika and when choosing the fresh chillies find ones which are medium hot, such as jalapeno or anaheim.

2 tbsp groundnut or sunflower oil

500 g/1 lb 2 oz skinless boneless chicken
  breasts, cut into cubes

2 kaffir lime leaves, roughly torn

1 lemon grass stalk, finely chopped

225 ml/8 fl oz canned
  coconut milk

16 baby aubergines, halved

2 tbsp Thai fish sauce

fresh Thai basil sprigs, to garnish

kaffir lime leaves, thinly sliced,
  to garnish

GREEN CURRY PASTE

16 fresh green chillies

2 shallots, sliced

4 kaffir lime leaves

1 lemon grass stalk, chopped

2 garlic cloves, chopped

1 tsp cumin seeds

1 tsp coriander seeds

1 tbsp grated fresh ginger or galangal

1 tsp grated lime rind

5 black peppercorns

1 tbsp sugar

salt

2 tbsp groundnut or sunflower oil

Heat 2 tablespoons of oil in a preheated wok or large heavy-based frying pan. Add 2 tablespoons of the curry paste and stir-fry briefly until all the aromas are released. Add the chicken, lime leaves and lemon grass and stir-fry for 3–4 minutes, until the meat is beginning to colour.

Add the coconut milk and aubergines and simmer gently for 8–10 minutes, or until tender. Stir in the fish sauce and serve immediately, garnished with Thai basil sprigs and lime leaves.

First make the curry paste. Deseed the chillies if you like and roughly chop. Place all the paste ingredients except the oil in a mortar and pound with a pestle. Alternatively, process in a food processor. Gradually blend in the oil.

212 *Thai green chicken curry with peppers*

Replace the baby aubergines with 3 green peppers, sliced, which will enhance the green colour of the curry. If you don't have any coconut milk you can use creamed coconut in a block, which, if you keep it well wrapped in the fridge, will last for months.

213 Azerbaijani lamb pilau

2–3 tbsp vegetable oil

650 g/1 lb 7 oz boneless lamb shoulder, cut into 2.5-cm/1-inch cubes

2 onions, roughly chopped

1 tsp ground cumin

200 g/7 oz arborio rice

1 tbsp tomato purée

1 tsp saffron threads

100 ml/3½ fl oz pomegranate juice

850 ml/1½ pints lamb stock, chicken stock or water

115 g/4 oz no-soak dried apricots or prunes, halved

2 tbsp raisins

salt and pepper

2 tbsp shredded fresh mint and 2 tbsp shredded fresh watercress, to garnish

Heat the oil in a large flameproof casserole or saucepan over a high heat. Add the lamb, in batches, and cook over a high heat, turning frequently, for 7 minutes, or until lightly browned. Add the onions, reduce the heat to medium and cook for 2 minutes, or until beginning to soften. Add the cumin and rice and cook, stirring to coat, for 2 minutes, or until the rice is translucent. Stir in the tomato purée and the saffron threads. Add the pomegranate juice and stock. Bring to the boil, stirring. Stir in the apricots and raisins. Reduce the heat to low, cover, and simmer for 20–25 minutes, or until the lamb and rice are tender and all of the liquid has been absorbed. Season to taste with salt and pepper, then sprinkle over the mint and watercress and serve from the casserole.

214 Hot Azerbaijani lamb pilau

The pilau above is a very lightly spiced fragrant dish – for more heat, add ½ teaspoon each of ground cinnamon, chilli powder and 1 teaspoon of fresh chopped ginger, all towards the end of the onions' cooking time. You can also replace the saffron with turmeric if you do not have saffron to hand.

215 Rogan josh

4 tbsp sunflower or olive oil

1 large onion, roughly chopped

5-cm/2-inch piece fresh ginger, peeled and roughly chopped

5 large garlic cloves, roughly chopped

400 g/14 oz canned tomatoes

3 brown cardamom pods

2 bay leaves

1 tbsp ground coriander

1 tsp ground turmeric

1 tsp chilli powder

700 g/1 lb 9 oz boned leg of lamb, cut into 2.5-cm/1-inch cubes

150 g/5½ oz natural yogurt

2 tsp gram flour

1 tsp salt, or to taste

1 tbsp tomato purée

125 ml/4 fl oz warm water

1 tsp ghee or unsalted butter

1 tsp garam masala

½ tsp ground nutmeg

2 tbsp chopped fresh coriander

naan bread or boiled basmati rice, to serve

Heat 2 tablespoons of the oil in a medium-sized, heavy-based saucepan over a medium heat. Add the onion, ginger and garlic and cook, stirring frequently, for 5 minutes, or until lightly coloured. Remove from the heat and squeeze out as much excess oil as possible. Transfer the mixture to a blender or food processor with the tomatoes, blend to a purée and set aside.

Return the saucepan to a low heat and add the remaining oil. Add the cardamom pods and bay leaves and leave to sizzle gently for 20–25 seconds, then add the ground coriander, turmeric and chilli powder.

Cook, stirring, for 1 minute, then add the tomato mixture. Increase the heat to medium and continue to cook for 10–12 minutes, until the oil separates from the spice paste, reducing the heat to low towards the last 2–3 minutes. Add the lamb and increase the heat slightly.

Cook, stirring, until the meat changes colour. Put the yogurt and gram flour in a bowl and beat with a fork or wire whisk until smooth. Reduce the heat slightly and stir the yogurt mixture, 2 tablespoons at a time, into the meat mixture. Add the salt and tomato purée. Reduce the heat to low, cover and cook for 30 minutes, stirring occasionally. Add the water and bring it to a slow simmer. Re-cover and cook for a further 20–25 minutes, until the meat is tender. Melt the ghee in a small saucepan over a low heat, add the garam masala and nutmeg and cook, stirring, for 30 seconds. Pour the spiced butter over the curry and stir in half the chopped fresh coriander. Remove from the heat and serve garnished with the remaining fresh coriander, accompanied by naan or plain boiled basmatic rice.

216 Rogan josh with yogurt

You can omit the yogurt/gram flour mixture from the curry if you want to retain its rich colour, and simply garnish the finished curry with 1 tablespoon of yogurt per portion.

700 g/1 lb 9 oz boneless shoulder of
lamb, trimmed and cut into 5-cm/
2-inch cubes
1 tbsp garlic and ginger purée
5 green cardamom pods
200 g/7 oz yellow lentils (toor dal)
100 g/3½ oz pumpkin, peeled,
deseeded and chopped
1 carrot, thinly sliced
1 fresh green chilli, deseeded
and chopped
1 tsp fenugreek powder
500 ml/18 fl oz water
1 large onion, thinly sliced
30 g/1 oz ghee or 2 tbsp vegetable or
groundnut oil
2 garlic cloves, crushed
salt
chopped fresh coriander, to garnish

DHANSAK MASALA
1 tsp garam masala
½ tsp ground coriander
½ tsp ground cumin
½ tsp chilli powder
½ tsp ground turmeric
¼ tsp ground cardamom
¼ tsp ground cloves

Put the lamb and 1 teaspoon of salt in a large saucepan with enough water to cover and bring to the boil. Reduce the heat and simmer, skimming the surface as necessary. Stir in the garlic and ginger purée and cardamom pods and continue simmering for a total of 30 minutes.

Meanwhile, put the lentils, pumpkin, carrot, chilli and fenugreek powder in a large saucepan and pour over the water. Bring to the boil, stirring occasionally, then reduce the heat and simmer for 20–30 minutes, until the lentils and carrot are very tender. Stir in a little extra water if the lentils look as though they will catch on the base of the pan.

Leave the lentil mixture to cool slightly, then pour it into a food processor and whizz until thick. While the lamb and lentils are cooking, put the onion in a bowl, sprinkle with 1 teaspoon of salt and leave to stand for about 5 minutes, before squeezing out the moisture.

Melt the ghee in a flameproof casserole or large frying pan with a tight-fitting lid over a high heat. Add the onion and cook, stirring constantly, for 2 minutes. Remove one third of the onion and continue frying the rest for a further 1–2 minutes, until golden brown. Use a slotted spoon to immediately remove the onion from the pan, as it will continue to darken as it cools.

Return the one third of the onion to the pan with the garlic. Stir in all the dhansak masala ingredients and cook for 2 minutes. Add the cooked lamb and stir for a further 2 minutes. Add the lentil sauce and simmer over a medium heat to warm through. Adjust the seasoning, if necessary. Sprinkle with the remaining onion, garnish with fresh coriander and serve.

218 *Quick lamb dhansak*

To serve 4, simmer 150 g/ 5 oz red lentils, 1 small chopped butternut squash, 1 large onion and 400 g/14 oz can chopped tomatoes with 1 teaspoon of ground turmeric and 300 ml/10½ fl oz water for 30 minutes. Saute 600 g/1lb 5 oz lamb cubes in 2 tablespoons of oil with 1 level teaspoon each of ground coriander, cumin and cardamom for 2 minutes, stir in 2 teaspoons each of fresh chopped ginger and garlic and 2 hot fresh chopped chillies. Add contents of first pan and simmer with lid on for 45 minutes or until lamb is tender. Stir in 1 teaspoon of garam masala and coriander leaves 2 minutes before serving.

Lamb pasanda

SERVES 4–6

600 g/1 lb 5 oz boneless shoulder or leg of lamb

2 tbsp garlic and ginger purée

55 g/2 oz ghee or 4 tbsp vegetable or groundnut oil

3 large onions, chopped

1 fresh green chilli, deseeded and chopped

2 green cardamom pods, bruised

1 cinnamon stick, broken in half

2 tsp ground coriander

1 tsp ground cumin

1 tsp ground turmeric

250 ml/9 fl oz water

150 ml/5 fl oz double cream

4 tbsp ground almonds

1½ tsp salt

1 tsp garam masala

paprika and toasted flaked almonds, to garnish

Cut the meat into thin slices, then place the slices between clingfilm and pound with a rolling pin or meat mallet to make them even thinner. Put the slices in a bowl, add the garlic and ginger purée and rub the paste into the lamb. Cover and set aside in a cool place to marinate for 2 hours.

Melt the ghee in a large frying pan with a tight-fitting lid over a medium–high heat. Add the onions and chilli and cook, stirring, for 5–8 minutes, until the onions are golden brown. Stir in the spices and continue stirring for 2 minutes, or until they are aromatic. Add the meat to the pan and cook, stirring occasionally, for 5 minutes, until brown on all sides and the fat begins to separate.

Stir in the water and bring to the boil, still stirring. Reduce the heat to its lowest setting, cover the pan and simmer for 40 minutes, or until the meat is tender.

When the lamb is tender, stir the cream and ground almonds together in a bowl. Beat in 6 tablespoons of the hot cooking liquid from the pan, then gradually beat this mixture back into the pan. Stir in the salt and garam masala. Continue to simmer for 5 minutes, uncovered, stirring occasionally. Garnish with a sprinkling of paprika and toasted flaked almonds and serve.

220 *Lamb pasanda with curry powder*

You can save time by using 1 tablespoon of a ready-made curry powder, medium strength, to replace the fresh chilli and the cardamon, cinnamon, coriander, cumin and turmeric. Add the powder towards the end of the onion cooking time and stir to release the aromas before adding meat.

221 *Peshawar-style lamb curry*

SERVES 4

4 tbsp sunflower or olive oil

2.5-cm/1-inch piece cinnamon stick

5 green cardamom pods, bruised

5 cloves

2 bay leaves

700 g/1 lb 9 oz boneless leg of lamb, cut into 2.5-cm/1-inch cubes

1 large onion, finely chopped

2 tsp ginger purée

2 tsp garlic purée

1 tbsp tomato purée

1 tsp ground turmeric

1 tsp ground coriander

1 tsp ground cumin

125 g/4½ oz thick set natural yogurt

2 tsp gram flour or cornflour

½–1 tsp chilli powder

150 ml/5 fl oz warm water

1 tbsp chopped fresh mint leaves

2 tbsp chopped fresh coriander leaves

Indian bread, to serve

In a medium saucepan, heat the oil over a low heat and add the cinnamon, cardamom, cloves and bay leaves. Let them sizzle for 25–30 seconds, then add the meat, increase the heat to medium–high and cook until the meat begins to brown and all the natural juices have evaporated. Add the onion and ginger and garlic purées, cook for 5–6 minutes, stirring regularly, then add the tomato purée, turmeric, ground coriander and cumin. Continue to cook for 3–4 minutes.

Whisk together the yogurt, gram flour and chilli powder and add to the meat. Reduce the heat to low, add the warm water, cover and simmer, stirring so that the sauce does not stick to the base of the pan, for 45–50 minutes, or until the meat is tender. Simmer uncovered, if necessary, to thicken the sauce to a desired consistency.

Stir in the fresh mint and coriander, remove from the heat and serve with Indian bread.

222 *Easy Peshawar-style lamb curry*

For an easy version, marinate the cubed lamb leg in the oil for several hours with ½ teaspoon of ground cinnamon, seeds from 5 cardamom pods, ½ teaspoon of ground cloves, 1 chopped bay leaf, 2 teaspoons of ginger, 2 teaspoons of garlic, 1 teaspoon each of turmeric, coriander and cumin. Baste several times. Remove lamb from dish and set aside – blend all spices in a food processor or blender with the oil and chopped onion until smooth. Heat a frying pan with 1 tablespoon of oil and cook lamb and spice mix over a medium–high heat for 3 minutes, then add tomato purée and a little water, and cook for 15 minutes more. Stir in yogurt, mint and coriander.

Red lamb curry

SERVES 4

500 g/1 lb 2 oz boneless lean leg of lamb
2 tbsp vegetable oil
1 large onion, sliced
2 garlic cloves, crushed
2 tbsp red curry paste
150 ml/5 fl oz coconut milk
1 tbsp soft light brown sugar
1 large red pepper, deseeded and thickly
   sliced

125 ml/4 fl oz lamb or beef stock
1 tbsp Thai fish sauce
2 tbsp lime juice
225 g/8 oz canned water chestnuts, drained
2 tbsp chopped fresh coriander
2 tbsp chopped fresh basil, plus extra
   leaves to garnish
salt and pepper
boiled jasmine rice, to serve

Trim the meat and cut it into 3-cm/1¼-inch cubes. Heat the oil in a large frying pan or preheated wok over a high heat and stir-fry the onion and garlic for 2–3 minutes, or until softened. Add the meat and stir-fry until lightly browned.

Stir in the curry paste and cook for a few seconds, then add the coconut milk and sugar and bring to the boil. Reduce the heat and simmer for 15 minutes, stirring occasionally.

Stir in the pepper, stock, fish sauce and lime juice. Cover and simmer for a further 15 minutes, or until the meat is tender.

Add the water chestnuts, coriander and basil and adjust the seasoning to taste. Serve, garnished with basil leaves, with jasmine rice.

224 *Red duck or beef curry*

This curry can also be made with other lean meats. Try replacing the lamb with trimmed duck breasts or pieces of lean beef steak. You can also use braising beef but increase the cooking time to at least 1 hour.

225 *Red curry pork with peppers*

SERVES 4

2 tbsp vegetable or groundnut oil
1 onion, roughly chopped
2 garlic cloves, chopped
450 g/1 lb pork fillet, thickly sliced
1 red pepper, deseeded and cut into
   squares
175 g/6 oz mushrooms, quartered

2 tbsp Thai red curry paste
115 g/4 oz creamed coconut, chopped
300 ml/½ pint pork or vegetable stock
2 tbsp Thai soy sauce
4 tomatoes, peeled, deseeded and chopped
handful of fresh coriander, chopped
boiled noodles or rice, to serve

Heat the oil in a wok or large frying pan and fry the onion and garlic for 1–2 minutes, until they are softened but not browned. Add the pork slices and stir-fry for 2–3 minutes until browned. Add the pepper, mushrooms and curry paste. Dissolve the coconut in the stock and add with the soy sauce. Bring to the boil and simmer for 4–5 minutes until the liquid has reduced and thickened. Add the tomatoes and coriander and cook for 1–2 minutes before serving with noodles or rice.

226 *Red curry pork with courgette*

Replace the mushrooms with 1 medium courgette, thinly sliced.

227 Burmese pork curry

700 g/1 lb 9 oz boneless leg of pork,
   fat trimmed and cut into
   2.5-cm/1-inch cubes
2 tbsp dry white wine
1 tsp salt, or to taste
8 large garlic cloves, roughly chopped
5-cm/2-inch piece fresh ginger,
   roughly chopped
2 fresh red chillies, roughly chopped

1 large onion, roughly chopped
1 tsp ground turmeric
½ –1 tsp chilli powder
3 tbsp groundnut oil
1 tbsp sesame oil
200 ml/7 fl oz warm water
1 fresh green chilli, deseeded and cut into
   julienne strips, to garnish

Mix the pork, wine and salt in a non-metallic bowl and set aside for 1 hour. Put the garlic, ginger, chillies and onion in a food processor or blender and blend until the ingredients are mushy. Transfer to a bowl and stir in the spices. Heat both oils in a medium heavy-based saucepan over a medium heat and add the puréed ingredients. Stir and cook for 5–6 minutes, reduce the heat to low and continue to cook for a further 8–10 minutes, sprinkling over a little water from time to time to prevent the spices from sticking. Add the marinated pork, increase the heat to medium–high and stir until the meat changes colour. Pour in the warm water, bring to the boil, reduce the heat to low, cover and cook for 1 hour 10 minutes, stirring several times during the last 15–20 minutes to prevent the sauce from sticking. Remove from the heat and garnish.

228 Burmese chicken curry

Make the same recipe as for pork but use 700 g/1lb 9 oz skinless chicken fillet, sliced, instead, and reduce cooking time by 5 minutes.

229 Pork vindaloo

2–6 dried red chillies (long slim variety),
   torn into 2–3 pieces
5 cloves
2.5-cm/1-inch piece cinnamon stick,
   broken up
4 green cardamom pods
½ tsp black peppercorns
½ mace blade
¼ nutmeg, lightly crushed
1 tsp cumin seeds
½ tsp coriander seeds
½ tsp fenugreek seeds
2 tsp garlic purée
1 tbsp ginger purée

3 tbsp cider vinegar or
   white wine vinegar
1 tbsp tamarind juice or juice of ½ lime
700 g/1 lb 9 oz boneless leg of pork, cut
   into 2.5-cm/1-inch cubes
4 tbsp sunflower or olive oil, plus 2 tsp
2 large onions, finely chopped
250 ml/9 fl oz warm water, plus 4 tbsp
1 tsp salt, or to taste
1 tsp soft dark brown sugar
2 large garlic cloves, finely sliced
8–10 fresh or dried curry leaves
cooked basmati rice, to serve

Grind the first 10 ingredients (all the spices) to a fine powder in a coffee grinder. Transfer the ground spices to a bowl and add the garlic and ginger purées, vinegar and tamarind juice. Mix together to form a paste.

Put the pork in a large non-metallic bowl and rub about one quarter of the spice paste into the meat. Cover and leave to marinate in the refrigerator for 30–40 minutes. Heat the 4 tablespoons of oil in a medium heavy-based saucepan over a medium heat, add the onions and cook, stirring frequently, for 8–10 minutes, until lightly browned. Add the remaining spice paste and cook, stirring constantly, for 5–6 minutes. Add 2 tablespoons of the warm water and cook until it evaporates. Repeat with another 2 tablespoons of water.

Add the marinated pork and cook over medium–high heat for 5–6 minutes, until the meat changes colour. Add the salt, sugar and the remaining 250 ml/9 fl oz warm water. Bring to the boil, then reduce the heat to low, cover and simmer for 50–55 minutes, until the meat is tender.

Meanwhile, heat the 2 teaspoons of oil in a very small saucepan over a low heat. Add the sliced garlic and cook, stirring frequently, until it begins to brown. Add the curry leaves and leave to sizzle for 15–20 seconds. Stir the garlic mixture into the vindaloo. Remove from the heat and serve immediately with cooked basmati rice.

230 Beef vindaloo

Replace pork with the same weight of braising steak and increase cooking time to 1½ hours or until steak is meltingly tender.

231 Railway pork & vegetables

40 g/1½ oz ghee or 3 tbsp vegetable or
    groundnut oil
1 large onion, finely chopped
4 green cardamom pods
3 cloves
1 cinnamon stick
1 tbsp garlic and ginger purée
2 tsp garam masala
¼–½ tsp chilli powder

½ tsp ground asafoetida
2 tsp salt
600 g/1 lb 5 oz lean minced pork
1 potato, scrubbed and cut into
    5-mm/¼-inch dice
400 g/14 oz canned chopped tomatoes
125 ml/4 fl oz water
1 bay leaf
1 large carrot, coarsely grated

Melt the ghee in a flameproof casserole or large frying pan with a tight-fitting lid over a medium heat. Add the onion and cook, stirring occasionally, for 5–8 minutes, until golden brown. Add the cardamom pods, cloves and cinnamon stick and cook, stirring, for 1 minute.

Add the garlic and ginger purée, garam masala, chilli powder, asafoetida and salt and stir around for a further minute. Add the pork and cook for 5 minutes, or until no longer pink, using a wooden spoon to break up the meat. Add the potato, tomatoes, water and bay leaf and bring to the boil, stirring. Reduce the heat to the lowest level, cover tightly and simmer for 15 minutes. Stir in the carrot and simmer for a further 5 minutes, or until the potato and carrot are tender. Taste and adjust the seasoning, if necessary, and serve.

232 Railway lamb & vegetables

Lean minced lamb or beef can be used instead of the pork.

233 Pork with mixed green beans

2 tbsp vegetable or groundnut oil
2 shallots, chopped
225 g/8 oz pork fillet, thinly sliced
2.5-cm/1-inch piece fresh galangal,
    thinly sliced
2 garlic cloves, chopped
300 ml/10 fl oz chicken stock

4 tbsp chilli sauce
4 tbsp crunchy peanut butter
115 g/4 oz fine French beans, trimmed
115 g/4 oz frozen broad beans
115 g/4 oz runner beans, trimmed
    and sliced
crispy noodles, to serve

Heat the oil in a wok and stir-fry the shallots, pork, galangal and garlic until lightly browned.

Add the stock, chilli sauce and peanut butter and stir until the peanut butter has melted. Add all the beans and simmer the mixture for 3–4 minutes. Serve hot with crispy noodles.

234 Pork with beans & carrots

Use same recipe as above but replace broad beans and runner beans with 125 g/4½ oz sliced carrot and 100 g/3½ oz fresh beansprouts, adding the beansprouts for the last minute of cooking only.

235 French country casserole

2 tbsp sunflower oil
2 kg/4 lb 8 oz boneless leg of lamb,
  cut into 2.5-cm/1-inch cubes
6 leeks, sliced
1 tbsp plain flour
150 ml/5 fl oz rosé wine
300 ml/10 fl oz chicken stock
1 tbsp tomato purée
1 tbsp sugar
2 tbsp chopped fresh mint
115 g/4 oz ready-to-eat dried
  apricots, chopped
1 kg/2 lb 4 oz potatoes, sliced
3 tbsp melted unsalted butter
salt and pepper
fresh mint sprigs, to garnish

Preheat the oven to 180°C/350°F/ Gas Mark 4. Heat the oil in a large flameproof casserole. Add the lamb in batches and cook over a medium heat, stirring, for 5–8 minutes, or until browned. Transfer to a plate. Add the sliced leeks to the casserole and cook, stirring occasionally, for 5 minutes, or until softened. Sprinkle in the flour and cook, stirring, for 1 minute. Pour in the wine and stock and bring to the boil, stirring. Stir in the tomato purée, sugar, chopped mint and apricots and season to taste with salt and pepper.

Return the lamb to the casserole and stir. Arrange the potato slices on top and brush with the melted butter. Cover and bake in the preheated oven for 1½ hours.

Increase the oven temperature to 200°C/400°F/Gas Mark 6,

uncover the casserole and bake for a further 30 minutes, or until the potato topping is golden brown. Serve immediately, garnished with fresh mint sprigs.

236 French casserole with squash

Replace the dried apricots with 150 g/5½ oz butternut squash, chopped into small cubes. If you don't have any rosé wine you can use medium dry white wine instead.

237 Kidneys in mustard sauce

12 lambs' kidneys,
  skinned and halved
30 g/1 oz unsalted butter
1 tbsp sunflower oil
2 large shallots, chopped
1 garlic clove, very finely chopped
2 tbsp dry white wine

125 ml/4 fl oz chicken stock
  or lamb stock
250 ml/9 fl oz double cream
2 tbsp Dijon mustard, or to taste
salt and pepper
chopped fresh flat-leaf parsley,
  to garnish

Use a pair of kitchen scissors to remove the kidney cores. Melt the butter with the oil in a large sauté or frying pan over a medium–high heat. Add the kidney halves and fry, turning occasionally, for 3 minutes, or until brown all over, working in batches, if necessary, to avoid overcrowding the pan. Use a slotted spoon to transfer the kidney halves to a plate, then cover with foil, shiny-side down, set aside and keep warm.

Add the shallots and garlic to the fat in the pan and sauté for 2 minutes, or until the shallots are soft, but not coloured. Add the wine and boil until it reduces by half, scraping the sediment from the base of the pan.

Add the stock and boil again until reduced by half. Stir in the cream and mustard, reduce the heat to medium–low and return the kidneys to the pan. Cover and simmer for 5 minutes, or until the kidneys are cooked through.

Remove the kidneys from the pan and keep warm. Increase the heat under the sauce and leave it to bubble until it reduces and thickens. Add salt and pepper to taste, return the kidneys and stir them around. Sprinkle with the parsley and serve.

238 Kidneys in mustard sherry sauce

Use a medium dry sherry instead of the wine and substitute wholegrain mustard for the Dijon mustard.

Turkey, leek & cheese gratin

115 g/4 oz dried short macaroni
1 small egg, lightly beaten
2 tbsp butter
4 small leeks, green part included, finely sliced
2 carrots, diced
1 tbsp plain flour
¼ tsp freshly grated nutmeg
250 ml/9 fl oz chicken stock
225 g/8 oz diced cooked turkey or chicken
55 g/2 oz diced ham
3 tbsp chopped fresh flat-leaf parsley
100 g/3½ oz freshly grated Gruyère cheese
salt and pepper

Preheat the oven to 180°C/350°F/Gas Mark 4.

Cook the macaroni in plenty of boiling salted water until just tender. Drain and return to the saucepan. Stir in the egg and a knob of the butter, mixing well. Set aside.

Melt the remaining butter in a saucepan over a medium heat. Add the leeks and carrots. Cover and cook for 5 minutes, shaking the saucepan occasionally, until just tender.

Add the flour and nutmeg. Cook for 1 minute, stirring constantly. Pour in the stock. Bring to the boil and continue to stir. Stir in the turkey, ham and parsley. Season to taste with salt and pepper.

Spread half the turkey mixture over the base of a shallow baking dish. Spread the macaroni over the turkey. Top with the remaining turkey mixture. Sprinkle with the cheese.

Bake in the oven for 15–20 minutes. Serve the gratin when the cheese is golden and bubbling.

Beef & tomato gratin

350 g/12 oz fresh lean beef mince
1 large onion, finely chopped
1 tsp dried mixed herbs
1 tbsp plain flour
300 ml/10 fl oz beef stock
1 tbsp tomato purée
2 large tomatoes, thinly sliced
4 courgettes, thinly sliced

2 tbsp cornflour
300 ml/10 fl oz skimmed milk
150 ml/5 fl oz low-fat natural fromage frais
1 egg yolk
4 tbsp freshly grated Parmesan cheese
salt and pepper

Preheat the oven to 190°C/375°F/Gas Mark 5. In a shallow flameproof casserole, dry-fry the beef and onion for 4–5 minutes, or until browned.

Stir in the herbs, flour, stock and tomato purée, and season to taste with salt and pepper. Bring to the boil, then reduce the heat and simmer for 30 minutes, or until thickened. Cover with a layer of the sliced tomatoes and then add a layer of sliced courgettes. Set aside until required.

Blend the cornflour with a little of the milk in a small bowl. Pour the remaining milk into a saucepan and bring to the boil. Add the cornflour mixture and cook, stirring, for 1–2 minutes, or until thickened. Remove from the heat and beat in the fromage frais and egg yolk. Season well.

Spread the white sauce over the layer of courgettes. Place the dish on a baking sheet and sprinkle with Parmesan cheese. Bake in the oven for 25–30 minutes, or until golden brown. Serve immediately.

With mascarpone cheese topping

Another topping version is simply to beat together 450 g/1 lb mascarpone cheese with enough skimmed milk to thin to a thick sauce consistency, beat in the yolk of an egg and 25 g/1 oz grated Parmesan cheese. Spoon over the gratin and continue as above.

Spicy meat & chipotle hash

1 tbsp vegetable oil
1 onion, finely chopped
450 g/1 lb cooked meat, such as roast
pork or beef, cooled and
cut into strips
1 tbsp mild chilli powder
2 ripe tomatoes, deseeded and diced
about 250 ml/8 fl oz meat stock
½–1 canned chipotle chilli, mashed,
with a little of the marinade
chopped fresh coriander,
to garnish
warmed tortillas and soured cream,
to serve

Heat the oil in a frying pan. Add the onion and cook until softened, stirring occasionally. Add the meat and cook for about 3 minutes, or until lightly browned, stirring.

Add the chilli powder, tomatoes and stock and cook until the tomatoes reduce to a sauce; break up the meat a little as it cooks.

Add the chilli and continue to cook, stirring the meat and sauce together until they are blended. Garnish with fresh coriander and serve with warmed tortillas and soured cream to make tacos.

243 With sweet peppers

Chipotles are smoked Mexican chillies – you can buy them powdered or dried as well as in jars. A great addition to these tacos is 2–3 bottled, skinned sweet peppers. Chop finely and add to the pan with chilli.

244 Steak & kidney pudding

butter, for greasing
450 g/1 lb braising steak, trimmed and
cut into 2.5-cm/1-inch pieces
2 lambs' kidneys, cored and cut into
2.5-cm/1-inch pieces
55 g/2 oz plain flour
1 onion, finely chopped
115 g/4 oz large field mushrooms, sliced
1 tbsp chopped fresh parsley

300 ml/½ pint (approx) stock, or a
mixture of beer and water
salt and pepper

SUET PASTRY
350 g/12 oz self-raising flour
175 g/6 oz suet
225 ml/8 fl oz cold water
salt and pepper

Grease a 1.2-litre/2-pint pudding basin. Put the prepared meat with the flour and salt and pepper into a large polythene bag and shake well until all the meat is well coated. Add the onion, mushrooms, and the parsley and shake again.

For the pastry, mix the flour, suet and salt and pepper together. Add enough of the cold water to make a soft dough.

Keep a quarter of the dough to one side and roll the remainder out to form a circle big enough to line the pudding basin. Line the basin, making sure that there is a good 1 cm/½ inch hanging over the edge.

Place the meat mixture in the basin and pour in enough of the stock to cover the meat.

Roll out the remaining pastry to make a lid. Fold in the edges of the lining pastry, dampen them and place the lid on top. Seal firmly in place. Cover with a piece of greaseproof paper and then foil, with a pleat to allow for expansion during cooking, and seal well. Place in a steamer or large saucepan half-filled with boiling water. Simmer the pudding for 4–5 hours, topping up the water from time to time.

Remove the basin from the steamer and take off the coverings. Wrap a clean cloth around the basin and serve at the table.

245 Steak & onion pudding

Omit the mushrooms and kidney – increase amount of steak to 600g/1 lb 5 oz and double the amount of onion you use. Another tasty change is to add 2 teaspoons of mixed herbs to the suet mix before adding the water – stir the herbs thoroughly into the dry mix.

246 Chicken fajitas

3 tbsp olive oil, plus extra for drizzling
3 tbsp maple syrup or clear honey
1 tbsp red wine vinegar
2 garlic cloves, crushed
2 tsp dried oregano
1–2 tsp dried red chilli flakes
4 skinless, boneless chicken breasts
2 red peppers, deseeded and cut into
   2.5-cm/1-inch strips
salt and pepper
8 tortillas, warmed
green salad and guacamole, to serve

Place the oil, maple syrup, vinegar, garlic, oregano, chilli flakes and salt and pepper to taste in a large, shallow dish or bowl and mix together.

Slice the chicken across the grain into slices 2.5 cm/1 inch thick. Toss in the marinade until well coated. Cover and leave to chill in the refrigerator for 2–3 hours, turning occasionally. Heat a griddle pan until hot. Lift the chicken slices from the marinade with a slotted spoon, lay on the griddle pan and cook over medium–high heat for 3–4 minutes on each side, or until cooked through. Remove the chicken to a warmed serving plate and keep warm.

Add the peppers to the griddle pan, skin side down, and cook for 2 minutes on each side. Transfer to the serving plate. Serve immediately with the warmed tortillas, a green salad and guacamole.

247 Beef fajitas

Use the same recipe but replace the chicken with 500 g/1 lb 2 oz rump or other good quality steak, cut into thin strips.

248 Chicken hash with fried eggs

900 g/2 lb floury potatoes
4 skinless, boneless chicken breasts
2 tbsp vegetable oil
1 onion, finely chopped
1 garlic clove, finely chopped
2 tbsp chopped fresh parsley
4 eggs
salt and pepper

Cut the potatoes into 2-cm/¾-inch dice and cook in a large saucepan of lightly salted water for 5 minutes, or until just tender. Drain well.

Cut the chicken into 2-cm/¾-inch pieces. Heat half the oil in a large frying pan. Add the onion and garlic and cook, stirring, for 5 minutes, or until the onion and garlic has softened.

Add the chicken and season to taste with salt and pepper. Cook, stirring, for a further 5 minutes, or until the onion and chicken have browned. Add the drained potatoes and cook, stirring occasionally, for 10 minutes, or until the potatoes have browned. Stir in the parsley.

Meanwhile, in a separate frying pan, heat the remaining oil. Break the eggs individually into the hot oil and cook until set.

Divide the chicken hash between individual serving plates and top each one with a fried egg.

249 Ham hash with peas & fried eggs

Use above recipe but replace chicken breasts with 200 g/7 oz lean ham, chopped and add 125 g/4½ oz cooked petit pois. Add ham to the pan for the last 3 minutes of potato cooking time and stir in peas for the last minute.

2 tbsp plain flour
4 skinned chicken quarters
or portions
3 tbsp olive oil
1 red onion, chopped
2 garlic cloves, finely chopped
1 red pepper, deseeded and chopped
pinch of saffron threads
150 ml/5 fl oz chicken stock or a
mixture of chicken stock and dry
white wine
400 g/14 oz canned tomatoes,
chopped
4 sun-dried tomatoes in oil,
drained and chopped
225 g/8 oz portobello mushrooms,
sliced
115 g/4 oz black olives, stoned
4 tbsp lemon juice
salt and pepper
fresh basil leaves, to garnish

Preheat the oven to 180°C/350°F/Gas Mark 4. Place the flour on a shallow plate and season with salt and pepper. Coat the chicken in the flour. Heat the olive oil in a large flameproof casserole. Add the chicken and cook over a medium heat, turning frequently, for 5–7 minutes, until golden brown. Remove from the casserole and set aside.

Add the onion, garlic and red pepper to the casserole, reduce the heat and cook, stirring occasionally, for 5 minutes, until softened. Meanwhile, stir the saffron into the stock. Stir the tomatoes, the sun-dried tomatoes, mushrooms and olives into the casserole and cook, stirring occasionally, for 3 minutes. Pour in the stock and saffron mixture and the lemon juice.

Bring to the boil, then return the chicken to the casserole. Cover and cook in the oven for 1 hour, until the chicken is tender. Garnish with the basil leaves and serve immediately.

251 *Tuscan chicken with red peppers*

Omit the mushrooms and use 2 large red peppers instead. Use sun-dried tomato purée instead of the whole sun-dried tomatoes.

252 Braised Asian duck

3 tbsp soy sauce
¼ tsp Chinese five-spice powder
4 duck legs or breasts, cut into pieces
3 tbsp vegetable oil
1 tsp dark sesame oil
1 tsp finely chopped fresh ginger
1 large garlic clove, finely chopped
4 spring onions, white parts sliced
    thickly, green part shredded

2 tbsp rice wine or dry sherry
1 tbsp oyster sauce
3 whole star anise
2 tsp black peppercorns
450–600 ml/16 fl oz–1 pint chicken stock
    or water
2 tbsp cornflour
salt and pepper

Combine 1 tablespoon of the soy sauce, the five-spice powder, and salt and pepper to taste and rub over the duck pieces. Brown the duck pieces in a casserole with 2½ tablespoons of the vegetable oil, remove and transfer to a plate.

Drain the fat from the casserole and wipe out. Heat the sesame oil and remaining vegetable oil. Add the ginger and garlic. Cook for a few seconds. Add the white spring onion. Cook for a few seconds. Return the duck

to the casserole. Add the rice wine, oyster sauce, star anise, peppercorns and remaining soy sauce. Pour in enough stock to just cover. Bring to the boil, cover and simmer gently for 1½ hours, adding more water if necessary.

Mix the cornflour with 2 tablespoons of the cooking liquid to a smooth paste. Add to the remaining liquid, stirring until thickened. Garnish with the green spring onion shreds to serve.

253 Braised Asian guinea fowl

You can use guinea fowl or pheasant instead of the duck in this recipe. You can also use wild duck (mallard) but you will need 2 to serve 4 people.

254 Pork with plum sauce

600 g/1 lb 5 oz pork fillet
2 tbsp groundnut oil
1 orange pepper, deseeded and sliced
1 bunch spring onions, sliced
250 g/9 oz oyster mushrooms, sliced
300 g/10½ oz fresh beansprouts
2 tbsp dry sherry
150 ml/5 fl oz plum sauce
250 g/9 oz medium egg noodles
salt and pepper
chopped fresh coriander,
    to garnish

Add the orange pepper and stir-fry for 2 minutes, then add the spring onions, mushrooms and beansprouts. Stir-fry for 2–3 minutes, then add the sherry and plum sauce and heat until boiling. Season well with salt and pepper.

Meanwhile, cook the noodles in a saucepan of lightly salted boiling water for 4 minutes, until tender. Drain the noodles, then add to the wok and toss well.

Serve immediately, garnished with fresh coriander.

Slice the pork into long thin strips. Heat the oil in a wok and stir-fry the pork for 2–3 minutes.

255 Pork with plum sauce & cucumber

Omit the orange pepper. Cut one third of a cucumber in half lengthways and deseed, then cut into thin batons. When serving the pork and noodles, lightly toss the cucumber pieces into the dish before serving, to add a delicious freshness and crunch to the meal.

256 *Lamb & potato moussaka*

1 tbsp olive or vegetable oil
1 onion, finely chopped
1 garlic clove, crushed
350 g/12 oz lean lamb mince
250 g/9 oz mushrooms, sliced
425 g/15 oz canned chopped tomatoes
   with herbs
150 ml/5 fl oz lamb or vegetable stock
2 tbsp cornflour
2 tbsp water
1 large aubergine, sliced

500 g/1 lb 2 oz potatoes, parboiled
   for 10 minutes and sliced
2 eggs
115 g/4 oz soft cheese
150 ml/5 fl oz Greek-style yogurt
55 g/2 oz kefalotiri or pecorino cheese,
   grated
salt and pepper
fresh flat-leaf parsley, to garnish

Beat together the eggs, soft cheese and yogurt and season to taste with salt and pepper. Pour over the potatoes to cover them completely. Sprinkle with the grated cheese.

Bake in for 45 minutes or until the topping is set and golden brown. Garnish with parsley and serve.

Preheat the oven to 190°C/375°F/Gas Mark 5. Heat the oil in a saucepan, add the onion and garlic and cook for 3–4 minutes. Add the lamb and mushrooms and cook for 5 minutes, until browned. Stir in the tomatoes and stock, bring to the boil and simmer for 10 minutes. Mix the cornflour with the water to a smooth paste and stir into the pan. Cook, stirring constantly, until thickened. Spoon half the mixture into an ovenproof dish. Cover with the aubergine slices, then the remaining lamb mixture. Arrange the sliced potatoes on top.

257 *Lamb & aubergine moussaka*

The traditional moussaka is made using all aubergines and no potatoes. If you want to try this, use 2 large aubergines in the recipe and omit the potatoes, using half the aubergines in place of potatoes when you layer up. For an even tastier dish, brush aubergines with a little olive oil and grill for 2 minutes on each side before using.

258 *Leek & sausage tortilla*

115 g/4 oz chorizo sausage
2 tbsp olive oil
4 leeks, thinly sliced

½ red pepper, deseeded and chopped
6 eggs
salt and pepper

Slice the sausage. Heat the oil in a large frying pan. Add the leeks and cook over a medium heat, stirring occasionally, for 5 minutes, or until softened. Add the red pepper and sausage slices and cook for 5 minutes.

Beat the eggs in a bowl and season to taste with salt and pepper. Pour the eggs into the frying pan and cook for a few seconds. Loosen any egg that has set at the edge of the pan with a palette knife and tilt the pan to let the uncooked egg run underneath.

Continue cooking until the underside has set. Remove the frying pan from the heat, place an upside-down plate on top and, holding the two together, invert the tortilla on to the plate. Slide it back into the frying pan and cook for a further 2 minutes, until the second side has set. Slide the tortilla out of the frying pan and on to a plate. Cut into wedges to serve.

259 *Sausage & onion tortilla*

Omit the leeks and replace with 2 onions, very thinly sliced.

260 *Sausage & courgette tortilla*

Omit leeks. Fry 2 thinly sliced courgettes in the oil until golden and soft; add 1 tablespoon of fresh chopped mint to the eggs before adding to the pan.

Pork chops with peppers & sweetcorn   SERVES 4

1 tbsp sunflower oil
4 pork chops, trimmed of visible fat
1 onion, chopped
1 garlic clove, finely chopped
1 green pepper, deseeded and sliced

1 red pepper, deseeded and sliced
325 g/11½ oz canned sweetcorn
1 tbsp chopped fresh parsley
salt and pepper
mashed potatoes, to serve

Heat the oil in a large flameproof casserole. Add the pork chops in batches and cook over a medium heat, turning occasionally, for 5 minutes, or until browned. Transfer the chops to a plate with a slotted spoon.

Add the chopped onion to the casserole and cook, stirring occasionally, for 5 minutes, or until softened. Add the garlic and peppers and cook, stirring occasionally for a further 5 minutes. Stir in the sweetcorn with the can juices and the parsley, and season to taste with salt and pepper.

Return the chops to the casserole, spooning the vegetable mixture over them. Cover and simmer for 30 minutes, or until tender. Serve immediately with mashed potatoes.

262 *Chicken with peppers & sweetcorn*

Use 4 chicken breast fillets instead of the pork chops – these can be with the skin on, or you can remove the skin if preferred. If skin is on, brown well until golden and crisp.

263 *Pork & sausage bake*   SERVES 4

2 tbsp sunflower oil
25 g/1 oz butter
450 g/1 lb pork fillet or loin, cut into thin
    strips
1 large onion, chopped
1 red pepper, deseeded and sliced
1 orange pepper, deseeded and sliced

115 g/4 oz mushrooms, sliced
140 g/5 oz long-grain rice
425 ml/15 fl oz beef stock
225 g/8 oz smoked sausage, sliced
¼ tsp ground mixed spice
salt and pepper
2 tbsp chopped fresh parsley, to garnish

Preheat the oven to 180°C/350°F/Gas Mark 4. Heat the oil and butter in a large flameproof casserole. Add the pork and cook over a medium heat, stirring, for 5 minutes, until browned. Transfer to a plate.

Add the onion and cook over a low heat, stirring occasionally, for 5 minutes, or until softened. Add the peppers and cook, stirring frequently, for a further 4–5 minutes. Add the mushrooms and cook for 1 minute, then stir in the rice. Cook for 1 minute, or until the grains are well coated, then add the stock and bring to the boil.

Return the pork to the casserole, add the sausage and mixed spice and season to taste with salt and pepper.

Mix thoroughly, cover and cook in the oven for 1 hour, or until all the liquid has been absorbed and the meat is tender. Serve immediately, garnished with chopped parsley.

264 *Pork & paprika bake*

Omit the smoked sausage and instead add 1 teaspoon of smoked paprika to the pan when you stir in the rice.

Toad in the hole

oil, for greasing
115 g/4 oz plain flour
pinch of salt
1 egg, beaten

300 ml/½ pint milk
450 g/1 lb good quality pork sausages
1 tbsp vegetable oil

Grease a 20 x 25-cm/8 x 10-inch ovenproof dish or roasting tin.

Make the batter by sifting the flour and salt into a mixing bowl. Make a well in the centre and add the beaten egg and half the milk. Carefully stir the liquid into the flour until the mixture is smooth. Gradually beat in the remaining milk. Leave to stand for 30 minutes.

Preheat the oven to 220°C/425°F/Gas Mark 7.

Prick the sausages and place them in the dish. Sprinkle over the oil and cook the sausages in the oven for 10 minutes until they are beginning to colour and the fat has started to run and is sizzling.

Remove from the oven and quickly pour the batter over the sausages. Return to the oven and cook for 35–45 minutes until well risen and golden brown. Serve immediately.

266 Meatball toad in the hole

Replace the sausages with 450 g/1lb sausagemeat. Put it in a bowl with 2 tablespoons of fresh chopped parsley, salt, black pepper, ½ teaspoon of ground cumin and ½ teaspoon of dry mustard powder. Combine well and form into 8 balls. Proceed as for sausages in the above recipe.

Broad beans with Serrano ham

55 g/2 oz Serrano ham or prosciutto, pancetta or rindless smoked lean bacon
115 g/4 oz chorizo sausage, outer casing removed
4 tbsp Spanish olive oil
1 onion, finely chopped
2 garlic cloves, finely chopped

splash of dry white wine
450 g/1 lb frozen broad beans, thawed, or about 1.3 kg/3 lb fresh broad beans in their pods, shelled to give 450 g/1 lb
1 tbsp chopped fresh mint or dill, plus extra to garnish
pinch of sugar
salt and pepper

Using a sharp knife, cut the ham into small strips. Cut the chorizo into 2-cm/¾-inch cubes.

Heat the olive oil in a large heavy-based frying pan or ovenproof dish that has a lid. Add the onion and cook for 5 minutes or until softened and starting to brown.

If you are using pancetta or bacon, add it to the onion. Add the garlic and cook for 30 seconds. Pour the wine into the pan, increase the heat and let it bubble to evaporate the alcohol, then lower the heat. Add the broad beans, ham and chorizo, and cook for 1–2 minutes, stirring all the time to coat in the oil.

Cover the frying pan and let the beans simmer very gently in the oil, stirring from time to time, for 10–15 minutes or until the beans are tender. It may be necessary to add a little water to the frying pan during cooking, so keep an eye on it and add a splash if the beans appear to become too dry. Stir in the mint or dill and sugar. Season the dish with salt and pepper but taste first as you may find that it does not need any salt.

Transfer the broad beans to a large, warmed serving dish and serve piping hot, garnished with chopped mint or dill.

268 Broad beans with ham & potato

Add 350 g/12 oz cooked sliced potato to the pan with the onion, brown a little then continue with the recipe, adding 1 tablespoon of fresh chopped parsley to the pan with the mint.

1.6 kg–1.8 kg/3 lb 8 oz–4 lb rolled beef
   silverside or brisket
½ tbsp plain flour, plus extra for dusting
3 tbsp vegetable oil
1 onion, finely chopped
2 celery sticks, finely diced

2 carrots, finely diced
1 fresh bay leaf
1 heaped tsp dried thyme
150 ml/5 fl oz meat stock
300–350 ml/10–12 fl oz red wine
salt and pepper

Preheat the oven to 150°C/300°F/Gas Mark 2. Season the meat well with salt and pepper and dust with flour. Heat the oil in a flameproof casserole in which the meat fits snugly. Cook the meat on all sides until browned and transfer to a plate. Add the onion, celery and carrots to the casserole and cook until soft.

Return the meat to the casserole and add the bay leaf, thyme, stock and enough wine to come one third of the way up the meat. Bring to the boil, cover tightly with a lid and place in the preheated oven. Cook for 3–3½ hours, turning occasionally, and topping up the liquid, if necessary. Transfer the meat to a warmed serving platter and cover loosely with foil.

Using kitchen paper, remove any excess fat from the surface of the liquid in the casserole. Strain the remaining liquid into a saucepan and bring to the boil, adding any juices from the meat. Mix the flour to a thin paste with a little water and whisk into the liquid to thicken. Check the seasoning and adjust, if necessary. Pour a little of the sauce over the meat and serve the remainder in a jug.

270 *Lamb & red wine pot roast*

Try the same recipe using a rolled breast of lamb (to serve 3–4) or boned leg or shoulder (to serve 5–6). Add 1 teaspoon of chopped rosemary to the pan with the thyme.

271 *Pork & red wine pot roast*

Try a rolled, boned pork leg to serve 5–6. Add 2 teaspoons of chopped sage to the pan with the thyme.

2½ tbsp plain flour
1 tsp salt
¼ tsp pepper
1.6 kg/3 lb 8 oz rolled brisket
2 tbsp vegetable oil
2 tbsp butter
1 onion, finely chopped
2 celery sticks, diced
2 carrots, diced
1 tsp dill seed
1 tsp dried thyme or oregano
350 ml/12 fl oz red wine
150–225 ml/5–8 fl oz beef stock
4–5 potatoes, cut into large chunks
and boiled until just tender
fresh dill sprigs, to serve

Preheat the oven to 140°C/275°F/Gas Mark 1. Mix 2 tablespoons of the flour with the salt and pepper in a shallow dish. Dip the meat in the seasoned flour to coat. Heat the oil in a flameproof casserole and brown the meat all over. Transfer to a plate. Heat half the butter in the casserole, add the onion, celery, carrots, dill seed and thyme and cook for 5 minutes. Return the meat and juices to the casserole. Pour in the wine and enough stock to reach one third of the way up the meat. Bring to the boil and cover. Transfer to the oven and cook for 3 hours, turning every 30 minutes. After 2 hours, add the potatoes and more stock if needed. When ready, transfer the meat and vegetables to a warmed serving dish. Strain the cooking liquid into a saucepan. Mix the remaining butter and flour to a paste. Bring the cooking liquid to the boil. Whisk in small pieces of the flour/butter paste, continuing to whisk until the sauce is smooth. Pour the sauce over the meat and vegetables. Sprinkle with dill sprigs and serve.

273 *Beef in the pot with potatoes & dill*

Cut the beef into 5-cm/2-inch cubes before coating with seasoned flour and browning. Use 250 ml/9 fl oz red wine and 150 ml/5 fl oz beef stock, and reduce oven cooking time to 2 hours, adding the potatoes after 1½ hours.

Lemon & tarragon poussins

2 poussins
4 sprigs fresh tarragon
1 tsp oil
2 tbsp butter
rind of ½ lemon
1 tbsp lemon juice
1 garlic clove, crushed
salt and pepper
tarragon and lemon slices to garnish

Prepare the poussins, turn them breast-side down on a chopping board and cut them through the backbone using kitchen scissors. Crush each bird gently to break the bones so that they lie flat while cooking. Season each bird with salt to taste.

Turn them over and insert a sprig of tarragon under the skin over each side of the breast. Brush the poussins with oil, using a pastry brush, and place under a preheated hot grill about 13 cm/ 5 inches from the heat. Grill the poussins for about 15 minutes, turning half way, until they are lightly browned.

To make the glaze for the poussins, melt the butter in a saucepan, add the lemon rind and juice and the garlic, and season to taste. Brush the poussins with the glaze and cook for a further 15 minutes, turning them once and brushing regularly so that they stay moist.

Garnish the poussins with tarragon and lemon slices.

275 *Orange & rosemary poussins*

Replace the lemon rind and juice with orange rind and juice. Use 3 teaspoons of fresh chopped rosemary instead of the tarragon, beaten with 1 level tablespoon of softened butter. Put half under the skin of each poussin.

276 *Lime & basil poussins*

Replace lemon rind and juice with rind and juice of 2 fresh limes. Use 2 tablespoons of fresh basil leaves instead of tarragon and add 1 teaspoon of olive oil with the leaves when inserting under the poussin skins.

277 *Roasted chicken with sun-dried tomato pesto*

4 skinless, boneless chicken breasts, about
    800 g/1 lb 12 oz in total
1 tbsp olive oil
green salad and crusty bread, to serve

RED PESTO
125 g/4½ oz sun-dried tomatoes in oil
    (drained weight), chopped
2 garlic cloves, crushed
6 tbsp pine kernels, lightly toasted
150 ml/5 fl oz extra virgin olive oil

Preheat the oven to 200°C/400°F/ Gas Mark 6. For the red pesto, put the sun-dried tomatoes, garlic, 4 tablespoons of the pine kernels and the oil into a food processor and blend to a coarse paste.

Arrange the chicken in a large, ovenproof dish or roasting tin. Brush each breast with the oil, then place 1 tablespoon of red pesto over each breast. Using the back of a spoon, spread the pesto so that it covers the top of each breast. (This pesto recipe makes more than just the 4 tablespoons used here. Store the extra pesto in an airtight container in the refrigerator for up to 1 week.)

Roast the chicken in the preheated oven for 30 minutes, or until tender and the juices run clear when a skewer is inserted into the thickest part of the meat.

Sprinkle with the remaining pine kernels and serve with a green side salad and crusty bread.

278 *Chicken with tomato & olive pesto*

Add 12 stoned and finely chopped black olives (well drained and rinsed) and ½ tbsp olive oil to the pesto after processing; stir in well.

279 *Chicken with red pepper & chilli pesto*

Make the pesto with 2 skinned and cooked red peppers and 2 mild red chilli peppers, replacing all but 50 g/2 oz of the sun-dried tomatoes.

1.5 litres/2¾ pints chicken stock
1.5 litres/2¾ pints water
bouquet garni of 4 sprigs parsley,
   4 sprigs thyme and 4 bay leaves tied
   with string
1 tsp black peppercorns
150 g/5½ oz smoked streaky bacon,
   chopped into chunks
1 whole garlic bulb, halved
3 small leeks, trimmed and cut into
   large chunks
3 carrots, peeled and cut into large chunks
3 celery stalks, cut into large chunks
3 turnips, peeled and cut into large
   chunks
6 small onions
1 chicken, 2–2.5 kg/4 lb 8 oz–5 lb 8 oz
1 small head of cabbage, cut into 6 pieces
12 small new potatoes, scrubbed
salt and pepper

STUFFING
125 g/4½ oz stale bread or breadcrumbs
125 g/4½ oz chicken livers, finely
   chopped
1 shallot, finely chopped
1 egg
handful of parsley, finely chopped
125 g/4½ oz sausage meat
3 garlic cloves, crushed
½ tsp salt
pepper

SAUCE
125 g/4½ oz gherkins, finely chopped
4 tbsp extra virgin olive oil
1 tbsp Dijon mustard

Take a very large saucepan and add the stock, water, bouquet garni, peppercorns, bacon and all the vegetables, except the potatoes and cabbage, and season with salt and pepper. Bring to a very gentle simmer.

Meanwhile, put all the stuffing ingredients in a bowl and mix thoroughly. Season the cavity of the chicken with salt and pepper. Spoon in the stuffing and truss the chicken with string. Place in the pot with the stock, cover and simmer very gently for 1½ hours. Add the cabbage and potatoes, bring back to the boil and simmer for a further 20 minutes. Combine all the sauce ingredients in a bowl and mix well. Remove the chicken from the pan, wrap in foil and leave to rest. Check the seasoning, then ladle the broth into bowls and serve as a starter.

Carve the chicken and serve on a plate with the vegetables and broth and the sauce on the side.

281 *With extra sausage meat*

If you have no chicken livers, simply double the amount of sausage meat that you use in the stuffing.

282 *Chicken with 40 garlic cloves*

1.5–2 kg/3 lb 5 oz–4 lb 8 oz
   free-range chicken
½ lemon
40 whole large garlic cloves, peeled
2 tbsp olive oil
4 sprigs thyme
2 sprigs rosemary
4 sprigs parsley

1 large carrot, roughly chopped
2 celery sticks, roughly chopped
1 onion, roughly chopped
375 ml/13 fl oz white wine
salt and pepper

Preheat the oven to 200°C/400°F/Gas Mark 6. Stuff the chicken with the ½ lemon and 4 of the garlic cloves. Rub the chicken with a little oil and some salt and pepper. In a large casserole dish lay a bed of the remaining garlic cloves, the herbs, carrot, celery and onion, then place the chicken on top. Pour over the remaining oil and add the wine. Cover with a tight-fitting lid, place in the oven and bake for 1¼ hours.

Remove the chicken from the casserole and pierce with a skewer to check the juices run clear. Cover and keep warm. Remove the garlic cloves and discard. Place the casserole over a low heat and simmer the juices for 5 minutes to make a gravy. Strain, reserving the vegetables. Carve the chicken and serve with the vegetables.

283 *Golden chicken with 40 garlic cloves*

If you would like a golden chicken, heat 1 tablespoon of oil in a large frying pan and brown the breasts of the bird over high heat for a few minutes before adding to the casserole.

284 *Poussins with herbs & wine*

5 tbsp fresh brown breadcrumbs
200 g/7 oz low-fat fromage frais
5 tbsp chopped fresh parsley
5 tbsp snipped fresh chives
4 poussins
1 tbsp sunflower oil
675 g/1 lb 8 oz young spring
vegetables, such as carrots, courgettes,
sugar snap peas, baby corn and
turnips, cut into small chunks
125 ml/4 fl oz boiling chicken stock
2 tsp cornflour
150 ml/5 fl oz dry white wine
salt and pepper

Preheat the oven to 220°C/425°F/Gas Mark 7.

Mix the breadcrumbs, one third of the fromage frais and 2 tablespoons each of the parsley and chives together in a bowl. Season well with salt and pepper.

Spoon into the neck ends of the poussins. Place on a rack in a roasting tin, brush with the sunflower oil and season well with salt and pepper.

Roast the poussins in the oven for 30–35 minutes, or until the juices run clear when the thickest part of the meat is pierced with a skewer. Place the vegetables in a shallow ovenproof dish in a single layer and add half the remaining herbs with the stock.

Cover and bake in the oven for 25–30 minutes until tender. Lift the poussins onto a warmed serving plate and skim any fat from the juices in the tin. Add the vegetable juices and place the tin over a medium heat.

Blend the cornflour with the wine and whisk into the sauce with the remaining fromage frais. Whisk until boiling, then add the remaining herbs. Season to taste with salt and pepper. Spoon the sauce over the poussins and serve with the vegetables.

285 *Stuffed chicken with herbs & wine*

You can make the same recipe using a normal chicken of about 1.5 kg/ 3 lb 5 oz to serve four – stuff the bird as usual and roast in the oven for 1¼ hours or until the juices run clear.

Guinea fowl with cabbage

1 oven-ready guinea fowl, weighing
    1.25 kg/2 lb 12 oz
½ tbsp sunflower oil
½ apple, peeled, cored and chopped
several fresh flat-leaf parsley sprigs,
    stems bruised
1 large Savoy cabbage, coarse outer
    leaves removed, cored and quartered

1 thick piece of smoked belly of pork,
    weighing about 140 g/5 oz, rind
    removed and cut into thin lardons,
    or 140 g/5 oz unsmoked lardons
1 onion, sliced
1 bouquet garni
1½ tbsp chopped fresh flat-leaf parsley
salt and pepper

Preheat the oven to 240°C/475°F/Gas Mark 9. Rub the guinea fowl with the oil and season to taste inside and out with salt and pepper. Add the apple and parsley sprigs to the guinea fowl's cavity and truss to tie the legs together.

Place the guinea fowl in a roasting tin and roast in the oven for 20 minutes to colour the breasts. When the guinea fowl is a golden brown colour, reduce the oven temperature to 160°C/325°F/Gas Mark 3.

Meanwhile, bring a large saucepan of salted water to the boil. Add the cabbage and blanch for 3 minutes. Drain, rinse in cold water and pat dry. Place the lardons in a flameproof casserole over a medium–high heat and sauté until they give off their fat. Use a slotted spoon to remove the lardons and set aside.

Add the onion to the fat left in the casserole and cook, stirring frequently, for 5 minutes, or until the onion is tender, but not brown. Stir the bouquet garni into the casserole with a very little salt and a pinch of pepper, then return the lardons to the casserole.

Remove the guinea fowl from the oven. Add the cabbage to the casserole, top with the guinea fowl and cover the surface with a piece of wet greaseproof paper. Cover the casserole and put it in the oven for 45 minutes–1 hour, or until the guinea fowl is tender and the juices run clear when a skewer is inserted into the thickest part of the meat.

Remove the guinea fowl from the casserole and cut into serving portions. Stir the parsley into the cabbage and onion, then taste and adjust the seasoning if necessary. Serve the guinea fowl portions on a bed of cabbage and onion.

287 Pheasant with cabbage

You can use pheasant, chicken or even a small turkey breast (which may need longer cooking – test after 1½ hours) instead of the guinea fowl.

Lamb shanks

1 tsp coriander seeds
1 tsp cumin seeds
1 tsp ground cinnamon
1 fresh green chilli, deseeded and
    finely chopped
1 garlic bulb, separated into cloves
125 ml/4 fl oz groundnut or sunflower oil
grated rind of 1 lime
6 lamb shanks
2 onions, chopped

2 carrots, chopped
2 celery sticks, chopped
1 lime, chopped
about 700 ml/1¼ pints beef stock
    or water
1 tsp sun-dried tomato purée
2 fresh mint sprigs
2 fresh rosemary sprigs, plus extra
    to garnish
salt and pepper

Dry-fry the coriander and cumin seeds, then pound with the cinnamon, chilli and 2 garlic cloves using a pestle and mortar. Stir in half the oil and the lime rind. Rub the paste over the lamb and marinate for 4 hours. Preheat the oven to 200°C/400°F/Gas Mark 6.

Heat the remaining oil in a flameproof casserole and cook the lamb, turning frequently, until evenly browned. Chop the remaining garlic and add to the casserole with the onions, carrots, celery and lime, then pour in enough stock or water to cover.

Stir in the tomato purée, add the herbs and season. Cover and cook in the preheated oven for 30 minutes. Reduce the oven temperature to 160°C/325°F/Gas Mark 3 and cook for a further 3 hours, or until tender.

Transfer the lamb to a dish. Strain the cooking liquid to remove any solids, then return the liquid to the casserole. Boil until reduced and thickened. Serve the lamb with the sauce poured over it, garnished with rosemary sprigs.

289 Lamb shanks with red wine

You can replace half the beef stock with red wine for an even richer dish – the wine helps tenderize the lamb shanks as well.

Slow-cooked lamb with celeriac

1 leg of lamb, on the bone, weighing
2.5 kg/5 lb 8 oz
2 whole heads garlic
grated rind of 2 lemons and juice of 1
2 tbsp finely chopped fresh rosemary
3 tbsp extra virgin olive oil
3 shallots, roughly chopped
350 ml/12 fl oz dry white wine
1 kg/2 lb 4 oz celeriac, peeled and
cut into large chunks
salt and pepper

Score gently through the fat on the lamb in a diamond pattern. Put in a non-metallic dish. Separate the heads of garlic into cloves. Peel and crush 4 of the cloves and reserve the remainder.

Mix together the crushed garlic, lemon rind and juice and rosemary. Season well with salt and pepper and stir in the oil. Rub the mixture all over the surface of the meat. Cover and marinate in the refrigerator for several hours, or overnight.

Preheat the oven to 220°C/425°F/Gas Mark 7. Transfer the lamb to a roasting tin and pour over the marinade. Roast in the preheated oven for 20 minutes. Reduce the oven temperature to 190°C/375°F/Gas Mark 5. Add the reserved whole garlic cloves, shallots and wine, cover with foil and roast for a further 1 hour 40 minutes, basting occasionally. Remove the foil, add the celeriac and turn to coat in the pan juices. Cook with the lamb for a further 20 minutes.

Remove from the oven, lift out the lamb and keep warm. Return the celeriac to the oven and roast for a further 10–15 minutes, until golden. Carve the lamb and serve with the celeriac and garlic cloves, drizzling over the pan juices.

291 *Slow-cooked lamb with potatoes*

Instead of using celeriac, you can use 600 g/1lb 5 oz peeled potatoes, sliced into 1 cm-thick rounds and added for the last hour of lamb cooking time, along with 4 medium sticks celery, cut into 2.5-cm/1-inch slices.

292 *Roast lamb with orzo*

1 boned leg or shoulder of lamb, weighing
about 750 g/1 lb 10 oz
1/2 lemon, thinly sliced
1 tbsp chopped fresh oregano
4 large garlic cloves, 2 finely chopped and
2 thinly sliced
800 g/1 lb 12 oz canned chopped tomatoes
150 ml/5 fl oz cold water
pinch of sugar
1 bay leaf
2 tbsp olive oil
150 ml/5 fl oz boiling water
200 g/7 oz orzo or short-grain rice
salt and pepper

Preheat the oven to 180°C/350°F/Gas Mark 4. Untie the lamb and open out. Place the lemon slices along the middle and sprinkle over half the oregano, the chopped garlic, and salt and pepper to taste. Roll up the meat and tie with string. Cut slits in the lamb and insert the garlic slices.

Weigh the meat and calculate the cooking time, allowing 25 minutes per 450 g/1 lb, plus 25 minutes. Place the tomatoes, cold water, remaining oregano, the sugar, and bay leaf in a large roasting pan. Place the lamb on top, drizzle over the oil, and season to taste with salt and pepper. Roast the lamb in the oven for the calculated cooking time. Fifteen minutes before the lamb will be cooked, stir the boiling water and orzo into the tomatoes. Add a little extra water if the sauce seems too thick. Return to the oven for an additional 15 minutes, or until the lamb and orzo are tender and the tomatoes are reduced to a thick sauce. To serve, carve the lamb into slices and serve hot with the orzo and tomato sauce.

1 leg of lamb,
2.5–3 kg/5 lb 8 oz–6 lb 8 oz
250 ml/9 fl oz chicken stock
250 ml/9 fl oz red wine
1 tbsp redcurrant sauce

MARINADE
1 bulb of garlic, cloves separated
but unpeeled
5 lemons or blood oranges
1 tbsp fresh rosemary leaves, chopped
1 tbsp fresh thyme leaves
25 g/1 oz salt

TO SERVE
roast potatoes
glazed carrots
mint sauce

Remove the lamb from the refrigerator and pat dry with kitchen paper. Combine all the marinade ingredients in a food processor and blend to a paste. Place the lamb in a roasting tin

and cover with the paste so that it is completely encased. Cover loosely with foil and set aside in a cool place for an hour (or preferably in your refrigerator overnight).

If the lamb has been in the refrigerator, remove it 30 minutes before cooking. Preheat the oven to 200°C/400°F/Gas Mark 6. Put the foil-covered lamb into the oven and cook for 1¾ hours. Take it out of the roasting tin, leaving behind 2 tablespoons of the marinade paste, and leave it to rest in the foil for 15–20 minutes.

Meanwhile, put the roasting tin on the hob and simmer the marinade paste with the stock, wine and redcurrant sauce until reduced by about half.

Carve the lamb, discarding most of the paste, and serve with the gravy, roast potatoes, carrots and mint sauce.

294 *Pork roasted in an orange & thyme crust*

This marinade/crust is also nice used to coat a rolled loin of pork (use oranges) or a large chicken (use lemons) before roasting.

1 tbsp sunflower oil
750 g/1 lb 10 oz boned and rolled
pork loin joint
1 onion, finely chopped
500 g/1 lb 2 oz red cabbage, thick
stems removed and leaves shredded
2 large cooking apples, peeled, cored
and sliced
3 cloves
1 tsp brown sugar
3 tbsp lemon juice, and a thinly pared
strip of lemon rind
lemon wedges, to garnish

Preheat the oven to 160°C/325°F/Gas Mark 3. Heat the oil in a flameproof casserole. Add the pork and cook over a medium heat, turning frequently, for 5–10 minutes, or until browned. Transfer to a plate.

Add the onion to the casserole and cook over a low heat, stirring occasionally, for 5 minutes, or until softened. Add the cabbage, in batches, and cook, stirring, for 2 minutes. Transfer each batch (mixed with some onion) into a bowl with a slotted spoon. Add the apple slices, cloves and sugar to the bowl and mix well, then place about half the mixture in the base of the casserole. Top with the pork and add the remaining cabbage mixture. Sprinkle in the

lemon juice and add the strip of rind. Cover and cook in the preheated oven for 1½ hours.

Transfer the pork to a plate. Transfer the cabbage mixture to the plate with a slotted spoon and keep warm. Bring the cooking juices to the boil over a high heat and reduce slightly. Slice the pork and arrange on warmed serving plates, surrounded with the cabbage mixture. Spoon the cooking juices over the meat and serve with lemon wedges.

296 *Pork with red cabbage & vinegar*

Use 2 tablespoons of white or red wine vinegar instead of the lemon juice.

297 *Slow-roasted pork*

loin of pork, weighing 1.6 kg/
3 lb 8 oz, boned and rolled
4 garlic cloves, thinly sliced lengthways
1½ tsp finely chopped fennel fronds
or ½ tsp dried fennel

4 cloves
300 ml/10 fl oz dry white wine
300 ml/10 fl oz water
salt and pepper

Preheat the oven to 150°C/300°F/Gas Mark 2. Use a small, sharp knife to make incisions all over the pork, opening them out slightly to make little pockets. Place the garlic slices in a small sieve and rinse under cold running water to moisten. Spread out the fennel on a saucer and roll the garlic slices in it to coat. Slide the garlic slices and the cloves into the pockets in the pork. Season the meat all over to taste with salt and pepper.

Place the pork in a large ovenproof dish or roasting tin. Pour in the wine and water. Cook in the oven, basting the meat occasionally, for 2½–2¾ hours, until the pork is tender but still quite moist.

If you are serving the pork hot, transfer it to a carving board, cover with foil and leave to rest before cutting it into slices. If you are serving it cold, leave it to cool completely in the cooking juices before removing and slicing.

298 *Slow-roasted pork with rosemary*

Instead of the fennel – a lovely herb that some people may find is an acquired taste – you can use 2 teaspoons of fresh rosemary leaves, finely chopped, or 1 teaspoon of dried and ground rosemary. Add a drizzle of olive oil to the pockets when you add the garlic and herbs and make sure the slits are deep enough so they don't pop out during roasting.

299 *Pot-roast pork*

1 tbsp sunflower oil
55 g/2 oz butter
1 kg/2 lb 4 oz boned and rolled pork
loin joint
4 shallots, chopped
6 juniper berries
2 fresh thyme sprigs, plus extra
to garnish

150 ml/5 fl oz dry cider
150 ml/5 fl oz chicken stock or water
8 celery sticks, chopped
2 tbsp plain flour
150 ml/5 fl oz double cream
salt and pepper
freshly cooked peas, to serve

Heat the oil with half the butter in a heavy-based saucepan or flameproof casserole. Add the pork and cook over a medium heat, turning frequently, for 5–10 minutes, or until browned. Transfer to a plate.

Add the shallots to the saucepan and cook, stirring frequently, for 5 minutes, or until softened. Add the juniper berries and thyme sprigs and return the pork to the saucepan, with any juices that have collected on the plate. Pour in the cider and stock, season to taste with salt and pepper, then cover and simmer for 30 minutes. Turn the pork over and add the celery. Re-cover the pan and cook for a further 40 minutes.

Meanwhile, make a beurre manié by mashing the remaining butter with the flour in a small bowl. Transfer the pork and celery to a platter with a slotted spoon and keep warm. Remove and discard the juniper berries and thyme. Whisk the beurre manié, a little at a time, into the simmering cooking liquid. Cook, stirring constantly, for 2 minutes, then stir in the cream and bring to the boil.

Slice the pork and spoon a little of the sauce over it. Garnish with thyme sprigs and serve immediately with the celery, peas and remaining sauce.

300 *Pot-roast venison*

Try this recipe using a joint of venison rather than the pork for a special occasion. Replace the cider with dry white wine.

301 Shepherd's pie

SERVES 6

1 tbsp olive oil
2 onions, finely chopped
2 garlic cloves, finely chopped
675 g/1½ lb good quality lamb mince
2 carrots, finely chopped
1 tbsp plain flour
225 ml/8 fl oz beef or chicken stock
125 ml/4 fl oz red wine
Worcestershire sauce (optional)

MASHED POTATO
675 g/1½ lb floury potatoes, such as King
    Edwards, Maris Piper or Desirée,
    peeled and cut into chunks
55 g/2 oz butter
2 tbsp cream or milk
salt and pepper

Preheat the oven to 180°C/350°F/ Gas Mark 4. Heat the oil in a large casserole dish and fry the onion until softened, then add the garlic and stir well. Raise the heat and add the lamb. Cook quickly to brown the lamb all over, stirring continually. Add the carrot and season well with salt and pepper. Stir in the flour and add the stock and wine. Stir well and heat until simmering and thickened. Cover the casserole dish and cook in the oven for about 1 hour. Check the consistency from time to time and add a little more stock or wine if required. The meat mixture should be quite thick but not dry. Season with salt and pepper to taste and add a little Worcestershire sauce, if desired.

While the meat is cooking, make the mashed potato. Cook the potatoes in a large saucepan of boiling salted water for 15–20 minutes. Drain well and mash with a potato masher until smooth. Add the butter and cream and season well with salt and pepper.

Spoon the lamb mixture into an ovenproof serving dish and spread or pipe the potato on top.

Increase the oven temperature to 200°C/400°F/Gas Mark 6 and cook the pie for 15–20 minutes at the top of the oven until golden brown. You might like to finish it off under a medium grill for a really crisp brown topping to the potato.

302 With celery & leek

Add 2 sticks finely chopped celery and 1 small finely chopped leek to the pan with the onion to add even more flavour and bulk out your shepherd's pie. Add a little extra oil if necessary while frying.

303 Beef & vegetable stew with corn cobs

SERVES 4

450 g/1 lb braising beef steak
1½ tbsp plain flour
1 tsp hot paprika
1–1½ tsp chilli powder
1 tsp ground ginger
2 tbsp olive oil
1 large onion, cut into chunks
3 garlic cloves, sliced
2 celery sticks, sliced
225 g/8 oz carrots, chopped

300 ml/10 fl oz lager
300 ml/10 fl oz beef stock
350 g/12 oz potatoes, chopped
1 red pepper, deseeded and chopped
2 corn cobs, halved
115 g/4 oz tomatoes, quartered
115 g/4 oz shelled fresh or frozen peas
1 tbsp chopped fresh coriander
salt and pepper

Trim any fat or gristle from the beef and cut into 2.5-cm/1-inch chunks. Mix the flour and spices together. Toss the beef in the spiced flour until well coated.

Heat the oil in a large heavy-based saucepan and cook the onion, garlic and celery, stirring frequently, for 5 minutes, or until softened. Add the beef and cook over a high heat, stirring frequently, for 3 minutes, or until browned on all sides and sealed. Add the carrots, then remove from the heat. Gradually stir in the lager and stock, then return to the heat and bring to the boil, stirring. Reduce the heat, cover and simmer, stirring occasionally, for 1½ hours.

Add the potatoes and simmer for 15 minutes. Add the red pepper and corn cobs and simmer for 15 minutes, then add the tomatoes and peas and simmer for a further 10 minutes. Season to taste with salt and pepper, stir in the coriander and serve.

304 Beef & vegetable stew with squash

Omit paprika and chilli. Add 1 teaspoon each of mustard powder and thyme. Omit red pepper and add 250 g/9 oz butternut squash slices with the potato; omit the corn cobs and add 125 g/4 oz sliced green beans. Garnish with parsley.

305 Beef & vegetable stew with courgette

Add 1 teaspoon each of ground coriander and cumin seed instead of paprika and chilli. Omit the red pepper and add 1 large sliced courgette, and then add 125 g/4 oz broad beans instead of the corn cobs.

Beef bourguignon

2 tbsp olive oil	700 ml/1¼ pints red wine
175 g/6 oz unsmoked bacon, sliced into thin strips	350–450 ml/12–16 fl oz beef stock
1.3 kg/3 lb stewing beef, cut into 5-cm/2-inch pieces	bouquet garni sachet
2 carrots, sliced	1 tsp salt
2 onions, chopped	½ tsp pepper
2 garlic cloves, very finely chopped	3 tbsp butter
3 tbsp plain flour	350 g/12 oz pickling onions
	350 g/12 oz button mushrooms
	2 tbsp chopped fresh parsley

Heat the oil in a large flameproof casserole, add the bacon and lightly brown. Remove with a slotted spoon. Brown the beef, in batches, in the casserole, drain and set aside with the bacon.

Add the carrots and chopped onions to the casserole and cook for 5 minutes, or until softened. Add the garlic and cook until just coloured. Return the meat and bacon to the casserole. Sprinkle over the flour and cook for 1 minute, stirring. Add the wine and enough stock to cover, the bouquet garni and salt and pepper.

Bring to the boil, then reduce the heat, cover and simmer gently for 3 hours. Heat half the butter in a frying pan. Add the pickling onions, cover and cook until soft. Remove with a slotted spoon and keep warm. Add the remaining butter to the pan and cook the mushrooms. Remove and keep warm. Strain the casserole liquid into a saucepan. Wipe the casserole and tip in the meat, bacon, mushrooms and onions. Remove the surface fat from the cooking liquid and simmer for 1–2 minutes to reduce. Pour over the meat and vegetables. Serve sprinkled with parsley.

307 **Beef bourguignon with red onions**

Try using shiitake mushrooms and small red onions instead of the pickling onions and button mushrooms.

Beef goulash

2 tbsp vegetable oil	250 ml/9 fl oz beef stock
675 g/1 lb 8 oz stewing beef, cubed	1 fresh bay leaf
3 onions, finely chopped	3 tbsp chopped fresh parsley
1 green pepper, deseeded and diced	1 tbsp paprika
2 garlic cloves, very finely chopped	1 tsp salt
2 tbsp tomato purée	¼ tsp pepper
2 tbsp plain flour	rice, to serve
400 g/14 oz canned chopped tomatoes	soured cream, to serve

Heat the oil in a flameproof casserole over a medium–high heat. Add the beef and cook until evenly browned. Remove and transfer to a bowl with a slotted spoon and set aside. Add the onions and pepper to the casserole and cook, stirring occasionally, for 5 minutes, or until soft. Add the garlic and cook until just coloured. Stir in the tomato purée and flour. Cook for 1 minute, stirring constantly.

Return the beef to the casserole. Add the remaining ingredients and bring to the boil. Cover and simmer over a low heat for 2½ hours, stirring occasionally. Add water or more stock if necessary. Remove the lid and simmer for 15 minutes, stirring to prevent sticking, until the sauce has thickened and the meat is very tender. Serve with rice and a bowl of soured cream.

309 **Pork goulash**

You can use lean pork or chicken fillet to make goulash, too. In this case, cook the onions and pepper on low for 15 minutes before adding the meat back to the pan. Simmer for no more than 40 minutes.

Beef stew with garlic & shallots

SERVES 6

4 tbsp plain flour
1.3 kg/3 lb braising steak, cut into
    5-cm/2-inch cubes
4 tbsp sunflower oil
12 garlic cloves, lightly crushed
3 tbsp sherry vinegar

55 g/2 oz butter
850 g/1 lb 14 oz shallots
350 ml/12 fl oz dry red wine
salt and pepper
few fresh thyme sprigs, to garnish

Place the flour on a plate and season to taste with salt and pepper. Toss the steak in the flour to coat.

Heat 3 tablespoons of the oil in a large flameproof casserole dish and cook the steak, in batches, until browned all over. Remove with a slotted spoon and set aside.

Add the remaining oil to the casserole dish and cook the garlic, stirring frequently, until golden.

Add the vinegar and heat until evaporated. Remove the garlic and set aside.

Melt the butter in the casserole dish and cook the shallots over a low heat, stirring frequently, for 15 minutes. Remove the shallots from the casserole dish and set aside. Return the steak and garlic to the casserole dish. Add the wine and season. Bring to the boil, stirring. Reduce the heat, cover and simmer, stirring occasionally, for 1–1¼ hours. Return the shallots to the dish, cover and continue cooking for 45 minutes, or until the steak is tender. Garnish with thyme and serve.

311 Beef stir-fry with garlic & shallots

Cut 400 g/14 oz beef steak (rump or fillet) into slices. Fry over medium–high heat for 2 minutes in 1 tablespoon of olive oil then remove with a slotted spatula and set aside. Turn heat to medium. Add 3 sliced garlic cloves and 8 sliced shallots to the pan with a 10-g/½-oz knob of butter and fry for 4 minutes, adding 1 teaspoon of thyme leaves for the last minute. Turn heat up to full, add 1 tablespoon of sherry vinegar and 85 ml/3 fl oz red wine to pan with 1 teaspoon of Dijon mustard. Stir for 1 minute until reduced. Return meat to pan, stir for a few seconds to heat through. This recipe serves 2.

Beef in beer with herb dumplings

SERVES 6

2 tbsp sunflower oil
2 large onions, thinly sliced
8 carrots, sliced
4 tbsp plain flour
1.25 kg/2 lb 12 oz stewing steak,
    cut into cubes
425 ml/15 fl oz stout
2 tsp muscovado sugar
2 bay leaves
1 tbsp chopped fresh thyme
salt and pepper

HERB DUMPLINGS
115 g/4 oz self-raising flour
pinch of salt
55 g/2 oz shredded suet
2 tbsp chopped fresh parsley,
    plus extra to garnish
about 4 tbsp water

Preheat the oven to 160°C/325°F/Gas Mark 3. Heat the oil in a flameproof casserole. Add the onions and carrots and cook over a low heat, stirring occasionally, for 5 minutes, or until the onions are softened.

Meanwhile, place the flour in a polythene bag and season with salt and pepper. Add the stewing steak to the bag, tie the top and shake well to coat. Do this in batches, if necessary. Remove the vegetables from the casserole with a slotted spoon and reserve. Add the stewing steak to the casserole, in batches, and cook, stirring frequently, until browned all over.

Return all the meat and the onions and carrots to the casserole and sprinkle in any remaining seasoned flour. Pour in the stout and add the sugar, bay leaves and thyme. Bring to the boil, cover and transfer to the preheated oven to bake for 1¾ hours.

To make the herb dumplings, sift the flour and salt into a bowl. Stir in the suet and parsley and add enough of the water to make a soft dough. Shape into small balls between the palms of your hands. Add to the casserole and return to the oven for 30 minutes. Remove and discard the bay leaves. Serve immediately, sprinkled with chopped parsley.

313 Beef in beer with a crumb crust

Omit dumplings. In a bowl, combine 50 g/2 oz breadcrumbs with salt, pepper, 2 teaspoons of mixed herbs and 1 tablespoon of olive oil. Remove lid from the casserole 20 minutes before the end of cooking time, sprinkle the crumb mix over and return to the oven (without the lid on).

900 g/2 lb stewing beef, such as chuck
or leg, trimmed and cut into
5-cm/2-inch chunks
2 onions, thinly sliced
2 carrots, thickly sliced
4 large garlic cloves, bruised
1 large bouquet garni
4 juniper berries
500 ml/18 fl oz full-bodied dry red
wine, such as Fitou
2 tbsp brandy
2 tbsp olive oil
225 g/8 oz boned belly of pork,
rind removed
200 g/7 oz plain flour
2 x 10-cm/4-inch strips of
orange rind
85 g/3 oz black olives, stoned and
rinsed to remove any brine
beef stock, if necessary
90 ml/3 fl oz water
salt and pepper
chopped fresh flat-leaf parsley,
to garnish
finely grated orange rind, to garnish
freshly cooked pasta noodles, to serve

Put the beef in a large non-metallic bowl and add the onions, carrots, garlic, bouquet garni, juniper berries and seasoning. Pour over the wine, brandy and oil and stir.

Cover with clingfilm and marinate in the refrigerator for 24 hours. Remove the beef from the fridge 30 minutes before you plan to cook; preheat the oven to 160°C/325°F/Gas Mark 3. Cut the pork into 5-mm/¼-inch strips. Add the pork to a pan of boiling water and blanch for 3 minutes, then drain.

Remove the beef from the marinade and dry with kitchen paper. Put the beef and 3 tablespoons of the flour with salt and pepper in a polythene bag, close the top and shake until it is coated. Remove from the bag, shake off excess flour and set aside. Transfer half the pork to a 3.4-litre/6-pint flameproof casserole. Top with the beef and marinade, orange rind and olives.

Add the remaining pork. Top up with beef stock to cover the ingredients, if necessary. Mix the remaining flour with the water to form

a paste. Bring the casserole to the boil on top of the hob, then put the lid on and use your fingers to press the paste around the sides to seal. Transfer the casserole to the oven and cook for 1 hour. Reduce the temperature to 140°C/275°F/Gas Mark 1; cook for a further 3 hours.

Remove the casserole from the oven and cut off the seal. Use a knife to ensure the beef is tender. If not, re-cover and return to the oven; test again after 15 minutes. Using a metal spoon, skim any fat from the surface. Adjust the seasoning if necessary. Remove the bouquet garni, sprinkle the parsley and orange rind over the top, and serve with freshly cooked pasta noodles.

315 *Beef stew with olives & bacon*

Substitute 125 g/4½ oz unsmoked bacon lardons for the belly of pork.

750 g/1 lb 10 oz lean braising
  or stewing steak
2 tbsp vegetable oil
1 large onion, sliced
2–4 garlic cloves, crushed
1 tbsp plain flour
425 ml/15 fl oz tomato juice
400 g/14 oz canned tomatoes
1–2 tbsp sweet chilli sauce

1 tsp ground cumin
425 g/15 oz canned red kidney
  beans, drained
½ tsp dried oregano
1–2 tbsp chopped fresh parsley
salt and pepper
sprig of fresh parsley, to garnish
boiled rice, to serve

Preheat the oven to 160°C/325°F/Gas Mark 3. Cut the beef into 2-cm/¾-inch cubes. Heat the oil in a flameproof casserole. Fry the beef until browned. Remove from the casserole.

Add the onion and garlic to the casserole and cook until lightly browned. Stir in the flour and cook for 1–2 minutes. Stir in the tomato juice and tomatoes and bring to the boil. Return the beef to the casserole and add the chilli sauce, cumin and salt and pepper to taste. Cover and cook in the oven for 1½ hours, or until almost tender. Stir in the beans, oregano and parsley and adjust the seasoning to taste. Cover the casserole and return to the oven for 45 minutes. Garnish with the parsley sprig and serve with the boiled rice.

317 *With extra chillis*

The above chilli is of low to medium heat – for a hotter chilli, add 3 (or to taste) fresh hot (e.g. birds' eye) red chillies, finely chopped, to the pan with the garlic.

318 *With green peppers*

Add 1–2 fresh green peppers, cut into bite-sized pieces, to the pan with the onion and garlic.

319 Caribbean beef stew

450 g/1 lb braising steak
450 g/1 lb diced pumpkin or other
squash
1 onion, chopped
1 red pepper, deseeded and chopped
2 garlic cloves, finely chopped
2.5-cm/1-inch piece fresh ginger,
finely chopped

1 tbsp sweet or hot paprika
225 ml/8 fl oz beef stock
400 g/14 oz canned chopped tomatoes
400 g/14 oz canned pigeon peas, drained
and rinsed
400 g/14 oz canned black-eyed beans,
drained and rinsed
salt and pepper

Trim off any visible fat from the steak, then dice the meat. Heat a large, heavy-based saucepan without adding any extra fat. Add the meat and cook, stirring constantly, for a few minutes until golden all over.

Stir in the pumpkin, onion and red pepper and cook for 1 minute, then add the garlic, ginger, paprika, stock and tomatoes and bring to the boil.

Transfer the mixture to a slow cooker, cover and cook on low for 7 hours. Add the pigeon peas and black-eyed beans to the stew and season to taste with salt and pepper. Re-cover and cook on high for 30 minutes, then serve.

320 Caribbean lamb stew

The stew works very well with lamb instead of beef – use neck of lamb, and replace the beef stock with lamb stock.

321 Osso bucco

1 tbsp extra virgin olive oil
4 tbsp butter
2 onions, chopped
1 leek, sliced
3 tbsp plain flour
4 thick slices of veal shin (osso bucco)
300 ml/½ pint white wine

300 ml/½ pint veal or chicken stock
salt and pepper

GREMOLATA
2 tbsp chopped fresh parsley
1 garlic clove, finely chopped
grated rind of 1 lemon

Heat the oil and butter in a large heavy-based frying pan. Add the onions and leek and cook over a low heat, stirring occasionally, for 5 minutes, until softened. Spread out the flour on a plate and season with salt and pepper. Toss the pieces of veal in the flour to coat, shaking off any excess. Add the veal to the frying pan, increase the heat to high and cook until browned on both sides.

Gradually stir in the wine and stock and bring just to the boil, stirring constantly. Lower the heat, cover and simmer for 1¼ hours, or until the veal is very tender. Meanwhile, make the gremolata by mixing the parsley, garlic and lemon rind in a small bowl. Transfer the veal to a warmed serving dish with a slotted spoon. Bring the sauce to the boil and cook, stirring occasionally, until thickened and reduced. Pour the sauce over the veal, sprinkle with the gremolata and serve immediately.

322 Sautéed veal with gremolata

For a much quicker dish, just sauté 1 thinly sliced onion and 1 thinly sliced leek in the oil and butter until soft, then add veal escalopes to the pan and cook 3 minutes a side or until cooked through. Remove with slotted spoon and keep warm. Add 100 ml/3½ fl oz stock to the pan with seasoning, stir to reduce a little over high heat. Serve with the pan juices and gremolata.

Pepper pot-style stew

450 g/1 lb stewing steak
1½ tbsp plain flour
2 tbsp olive oil
1 Spanish onion, chopped
3–4 garlic cloves, crushed
1 fresh green chilli, deseeded and
chopped
3 celery sticks, sliced
4 whole cloves
1 tsp ground allspice
1–2 tsp hot pepper sauce, or to taste
600 ml/1 pint beef stock
225 g/8 oz deseeded and peeled
squash, such as acorn, cut into
small chunks
1 large red pepper, deseeded and
chopped
4 tomatoes, roughly chopped
115 g/4 oz okra, trimmed and halved

Trim any fat or gristle from the beef and cut into 2.5-cm/1-inch chunks. Toss the beef in the flour until well coated and reserve any remaining flour. Heat the oil in a large heavy-based saucepan and cook the onion, garlic, chilli and celery with the cloves and allspice, stirring frequently, for 5 minutes, or until softened.

Add the beef and cook over a high heat, stirring frequently, for 3 minutes, or until browned on all sides and sealed. Sprinkle in the reserved flour and cook, stirring constantly, for 2 minutes, then remove from the heat. Add the hot pepper sauce and gradually stir in the stock, then return to the heat and bring to the boil, stirring.

Reduce the heat, cover and simmer, stirring occasionally, for 1½ hours.

Add the squash and red pepper to the saucepan and simmer for a further 15 minutes. Add the tomatoes and okra and simmer for a further 15 minutes, or until the beef is tender. Serve the stew immediately.

324 *Pepper pot-style stew & sweet potatoes*

Replace the squash and red pepper with 2 medium sweet potatoes – about 400 g/14 oz in total. Peel, chop and add to the stew after about 1½ hours cooking time.

Rich beef stew

2 tbsp olive oil
25 g/1 oz butter
225 g/8 oz baby onions, peeled
and halved
600 g/1 lb 5 oz stewing steak, diced into
4-cm/1½-inch chunks
300 ml/10 fl oz beef stock
150 ml/5 fl oz red wine

4 tbsp chopped fresh oregano
1 tbsp sugar
1 orange
25 g/1 oz dried porcini mushrooms
4 tbsp warm water
225 g/8 oz fresh plum tomatoes
cooked rice or potatoes, to serve

Preheat the oven to 180°C/350°F/Gas Mark 4. Heat the oil and butter in a large frying pan. Add the onions and cook for 5 minutes, or until golden. Remove with a slotted spoon, set aside and keep warm. Add the beef to the pan and cook, stirring, for 5 minutes, or until browned all over. Return the onions to the pan and add the stock, wine, oregano and sugar, stirring to mix well. Transfer the mixture to an ovenproof casserole. Pare the rind from the orange and cut into strips. Slice the orange flesh into rings. Add the rings and rind to the casserole. Cook in the oven for 1¼ hours. Soak the mushrooms for 30 minutes in a small bowl containing the warm water. Peel and halve the tomatoes. Add the tomatoes, mushrooms and their soaking liquid to the casserole. Cook for 20 minutes, or until the beef is tender. Serve with rice or potatoes.

326 *Rich beef stew & sun-dried tomatoes*

Instead of fresh tomatoes, try using sun-dried tomatoes, cut into wide strips.

327 *Rich beef stew with fresh mushrooms*

Use 125 g/4½ oz fresh mushrooms – a dark-gilled meaty variety such as portobello or larger chestnut mushrooms would be ideal – instead of the dried mushrooms. Add to the pan with the orange rings.

1.8 kg/4 lb chicken pieces
2 tbsp paprika
2 tbsp olive oil
25 g/1 oz butter
450 g/1 lb onions, chopped
2 yellow peppers, deseeded and chopped
400 g/14 oz canned chopped tomatoes
225 ml/8 fl oz dry white wine
450 ml/16 fl oz chicken stock
1 tbsp Worcestershire sauce

½ tsp Tabasco sauce
1 tbsp finely chopped fresh parsley
325 g/11½ oz canned sweetcorn, drained
425 g/15 oz canned butter beans,
    drained and rinsed
2 tbsp plain flour
4 tbsp water
salt
freshly chopped parsley, to garnish

Season the chicken pieces with salt and dust with paprika. Heat the oil and butter in a flameproof casserole or large saucepan. Add the chicken pieces and cook over a medium heat, turning, for 10–15 minutes, or until golden. Transfer to a plate with a slotted spoon.

Add the onion and peppers to the casserole. Cook over a low heat, stirring occasionally, for 5 minutes, or until softened. Add the tomatoes, wine, stock, Worcestershire sauce, Tabasco sauce and parsley and bring to the boil, stirring. Return the chicken to the casserole, cover and simmer, stirring occasionally, for 30 minutes. Add the sweetcorn and beans to the casserole, partially re-cover and simmer for 30 minutes. Place the flour and water in a bowl and mix to make a paste. Stir a ladleful of the cooking liquid into the paste, then stir it into the stew. Cook, stirring frequently, for 5 minutes. Serve, garnished with parsley.

329 *Brunswick stew with cannellini beans*

Replace the butter beans with the same weight of cannellini beans, which are equally creamy.

330 *With pasta*

For an even heartier meal with no need for a side vegetable, add 200 g/7 oz (dry weight) small wholemeal pasta shapes to the dish when you add the sweetcorn and beans. Increase the amount of stock to 600 ml/1 pint as the pasta will absorb water during cooking. If when the stew is cooked it looks a bit dry, stir in a little boiling water.

Teriyaki steaks

4 beef steaks, about 150 g/5½ oz each
2 tbsp vegetable oil
200 g/7 oz fresh beansprouts
4 spring onions, trimmed and
 finely sliced
salt and pepper

TERIYAKI SAUCE
2 tbsp mirin (Japanese rice wine)
2 tbsp sake or pale dry sherry
4 tbsp dark soy sauce
1 tsp granulated or caster sugar

Season the steaks with salt and pepper to taste and set aside. For the sauce, combine the mirin, sake, soy sauce and sugar in a bowl, stirring well. Heat 1 tablespoon of the oil in a frying pan over a high heat. Add the beansprouts and fry quickly, tossing in the hot oil for 30 seconds. Remove from the pan and drain on kitchen paper. Add the remaining oil to the pan and, when hot, add the steaks. Cook for 1–3 minutes on each side, or until cooked to your liking. Remove from the pan and keep warm. Remove the pan from the heat and add the sauce and spring onions. Return to the heat and simmer for 2 minutes, stirring until the sauce thickens slightly and is glossy. Slice each steak and arrange on a bed of beansprouts. Spoon over the sauce and serve immediately.

332 *Teriyaki pork*

Instead of using beef steaks, try using pork steaks. Follow the same recipe, cooking the pork for 3 minutes on each side until just cooked through and the juices run clear when the meat is pierced with a skewer at the thickest point.

333 *Beef cobbler with chilli*

2 tbsp plain flour
900 g/2 lb stewing beef,
 cut into bite-sized chunks
2 tbsp chilli oil or olive oil
1 large onion, peeled and sliced
1 garlic clove, crushed
1 small red chilli, deseeded and chopped
1 courgette, sliced
1 red pepper, deseeded and cut into small
 chunks
150 g/5½ oz mushrooms, sliced
1 tbsp tomato purée
500 ml/18 fl oz red wine

250 ml/9 fl oz beef stock or vegetable
 stock
1 bay leaf
salt and pepper

COBBLER TOPPING
175 g/6 oz self-raising flour, plus extra
 for dusting
2 level tsp baking powder
pinch of cayenne pepper
3 tbsp butter
4–5 tbsp milk
salt

Preheat the oven to 160ºC/325ºF/ Gas Mark 3. Put the flour in a bowl, season with salt and pepper, then add the beef chunks and toss in the flour to coat. Heat half of the oil in a large flameproof casserole. Add the beef and cook, stirring, until the meat has browned all over and is sealed. Lift out with a slotted spoon, transfer to a plate and set aside.

Heat the remaining oil in the casserole, add the onion and garlic and cook over a medium heat, stirring, for 2 minutes until softened. Add the chilli, courgette, red pepper and mushrooms and cook, stirring, for another 3 minutes. Stir in the remaining seasoned flour and the tomato purée, then stir in the red wine,

scraping the bottom gently to deglaze the pan. Pour in the stock, add the bay leaf, then bring to the boil. Reduce the heat and cook over a low heat, stirring, until thickened. Return the beef to the pan, cover and bake in the preheated oven for 45 minutes.

Meanwhile, to make the cobbler topping, sift the flour, baking powder, cayenne pepper and a pinch of salt into a large mixing bowl. Rub in the butter until the mixture resembles fine breadcrumbs, then stir in enough of the milk to make a smooth dough. Transfer to a clean, lightly floured board, knead lightly,

then roll out to a thickness of about 1 cm/½ inch. Cut out rounds using a 5-cm/2-inch biscuit cutter.

Remove the casserole from the oven, remove and discard the bay leaf, and adjust the seasoning to taste. Arrange the dough rounds over the top, then return to the oven and bake for another 30 minutes, or until the cobbler topping has risen and is lightly golden. Serve hot.

334 *Chicken cobbler with chilli*

Try the same recipe but use 900 g/2 lb of chicken thigh fillets instead of the beef, and replace the beef or vegetable stock with chicken stock. Stewing venison also works well.

4 chicken quarters
2 tbsp sunflower oil
2 leeks
250 g/9 oz carrots, chopped
250 g/9 oz parsnips, chopped
2 small turnips, chopped
600 ml/1 pint chicken stock
3 tbsp Worcestershire sauce
2 fresh rosemary sprigs
salt and pepper

ROSEMARY DUMPLINGS
200 g/7 oz self-raising flour
100 g/3½ oz shredded suet
1 tbsp chopped fresh rosemary leaves
salt and pepper
about 2–3 tbsp cold water

Remove the skin from the chicken, if you prefer. Heat the oil in a large flameproof casserole or heavy-based saucepan. Add the chicken and fry until golden. Using a slotted spoon, remove the chicken from the casserole.

Drain off the excess fat. Slice the leeks and add to the casserole together with the carrots, parsnips and turnips. Cook for 5 minutes, or until the vegetables are lightly coloured. Return the chicken to the casserole. Add the stock, Worcestershire sauce and rosemary, season to taste with salt and pepper, then bring to the boil. Reduce the heat, cover

and simmer gently for 50 minutes, or until the chicken is tender and the juices run clear when a skewer is inserted into the thickest part of the meat.

To make the dumplings, mix together the flour, suet, rosemary and salt and pepper to taste in a large bowl. Stir in just enough water to form a firm dough. Form into 8 small balls between the palms of your hands and place on top of the chicken and vegetables. Cover and simmer for a further 10–12 minutes, or until the dumplings are well risen. Serve immediately.

336 *Braised chicken with swede & celeriac*

Replace the parsnips and turnips with swede and celeriac – use 250 g/9 oz swede and 1 small celeriac, peeled and chopped.

337 *Braised chicken & parsley dumplings*

Replace the rosemary in the dumplings with 2 tablespoons of fresh chopped parsley and 2 teaspoons of dried thyme.

338 Chicken & apple pot

4 chicken portions, about 150 g/5½ oz
  each, skinned if preferred
1 tbsp olive oil
1 onion, chopped
2 celery sticks, roughly chopped
1½ tbsp plain flour
300 ml/10 fl oz clear apple juice
150 ml/5 fl oz chicken stock
1 cooking apple, cored and quartered
2 bay leaves

1–2 tsp clear honey
1 yellow pepper, deseeded and cut
  into chunks
1 tbsp butter
1 large or 2 medium eating apples,
  cored and sliced
2 tbsp demerara sugar
salt and pepper
1 tbsp chopped fresh mint, to garnish

Preheat the oven to 190°C/375°F/Gas Mark 5. Lightly rinse the chicken and pat dry with kitchen paper. Heat the oil in a deep frying pan and cook the chicken over a medium–high heat, turning frequently, for 10 minutes, or until golden all over and sealed. Using a slotted spoon, transfer to an ovenproof casserole. Add the onion and celery to the frying pan and cook over a medium heat, stirring frequently, for 5 minutes, or until softened. Sprinkle in the flour and cook, stirring constantly, for 2 minutes, then remove from the heat.

Gradually stir in the apple juice and stock, then return to the heat and bring to the boil, stirring. Add the cooking apple, bay leaves and honey and season to taste with salt and pepper. Pour over the chicken in the casserole, cover and cook in the preheated oven for 25 minutes. Add the yellow pepper and cook for a further 10–15 minutes, or until the chicken is tender and the juices run clear when a skewer is inserted into the thickest part of the meat.

Meanwhile, preheat the grill to high. Melt the butter in a saucepan over a low heat. Line the grill pan with kitchen foil. Brush the eating apple slices with half the butter, sprinkle with a little sugar and cook under the grill for 2–3 minutes, or until the sugar has caramelized. Turn the slices over, brush with the remaining butter and sprinkle with the remaining sugar, then cook for a further 2 minutes. Serve the stew garnished with the mint and caramelized apple slices.

339 With Calvados

You could add a couple of tablespoons of Calvados – a dry apple brandy which comes from Normandy in France – to intensify the apple flavours in this dish.

340 Pork & apple pot

This casserole is equally good made with 4 large pork chops or pork steaks instead of the chicken.

341 Nutty chicken

3 tbsp sunflower oil
4 skinless chicken portions
2 shallots, chopped
1 tsp ground ginger
1 tbsp plain flour
425 ml/15 fl oz beef stock

55 g/2 oz walnut pieces
grated rind of 1 lemon
2 tbsp lemon juice
1 tbsp black treacle
salt and pepper
fresh watercress sprigs, to garnish

Heat the oil in a large, heavy-based frying pan. Season the chicken portions with salt and pepper and add to the pan. Cook over a medium heat, turning occasionally, for 5–8 minutes, until lightly golden all over. Transfer to a slow cooker.

Add the shallots to the pan and cook, stirring occasionally, for 3–4 minutes until softened. Sprinkle in the ginger and flour and cook, stirring constantly, for 1 minute. Gradually stir in the stock and bring to the boil, stirring constantly. Lower the heat and simmer for 1 minute, then stir in the nuts, lemon rind and juice and treacle.

Pour the sauce over the chicken. Cover and cook on low for 6 hours until the chicken is cooked through and tender. Adjust the seasoning if needed. Transfer the chicken to warm plates, spoon some of the sauce over each portion, garnish with watercress sprigs and serve immediately.

342 Quick nutty chicken

For a quicker version of this dish, use skinless, boneless chicken breast fillet, sliced. Follow step one but brown for only 3 minutes, then transfer the chicken to a plate and keep warm. Follow step two then return the chicken to the pan and simmer for 10 minutes before garnishing and serving.

Chicken Basquaise

1 chicken, weighing 1.3 kg/3 lb,
cut into 8 pieces
flour, for coating
3 tbsp olive oil
1 Spanish onion, thickly sliced
2 red, green or yellow peppers,
deseeded and cut lengthways
into thick strips
2 garlic cloves
150 g/5 oz chorizo sausage, skinned
and cut into 1-cm/
½-inch pieces
1 tbsp tomato purée
200 g/7 oz long-grain white rice
450 ml/16 fl oz chicken stock
1 tsp crushed dried chillies
½ tsp dried thyme
115 g/4 oz Bayonne or other
air-dried ham, diced
12 dry-cured black olives
2 tbsp chopped fresh parsley
salt and pepper

Pat the chicken pieces dry with kitchen paper. Put 2 tablespoons of flour in a polythene bag, season well with salt and pepper and add the chicken pieces. Seal the bag and shake to coat the chicken.

Heat 2 tablespoons of the oil in a large flameproof casserole over a medium–high heat. Add the chicken and cook, turning frequently, for 15 minutes, or until well browned all over. Transfer to a plate.

Heat the remaining oil in the casserole and add the onion and peppers. Reduce the heat to medium and stir-fry until beginning to colour and soften.

Add the garlic, chorizo and tomato purée and cook, stirring constantly, for about 3 minutes. Add the rice and cook, stirring to coat, for 2 minutes, or until the rice is translucent. Add the stock, crushed chillies and thyme, season to taste with salt and pepper and stir well.

Bring to the boil. Return the chicken to the casserole, pressing it gently into the rice. Cover and cook over a very low heat for 45 minutes, or until the chicken is cooked through and the rice is tender. Gently stir the ham, black olives and half the parsley into the rice mixture.

Re-cover and heat through for a further 5 minutes. Sprinkle with the remaining parsley and serve the casserole immediately.

344 *With green olives*

Instead of the black olives, you could use 12 large, tomato-stuffed green olives, sliced into rounds.

Chicken cacciatore

3 tbsp olive oil
1.8 kg/4 lb skinless chicken pieces
2 red onions, sliced
2 garlic cloves, finely chopped
400 g/14 oz canned chopped tomatoes
2 tbsp chopped fresh flat-leaf parsley

1 tbsp sun-dried tomato purée
150 ml/5 fl oz red wine
6 fresh basil leaves
salt and pepper
fresh basil sprigs, to garnish
pasta, to serve

Preheat the oven to 160°C/325°F/Gas Mark 3. Heat the olive oil in a flameproof casserole. Add the chicken and cook over a medium heat, stirring frequently, for 5–10 minutes, or until golden. Transfer to a plate with a slotted spoon.

Add the onions and garlic to the casserole and cook over a low heat, stirring occasionally, for 10 minutes, or until golden. Add the tomatoes, the parsley, tomato purée and wine, and tear in the basil leaves. Season to taste with salt and pepper.

Bring the mixture to the boil, then return the chicken to the casserole, pushing it down into the cooking liquid. Cover and cook in the preheated oven for 1 hour, or until the chicken is cooked through and tender. Garnish with fresh basil sprigs and serve immediately with pasta.

346 *With red pepper pesto*

To make the dish even tastier, stir in 1 tablespoon of red pepper pesto with the sun-dried tomato purée.

1 chicken, weighing 1.5 kg/3 lb 5 oz,
cut into 6 pieces
2 celery sticks, 1 broken in half and
1 finely chopped
1 carrot, chopped
2 onions, 1 sliced and 1 chopped
2 bay leaves
4 or groundnut oil
50 g/1¾ oz plain flour
2 large garlic cloves, crushed
1 green pepper, deseeded and diced
450 g/1 lb fresh okra, trimmed, then
cut crossways into 1-cm/½-inch slices
225 g/8 oz andouille sausage or Polish
kielbasa, sliced
2 tbsp tomato purée
1 tsp dried thyme
½ tsp cayenne pepper
400 g/14 oz canned peeled plum
tomatoes
salt and pepper
cooked long-grain rice, to serve

Put the chicken into a large saucepan with water to cover, place over a medium–high heat and bring to the boil, skimming the surface to remove the foam. When the foam stops rising, reduce the heat to medium, add the celery stick halves, carrot, sliced onion, 1 bay leaf and ¼ teaspoon of salt and simmer for 30 minutes, or until the chicken is tender and the juices run clear when a skewer is inserted into the thickest part of the meat. Remove the chicken, straining and reserving 1 litre/1¾ pints of the liquid. When the chicken is cool enough to handle, remove and discard the skin, bones and other ingredients. Cut the chicken flesh into bite-sized pieces and reserve.

Heat the oil in a large saucepan over a medium–high heat for 2 minutes. Reduce the heat to low, sprinkle in the flour and stir to make a roux. Stir constantly until the roux turns hazelnut-brown.

If black specks appear, it is burnt and you will have to start again. Add the chopped celery, chopped onion, garlic, green pepper and okra to the saucepan. Increase the heat to medium–high and cook, stirring frequently, for 5 minutes. Add the sausage and cook, stirring frequently, for 2 minutes. Stir in all the remaining ingredients, except the chicken, including the second bay leaf and the reserved cooking liquid.

Bring to the boil, crushing the tomatoes with a wooden spoon. Reduce the heat to medium–low and simmer, uncovered, for 30 minutes, stirring occasionally.

Add the chicken to the saucepan and simmer for a further 30 minutes. Taste and adjust the seasoning, if necessary. Discard the bay leaf, spoon the gumbo over the rice and serve.

348 *Chicken gumbo with chorizo*

If you can't find the andouille or Polish sausage, any smoked/spicy cured sausage will do – including chorizo or pepperoni.

349 *With prawns*

In New Orleans, where gumbo is a common dish, seafood is often added. Add 100 g/3½ oz uncooked large prawns for the last 5–6 minutes of cooking.

350 Chicken fricassee

1 tbsp plain flour
4 skinless, boneless chicken breasts, about
    140 g/5 oz each, trimmed of all visible
    fat and cut into 2-cm/¾-inch cubes
1 tbsp sunflower or corn oil
8 baby onions
2 garlic cloves, crushed
225 ml/8 fl oz chicken stock

2 carrots, diced
2 celery sticks, diced
225 g/8 oz frozen peas
1 yellow pepper, deseeded and diced
115 g/4 oz button mushrooms, sliced
125 ml/4 fl oz low-fat natural yogurt
3 tbsp chopped fresh parsley
salt and white pepper

Spread out the flour on a dish and season with salt and pepper. Add the chicken and, using your hands, coat in the flour. Heat the oil in a heavy-based saucepan. Add the onions and garlic and cook over a low heat, stirring occasionally, for 5 minutes. Add the chicken and cook, stirring, for 10 minutes, or until just beginning to colour.

Gradually stir in the stock, then add the carrots, celery and peas. Bring to the boil, then reduce the heat, cover and simmer for 5 minutes. Add the yellow pepper and the mushrooms, cover and simmer for a further 10 minutes.

Stir in the yogurt and chopped parsley and season to taste with salt and pepper. Cook for 1–2 minutes, or until heated through, then transfer to 4 large, warmed serving plates and serve immediately.

351 Creamy chicken fricassee

For an even creamier but still healthy casserole, replace the low-fat yogurt with Greek yogurt.

352 Chicken fricassee with French beans

Replace the yellow pepper with 100 g/3½ oz French beans.

353 Chicken Madeira French-style

25 g/1 oz butter
20 shallots
250 g/9 oz carrots, sliced
250 g/9 oz rindless bacon, chopped
250 g/9 oz button mushrooms
1 chicken, weighing 1.5 kg/ 3 lb 5 oz
425 ml/15 fl oz white wine

25 g/1 oz plain flour, seasoned
425 ml/15 fl oz chicken stock
1 bouquet garni
150 ml/5 fl oz Madeira wine
salt and pepper
mashed potatoes, to serve

Heat the butter in a large flameproof casserole. Add the shallots, carrots, bacon and mushrooms and fry for 3 minutes, stirring frequently. Transfer to a plate and reserve. Add the chicken to the casserole and cook until browned all over.

Add the reserved vegetables and bacon to the casserole. Add the white wine and cook until reduced. Sprinkle with the seasoned flour, stirring to avoid lumps forming. Add the stock, salt and pepper to taste and the bouquet garni. Cover and simmer for 2 hours, or until the chicken is tender and the juices run clear when a skewer is inserted into the thickest part of the meat. About 30 minutes before the end of the cooking time, add the Madeira wine and continue cooking, uncovered.

Just before serving, remove and discard the bouquet garni. Carve the chicken and serve with mashed potatoes.

354 With herbs

You can add any combination of herbs to this recipe – chervil is a popular herb in French cuisine, but add it at the end of cooking so that its delicate flavour is not lost. Other herbs that work well are parsley and tarragon.

355 Chicken Marsala Italian-style

You can replace the Madeira wine with Marsala wine, a wine from Italy which tastes quite similar, or you can even use a medium sweet sherry.

55 g/2 oz butter
2 tbsp olive oil
2 rindless, thick streaky bacon rashers, chopped
115 g/4 oz baby onions, peeled
1 garlic clove, finely chopped
1.8 kg/4 lb chicken pieces
400 ml/14 fl oz dry white wine
300 ml/10 fl oz chicken stock
1 bouquet garni
25 g/1 oz plain flour
115 g/4 oz button mushrooms
salt and pepper
fresh mixed herbs, to garnish

Preheat the oven to 160°C/325°F/Gas Mark 3. Melt half the butter with the oil in a flameproof casserole. Add the bacon and cook over a medium heat, stirring, for 5–10 minutes, or until golden brown. Transfer the bacon to a large plate. Add the onions and garlic to the casserole and cook over a low heat, stirring occasionally, for 10 minutes, or until golden. Transfer to the plate.

Add the chicken and cook over a medium heat, stirring constantly, for 8–10 minutes, or until golden. Transfer to the plate. Drain off any excess fat. Stir in the wine and stock and bring to the boil, scraping any sediment off the base. Add the bouquet garni and season to taste with salt and pepper. Return the bacon, onions and chicken to the casserole. Cover and cook in the oven for 1 hour. Add the mushrooms, re-cover and cook for 15 minutes. Meanwhile, make a beurre manié by mashing the remaining butter with the flour in a small bowl. Remove the casserole from the oven and set over a medium heat. Remove and discard the bouquet garni. Whisk in the beurre manié, a little at a time. Bring to the boil, stirring, then serve, garnished with fresh herb sprigs.

357 *Quick chicken in white wine*

Although the pieces of chicken on the bone add flavour to the finished dish, to save time you can make a quicker version with all the same tastes, which is also lower in fat. Follow the recipe above to brown the bacon, onions and garlic, but using a large lidded frying pan. Remove from pan with a slotted spoon and reserve.

Slice 4 skinless chicken breasts each into 5, add to pan (with a little extra oil if needed), and cook over medium heat for 2 minutes stirring once or twice until tinged gold. Remove to the plate with the bacon and onion.

Pour 100 ml/3½ fl oz wine into the pan and bring to boil, then add 100 ml/3½ fl oz stock and boil again. Add bouquet garni, seasoning and mushrooms and simmer for 5 minutes, then return chicken, bacon and onion to the pan, stir to combine and cook, covered, for 20 minutes. Remove bouquet garni. Mix 1 heaped teaspoon of cornflour with a little cold water and add to pan. Cook, stirring, for 2 minutes to thicken the sauce.

1 tbsp olive oil
1 onion, cut into small wedges
2–4 garlic cloves, sliced
450 g/1 lb skinless, boneless chicken breast, diced
1 tsp ground cumin
2 cinnamon sticks, lightly bruised
1 tbsp plain wholemeal flour
225 g/8 oz aubergine, diced
1 red pepper, deseeded and chopped
85 g/3 oz button mushrooms, sliced
1 tbsp tomato purée
600 ml/1 pint chicken stock
280 g/10 oz canned chickpeas, drained and rinsed
55 g/2 oz ready-to-eat dried apricots, chopped
salt and pepper
1 tbsp chopped fresh coriander, to garnish

Heat the oil in a large saucepan over a medium heat, add the onion and garlic and cook for 3 minutes, stirring frequently. Add the chicken and cook, stirring constantly, for a further 5 minutes, or until sealed on all sides. Add the cumin and cinnamon sticks to the saucepan halfway through sealing the chicken.

Sprinkle in the flour and cook, stirring constantly, for 2 minutes. Add the aubergine, red pepper and mushrooms and cook for a further 2 minutes, stirring constantly. Blend the tomato purée with the stock, stir into the saucepan and bring to the boil. Reduce the heat and add the chickpeas and apricots. Cover and simmer for 15–20 minutes, or until the chicken is tender. Season with salt and pepper to taste and serve immediately, sprinkled with coriander.

359 *Chicken tagine with flaked almonds*

You can omit the mushrooms and add 70 g/2½ oz toasted flaked almonds to the dish to serve.

360 *With harissa*

For a lovely spicy finish, stir in 2–3 teaspoons of harissa paste (a red Moroccan paste) for the last 5 minutes of cooking.

361 *Chicken tagine with sultanas & dates*

You can replace half of the apricots with sultanas, or even use half sultanas, half stoned, semi-dried dates, chopped, instead of the apricots.

362 *Coq au vin*

55 g/2 oz butter
2 tbsp olive oil
1.8 kg/4 lb chicken pieces
115 g/4 oz rindless smoked bacon,
cut into strips
115 g/4 oz baby onions
115 g/4 oz chestnut mushrooms,
halved
2 garlic cloves, finely chopped
2 tbsp brandy
225 ml/8 fl oz red wine
300 ml/10 fl oz chicken stock
1 bouquet garni
2 tbsp plain flour
salt and pepper
bay leaves, to garnish

Melt half the butter with the olive oil in a large flameproof casserole. Add the chicken and cook over a medium heat, stirring, for 8–10 minutes, or until golden brown all over. Add the bacon, onions, mushrooms and garlic.

Pour in the brandy and set it alight. When the flames have died down, add the wine, stock and bouquet garni and season to taste with salt and pepper. Bring to the boil, reduce the heat and simmer for 1 hour, or until the chicken pieces are cooked through and tender. Meanwhile, make a beurre manié by mashing the remaining butter with the flour in a bowl.

Remove and discard the bouquet garni. Transfer the chicken to a plate and keep warm. Stir the beurre manié into the casserole, a little at a time. Bring to the boil, return the chicken to the casserole and serve immediately, garnished with bay leaves.

363 *Coq au vin with extra red wine*

If you are feeling generous you can, in fact, omit the chicken stock and use all red wine as the liquid for this casserole. Cremini mushrooms are virtually identical to chestnut mushrooms, so you can use those, or you could use sliced portobellos or even chanterelles.

364 *Country chicken bake*

2 tbsp sunflower oil
4 chicken quarters
16 small whole onions
3 celery sticks, sliced
400 g/14 oz canned red kidney beans,
rinsed and drained
4 tomatoes, quartered
200 ml/7 fl oz dry cider or chicken stock
4 tbsp chopped fresh parsley
1 tsp paprika
55 g/2 oz butter
12 slices French bread
salt and pepper

Preheat the oven to 200°C/400°F/Gas Mark 6. Heat the oil in a large flameproof casserole. Add the chicken quarters, 2 at a time, and fry until golden. Using a slotted spoon, remove the chicken from the casserole and reserve until required.

Add the onions and fry, turning occasionally, until golden brown. Add the celery and cook for 2–3 minutes. Return the chicken to the casserole, then stir in the beans, tomatoes, cider or stock and half the parsley. Season to taste with salt and pepper and sprinkle with the paprika. Cover and cook in the oven for 20–25 minutes, or until the chicken is tender and the juices run clear when a skewer is inserted into the thickest part of the meat. Mix the remaining parsley and butter together, then spread evenly over the French bread.

Uncover the casserole, arrange the bread slices overlapping on top and bake for a further 10–12 minutes, or until golden and crisp.

365 *Country chicken bake with lentils*

Use 150 g/5½ oz (dry weight) red lentils instead of the kidney beans and add 125 ml/4 fl oz chicken stock to the cider, as the lentils will absorb liquid. Add a little boiling water at the end of the cooking time if the casserole looks dry.

450 g/1 lb skinless, boneless chicken
1½ tbsp plain flour
1 tbsp olive oil
1 onion, cut into wedges
2 celery sticks, sliced
150 ml/5 fl oz orange juice
300 ml/10 fl oz chicken stock
1 tbsp light soy sauce
1–2 tsp clear honey
1 tbsp grated orange rind
1 orange pepper, deseeded and
chopped
225 g/8 oz courgettes, sliced into
half moons
2 small corn cobs, halved
1 orange, peeled and segmented
salt and pepper
1 tbsp chopped fresh parsley,
to garnish

Lightly rinse the chicken and pat dry with kitchen paper. Cut into bite-sized pieces. Season the flour well with salt and pepper. Toss the chicken in the seasoned flour until well coated and reserve any remaining seasoned flour.

Heat the oil in a large heavy-based frying pan and cook the chicken over a high heat, stirring frequently, for 5 minutes, or until golden on all sides and sealed. Using a slotted spoon, transfer the chicken to a plate. Add the onion and celery to the frying pan and cook over a medium heat, stirring frequently, for 5 minutes, or until softened. Sprinkle in the reserved seasoned flour and cook, stirring constantly, for 2 minutes, then remove from the heat. Gradually stir in the orange juice, stock, soy sauce and honey, followed by the orange rind, then return to the heat and bring to the boil, stirring.

Return the chicken to the frying pan. Reduce the heat, cover and simmer, stirring occasionally, for 15 minutes. Add the orange pepper, courgettes and corn cobs and simmer for a further 10 minutes, or until the chicken and vegetables are tender. Add the orange segments, stir well and heat for 1 minute. Serve, garnished with the parsley.

367 *Florida pork*

Use 450 g/1 lb of pork fillet instead of the chicken.

368 *Florida lamb*

Use lamb fillet instead of the chicken. Omit the orange, and add the juice of ½ lemon to the pan for the last 10 minutes of cooking time.

369 Hunter's chicken

15 g/½ oz unsalted butter
2 tbsp olive oil
1.8 kg/4 lb skinned, unboned chicken
   portions
2 red onions, sliced
2 garlic cloves, finely chopped
400 g/14 oz canned chopped tomatoes
2 tbsp chopped fresh flat-leaf parsley
6 fresh basil leaves, torn
1 tbsp sun-dried tomato purée
150 ml/5 fl oz red wine
225 g/8 oz mushrooms, sliced
salt and pepper

Preheat the oven to 160°C/325°F/Gas Mark 3. Heat the butter and oil in a flameproof casserole and cook the chicken over a medium–high heat, turning frequently, for 10 minutes, or until golden all over and sealed. Using a slotted spoon, transfer to a plate. Add the onions and garlic to the casserole and cook over a low heat, stirring occasionally, for 10 minutes, or until softened and golden. Add the tomatoes, the herbs, sun-dried tomato purée and wine, and season to taste with salt and pepper. Bring to the boil, then return the chicken portions to the casserole, pushing them down into the sauce.

Cover and cook in the preheated oven for 50 minutes. Add the mushrooms and cook for a further 10 minutes, or until the chicken is tender and the juices run clear when a skewer is inserted into the thickest part of the meat. Serve immediately.

370 Hunter's game

Try any game bird in this recipe instead of chicken – particularly good would be pheasant or guinea fowl. Use 1 whole large bird, jointed. You can also use 1.8 kg/4 lb shin of veal and increase simmering time to 1¼ hours.

371 Italian-style roast chicken

1 chicken weighing 2.5 kg/5 lb 8 oz
fresh rosemary sprigs
175 g/6 oz feta cheese, coarsely grated
2 tbsp sun-dried tomato purée
55 g/2 oz butter, softened
1 bulb garlic
1 kg/2 lb 4 oz new potatoes, halved
   if large
1 each red, green and yellow pepper,
   deseeded and cut into chunks
3 courgettes, thinly sliced
2 tbsp olive oil
2 tbsp plain flour
600 ml/1 pint chicken stock
salt and pepper

sun-dried tomato purée, butter and pepper to taste, then spoon under the skin. Put the chicken in a large roasting tin, cover with foil and cook in the preheated oven, for 20 minutes per 500 g/1 lb 2 oz, plus 20 minutes. Break the garlic bulb into cloves but do not peel.

Add the vegetables and garlic to the chicken after 40 minutes. Drizzle with oil, tuck in a few stems of rosemary and season. Cook for the remaining calculated time, removing the foil for the last 40 minutes to brown the chicken. Transfer the chicken to a serving platter. Place some of the vegetables around the chicken and transfer the remainder to a warmed serving dish. Spoon the fat out of the roasting tin (it will be floating on top) and stir the flour into the remaining cooking juices.

Place the roasting tin on top of the hob and cook over medium heat for 2 minutes, then gradually stir in the stock. Bring to the boil, stirring until thickened. Strain into a gravy boat and serve with the chicken and vegetables.

Preheat the oven to 190°C/375°F/Gas Mark 5. Rinse the chicken inside and out with cold water and drain well. Carefully cut between the skin and the top of the breast meat using a small pointed knife. Slide a finger into the slit and enlarge it to form a pocket. Continue until the skin is completely lifted away from both breasts and the top of the legs. Chop the leaves from 3 rosemary stems. Mix with the feta cheese,

372 Creamy Italian-style roast chicken

Try using mascarpone or ricotta cheese instead of the feta for a creamy result, which makes the breast especially succulent and gives a delicious gravy.

Jamaican hotpot

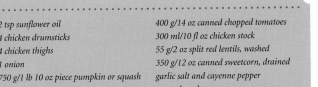

2 tsp sunflower oil
4 chicken drumsticks
4 chicken thighs
1 onion
750 g/1 lb 10 oz piece pumpkin or squash
1 green pepper
2.5-cm/1-inch piece fresh ginger, finely chopped

400 g/14 oz canned chopped tomatoes
300 ml/10 fl oz chicken stock
55 g/2 oz split red lentils, washed
350 g/12 oz canned sweetcorn, drained
garlic salt and cayenne pepper
crusty bread, to serve

Preheat the oven to 190°C/375°F/ Gas Mark 5. Heat the oil in a large flameproof casserole. Add the chicken joints and fry until golden brown, turning frequently. Using a sharp knife, slice the onion, then peel and dice the pumpkin and deseed and slice the green pepper.

Drain any excess fat from the casserole and add the onion, pumpkin and pepper. Gently fry for a few minutes until lightly browned. Add the ginger, tomatoes, stock and lentils. Season lightly with garlic salt and cayenne pepper. Cover the casserole and cook in the oven for 1 hour, or until the vegetables and chicken are tender and the chicken juices run clear when a skewer is inserted into the thickest part of the meat.

Add the drained sweetcorn and cook for a further 5 minutes. Taste and adjust the seasoning, if necessary, then serve with crusty bread.

374 Jamaican hotpot with allspice

If you can't find fresh root ginger, add 1 teaspoon of ground allspice for a fragrant aroma. If squash or pumpkin is not available, swede makes a very good substitute.

375 Jamaican hotpot with chicken thighs

You don't have to use both chicken thighs and drumsticks – you can use 8 thighs if you prefer. The leg meat is better in this dish than breast meat as it stays more moist and has a stronger flavour.

376 Jambalaya

2 tbsp vegetable oil
2 onions, roughly chopped
1 green pepper, deseeded and roughly chopped
2 celery sticks, roughly chopped
3 garlic cloves, finely chopped
2 tsp paprika
300 g/10½ oz skinless, boneless chicken breasts, chopped
100 g/3½ oz kabanos sausages, chopped
3 tomatoes, peeled and chopped
450 g/1 lb long-grain rice
850 ml/1½ pints hot chicken or fish stock
1 tsp dried oregano
2 bay leaves
12 large raw prawns
4 spring onions, finely chopped
2 tbsp chopped fresh parsley
salt and pepper
chopped fresh herbs, to garnish

Heat the vegetable oil in a large frying pan over a low heat. Add the onions, pepper, celery and garlic and cook for 8–10 minutes until all the vegetables have softened. Add the paprika and cook for a further 30 seconds. Add the chicken and sausages and cook for 8–10 minutes until lightly browned. Add the tomatoes and cook for 2–3 minutes until they have collapsed. Add the rice to the pan and stir well. Pour in the hot stock, oregano and bay leaves and stir well. Cover and simmer for 10 minutes. Add the prawns and stir. Cover again and cook for a further 6–8 minutes until the rice is tender and the prawns are cooked through. Stir in the spring onions and parsley and season to taste. Transfer to a serving dish, garnish with the fresh herbs and serve.

377 Jambalaya with chorizo or ham

Kabanos sausage is a spicy cured sausage from Poland. You can substitute it with chorizo from Spain or another sausage of your choice, or you can use the same weight of cubed ham.

378 Louisiana chicken

5 tbsp sunflower oil
4 chicken portions
55 g/2 oz plain flour
1 onion, chopped
2 celery sticks, sliced
1 green pepper, deseeded and chopped
2 garlic cloves, finely chopped
2 tsp chopped fresh thyme

2 fresh red chillies, deseeded and finely chopped
400 g/14 oz canned chopped tomatoes
300 ml/10 fl oz chicken stock
salt and pepper
lamb's lettuce, to garnish
chopped fresh thyme, to garnish

Heat the oil in a large heavy-based saucepan or flameproof casserole. Add the chicken and then cook over a medium heat, stirring, for 5–10 minutes, or until golden. Transfer the chicken to a plate with a slotted spoon.

Stir the flour into the oil and cook over a very low heat, stirring constantly, for 15 minutes, or until light golden. Do not let it burn. Immediately, add the onion, celery and green pepper and cook, stirring constantly, for 2 minutes. Add the garlic, thyme and chillies and cook, stirring, for 1 minute. Stir in the tomatoes, then gradually stir in the stock. Return the chicken pieces to the saucepan, cover and simmer for 45 minutes, or until the chicken is cooked through and tender. Season to taste with salt and pepper, transfer to warmed serving plates and serve immediately, garnished with some lettuce leaves and a sprinkling of chopped thyme.

379 With rice

To make a filling one-pot meal, stir 175 g/6 oz long-grain rice into the pot after the vegetables have finished sautéeing in the oil. Carry on with the recipe but add 500 ml/18 fl oz stock as the rice will absorb liquid. Add a little more boiling water to the pan towards the end of cooking time if it looks too dry.

380 Mexican chicken, chilli & potato pot

2 tbsp vegetable oil
450 g/1 lb skinless, boneless chicken breasts, cubed
1 onion, finely chopped
1 green pepper, deseeded and finely chopped
1 potato, diced
1 sweet potato, diced
2 garlic cloves, very finely chopped
1–2 fresh green chillies, deseeded and very finely chopped
200 g/7 oz canned chopped tomatoes
½ tsp dried oregano
½ tsp salt
¼ tsp pepper
4 tbsp chopped fresh coriander
450 ml/16 fl oz chicken stock

Heat the oil in a large heavy-based saucepan over a medium–high heat. Add the chicken and cook until lightly browned. Reduce the heat to medium. Add the onion, pepper, potato and sweet potato. Cover and cook, stirring occasionally, for 5 minutes, or until the vegetables begin to soften.

Add the garlic and chillies and cook for 1 minute. Stir in the tomatoes, oregano, salt, pepper and half the coriander and cook for 1 minute. Pour in the stock. Bring to the boil, then cover and simmer over a medium–low heat for 15–20 minutes, or until the chicken is cooked through and the vegetables are tender.

Sprinkle with the remaining coriander just before serving.

381 With sweetcorn & coriander

Stir in 200 g/7 oz sweetcorn with the tomatoes. For added warmth, stir in ½ teaspoon of ground coriander seed with the oregano.

4 chicken portions, about 150 g/5½ oz
  each
1 tbsp plain flour
2½ tbsp olive oil
8–12 shallots, halved if large
2–4 garlic cloves, sliced
400 ml/14 fl oz chicken stock
50 ml/2 fl oz sherry

few sprigs fresh thyme, plus 1 tbsp
  chopped fresh thyme, to garnish
115 g/4 oz cherry tomatoes
115 g/4 oz baby corn, halved lengthways
2 large slices white or wholemeal bread
salt and pepper

Lightly rinse the chicken and pat dry with kitchen paper. Season the flour well with salt and pepper. Toss the chicken in the seasoned flour until well coated and reserve any remaining seasoned flour.

Heat 1 tablespoon of the oil in a large deep frying pan and cook the chicken over a medium–high heat, turning frequently, for 10 minutes, or until golden all over and sealed. Using a slotted spoon, transfer to a plate.

Add the shallots and garlic to the frying pan and cook over a medium heat, stirring frequently, for 5 minutes, or until softened. Sprinkle in the reserved seasoned flour and cook, stirring constantly, for 2 minutes, then remove from the heat. Gradually stir in the stock followed by the sherry, then return to the heat and bring to the boil, stirring.

Return the chicken to the frying pan and add the thyme sprigs. Reduce the heat, cover and simmer, stirring occasionally, for 40 minutes. Add the tomatoes and baby corn and simmer for a further 10 minutes, or until the chicken is tender and the juices run clear when a skewer is inserted into the thickest part of the meat.

Meanwhile, cut the bread into small cubes. Heat the remaining oil in a frying pan and fry the bread, stirring frequently, for 4–5 minutes, or until golden. Serve the stew garnished with the chopped thyme and the croûtons.

383 *Poulet Marengo with French beans*

Omit the baby corn and add 115 g/4 oz French beans to the pot instead.

384 *With a herby breadcrumb topping*

Instead of croûtons, try adding a crumb mix. Combine 50 g/2 oz stale breadcrumbs with 2 teaspoons of finely chopped fresh oregano leaves, 1 tablespoon of fresh chopped parsley and 1 teaspoon of finely grated lemon rind. Stir in a small non-stick frying pan with 1 tablespoon of olive oil until the crumbs begin to turn golden then sprinkle over the finished casserole.

385 Red hot chilli chicken

2 tbsp groundnut or sunflower oil
½ tsp cumin seeds
1 onion, chopped
2 curry leaves
1 tsp ground cumin
1 tsp ground coriander
½ tsp ground turmeric
400 g/14 oz canned chopped tomatoes
150 ml/5 fl oz chicken stock
4 skinless, boneless chicken breasts
1 tsp garam masala
fresh mint sprigs, to garnish
freshly cooked rice, to serve

CHILLI PASTE
1 tbsp curry paste
2 fresh green chillies, chopped
5 dried red chillies
2 tbsp tomato purée
2 garlic cloves, chopped
1 tsp chilli powder
pinch of sugar
pinch of salt

To make the chilli paste, place the curry paste, fresh and dried chillies, tomato purée, garlic, chilli powder and sugar in a blender or food processor and add a pinch of salt. Process until mixture turns into a smooth paste.

Heat the oil in a large heavy-based saucepan. Add the cumin seeds and cook over a medium heat, stirring constantly, for 2 minutes, or until they begin to pop and release their aroma.

Add the onion and curry leaves and cook, stirring, for 5 minutes. Add the chilli paste and cook for 2 minutes, then stir in the ground cumin, coriander and turmeric and cook for a further 2 minutes.

Add the tomatoes and the stock. Bring to the boil, then reduce the heat and simmer for 5 minutes.

Add the chicken and garam masala, cover and simmer gently for 20 minutes, or until the chicken is cooked through and tender. Serve immediately with rice and garnished with fresh mint sprigs.

386 Quick red hot chilli chicken

In a bowl, combine 2 tablespoons of harissa paste with 2 tablespoons of tomato purée. Sauté 1 chopped onion in 2 tablespoons of groundnut oil over a medium heat with 2 curry leaves for 5 minutes. Add the paste/purée mix, then stir for 1 minute. Add 400 g/14 oz canned chopped tomatoes, 150 ml/5 fl oz stock, and simmer for 5 minutes. Add 4 chicken breast fillets and 1 teaspoon of garam masala, stir, cover, and cook for 20 minutes.

387 Tarragon chicken

4 skinless, boneless chicken breasts, about 175 g/6 oz each
125 ml/4 fl oz dry white wine
225–300 ml/8–10 fl oz chicken stock
1 garlic clove, finely chopped
1 tbsp dried tarragon
175 ml/6 fl oz double cream
1 tbsp chopped fresh tarragon
salt and pepper
fresh tarragon sprigs, to garnish

Season the chicken with salt and pepper and place in a single layer in a large heavy-based frying pan. Pour in the wine and enough chicken stock just to cover and add the garlic and dried tarragon. Bring to the boil, reduce the heat and cook gently for 10 minutes, or until the chicken is tender and cooked right through.

Remove the chicken with a slotted spoon or tongs, cover and keep warm. Strain the poaching liquid through a sieve into a clean frying pan and skim off any fat from the surface. Bring to the boil and cook for 12–15 minutes, or until reduced by about two-thirds. Stir in the cream, return to the boil and cook until reduced by about half. Stir in the fresh tarragon. Slice the chicken breasts and arrange on warmed plates. Spoon over the sauce, garnish with tarragon sprigs and serve immediately.

388 Easy herbed chicken

If you haven't any fresh tarragon you can make a similar and equally tasty herbed chicken and wine dish using fresh parsley. Omit both the dried and fresh tarragon from the recipe and use 3 tablespoons of finely chopped fresh parsley, added to the pan with the cream. Increase the amount of garlic to 2 cloves.

389 Springtime chicken cobbler

1 tbsp oil
8 skinless chicken drumsticks
1 small onion, sliced
350 g/12 oz baby carrots
2 baby turnips
125 g/4½ oz fresh or frozen peas
1 tsp cornflour
300 ml/10 fl oz chicken stock
2 bay leaves
salt and pepper

COBBLER TOPPING
250 g/9 oz wholemeal plain flour,
    plus extra for dusting
2 tsp baking powder
25 g/1 oz sunflower soft margarine
2 tsp dry mustard
55 g/2 oz Cheddar cheese, grated
2–3 tbsp skimmed milk, plus extra for
    brushing
sesame seeds, for sprinkling

Preheat the oven to 200°C/400°F/ Gas Mark 6. Heat the oil in a large flameproof casserole. Add the chicken and fry, turning frequently, until golden brown. Drain well and remove. Add the onion to the casserole and sauté for 2–3 minutes, or until softened. Cut the carrots and turnips into equal-sized pieces. Add to the casserole with the peas and chicken. Blend the cornflour with a little of the stock in a small saucepan, then stir in the remainder of the stock and heat gently, stirring, until boiling. Pour into the casserole and add the bay leaves and salt and pepper to taste.

Cover the casserole and bake in the oven for 50–60 minutes, or until the chicken is tender and the juices run clear when a skewer is inserted into the thickest part of the meat.

For the topping, sift the flour and baking powder into a large bowl, then mix in the margarine with a fork. Stir in the mustard, cheese and enough milk to form a fairly soft dough. Roll out on a lightly floured work surface.

Cut out 16 rounds with a 4-cm/1½-inch cutter. Uncover the casserole and arrange the rounds on top. Brush with milk and sprinkle with sesame seeds. Bake for a further 20 minutes, or until the topping is golden and firm.

390 Springtime chicken pie

Instead of the cobbler topping, roll out 350 g/12 oz ready-made puff pastry to approximately ½ cm/¼ inch thick. Use a 4-cm/1½-inch cutter to make 16 rounds and add to the top of the casserole. Brush with beaten egg or milk. Bake for 15–20 minutes (without lid on) until pastry is puffed up and golden.

391 Duck jambalaya-style stew

4 duck breasts, about
    150 g/5½ oz each
2 tbsp olive oil
225 g/8 oz piece gammon, cut into
    small chunks
225 g/8 oz chorizo, outer casing
    removed
1 onion, chopped
3 garlic cloves, chopped
3 celery sticks, chopped
1–2 fresh red chillies, deseeded
    and chopped
1 green pepper, deseeded and chopped
600 ml/1 pint chicken stock
1 tbsp chopped fresh oregano
400 g/14 oz canned chopped tomatoes
1–2 tsp hot pepper sauce, or to taste
chopped fresh flat-leaf parsley,
    to garnish
green salad, to serve
freshly cooked rice, to serve

Remove and discard the skin and any fat from the duck breasts. Cut into bite-sized pieces. Heat half the oil in a deep frying pan and cook the duck, gammon and chorizo over a high heat, stirring frequently, for 5 minutes, or until browned all over and sealed. Using a slotted spoon, remove from the frying pan and set aside. Add the onion, garlic, celery and chillies to the frying pan and cook over a medium heat, stirring frequently, for 5 minutes. Add the green pepper, then stir in the stock, oregano, tomatoes and hot pepper sauce. Bring to the boil, then reduce the heat and return the meat to the pan. Cover and simmer, stirring occasionally, for 20 minutes, or until the duck and gammon are tender. Garnish with parsley and serve accompanied by a green salad and rice.

4 duck portions, about
150 g/5½ oz each, most of fat
removed and discarded
1 tbsp olive oil, plus 1–2 tsp
1 red onion, cut into wedges
2–3 garlic cloves, chopped
1 large carrot, chopped
2 celery sticks, chopped
2 tbsp plain flour
300 ml/10 fl oz red wine,
such as Claret
2 tbsp brandy (optional)
150–200 ml/5–7 fl oz stock or water
7.5-cm/3-inch strip of orange rind
2 tsp redcurrant jelly
115 g/4 oz sugar snap peas
115 g/4 oz button mushrooms
salt and pepper
1 tbsp chopped fresh parsley,
to garnish

Lightly rinse the duck and pat dry with kitchen paper. Heat a large, deep frying pan for 1 minute until warm but not piping hot. Put the duck in the frying pan and gently heat until the fat starts to run. Increase the heat a little, then cook, turning over halfway through, for 5 minutes, or until browned on both sides and sealed. Using a slotted spoon, transfer to a flameproof casserole.

Add 1 tablespoon of the oil if there is little duck fat in the frying pan and cook the onion, garlic, carrot and celery, stirring frequently, for 5 minutes, or until softened. Sprinkle in the flour and cook, stirring constantly, for 2 minutes, then remove the frying pan from the heat.

Gradually stir in the wine, brandy (if using), and stock, then return to the heat and bring to the boil, stirring. Season to taste with salt and pepper, then add the orange rind and redcurrant jelly. Pour over the duck portions in the casserole, cover and simmer, stirring occasionally, for 1–1¼ hours.

Cook the sugar snap peas in a saucepan of boiling water for 3 minutes, then drain and add to the stew. Meanwhile, heat 1–2 teaspoons of the olive oil in a small saucepan and cook the mushrooms, stirring frequently, for 3 minutes, until they begin to soften. Add to the stew. Cook the stew for a further 5 minutes, or until the duck is tender. Serve garnished with the parsley.

393 *Duck & white wine stew*

For a delicate but equally tasty stew, replace the red wine with dry white wine, and use apple jelly instead of redcurrant jelly.

394 Chorizo & mussel stew

1 kg/2 lb 4 oz mussels
2 tbsp olive oil
500 g/1 lb 2 oz chorizo sausage
(preferably raw), chopped into
1-cm/½-inch slices
250 g/9 oz bacon (in 1 piece if
possible), roughly chopped
3 large garlic cloves, chopped
40 g/1½ oz butter
½ tsp hot smoked paprika
1 small jar sweet piquillo peppers,
drained, or
1 large red pepper, roughly chopped
150 ml/5 fl oz white wine
250 ml/9 fl oz chicken stock
large handful of parsley, finely
chopped
lots of crusty fresh bread, to serve

Clean and debeard the mussels, discarding any that don't close when tapped, or that are broken.

Place a large casserole over a high heat and add the olive oil. When hot, add the chorizo and the bacon and fry for about 10 minutes, until they just start to brown. Reduce the heat, add the garlic, butter, paprika and peppers and fry for a further 2–3 minutes, until soft.

Add the mussels, wine and chicken stock, increase the heat to high and put the lid on. The mussels will start to open as soon as the stew starts to bubble. They need to cook for about 1 minute after they have all opened. Discard any that remain closed.

Ladle into large bowls with the juices, scatter over the parsley and serve with some good, fresh bread.

395 Chorizo & seafood stew

Use 800 g/1¾ lb frozen mixed seafood (available from most supermarkets) instead of the fresh mussels for a quicker option. These packs usually contain a mixture of mussels (shell off), squid, prawns and octopus. Thaw and add instead of the fresh mussels and simmer for 5 minutes, very gently.

396 Chicken with vegetables & coriander rice

SERVES 4

2 tbsp vegetable or groundnut oil
1 red onion, chopped
2 garlic cloves, chopped
2.5-cm/1-inch piece fresh ginger,
peeled and chopped
2 skinless, boneless chicken breasts,
cut into strips
115 g/4 oz button mushrooms
400 g/14 oz canned coconut milk
55 g/2 oz sugar snap peas, trimmed and
halved lengthways

2 tbsp soy sauce
1 tbsp fish sauce

RICE
1 tbsp vegetable or groundnut oil
1 red onion, sliced
350 g/12 oz rice, cooked and cooled
250 g/8 oz pak choy, torn into
large pieces
handful of fresh coriander, chopped
2 tbsp Thai soy sauce

Heat the oil in a wok or large frying pan and fry the onion, garlic and ginger together for 1–2 minutes. Add the chicken and mushrooms and fry over a high heat until browned. Add the coconut milk, sugar snap peas and sauces and bring to the boil. Simmer gently for 4–5 minutes until tender. Heat the oil for the rice in a separate wok or large frying pan and fry the onion until softened but not browned.

Add the cooked rice, pak choy and fresh coriander and heat gently until the leaves have wilted and the rice is hot. Sprinkle over the soy sauce and serve immediately with the chicken.

397 Chicken with broccoli & coriander rice

Try replacing the sugar snap peas with small florets of broccoli or with halved French beans.

Lamb stew with chickpeas

6 tbsp olive oil
225 g/8 oz chorizo sausage, cut into
5-mm/¹⁄₄-inch thick slices, casings
removed
2 large onions, chopped
6 large garlic cloves, crushed
900 g/2 lb boned leg of lamb, cut into
5-cm/2-inch cubes
250 ml/9 fl oz lamb stock or water
125 ml/4 fl oz red wine, such as Rioja
or Tempranillo
2 tbsp sherry vinegar
800 g/1 lb 12 oz canned chopped
tomatoes
4 sprigs fresh thyme, plus extra to
garnish
2 bay leaves
¹⁄₂ tsp sweet Spanish paprika
800 g/1 lb 12 oz canned chickpeas,
rinsed and drained
salt and pepper

Preheat the oven to 160°C/325°F/ Gas Mark 3. Heat 4 tablespoons of the oil in a large heavy-based flameproof casserole over a medium–high heat. Reduce the heat, add the chorizo and fry for 1 minute and then set aside. Add the onions to the casserole and fry for 2 minutes, then add the garlic and continue frying for 3 minutes, or until the onions are soft, but not brown. Remove from the casserole and set aside. Heat the remaining 2 tablespoons of oil in the casserole. Add the lamb cubes in a single layer without over-crowding the casserole, and fry until browned on each side; work in batches, if necessary.

Return the onion mixture to the casserole with all the lamb and chorizo. Stir in the stock, wine, vinegar, tomatoes and add salt and pepper to taste. Bring to the boil, scraping any glazed bits from the base of the casserole. Reduce the heat and stir in the thyme, bay leaves and paprika.

Transfer to the preheated oven and cook, covered, for 40–45 minutes until the lamb is tender. Stir in the chickpeas and return to the oven, uncovered, for 10 minutes, or until they are heated through and the juices are reduced. Taste and adjust the seasoning. Serve garnished with thyme.

399 Chicken stew with chickpeas

Replace the lamb in the above recipe with 800 g/1 lb 12 oz chicken fillet – thigh is good. Cut each thigh in half and fry in the oil after the onions, until lightly golden; continue with recipe.

---

400 Lamb stew with red peppers

450 g/1 lb lean boneless lamb, such as leg
of lamb or fillet
1¹⁄₂ tbsp plain flour
1 tsp ground cloves
1–1¹⁄₂ tbsp olive oil
1 onion, sliced
2–3 garlic cloves, sliced
300 ml/10 fl oz orange juice
150 ml/5 fl oz lamb stock or chicken stock

1 cinnamon stick, bruised
2 sweet (pointed, if available) red
peppers, deseeded and sliced into rings
4 tomatoes
salt and pepper
few fresh sprigs coriander, plus 1 tbsp
chopped fresh coriander, to garnish

Preheat the oven to 190°C/375°F/ Gas Mark 5. Trim any fat or gristle from the lamb and cut into thin strips. Mix the flour and cloves together. Toss the lamb in the spiced flour until well coated and reserve any remaining spiced flour. Heat 1 tablespoon of the oil in a heavy-based frying pan and cook the lamb over a high heat, stirring frequently, for 3 minutes, or until browned on all sides and sealed. Using a slotted spoon, transfer to an ovenproof casserole.

Add the onion and garlic to the frying pan and cook over a medium heat, stirring frequently, for 3 minutes, adding the extra oil if necessary. Sprinkle in the reserved spiced flour and cook, stirring constantly, for 2 minutes, then remove from the heat.

Gradually stir in the orange juice and stock, then return to the heat and bring to the boil, stirring. When boiling, pour over the lamb in the casserole, add the cinnamon stick, red peppers, tomatoes and coriander sprigs and stir well. Cover and cook in the preheated oven for 1¹⁄₂ hours, or until the lamb is tender.

Discard the cinnamon stick and adjust the seasoning to taste. Serve garnished with the chopped fresh coriander.

401 Spicy lamb stew with red peppers

Try using ¹⁄₂ teaspoon each of ground cumin and coriander seed instead of the cloves to spice up the flour.

402 Lamb with courgettes & tomatoes

4–8 lamb chops	400 g/14 oz canned tomatoes
2 tbsp olive oil	pinch of sugar
1 onion, finely chopped	250 g/9 oz courgettes, sliced
1 garlic clove, finely chopped	2 tbsp chopped fresh thyme
4 tbsp ouzo (optional)	salt and pepper

Season the lamb chops with pepper. Heat the oil in a large flameproof casserole, add the onion and garlic and fry for 5 minutes or until softened. Add the lamb chops and fry until browned on both sides. Stir in the ouzo, if using, then add the tomatoes, sugar, courgettes, thyme and salt.

Bring to the boil and then simmer for 30–45 minutes, stirring occasionally and turning the chops once during cooking, until the lamb and courgettes are tender. If necessary, add a little water during cooking.

403 Lamb with courgettes & potatoes

Instead of the ouzo, add 4 tablespoons of dry white wine. For a heartier meal, slice some cooked potatoes into thin rounds and add with the courgettes.

404 Lamb with mint

2 tbsp sunflower oil	200 g/7 oz canned chopped tomatoes
1 onion, chopped	1 tbsp chopped fresh mint
1 garlic clove, finely chopped	85 g/3 oz fresh or frozen peas
1 tsp grated fresh ginger	2 carrots, sliced into thin batons
1 tsp ground coriander	1 fresh green chilli, deseeded and finely
1/2 tsp chilli powder	chopped
1/4 tsp ground turmeric	1 tbsp chopped fresh coriander
pinch of salt	fresh mint sprigs, to garnish
350 g/12 oz fresh lamb mince	

Heat the oil in a large heavy-based frying pan or flameproof casserole. Add the onion and cook over a low heat, stirring occasionally, for 10 minutes, or until golden.

Meanwhile, place the garlic, ginger, ground coriander, chilli powder, turmeric and salt in a small bowl and mix well. Add the spice mixture to the frying pan and cook, stirring constantly, for 2 minutes. Add the lamb and cook, stirring frequently, for 8–10 minutes, or until it is broken up and browned.

Add the tomatoes, the mint, peas, carrots, chilli and fresh coriander. Cook, stirring constantly, for 3–5 minutes, then serve immediately, garnished with fresh mint sprigs.

405 Lamb with mint & leeks

Instead of the carrots, finely chop 2 leeks and add to the pan with the onion.

127

Lamb with pears

1 tbsp olive oil
1 kg/2 lb 4 oz best end of neck lamb
    cutlets, trimmed of visible fat
6 pears, peeled, cored and quartered
1 tsp ground ginger

4 potatoes, diced
4 tbsp dry cider
450 g/1 lb green beans, trimmed
salt and pepper
2 tbsp snipped fresh chives,
    to garnish

Preheat the oven to 160°C/325°F/Gas Mark 3. Heat the olive oil in a flameproof casserole over a medium heat. Add the lamb and cook, turning frequently, for 5–10 minutes, or until browned on all sides.

Arrange the pear quarters on top, then sprinkle over the ginger. Cover with the potatoes. Pour in the cider and season to taste with salt and pepper. Cover and cook in the preheated oven for 1¼ hours.

Remove the casserole from the oven and add the beans, then re-cover and return to the oven for a further 30 minutes. Taste and adjust the seasoning. Sprinkle with the chives and serve.

407 Lamb with pineapple

Instead of the pears use 1 peeled, cored and quartered pineapple and replace half of the cider with pineapple juice.

408 Lamb with tomatoes, artichokes & olives

4 tbsp Greek-style yogurt
grated rind of 1 lemon
2 garlic cloves, crushed
3 tbsp olive oil
1 tsp ground cumin
700 g/1 lb 9 oz lean boneless lamb,
    cubed
1 onion, thinly sliced
150 ml/5 fl oz dry white wine
450 g/1 lb tomatoes, roughly chopped
1 tbsp tomato purée
pinch of sugar
2 tbsp chopped fresh oregano or 1 tsp
    dried oregano
2 bay leaves
85 g/3 oz kalamata olives
400 g/14 oz canned artichoke hearts,
    drained and halved
salt and pepper

Put the yogurt, lemon rind, garlic, 1 tablespoon of the olive oil, cumin, salt and pepper in a large bowl and mix together.

Add the lamb and toss together until the lamb is coated in the yogurt mixture. Cover and marinate for at least 1 hour.

Heat 1 tablespoon of the olive oil in a large flameproof casserole. Add the lamb in batches and fry for about 5 minutes, stirring frequently, until browned on all sides. Using a slotted spoon, remove the meat from the casserole and set aside.

Add the remaining tablespoon of oil to the casserole with the onion and fry for 5 minutes or until softened. Pour the wine into the casserole, stirring in any glazed bits from the bottom, and bring to the boil. Reduce the heat and return the meat to the casserole, then stir in the tomatoes, tomato purée, sugar, oregano and bay leaves.

Cover the casserole with a lid and simmer for about 1½ hours, until the lamb is tender. Stir in the olives and artichoke hearts and simmer for another 10 minutes. Serve hot.

409 Lamb with tomatoes, beans & capers

Replace the artichokes with 300 g/11 oz broad beans, added to the pan for the last half hour of simmering time. Omit the olives and add 1 tablespoon of rinsed capers for the last 5 minutes.

Lancashire hotpot

900 g/2 lb best end lamb chops
3 lambs' kidneys
55 g/2 oz butter
900 g/2 lb floury potatoes, such as
    King Edwards or Maris Piper,
    peeled and sliced
3 onions, halved and finely sliced

2 tsp fresh thyme leaves
1 tsp finely chopped fresh rosemary
600 ml/1 pint chicken stock
salt and pepper

Preheat the oven to 160°C/325°F/Gas Mark 3. Trim the chops of any excess fat. Cut the kidneys in half, remove the core and cut into quarters. Season all the meat well. Butter a large, shallow ovenproof dish or deep roasting tin with half the butter and arrange a layer of potatoes in the bottom. Layer up the onions and meat, adding the herbs and salt and pepper between each layer. Finish with a neat layer of overlapping potatoes. Pour in most of the stock so that it covers the meat. Melt the remaining butter and brush the top of the potato with it. Reserve any remaining butter. Cover with foil and cook in the oven for 2 hours.

    Uncover the hotpot and brush the potatoes again with the melted butter. Return the hotpot to the oven and cook for a further 30 minutes, allowing the potatoes to get brown and crisp. You may need to increase the temperature if not browning sufficiently, or pop under a hot grill. Serve the hotpot at the table, making sure that everyone gets a good helping of crusty potato and the meat.

411 ### With Worcestershire sauce

You can, if you prefer, omit the kidneys – not all Lancashire Hotpot recipes from past times include them. For more flavour add a dash of Worcestershire sauce – which isn't traditional!

412 ## Irish stew

4 tbsp plain flour
1.3 kg/3 lb middle neck of lamb,
    trimmed of visible fat
3 large onions, chopped
3 carrots, sliced

450 g/1 lb potatoes, quartered
½ tsp dried thyme
850 ml/1½ pints hot beef stock
salt and pepper
2 tbsp chopped fresh parsley, to garnish

Preheat the oven to 160°C/325°F/Gas Mark 3. Spread the flour on a plate and season with salt and pepper. Roll the pieces of lamb in the flour to coat, shaking off any excess, and arrange in the base of a casserole. Layer the onions, carrots and potatoes on top of the lamb. Sprinkle in the thyme and pour in the stock, then cover and cook in the preheated oven for 2½ hours. Garnish with the chopped fresh parsley and serve straight from the casserole.

413 ### Irish stew with lamb chops

Use 8 loin lamb chops instead of the neck of lamb. Put the carrots and onions in the base of the lightly-oiled casserole then add the lamb. Cut the potatoes into 1-cm/½-inch thick rounds and cover the lamb. Add the stock and thyme.

Spring lamb stew

500 g/1 lb 2 oz boneless shoulder of
lamb, cut into 5-cm/2-inch chunks
250 g/9 oz best end of neck lamb,
chopped
2 tbsp caster sugar
140 g/5 oz unsalted butter
2 tbsp sunflower oil
2 tbsp plain flour
1 tbsp tomato purée
3 vine-ripened tomatoes, peeled,
deseeded and chopped
3 garlic cloves, crushed
2 onions, chopped
600 ml/1 pint chicken or vegetable
stock
1 bouquet garni
200 g/7 oz baby turnips, peeled
but left whole
200 g/7 oz baby carrots, scrubbed or
peeled but left whole or chopped,
depending on how young they are
200 g/7 oz pickling onions, peeled but
left whole
200 g/7 oz small new potatoes, peeled
but left whole
100 g/3½ oz shelled peas
salt and pepper

Preheat the oven to 190°C/375°F/Gas Mark 5. Season the lamb with
1 tablespoon of the sugar and salt and pepper to taste.

Melt 85 g/3 oz of the butter with the oil in a large flameproof
casserole over a medium–high heat. Add the pieces of lamb shoulder
and sauté until brown on all sides, working in batches as necessary.
Remove the meat from the casserole as it browns and set aside. Add the
pieces of lamb neck to the casserole and brown, then add them to the
shoulder meat.

Pour off all but 2 tablespoons of the fat in the casserole. Return the
meat to the casserole, sprinkle with the flour and sauté over a medium
heat for 5 minutes, or until the flour browns.

Add the tomato purée, tomatoes, garlic, chopped onions and stock
and bring to the boil, skimming the surface if necessary. Add the
bouquet garni and season to taste with salt and pepper. Cover the
casserole and transfer it to the oven to cook for 45 minutes.

Meanwhile, put the turnips, carrots and pickling onions in a large
sauté or frying pan over a medium–high heat. Add the remaining butter
and sugar, salt and pepper to taste and just enough water to cover the
vegetables. Bring to the boil, then reduce the heat and simmer until the
liquid evaporates and the vegetables are covered with a glaze, shaking
the pan frequently.

After the stew has cooked for 45 minutes, add the glazed vegetables
and the potatoes, re-cover the casserole and cook for a further 35 minutes.
Add the peas and continue cooking for a further 10 minutes until the
meat and all the vegetables are tender.

Use a large metal spoon to remove any excess fat from the surface.
If the juices seem too thin, remove the meat and vegetables and keep
warm while you boil the juices to reduce, then return the meat and
vegetables to the casserole. Adjust the seasoning if necessary. Discard
the bouquet garni before serving.

Tagine of lamb with apricots, prunes & honey

- 1 kg/2 lb 4 oz shoulder of lamb, trimmed and cubed
- 2–3 tbsp olive or argan oil
- 25 g/1 oz fresh ginger, peeled and chopped
- large pinch of saffron threads
- 2 tsp ground cinnamon
- 1 onion, finely chopped
- 2–3 garlic cloves, chopped
- 175 g/6 oz ready-to-eat stoned prunes, soaked in lukewarm water for 1 hour
- 175 g/6 oz ready-to-eat apricots, soaked in lukewarm water for 1 hour
- 2 tbsp runny honey
- salt and pepper
- plain, buttery couscous, to serve
- salad, to serve

Put the lamb in a large tagine or a heavy-based flameproof casserole. Add the oil, ginger, saffron, cinnamon, onion, garlic and salt and pepper to taste. Pour in enough water to cover. Cover and simmer gently for almost 2 hours, topping up the water if necessary, until the meat is very tender.

Drain the prunes and apricots and add them to the tagine. Stir in the honey, re-cover and simmer for a further 30 minutes, or until the sauce has reduced. Serve hot with plain, buttery couscous and a salad.

416 Tagine of lamb with figs & peaches

Omit prunes and apricots. Add 100 g/3½ oz fresh quartered figs and 125 g/4 oz dried peaches. Use only 1 tablespoon of runny honey.

417 Tagine of lamb with dates & squash

Omit prunes. Add 100 g/3½ oz semi-dried dates, chopped, and use only 85 g/3 oz apricots. Peel and chop 250 g/9 oz orange-fleshed squash and add to the tagine with the fruit and the juice of half a lemon.

418 Basque pork & beans

- 200 g/7 oz dried cannellini beans, soaked in cold water overnight
- olive oil, for frying
- 600 g/1 lb 5 oz boneless leg of pork, cut into 5-cm/2-inch chunks
- 1 large onion, sliced
- 3 large garlic cloves, crushed
- 400 g/14 oz canned chopped tomatoes
- 2 green peppers, deseeded and sliced
- finely grated rind of 1 large orange
- salt and pepper
- finely chopped fresh parsley, to garnish

Preheat the oven to 180°C/350°F/Gas Mark 4. Drain the beans and put in a large saucepan with fresh water to cover. Bring to the boil and boil rapidly for 10 minutes. Reduce the heat and simmer for 20 minutes. Drain.

Add enough oil to cover the base of a frying pan in a very thin layer. Heat the oil over a medium heat, add a few pieces of the pork and fry on all sides until brown. Remove from the pan and set aside. Repeat with the remaining pork.

Add 1 tablespoon of oil to the frying pan, if necessary, then add the onion and cook for 3 minutes. Stir in the garlic and cook for a further 2 minutes. Return the pork to the pan. Add the tomatoes and bring to the boil. Reduce the heat and stir in the pepper slices, orange rind and the drained beans. Season to taste with salt and pepper.

Transfer to a casserole. Cover the casserole and cook in the oven for 45 minutes, or until the beans and pork are tender. Sprinkle with chopped parsley and serve immediately straight from the casserole.

419 Basque pork sausages & beans

Instead of using cubed pork this dish is nice made with 600 g/1 lb 5 oz good quality pork and herb sausages, e.g. Cumberland. Brown them in the same way as you would the pork.

2 large pork hand and spring

2 large garlic cloves, sliced

3 tbsp olive oil

2 carrots, finely chopped

2 celery sticks, finely chopped

1 large onion, finely chopped

2 fresh thyme sprigs, broken into pieces

2 fresh rosemary sprigs, broken into pieces

1 large bay leaf

225 ml/8 fl oz dry white wine

225 ml/8 fl oz water

20 pickling onions

salt and pepper

roughly chopped fresh flat-leaf parsley,
    to garnish

Preheat the oven to 160°C/325°F/Gas Mark 3. Using the tip of a sharp knife, make slits all over the pork and insert the garlic slices. Heat 1 tablespoon of the oil in a flameproof casserole over a medium heat. Add the carrots, celery and onion. Cook, stirring occasionally, for 10 minutes, or until softened.

Place the pork on top of the vegetables. Sprinkle the thyme and rosemary over the meat. Add the bay leaf, wine and water and season to taste with pepper.

Bring to the boil, then remove the casserole from the heat. Cover the casserole tightly and cook in the oven for 3½ hours, or until the meat is very tender.

Meanwhile, put the onions in a heatproof bowl, pour over boiling water to cover and set aside for 1 minute. Drain, then slip off all the skins. Heat the remaining oil in a large heavy-based frying pan. Add the onions, partially cover and cook over a low heat for 15 minutes, shaking the pan occasionally, until the onions are just beginning to turn golden.

When the pork is tender, add the onions to the casserole and return to the oven for a further 15 minutes. Remove the pork and onions from the casserole and keep warm. Using a large, metal spoon, skim off as much fat as possible from the surface of the cooking liquid. Strain the cooking liquid into a bowl, pressing down lightly to extract the flavour; reserve the strained vegetables. Adjust the seasoning.

Cut the pork from the bones, if wished, then arrange on a serving platter with the onions and strained vegetables. Spoon the sauce over and garnish with parsley.

421 *Country roast belly of pork*

This has similar flavours but uses belly, which becomes deliciously tender with wonderful crackling. Take a 1.5 kg/3 lb 5 oz belly of pork; score the rind with a sharp knife and rub in salt. Roast at 220°C/425°F/Gas Mark 7 for 30 minutes until skin begins to 'crackle' (puff up and become crisp and golden). Turn heat down to 180°C/350°F/Gas Mark 4, roast for a further hour then remove pork, add 675 g/1½ lb thick slices of onion, carrot and celery to the pan with 10 unpeeled garlic cloves and 1 level teaspoon of thyme leaves, all tossed in 1½ tablespoons of groundnut oil. Set the pork back on top of vegetables and cook for a further hour. Remove pork from pan and set aside in a warm place to rest. Skim most of the fat from the pan then add 350 ml/12 fl oz chicken stock and simmer vegetables for 10 minutes. Push through sieve, discard sieve contents and return the liquid to the pan, bring to boil and reduce a little. Serve with the pork, cut into four.

Paprika pork

SERVES 4

675 g/1 lb 8 oz pork fillet
2 tbsp sunflower oil
25 g/1 oz butter
1 onion, chopped
1 tbsp paprika
25 g/1 oz plain flour

300 ml/10 fl oz chicken stock
4 tbsp dry sherry
115 g/4 oz mushrooms, sliced
150 ml/5 fl oz soured cream
salt and pepper

Cut the pork into 4-cm/1½-inch cubes. Heat the oil and butter in a large saucepan. Add the pork and cook over a medium heat, stirring, for 5 minutes, or until browned. Transfer to a plate using a slotted spoon.

Add the chopped onion to the saucepan and cook, stirring occasionally, for 5 minutes, or until softened. Stir in the paprika and flour and cook, stirring constantly, for 2 minutes. Gradually stir in the stock and bring to the boil, stirring constantly. Return the pork to the saucepan, add the sherry and sliced mushrooms and season to taste with salt and pepper. Cover and simmer gently for 20 minutes, or until the pork is tender. Stir in the soured cream and serve.

423 *Paprika pork with red pepper*

Try replacing the mushrooms with 1 thinly sliced red pepper – add to the pan with the onion.

Gammon cooked in cider

SERVES 6

1 kg/2 lb 4 oz boneless gammon joint
1 onion, halved
4 cloves
6 black peppercorns
1 tsp juniper berries

1 celery stick, chopped
1 carrot, sliced
1 litre/1¾ pints medium cider
fresh vegetables, to serve

Place a trivet or rack in a slow cooker, if you like, and stand the gammon on it. Otherwise just place the gammon in the cooker. Stud each of the onion halves with 2 cloves and add to the cooker with the peppercorns, juniper berries, celery and carrot.

Pour in the cider, cover and cook on low for 8 hours until the meat is tender. Remove the gammon from the cooker and place on a board. Tent with foil and leave to stand for 10–15 minutes. Discard the cooking liquid and flavourings.

Cut off any rind and fat from the gammon joint, then carve into slices and serve with fresh vegetables.

425 *Quick gammon cooked in cider*

For people in more of a hurry, try this gammon and cider recipe cooked on the hob in less than 30 minutes. Slice 1 onion, cut 1 celery stick and 1 carrot into thin batons, chop 2 garlic cloves, and fry in 1 tablespoon of groundnut oil over medium–low heat until everything is soft and the onion just turning golden. Push the vegetables to the edges and add 2 gammon steaks to the pan, seasoned with black pepper. Fry over medium heat until cooked through, turning halfway. Pour 200 ml/7 fl oz medium dry cider into the pan and allow to bubble and reduce a little. Stir in 2 tablespoons of crème fraîche, check seasoning (you may need to add a little salt) and serve. This recipe serves 2.

350 g/12 oz lean pork fillet
1 tbsp vegetable oil
1 onion, chopped
2 garlic cloves, crushed
25 g/1 oz plain flour
2 tbsp tomato purée
425 ml/15 fl oz chicken or vegetable stock
125 g/4½ oz button mushrooms, sliced

1 large green pepper, deseeded and diced
½ tsp ground nutmeg, plus extra to garnish
4 tbsp low-fat natural yogurt, plus extra to serve
salt and pepper
freshly boiled white rice, to serve

Trim away any excess fat and membrane from the pork fillet, then cut the meat into slices 1 cm/½ inch thick.

Heat the oil in a large saucepan over a medium heat, add the pork, chopped onion and garlic and cook for 4–5 minutes, or until lightly browned.

Stir in the flour and tomato purée, then pour in the stock and stir to mix thoroughly.

Add the mushrooms, green pepper, salt and pepper to taste and nutmeg. Bring to the boil, then cover and simmer for 20 minutes, or until the pork is cooked through.

Remove the pan from the heat, cool slightly and stir in the yogurt. Serve the pork and sauce on a bed of rice, topped with an extra spoonful of yogurt and garnished with a dusting of nutmeg.

427 *With brandy & hot paprika*

For an even tastier dish, add 1–2 tablespoons of brandy to the pan just before you stir in the flour. You can also add ½ teaspoon of hot paprika at the same time for a hint of spice.

428 *Pork with cinnamon & fenugreek*

SERVES 4

1 tsp ground coriander
1 tsp ground cumin
1 tsp chilli powder
1 tbsp dried fenugreek leaves
1 tsp ground fenugreek
150 ml/5 fl oz natural yogurt
450 g/1 lb diced pork fillet
4 tbsp ghee or vegetable oil
1 large onion, sliced

5-cm/2-inch piece fresh ginger, finely chopped
4 garlic cloves, finely chopped
1 cinnamon stick
6 green cardamom pods
6 whole cloves
2 bay leaves
175 ml/6 fl oz water
salt

Mix the coriander, cumin, chilli powder, dried fenugreek, ground fenugreek and yogurt together in a small bowl. Place the pork in a large, shallow non-metallic dish and add the spice mixture, turning well to coat. Cover with clingfilm and leave to marinate in the refrigerator for 30 minutes.

Melt the ghee in a large heavy-based saucepan. Cook the onion over a low heat, stirring occasionally, for 5 minutes, or until soft. Add the ginger, garlic, cinnamon stick, cardamom pods, cloves and bay leaves and cook, stirring constantly, for 2 minutes, or until the spices give off their aroma. Add the meat with its marinade and the water, and season to taste with salt. Bring to the boil, reduce the heat, cover and simmer for 30 minutes.

Transfer the meat mixture to a preheated wok or large heavy-based frying pan and cook over a low heat, stirring constantly, until dry and tender. If necessary, occasionally sprinkle with a little water to prevent it from sticking to the wok. Serve immediately.

429 *Lamb with cinnamon & fenugreek*

This recipe would also work well with lean lamb or rump steak instead of the pork, if you prefer.

430 Pork with prunes

SERVES 4

16 ready-to-eat prunes
4 tbsp brandy or Madeira
2 tbsp water
600 g/1 lb 5 oz pork fillet
30 g/1 oz unsalted butter

1 tbsp sunflower oil
125 ml/4 fl oz double cream
    or crème fraîche
squeeze of lemon juice
salt and pepper

Put the prunes in a saucepan with 2 tablespoons of the brandy and the water and simmer over a low heat, uncovered, for 10 minutes, or until the prunes are very tender, but still holding their shape. Strain off any excess liquid and set the prunes aside. Cut the pork fillet into 2-cm/¾-inch slices and season to taste with salt and pepper. Melt the butter with the oil in a large sauté or frying pan over a medium–high heat. Add the pork slices and fry for 2–3 minutes on each side until cooked through, working in batches if necessary.

Return all the pork slices to the pan and remove the pan from the heat. Warm the remaining brandy in a ladle or small saucepan, ignite and pour it over the pork slices to flambé.

When the flames die down, stir in the cream and bring to the boil, stirring constantly, until reduced.

Add the prunes to the pan and warm through. Season to taste with salt and pepper and a little lemon juice.

431 Game with prunes

Prunes also complement other rich meats such as game birds (pheasant, guinea fowl, partridge) and rabbit. Use the breast meat from any of these birds in the recipe above. You can also use chicken – a corn-fed chicken would be particularly good.

432 Pork & vegetable ragout

SERVES 4

450 g/1 lb lean boneless pork
1½ tbsp plain flour
1 tsp ground coriander
1 tsp ground cumin
1½ tsp ground cinnamon
1 tbsp olive oil
1 onion, chopped
400 g/14 oz canned chopped tomatoes
2 tbsp tomato purée
300–450 ml/10–16 fl oz chicken stock
225 g/8 oz carrots, chopped
350 g/12 oz squash, such as kabocha, peeled, deseeded and chopped
225 g/8 oz leeks, sliced, blanched and drained
115 g/4 oz okra, trimmed and sliced
salt and pepper
fresh parsley sprigs, to garnish
couscous, to serve

Trim off and discard any fat or gristle from the pork and cut the meat into thin strips about 5 cm/2 inches long. Mix the flour and spices together. Toss the pork in the spiced flour until well coated and reserve any remaining spiced flour.

Heat the oil in a large heavy-based saucepan and cook the onion, stirring frequently, for 5 minutes, or until softened. Add the pork and cook over a high heat, stirring frequently, for 5 minutes, or until browned on all sides and sealed.

Sprinkle in the reserved spiced flour and cook, stirring constantly, for 2 minutes, then remove from the heat. Gradually stir in the tomatoes. Blend the tomato purée with a little of the stock in a jug and gradually stir into the saucepan, then stir in half the remaining stock. Add the carrots, then return to the heat and bring to the boil, stirring. Reduce the heat, cover and simmer, stirring occasionally, for 1½ hours.

Add the squash and cook for a further 15 minutes. Add the leeks and okra, and the remaining stock if you prefer a thinner ragout. Simmer for a further 15 minutes, or until the pork and vegetables are tender.

Season to taste with salt and pepper, then garnish with fresh parsley and serve with couscous.

433 Pork & sweet potato ragout

Replace the squash with peeled and diced sweet potato; add 125 g/4½ oz blanched broccoli florets to the pan with the leeks.

2 tbsp olive oil
225 g/8 oz coarse-textured pure pork
  sausages, skinned and cut into chunks
2 onions, finely chopped
4 carrots, thickly sliced
6 potatoes, cut into chunks
2 large garlic cloves, very finely chopped

2 tsp chopped fresh rosemary
2 tsp chopped fresh thyme or oregano
1.2 kg/2 lb 10 oz canned chopped
  tomatoes
salt and pepper
2 tbsp chopped fresh flat-leaf parsley,
  to garnish

Heat the oil in a large heavy-based saucepan over a medium–high heat. Add the sausage and cook until browned. Remove from the saucepan with a slotted spoon and set aside.

Reduce the heat to medium. Add the onions, carrots, potatoes, garlic, rosemary and thyme to the saucepan. Cover and cook gently for 10 minutes, stirring occasionally.

Return the sausage to the saucepan. Add the tomatoes and bring to the boil. Season to taste with salt and pepper. Cover and simmer over a medium–low heat, stirring occasionally, for 45 minutes, or until the vegetables are tender. Sprinkle with the parsley just before serving.

435 *Sausage, tomato & bean hotpot*

For a dish that children will enjoy, replace 1 can of tomatoes with a 400-g/14-oz can of baked beans in tomato sauce.

plain flour, for coating
450 g/1 lb boneless pork, cut into
  2.5-cm/1-inch cubes
1 tbsp vegetable oil
225 g/8 oz chorizo sausage, outer
casing removed, cut into bite-sized
  chunks
1 onion, coarsely chopped
4 garlic cloves, finely chopped
2 celery sticks, chopped
1 cinnamon stick, broken
2 bay leaves
2 tsp allspice
2 carrots, sliced
2–3 fresh red chillies, deseeded and
  finely chopped
6 ripe tomatoes, peeled and chopped
1 litre/1¾ pints pork or vegetable stock
2 sweet potatoes, cut into chunks
sweetcorn kernels, cut from 1 fresh
  corn cob
1 tbsp chopped fresh oregano
salt and pepper
fresh oregano, to garnish

Season the flour well with salt and pepper and toss the pork in it to coat. Heat the oil in a large, heavy-based saucepan or ovenproof casserole. Add the chorizo and lightly brown. Remove with a slotted spoon and set aside. Add the pork, in batches, and cook until browned all over. Remove with a slotted spoon and set aside. Add the onion, garlic and celery to the pan and cook for 5 minutes. Add the spices and cook, stirring, for 2 minutes. Add the pork, carrots, chillies, tomatoes and stock. Bring to the boil, then reduce the heat, cover and simmer for 1 hour, or until the pork is tender. Return the chorizo to the pan with the sweet potatoes, sweetcorn, oregano and salt and pepper. Cover and simmer for a further 30 minutes. Serve garnished with oregano.

437 *Spicy pork & peppers hotpot*

Omit the carrot and add 2 orange sweet peppers, sliced, instead.

2 tbsp extra virgin olive oil
500 g/1 lb 2 oz Italian sausages
140 g/5 oz smoked pancetta or lean
   bacon, diced
2 red onions, chopped
2 garlic cloves, finely chopped
225 g/8 oz dried borlotti beans, covered
   and soaked overnight in cold water
2 tsp finely chopped fresh rosemary
2 tsp chopped fresh sage
300 ml/10 fl oz dry white wine
salt and pepper
fresh rosemary sprigs, to garnish
crusty bread, to serve

Heat the oil in a flameproof casserole. Add the sausages and cook over a low heat, turning frequently, for 10 minutes, or until browned all over. Remove from the casserole and set aside.

Add the pancetta to the casserole, increase the heat to medium and cook, stirring frequently, for 5 minutes, or until golden brown. Remove with a slotted spoon and set aside.

Add the onions to the casserole and cook over a low heat, stirring occasionally, for 5 minutes, until softened. Add the garlic and cook for a further 2 minutes.

Preheat the oven to 140°C/275°F/Gas Mark 1. Drain the beans and set aside the soaking liquid. Add the beans to the casserole, then return the sausages and pancetta. Gently stir in the herbs and pour in the wine.

Measure the reserved soaking liquid and add 300 ml/10 fl oz to the casserole. Season to taste with salt and pepper. Bring to the boil over a low heat and boil for 15 minutes, then transfer to the oven and cook for 2³/₄ hours.

Remove the casserole from the oven and ladle the sausages and beans onto 4 warmed plates. Garnish with the rosemary sprigs and serve immediately with crusty bread.

439 *Sausages with cannellini beans*

Replace the dried borlotti beans with the same weight of either cannellini beans or flageolet beans – both are Italian and very good in this dish.

450–550 g/1–1 lb 4 oz lean gammon
2¹/₂ tbsp olive oil, plus 1–2 tsp
1 onion, chopped
2–3 garlic cloves, chopped
2 celery sticks, chopped
175 g/6 oz sliced carrots
1 cinnamon stick, bruised
¹/₂ tsp ground cloves
¹/₄ tsp freshly grated nutmeg
1 tsp dried oregano
450 ml/16 fl oz chicken stock or
   vegetable stock
1–2 tbsp maple syrup
3 large spicy sausages, or about
   225 g/8 oz chorizo
400 g/14 oz canned black-eyed beans
   or broad beans
1 orange pepper
1 tbsp cornflour
   pepper

Trim off any fat or skin from the gammon and cut into 4-cm/1¹/₂-inch chunks. Heat 1 tablespoon of oil in a heavy-based saucepan or flameproof casserole and cook the gammon over a high heat, stirring frequently, for 5 minutes, or until browned on all sides and sealed. Using a slotted spoon, remove from the saucepan and set aside.

Add the onion, garlic, celery and carrots to the saucepan with a further 1 tablespoon of oil and cook over a medium heat, stirring frequently, for 5 minutes, or until softened. Add all the spices, season with pepper to taste, and cook, stirring constantly, for 2 minutes. Return the gammon to the saucepan. Add the dried oregano, stock, and maple syrup to taste, then bring to the boil, stirring.

Reduce the heat, cover and simmer, stirring occasionally, for 1 hour. Heat the remaining ¹/₂ tablespoon of oil in a frying pan and cook the sausages, turning frequently, until browned all over.

Remove and cut each into 3–4 chunks, then add to the saucepan. Drain and rinse the beans, then drain again. Deseed and chop the orange pepper. Add the beans and pepper to the pan, and simmer for a further 20 minutes.

Blend 2 tablespoons of water with the cornflour and stir into the stew. Cook for 3–5 minutes. Discard the cinnamon stick and serve immediately.

441 *Ham with red lentils*

Try using red lentils (you can buy them canned but they are easy to cook – simmer for 20–25 minutes, drain) instead of the black-eyed beans. They go very well with ham, pork or bacon.

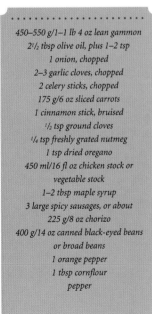

Maltese rabbit with fennel

5 tbsp olive oil
2 large fennel bulbs, sliced
2 carrots, diced
1 large garlic clove, crushed
1 tbsp fennel seeds
about 4 tbsp plain flour
2 wild rabbits, jointed
225 ml/8 fl oz dry white wine
225 ml/8 fl oz water
1 bouquet garni of 2 fresh flat-leaf
parsley sprigs,
1 fresh rosemary sprig and 1 bay leaf,
tied in a 7.5-cm/3-inch piece of celery
salt and pepper
finely chopped fresh flat-leaf parsley
or coriander, to garnish
fresh rosemary sprigs, to garnish
thick, crusty bread, to serve

Heat 3 tablespoons of the oil in a large flameproof casserole over a medium heat. Add the fennel and carrots and cook, stirring occasionally, for 5 minutes. Stir in the garlic and fennel seeds and cook for a further 2 minutes, or until the fennel is tender. Remove the fennel and carrots from the casserole with a slotted spoon and set aside.

Put the flour in a polythene bag and season to taste with salt and pepper. Add 2 rabbit pieces and shake to lightly coat, then shake off any excess flour. Continue until all the pieces of rabbit are coated, adding more flour if necessary.

Add the remaining oil to the casserole. Fry the rabbit pieces for 5 minutes on each side, or until golden brown, working in batches. Remove the rabbit from the casserole.

Pour in the wine and bring to the boil, stirring to scrape up all the sediment from the bottom. Return the rabbit pieces, fennel and carrots to the casserole and pour in the water. Add the bouquet garni and season to taste with salt and pepper.

Bring to the boil, then reduce the heat, cover and simmer for 1¼ hours, or until the rabbit is tender. Discard the bouquet garni. Garnish with herbs and serve with lots of bread to mop up the juices.

443 Chicken with fennel

Use the above recipe but substitute 1 well-flavoured (e.g. organic) chicken, skin removed and jointed into 10 pieces (2 thigh, 2 drumstick, 4 breast and 2 wing), for the two rabbits.

444 Turkey in a piquant sauce

2 tbsp plain flour	400 g/14 oz canned chopped tomatoes
1 kg/2 lb 4 oz turkey pieces	1 bouquet garni
25 g/1 oz butter	150 ml/5 fl oz chicken stock
1 tbsp sunflower oil	salt and pepper
2 onions, sliced	2 tbsp chopped fresh flat-leaf parsley,
1 garlic clove, finely chopped	to garnish
1 red pepper, deseeded and sliced	salad, to serve

Spread the flour on a plate and season with salt and pepper. Coat the turkey pieces in the seasoned flour, shaking off any excess.

Melt the butter with the oil in a flameproof casserole or large saucepan. Add the turkey and cook over a medium heat, stirring, for 5–10 minutes, or until golden. Transfer the turkey pieces to a plate with a slotted spoon and keep warm. Add the onions, garlic and red pepper to the casserole and cook, stirring occasionally, for 5 minutes, or until softened. Sprinkle in any remaining flour and cook, stirring constantly, for 1 minute.

Return the turkey pieces to the casserole, then add the tomatoes and the bouquet garni and stock. Bring to the boil, stirring constantly, then cover and simmer for 1¼ hours, or until the turkey is cooked through and tender.

Transfer the turkey to a serving platter with a slotted spoon. Remove and discard the bouquet garni. Return the sauce to the boil and cook until reduced and thickened. Season to taste with salt and pepper and pour over the turkey. Garnish with parsley and serve with salad.

445 Chicken in a piquant sauce

Chicken, veal or pork escalopes would work well in this recipe. You can also add 1 tablespoon of balsamic vinegar to the sauce to increase piquancy.

446 Pheasant with mushrooms

15 g/½ oz dried ceps or porcini
mushrooms
1 pheasant, about 1.25 kg/2 lb 12 oz
2 tbsp plain flour
2 tbsp olive oil
1 onion, chopped
1 large carrot, thinly sliced
2 celery sticks, sliced
475 ml/17 fl oz chicken stock
1 fresh bouquet garni
1–2 tsp redcurrant jelly
2–3 tbsp port
1 tbsp butter or margarine
115 g/4 oz sliced mushrooms
85 g/3 oz no-soak prunes, chopped
salt and pepper
1 tbsp chopped fresh parsley,
to garnish

TO SERVE
creamed potato and parsnip mash
red cabbage
peas

Preheat the oven to 350°F/180°C/ Gas Mark 4. Put the dried mushrooms in a heatproof jug, then cover with almost boiling water and leave to stand for 20 minutes to soak.

Discard any excess fat from the pheasant, then lightly rinse and pat dry with paper towels, and cut into 4 pieces. Season the flour well with salt and pepper. Toss the pheasant in the seasoned flour until well coated and reserve any remaining seasoned flour.

Heat all but 2 teaspoons of the oil in a large frying pan and cook the pheasant over medium–high heat, turning frequently, for 10 minutes, or until browned all over and sealed. Using a slotted spoon, transfer the pheasant to an ovenproof casserole. Add the remaining oil to the frying pan and cook the onion, carrot and celery over medium heat, stirring frequently, for 5 minutes, or until softened. Sprinkle in the reserved seasoned flour and cook, stirring constantly, for 2 minutes, then remove from the heat.

Gradually stir in the stock followed by the soaked dried mushrooms and their soaking liquid, then return to the heat and bring to a boil, stirring.

Pour over the pheasant in the casserole and add the bouquet garni, redcurrant jelly and port. Cover and cook in the preheated oven for 1½ hours.

Melt the butter in a pan and cook the mushrooms, stirring frequently, for 3 minutes, or until beginning to soften.

Add to the casserole with the prunes and cook for an additional 15–20 minutes, or until the pheasant is tender.

Serve garnished with chopped parsley, accompanied by the potato and parsnip mash, red cabbage and peas.

447 Pheasant with mushrooms & chestnuts

Omit the prunes and add 85 g/3 oz ready-cooked sweet chestnuts, roughly chopped, to the pan with the mushrooms.

448 Baby broad beans & chorizo

2 tbsp olive oil
250 g/9 oz fresh chorizo sausage
4 spring onions, sliced
3 garlic cloves, crushed
100 ml/3½ fl oz chicken stock or
vegetable stock, warmed
2 kg/4 lb 8 oz young broad beans in
their pods, or about 750 g/1 lb 10 oz
podded frozen baby broad beans
1 large handful fresh mint, chopped
salt and pepper
toasted sourdough bread, to serve

Chop the chorizo sausage into finger-thick rounds. Place a heavy-based frying pan over a medium heat and add the olive oil. When it's shimmering hot, add the chorizo and brown it on all sides for about 15 minutes. Remove it from the pan and set aside. Reduce the heat, add the spring onions and garlic and fry for a further 5 minutes. Add the stock and broad beans and simmer for 3–5 minutes until the beans are just tender. Add the mint and the cooked chorizo, stir through and season with salt and pepper. Serve, with some sourdough toast on the side.

449 Baby broad beans, artichoke & chorizo

Add 250 g/9 oz quartered artichoke hearts (from a drained jar) to the pan with the broad beans. You can also add 100 g/3½ oz French beans, halved.

450 Mexican turkey

SERVES 4

55 g/2 oz plain flour
4 turkey breast fillets
3 tbsp corn oil
1 onion, thinly sliced
1 red pepper, deseeded and sliced
300 ml/10 fl oz chicken stock
25 g/1 oz raisins
4 tomatoes, peeled, deseeded and chopped

1 tsp chilli powder
½ tsp ground cinnamon
pinch of ground cumin
25 g/1 oz plain chocolate, finely chopped
    or grated
salt and pepper
sprigs of fresh coriander, to garnish

Preheat the oven to 160°C/325°F/ Gas Mark 3. Spread the flour on a plate and season with salt and pepper. Coat the turkey fillets in the seasoned flour, shaking off any excess. Reserve any remaining seasoned flour.

Heat the oil in a flameproof casserole. Add the fillets and cook over a medium heat, turning occasionally, for 5–10 minutes, or until golden. Transfer to a plate with a slotted spoon.

Add the onion and red pepper to the casserole. Cook over a low heat, stirring occasionally, for 5 minutes, or until softened. Sprinkle in the remaining seasoned flour and cook, stirring constantly, for 1 minute.

Gradually stir in the stock, then add the raisins, chopped tomatoes, chilli powder, cinnamon, cumin and chocolate. Season to taste with salt and pepper. Bring to the boil, stirring constantly.

Return the turkey to the casserole, cover and cook in the preheated oven for 50 minutes. Serve immediately, garnished with sprigs of coriander.

451 Mexican beef

Make the recipe using 4 beef fillet steaks or chicken breast fillets; it is equally good.

452 Italian turkey steaks

SERVES 4

1 tbsp olive oil
4 turkey escalopes or steaks
2 red peppers, deseeded and sliced
1 red onion, sliced
2 garlic cloves, finely chopped
300 ml/10 fl oz passata
150 ml/5 fl oz medium white wine

1 tbsp chopped fresh marjoram
400 g/14 oz canned cannellini beans,
    drained and rinsed
3 tbsp fresh white breadcrumbs
salt and pepper
fresh basil sprigs, to garnish

Preheat the grill to medium. Heat the oil in a flameproof casserole or heavy-based frying pan. Add the turkey escalopes and cook over a medium heat for 5–10 minutes, turning occasionally, until golden.

Transfer to a plate. Add the red peppers and onion to the frying pan and cook over a low heat, stirring occasionally, for 5 minutes, or until softened. Add the garlic and cook for a further 2 minutes. Return the turkey to the frying pan and add the passata, wine and marjoram. Season to taste with salt and pepper. Bring to the boil, then reduce the heat, cover and simmer, stirring occasionally, for 25–30 minutes, or until the turkey is cooked through and tender. Stir in the cannellini beans and simmer for a further 5 minutes. Sprinkle the breadcrumbs over the top and place under the preheated grill for 2–3 minutes, or until golden. Serve, garnished with fresh basil sprigs.

453 Italian turkey steaks with courgette

Omit the cannellini beans and add 2 courgettes, thinly sliced into rounds, and 1 extra tablespoon of oil to the pan with the red peppers.

Beef chop suey

MARINADE
1 tbsp Shaoxing rice wine
pinch of white pepper
pinch of salt
1 tbsp light soy sauce
½ tsp sesame oil

CHOP SUEY
450 g/1 lb ribeye or sirloin steak, thinly sliced
1 head of broccoli, cut into small florets
2 tbsp vegetable or groundnut oil
1 onion, thinly sliced
2 sticks celery, thinly sliced on the diagonal
225 g/8 oz mangetout, sliced in half lengthways
55 g/2 oz fresh or canned bamboo shoots, rinsed and julienned (if using fresh, boil in water first for 30 minutes)
8 water chestnuts, thinly sliced
225 g/8 oz mushrooms, thinly sliced
1 tbsp oyster sauce
1 tsp salt

Combine all the marinade ingredients in a bowl and marinate the beef for at least 20 minutes. Blanch the broccoli in a large pan of boiling water for 30 seconds. Drain and set aside. In a preheated wok or deep pan, heat 1 tablespoon of the oil and stir-fry the beef until the colour has changed. Remove and set aside.

Wipe out the wok or pan with kitchen paper. In the clean wok or deep pan, heat the remaining oil and stir-fry the onion for 1 minute. Add the celery and broccoli and cook for 2 minutes. Add the mangetout, bamboo shoots, water chestnuts and mushrooms and cook for 1 minute. Add the beef, season with the oyster sauce and salt and serve.

455 Beef chop suey with cabbage & carrot

Chop suey means 'bits and pieces' and is ideal for using up leftovers. Replace the broccoli and mangetout with shredded Chinese cabbage and carrot.

456 With beansprouts & noodles

For a heartier meal, add 125 g/4½ oz fresh beansprouts and 250 g/9 oz cooked egg thread noodles to the cooked dish – stir for 2 minutes over heat.

457 Pork & prawn chop suey

Replace the beef with 400 g/14 oz pork fillet, thinly sliced, and add 100 g/3½ oz peeled cooked prawns for the last 2 minutes of cooking time. You can also use baby corn instead of the bamboo shoots, if liked.

Beef with onions & broccoli

2 tbsp vegetable or groundnut oil
2 tbsp Thai green curry paste
2 x 175-g/6-oz sirloin steaks, thinly sliced
2 onions, sliced
6 spring onions, chopped
2 shallots, finely chopped

225 g/8 oz head of broccoli, cut into florets
400 ml/14 fl oz coconut milk
3 kaffir lime leaves, roughly chopped
4 tbsp chopped fresh coriander
few Thai basil leaves

Heat the oil in a wok and stir-fry the curry paste for 1–2 minutes. Add the meat, in batches if necessary, and stir-fry until starting to brown.

Add the onions, spring onions and shallots, and stir-fry for 2–3 minutes. Add the broccoli and stir-fry for 2–3 minutes. Pour in the coconut milk, add the lime leaves and bring to the boil. Simmer gently for 8–10 minutes, until the meat is tender. Stir in the coriander and basil and serve immediately.

459 Spicy beef with potato

450 g/1 lb beef fillet
2 tbsp Thai soy sauce
2 tbsp fish sauce
2 tbsp vegetable or peanut oil
3–4 coriander roots, chopped
1 tbsp crushed black peppercorns
2 garlic cloves, chopped
1 tbsp soft light brown sugar
350 g/12 oz potatoes, diced
150 ml/5 fl oz water
bunch of spring onions, chopped
225 g/8 oz baby spinach leaves
cooked rice or noodles, to serve

Cut the beef into thick slices and place in a shallow dish. Put the soy sauce, fish sauce, 1 tablespoon of the oil, the coriander roots, peppercorns, garlic and sugar in a food processor and process to a thick paste. Scrape the paste into the dish and toss the beef to coat. Cover with clingfilm and set aside to marinate in the refrigerator for at least 3 hours, and preferably overnight.

Heat the remaining oil in a wok. Lift the beef out of the marinade, reserving the marinade, and cook for 3–4 minutes on each side, until browned. Add the reserved marinade and the potatoes with the measured water and gradually bring to the boil. Simmer for 6–8 minutes, or until the potatoes are tender.

Add the spring onions and spinach. Cook gently until the greens have wilted. Serve immediately with rice or noodles.

460 Spicy beef with potato & chard

Replace the spinach with the same weight of either chard or Chinese cabbage. Or use thinly sliced spring greens, which will need a little longer in the pan to make them tender.

461 Chicken chow mein

250 g/9 oz dried medium Chinese egg noodles
2 tbsp sunflower oil
280 g/10 oz cooked chicken breasts, shredded
1 garlic clove, finely chopped
1 red pepper, deseeded and thinly sliced
100 g/3½ oz shiitake mushrooms, sliced
6 spring onions, sliced
100 g/3½ oz beansprouts
3 tbsp soy sauce
1 tbsp sesame oil

Place the noodles in a large bowl or dish and break them up slightly. Pour enough boiling water over the noodles to cover and set aside while preparing the other ingredients.

Preheat a wok over a medium heat. Add the sunflower oil and swirl it around to coat the sides of the wok. When the oil is hot, add the shredded chicken, garlic, red pepper, mushrooms, spring onions and beansprouts to the wok and stir-fry for about 5 minutes.

Drain the noodles thoroughly then add them to the wok, toss well and stir-fry for a further 5 minutes. Drizzle over the soy sauce and sesame oil and toss until thoroughly combined. Transfer to warmed serving bowls and serve immediately.

462 With Chinese five spice

Add 1 teaspoon of Chinese five spice to the pan just before you add the chicken, etc. and stir for a few seconds to release the aromas.

Thai spiced chicken with courgettes

SERVES 4

1 tbsp olive oil
1 clove garlic, finely chopped
2.5-cm/1-inch piece fresh ginger, peeled and finely chopped
1 small fresh red chilli, deseeded and finely chopped
350 g/12 oz skinless, boneless chicken breasts, cut into thin strips
1 tbsp Thai 7-spice seasoning
1 red pepper and 1 yellow pepper, deseeded and sliced
2 courgettes, thinly sliced
227 g/8 oz canned bamboo shoots, drained
2 tbsp dry sherry or apple juice
1 tbsp light soy sauce
2 tbsp chopped fresh coriander, plus extra to garnish
salt and pepper

Heat the olive oil in a non-stick wok or large frying pan. Add the garlic, ginger and chilli and stir-fry for 30 seconds to release the flavours.

Add the chicken and Thai seasoning and stir-fry for about 4 minutes or until the chicken has coloured all over. Add the peppers and courgettes and stir-fry for 1–2 minutes or until slightly softened.

Stir in the bamboo shoots and stir-fry for a further 2–3 minutes or until the chicken is cooked through and tender. Add the sherry or apple juice, soy sauce and seasoning and sizzle for 1–2 minutes.

Stir in the chopped coriander and serve immediately, garnished with extra coriander.

---

464 Asian pork

SERVES 4

450 g/1 lb lean boneless pork
1½ tbsp plain flour
1–2 tbsp olive oil
1 onion, cut into small wedges
2–3 garlic cloves, chopped
2.5-cm/1-inch piece fresh ginger, peeled and grated
1 tbsp tomato purée
300 ml/10 fl oz chicken stock
225 g/8 oz canned pineapple chunks in natural juice
1–1½ tbsp dark soy sauce
1 red pepper, deseeded and sliced
1 green pepper, deseeded and sliced
1½ tbsp balsamic vinegar
4 spring onions, sliced on the diagonal, to garnish

Trim off any fat or gristle from the pork and cut into 2.5-cm/1-inch chunks. Toss the pork in the flour until well coated and reserve any remaining flour.

Heat the oil in a large heavy-based saucepan and cook the onion, garlic and ginger, stirring frequently, for 5 minutes, or until softened. Add the pork and cook over a high heat, stirring frequently, for 5 minutes, or until browned on all sides and sealed.

Sprinkle in the reserved flour and cook, stirring constantly, for 2 minutes, then remove from the heat. Blend the tomato purée with the stock in a heatproof jug and gradually stir into the saucepan.

Remove the pineapple chunks from their juice and stir the juice into the saucepan. Add the soy sauce to the saucepan, then return to the heat and bring to the boil, stirring. Reduce the heat, cover and simmer, stirring occasionally, for 1 hour.

Add the peppers and cook for a further 15 minutes, or until the pork is tender. Stir in the vinegar and the pineapple and heat through for 5 minutes. Serve sprinkled with the spring onions.

465 Asian lamb

The flavours in this recipe work really well with lamb, too – add 450 g/1 lb lean lamb cubes to the pan instead of the pork and use lamb stock if you have it rather than chicken stock.

Hoisin pork with garlic noodles

250 g/9 oz dried thick Chinese egg
    noodles, or Chinese wholemeal egg
    noodles
450 g/1 lb pork fillet, thinly sliced
1 tsp sugar
1 tbsp peanut or corn oil
4 tbsp rice vinegar

4 tbsp white wine vinegar
4 tbsp bottled hoisin sauce
2 spring onions, sliced on the diagonal
about 2 tbsp garlic-flavoured corn oil
2 large garlic cloves, thinly sliced
chopped fresh coriander, to garnish

Start by boiling the noodles for 3 minutes, until soft. Alternatively, cook according to the packet instructions. Drain well, rinse under cold water to stop the cooking and drain again, then set aside.

Meanwhile, sprinkle the pork slices with the sugar and use your hands to toss together. Heat a wok over a high heat. Add the oil and heat until it shimmers. Add the pork and stir-fry for about 3 minutes, until the pork is cooked through and is no longer pink. Use a slotted spoon to remove the pork from the wok and keep warm. Add both vinegars to the wok and boil until they are reduced to 5 tablespoons. Pour in the hoisin sauce with the spring onions and let it bubble until reduced by half. Add to the pork and stir together.

Quickly wipe out the wok and reheat. Add the garlic-flavoured oil and heat until it shimmers. Add the garlic slices and stir round for about 30 seconds, until they are golden and crisp, then use a slotted spoon to scoop them out of the wok and set aside.

Add the noodles to the wok and stir them round to warm them through. Divide the noodles between 4 plates, top with the pork and onion mixture and sprinkle over the garlic slices and chopped coriander.

467 With cashew nuts or peanuts

Stir 1 tablespoon of cashew or peanut butter into the pan with the hoisin sauce for a delicious flavour. Add 50 g/2 oz cashew nut halves or peanuts to the dish before serving.

---

468 Pork with peppers

1 tbsp vegetable or peanut oil
1 tbsp chilli oil
450 g/1 lb pork fillet, thinly sliced
2 tbsp green chilli sauce
6 spring onions, sliced
2.5-cm/1-inch piece fresh ginger,
    thinly sliced
1 red pepper, deseeded and sliced
1 yellow pepper, deseeded and sliced
1 orange pepper, deseeded and sliced
1 tbsp fish sauce
2 tbsp Thai soy sauce
juice of ½ lime
4 tbsp chopped fresh parsley
cooked flat rice noodles, to serve

Heat both the oils in a wok. Add the pork, in batches, and stir-fry until browned all over. Remove with a slotted spoon and set aside.

Add the chilli sauce, spring onions and ginger to the wok and stir-fry for 1–2 minutes. Add the peppers and stir-fry for 2–3 minutes.

Return the meat to the wok, stir well and add the fish sauce, soy sauce and lime juice. Cook for a further 1–2 minutes, then stir in the parsley and serve with flat rice noodles.

469 Beef with peppers

This dish works just as well if you use 450 g/1lb thinly sliced fillet of beef instead of the pork.

470 Sour & spicy pork

55 g/2 oz dried Chinese cloud
  ear mushrooms
100 g/3½ oz baby corn, halved
  lengthways
2 tbsp honey
1 tbsp tamarind paste
4 tbsp boiling water
2 tbsp dark soy sauce
1 tbsp rice vinegar
2 tbsp groundnut or maize oil

1 large garlic clove, very finely chopped
1-cm/½-inch piece fresh ginger, peeled
  and very finely chopped
½ tsp dried red pepper flakes, or to taste
350 g/12 oz pork fillet, thinly sliced
4 spring onions, thickly sliced on the
  diagonal
1 green pepper, deseeded and sliced
250 g/9 oz fresh Hokkien noodles
chopped fresh coriander, to garnish

Soak the mushrooms in enough boiling water to cover for about 20 minutes, until they are tender. Drain them well, then cut off and discard any thick stems, and slice the cups if they are large.

Meanwhile, bring a large saucepan of lightly salted water to the boil, add the baby corn and blanch for 3 minutes. Drain the baby corn and run it under cold running water to stop the cooking, then set aside. Put the honey and tamarind paste in a small bowl and stir in the water, stirring until the paste dissolves. Stir in the soy sauce and rice vinegar and set aside.

Heat a wok over high heat. Add 1 tablespoon of the oil and heat until it shimmers. Add the garlic, ginger and red pepper flakes and stir-fry for about 30 seconds. Add the pork and continue stir-frying for 2 minutes.

Add the remaining oil to the wok and heat. Add the spring onions, pepper, mushrooms and baby corn, and the tamarind mixture, and stir-fry for a further 2–3 minutes, until the pork is cooked through and the vegetables are tender, but still firm to the bite. Add the noodles and use 2 forks to mix all the ingredients together. Sprinkle with coriander.

471 Sour & spicy pork with sweetcorn

You can use sweetcorn instead of the baby corn if you like – they will need blanching for just 2 minutes, or not at all if they are thawed from frozen. You can also try adding 85 g/3 oz halved French beans to the recipe, with the pepper.

472 Stir-fried turkey with cranberry glaze

450 g/1 lb boneless turkey breast
2 tbsp sunflower oil
15 g/½ oz stem ginger
50 g/1¼ oz fresh or frozen cranberries
100 g/3½ oz canned chestnuts
4 tbsp cranberry sauce
3 tbsp light soy sauce
salt and pepper

Remove any skin from the turkey breast. Using a sharp knife, thinly slice the turkey breast. Heat the sunflower oil in a large preheated wok or heavy-based frying pan.

Add the turkey to the wok and stir-fry for 5 minutes, or until cooked through.

Drain off the syrup from the stem ginger and chop finely. Add the ginger and the cranberries to the wok and stir-fry for 2–3 minutes, or until the cranberries have softened. Add the chestnuts, cranberry sauce and soy sauce, season to taste with salt and pepper and allow to bubble for 2–3 minutes.

Transfer the glazed turkey stir-fry to warmed serving dishes and serve immediately.

473 Stir-fried chicken with cranberry glaze

You can replace the turkey with chicken breast or even use duck breast fillet for a tasty change.

Turkey with bamboo shoots & water chestnuts

MARINADE
4 tbsp sweet sherry
1 tbsp lemon juice
1 tbsp soy sauce
2 tsp grated fresh ginger
1 clove garlic, crushed

STIR-FRY
450 g/1 lb turkey breast, cubed
1 tbsp sesame oil
2 tbsp vegetable oil
125 g/4½ oz small mushrooms, cut into halves
1 green pepper, cut into strips
1 courgette, thinly sliced
4 spring onions, cut into quarters
115 g/4 oz canned bamboo shoots, drained
115 g/4 oz canned sliced water chestnuts, drained
cooked noodles or rice, to serve

Blend the sherry, lemon juice, soy sauce, ginger and garlic in a bowl, then add the turkey and stir. Cover the dish with clingfilm and refrigerate for 3–4 hours.

In a wok, add the oils and heat slowly. Remove the turkey from the marinade with a slotted spoon (reserving the marinade) and stir-fry a few pieces at a time until browned. Remove the turkey from the wok and set aside. Add the mushrooms, green pepper and courgette to the wok and stir-fry for 3 minutes. Add the spring onions and stir-fry for 1 minute more. Add the bamboo shoots and water chestnuts to the wok, then the turkey along with half of the reserved marinade.

Stir over a medium–high heat for another 2–3 minutes. Serve immediately over noodles or rice.

475 *Turkey with bamboo shoots & carrot*

You can vary this dish according to what ingredients you have to hand – for example, replace the green pepper with a sliced carrot; use celery instead of the courgette, or replace the sherry with rice wine and 1 teaspoon of sugar.

Turkey, broccoli & pak choi stir-fry

450 g/1 lb turkey breast, cut into strips
1 tbsp vegetable oil
1 head of broccoli, cut into florets
2 heads of pak choi, leaves washed and separated
1 red pepper, thinly sliced
50 ml/2 fl oz chicken stock
cooked rice, to serve

MARINADE
1 tbsp soy sauce
1 tbsp honey
2 cloves garlic, crushed

To make the marinade, combine the soy sauce, honey and garlic in a medium-sized bowl. Add the turkey and toss to coat. Cover the bowl with clingfilm and marinate in the refrigerator for 2 hours.

Put a wok or large frying pan over a medium–high heat and add the oil; heat for 1 minute. Add the turkey and stir-fry for 3 minutes or until the turkey is opaque. Remove with a slotted spoon, set aside and keep warm.

Add the broccoli, pak choi and the red pepper to the pan and stir-fry for 2 minutes. Add the stock and continue to stir-fry for 2 minutes or until the vegetables are crisp yet tender.

Return the turkey to the wok and cook briefly to reheat. Serve immediately with some freshly cooked rice.

477 *Turkey & cabbage stir-fry*

You can replace the pak choi with Chinese cabbage, Savoy cabbage or spinach, if you prefer. Or you can omit it altogether and use 2 red peppers instead of 1.

Cheesy courgette & ham gratin

16 baby courgettes (about 500 g/
1 lb 2 oz total weight)
55 g/2 oz butter
40 g/1½ oz plain white flour
600 ml/1 pint milk
1 tsp Dijon mustard
115 g/4 oz mature Cheddar cheese,
grated
8 fairly thin slices lean smoked
or unsmoked cooked ham
40 g/1½ oz fresh white or wholemeal
breadcrumbs
salt and pepper
snipped fresh chives or parsley,
to garnish

Lightly grease a shallow ovenproof dish and set aside. Cook the courgettes in a saucepan of boiling water for 4–5 minutes or until tender. Drain well, set aside and keep warm.

Meanwhile, melt 40 g/1½ oz of the butter in a separate saucepan, then stir in the flour and cook gently for 1 minute, stirring. Remove the pan from the heat and gradually whisk in the milk. Return to the heat and bring gently to the boil, stirring continuously, until the sauce comes to the boil and thickens. Simmer for 2–3 minutes, stirring. Remove the pan from the heat and stir in the Dijon mustard and 85 g/3 oz of the cheese. Season to taste with salt and pepper.

Preheat the grill to medium–high. Cut each slice of ham in half crossways, then wrap a half slice of ham around each courgette. Place the ham-wrapped courgettes in a single layer in the prepared dish and pour the cheese sauce evenly over the top to cover. Mix together the remaining cheese and the breadcrumbs and sprinkle evenly over the cheese sauce. Dot with the remaining butter, then place under the grill for a few minutes until lightly browned. Garnish with chives and serve.

479 Cheesy courgette & bacon gratin

Cut up 6 rashers of lean smoked back bacon into thin strips, dry-fry in a non-stick pan brushed with oil for 3 minutes and add to the gratin instead of the ham. You can also use half Parmesan, half Cheddar cheese.

480 Cheesy courgette & chicken gratin

Use 300 g/10½ oz cooked chicken meat (no skin), sliced into bite-sized pieces instead of the ham.

Duck legs with olives

4 duck legs, all visible fat removed
and discarded
800 g/1 lb 12 oz canned chopped
tomatoes
8 garlic cloves, peeled, but left whole
1 large onion, chopped
1 carrot, peeled and finely chopped

1 celery stick, finely chopped
3 sprigs fresh thyme
100 g/3½ oz Spanish green olives in
brine, stuffed with pimientos, garlic
or almonds, drained and rinsed
1 tsp finely grated orange rind
salt and pepper

Put the duck legs in the bottom of a flameproof casserole or a large heavy-based frying pan with a tight-fitting lid, over a medium–low heat. Add the tomatoes, garlic, onion, carrot, celery, thyme and olives and stir together. Season with salt and pepper to taste.

Turn the heat to high and cook, uncovered, until the ingredients begin to bubble. Reduce the heat to low, cover tightly and simmer for 1¼–1½ hours until the duck is very tender. Check occasionally and add a little water if the mixture appears to be drying out.

When the duck legs are tender, transfer them to a serving platter, cover and keep hot in a warmed oven. Leave the rest of the casserole uncovered, increase the heat to medium and cook, stirring, for about 10 minutes until the mixture forms a sauce. Stir in the orange rind, then adjust the seasoning if necessary. Remove the cooked, tender garlic cloves, mash with a fork and spread over the duck legs.

Spoon the sauce over the top and serve immediately.

482 Chicken legs with olives

Use the previous recipe but omit the duck and use 4 chicken legs instead – organic or free range legs will have most flavour and are more fatty, which is useful in this dish.

483 Duck legs with olives & squash

This recipe also works very well if you use 200 g/7 oz butternut squash, chopped into approximately 1-cm/½-inch cubes, instead of the carrot.

Fish and Seafood

Squid with parsley & pine kernels

85 g/3 oz sultanas
5 tbsp olive oil
6 tbsp chopped fresh flat-leaf parsley,
  plus extra to garnish
2 garlic cloves, finely chopped
800 g/1 lb 12 oz prepared squid, sliced,
  or squid rings

125 ml/4 fl oz dry white wine
500 g/1 lb 2 oz passata
pinch of chilli powder
85 g/3 oz pine kernels, finely chopped
salt

Place the sultanas in a small bowl, cover with lukewarm water and set aside for 15 minutes to plump up.

Meanwhile, heat the olive oil in a heavy-based saucepan. Add the parsley and garlic and cook over a low heat, stirring frequently, for 3 minutes. Add the squid and cook, stirring occasionally, for 5 minutes.

Increase the heat to medium, pour in the wine and cook until it has almost completely evaporated. Stir in the passata and season to taste with chilli powder and salt. Lower the heat again, cover and simmer gently, stirring occasionally, for 45–50 minutes, until the squid is almost tender.

Drain the sultanas and stir them into the saucepan with the pine kernels. Let simmer for a further 10 minutes, then serve immediately garnished with the reserved chopped parsley.

485 Sardines with parsley & pine kernels

Try using fresh sardines (filleted if you like) instead of the squid. Fillets will cook in 2 minutes, unfilleted sardines in 5 minutes.

Celery & salt cod casserole

250 g/9 oz salt cod, soaked overnight
1 tbsp oil
4 shallots, finely chopped
2 garlic cloves, chopped
3 celery sticks, chopped
400 g/14 oz canned chopped tomatoes

150 ml/5 fl oz fish stock
50 g/1¾ oz pine kernels
2 tbsp roughly chopped fresh tarragon
2 tbsp capers
crusty bread or mashed potatoes, to serve

Drain the salt cod, rinse it under plenty of cold running water and drain again thoroughly. Remove and discard any skin and bones. Pat the fish dry with kitchen paper and then cut it into chunks.

Heat the oil in a large frying pan. Add the shallots and garlic and cook for 2–3 minutes. Add the celery and cook for a further 2 minutes, then add the tomatoes and stock. Bring the mixture to the boil, then reduce the heat and simmer for 5 minutes. Add the fish and cook for 10 minutes, or until tender.

Meanwhile, preheat the grill. Place the pine kernels on a baking tray. Place under the hot grill and toast for 2–3 minutes, or until golden.

Stir the tarragon, capers and pine kernels into the fish casserole and heat gently to warm through. Transfer to serving plates and serve with fresh crusty bread or mashed potatoes.

487 Celery & tuna casserole

You could use fresh tuna steaks instead of the salt cod and cook in exactly the same way. Try using fresh chopped parsley instead of the tarragon.

Mediterranean fish casserole

2 tbsp olive oil
1 red onion, peeled and sliced
2 garlic cloves, peeled and chopped
2 red peppers
400 g/14 oz canned chopped tomatoes
1 tsp chopped fresh oregano or marjoram
a few saffron strands soaked in 1 tbsp
    warm water for 2 minutes
450 g/1 lb white fish (cod, haddock or
    hake), skinned and boned

300 ml/10 fl oz fish stock or
    vegetable stock
450 g/1 lb prepared squid, cut into rings
115 g/4 oz cooked peeled prawns
salt and pepper
2 tbsp chopped fresh parsley, to garnish
chunky bread, to serve

Heat the oil in a frying pan and fry the onion and garlic over a medium heat for 2–3 minutes until beginning to soften. Deseed and thinly slice the peppers and add to the pan. Continue to cook over a low heat for a further 5 minutes. Add the tomatoes with the oregano and saffron and stir well.

Preheat the oven to 200°C/400°F/Gas Mark 6. Cut the white fish into 3-cm/1¼-inch pieces and place in the casserole dish. Pour in the fried vegetable mixture and the stock, stir well and season to taste with salt and pepper. Cover and cook in the centre of the oven for about 30 minutes, until the fish is tender and cooked. Add the squid and cook for 2 minutes, then add the prawns to heat through. Serve in warmed bowls garnished with the parsley, and chunky bread to mop up the juices.

Seafood hotpot with red wine & tomatoes

350 g/12 oz mussels, scrubbed and
    debearded
4 tbsp olive oil
1 onion, finely chopped
1 green pepper, deseeded and chopped
2 garlic cloves, very finely chopped
5 tbsp tomato purée
1 tbsp chopped fresh flat-leaf parsley
1 tsp dried oregano
400 g/14 oz canned chopped tomatoes

225 ml/8 fl oz dry red wine
450 g/1 lb firm white fish (such as cod or
    monkfish), cut into 5-cm/2-inch pieces
115 g/4 oz scallops, halved
115 g/4 oz raw prawns, peeled and
    deveined
200 g/7 oz canned crabmeat
salt and pepper
10–15 fresh basil leaves, shredded,
    to garnish

Discard any mussels with broken shells or that don't close when tapped. Heat the oil in a heavy-based saucepan or flameproof casserole over a medium heat.

Add the onion and green pepper and cook for 5 minutes, or until beginning to soften. Stir in the garlic, tomato purée and herbs and cook for 1 minute, stirring.

Pour in the tomatoes and wine. Season to taste with salt and pepper. Bring to the boil, then cover and simmer for 30 minutes. Add the fish, cover and simmer for 15 minutes. Add the mussels, scallops, prawns and crabmeat. Cover and cook for 15 minutes. Discard any mussels that remain closed. Stir in the basil just before serving.

490 *Seafood hotpot with red wine & bacon*

Omit the prawns and crab and instead fry 175 g/6 oz smoked back bacon, cut into strips, in 2 teaspoons of oil until golden, then add to the pot for the last 5 minutes of cooking time.

491 *Tuna & noodle casserole*

SERVES 4–6

200 g/7 oz dried ribbon egg pasta,
such as tagliatelle
25 g/1 oz butter
55 g/2 oz fine fresh breadcrumbs
400 ml/14 fl oz canned condensed
cream of mushroom soup
125 ml/4 fl oz milk
2 celery sticks, chopped
1 red pepper, deseeded and chopped
1 green pepper, deseeded and chopped
140 g/5 oz mature Cheddar cheese,
roughly grated
2 tbsp chopped fresh parsley
200 g/7 oz canned tuna in oil,
drained and flaked
salt and pepper

Preheat the oven to 200°C/400°F/ Gas Mark 6. Bring a large saucepan of salted water to the boil. Add the pasta, return to the boil and cook for 2 minutes less than specified on the packet instructions.

Meanwhile, melt the butter in a separate small saucepan. Stir in the breadcrumbs, then remove from the heat and set aside.

Drain the pasta well and set aside. Pour the soup into the pasta saucepan over a medium heat, then stir in the milk, celery, peppers, half the cheese and all the parsley.

Add the tuna and gently stir in so that the flakes don't break up. Season to taste with salt and pepper. Heat just until small bubbles appear around the edge of the mixture – do not boil.

Stir the pasta into the saucepan and use 2 forks to mix all the ingredients together. Spoon the mixture into an ovenproof dish that is also suitable for serving and spread it out.

Stir the remaining cheese into the buttered breadcrumbs, then

sprinkle over the top of the pasta mixture. Bake in the preheated oven for 20–25 minutes until the topping is golden. Remove from the oven, then leave to stand for 5 minutes before serving straight from the dish.

492 *Tuna & noodle casserole with celery*

If you like the flavour of celery, use canned condensed cream of celery soup instead of the mushroom soup. You can also replace the celery sticks with 200 g/7 oz canned, drained sweetcorn.

493 *Tuna & noodle casserole with beans*

Omit the peppers and instead use 150 g/5½ oz sliced green beans – either runner beans or French-type beans, cut into 5-cm/2-inch pieces. Blanch for 2 minutes in boiling water and drain before using.

494 *Mixed fish cobbler with dill*

SERVES 4

2 tbsp butter
2 large leeks, trimmed and sliced
150 g/5½ oz white mushrooms, sliced
2 courgettes, sliced
4 large tomatoes, peeled and chopped
1 tbsp chopped fresh dill
100 ml/3½ fl oz white wine
200 ml/7 fl oz fish stock
4 tsp cornflour
225 g/8 oz cod, cut into bite-sized
chunks
225 g/8 oz haddock, cut into
bite-sized chunks
salt and pepper

COBBLER TOPPING
175 g/6 oz self-raising flour,
plus extra for dusting
2 level tsp baking powder
1 tbsp chopped fresh dill
3 tbsp butter
4–5 tbsp milk
salt

Preheat the oven to 200°C/400°F/ Gas Mark 6. Melt the butter in a large flameproof casserole over a low heat. Add the leeks and cook, stirring, for 2 minutes until slightly softened. Add the mushrooms, courgettes, tomatoes and dill, and cook, stirring, for another 3 minutes. Stir in the

white wine and stock, bring to the boil, then reduce the heat to a simmer. Mix the cornflour with a little water to form a paste, then stir it into the casserole. Cook, stirring constantly, until thickened, then season with salt and pepper and remove from the heat.

To make the cobbler topping, sift the flour, baking powder and a pinch of salt into a large mixing bowl. Stir in the dill, then rub in the butter until the mixture resembles fine breadcrumbs. Stir in enough of the milk to make a

smooth dough. Transfer to a clean, lightly floured board, knead lightly, then roll out to a thickness of about 1 cm/½ inch. Cut out rounds using a 5-cm/2-inch biscuit cutter. Add the cod and haddock to the casserole and stir gently to mix.

Arrange the dough rounds over the top, then return to the oven and bake for another 30 minutes, or until the cobbler topping has risen and is lightly golden. Remove from the oven and serve hot.

495 *Mixed fish cobbler with fennel*

Replace the cod with smoked cod and replace half the haddock with salmon fillet. If you don't have any dill, you can use snipped fennel leaves instead – it has a similar flavour and aroma.

496 Quick & creamy fish pie

SERVES 4

1 tbsp olive oil
2 shallots, finely chopped
150 ml/5 fl oz dry white wine or
    fish stock
1 bay leaf
200 g/7 oz closed cup mushrooms,
    thickly sliced
100 g/3½ oz crème fraîche

500 g/1 lb 2 oz firm white fish (such as
    cod or monkfish), cut into chunks
175 g/6 oz cooked peeled prawns
175 g/6 oz frozen peas
40 g/1½ oz butter, melted
150 g/5½ oz fresh white breadcrumbs
salt and pepper
chopped fresh parsley, to garnish

Heat the oil in an ovenproof saucepan or a shallow flameproof casserole and fry the shallots for 2–3 minutes, until softened.

Add the wine, bay leaf and mushrooms and simmer for 2 minutes, stirring occasionally. Stir in the crème fraîche and add the fish. Season to taste with salt and pepper. Bring to the boil, cover and simmer for 5–6 minutes, until the fish is almost cooked. Remove and discard the bay leaf, then add the prawns and peas and bring back to the boil. Meanwhile, re-melt the butter in a separate saucepan, if necessary, and stir in the breadcrumbs. Preheat the grill to medium.

Spread the breadcrumbs over the top of the fish mixture. Place the saucepan under the preheated grill for 3–4 minutes, until the topping is golden brown and bubbling. Sprinkle with fresh parsley and serve hot.

497 Quick & creamy fish pie with potato

If you have any leftover mashed potato, you can replace the crumb topping by smoothing the mash over the fish, then sprinkle 50 g/2 oz grated Cheddar cheese over the top before browning under the grill.

498 Monkfish ragout

SERVES 4–6

2 tbsp olive oil
1 small onion, finely chopped
1 red pepper, deseeded and cut into
    2.5-cm/1-inch pieces
115 g/4 oz mushrooms, finely sliced
3 garlic cloves, very finely chopped
1 tbsp tomato purée
2 tbsp chopped fresh flat-leaf parsley
½ tsp dried oregano

400 g/14 oz canned chopped tomatoes
150 ml/5 fl oz dry red wine
550 g/1 lb 4 oz monkfish, skinned
    and cubed
1 yellow or green courgette, sliced
salt and pepper
6–8 fresh basil leaves, shredded,
    to garnish
crusty bread, to serve

Heat the oil in a heavy-based saucepan or flameproof casserole over a medium heat. Add the onion, pepper and mushrooms and cook for 5 minutes, or until beginning to soften.

Stir in the garlic, tomato purée, parsley and oregano. Cook together for 1 minute. Pour in the tomatoes and wine. Season with salt and pepper to taste. Bring the mixture to the boil, then simmer gently for 10–15 minutes, or until slightly thickened.

Add the monkfish and the courgette slices. Cover and simmer for 15 minutes, or until the monkfish is cooked and the courgette is tender but still brightly coloured. Sprinkle with the basil and serve with crusty bread.

499 Monkfish ragout with squash

Summer squash such as patty pan, with its creamy coloured delicate flesh, makes a good replacement for the courgette in this ragout. You can also use white or dry rosé wine instead of the red wine.

153

500 *Goan-style seafood curry*

3 tbsp vegetable or groundnut oil
1 tbsp black mustard seeds
12 fresh curry leaves or 1 tbsp dried
6 shallots, finely chopped
1 garlic clove, crushed
1 tsp ground turmeric
½ tsp ground coriander
¼–½ tsp chilli powder
140 g/5 oz creamed coconut, grated and
   dissolved in 300 ml/10 fl oz boiling water

500 g/1 lb 2 oz skinless, boneless
   white fish (such as monkfish or
   cod), cut into large chunks
450 g/1 lb large raw prawns, peeled
   and deveined
finely grated rind and juice of 1 lime
salt
lime wedges, to serve

Heat the oil in a wok or large frying pan over a high heat. Add the mustard seeds and stir them around for about 1 minute, or until they jump. Stir in the curry leaves.

Add the shallots and garlic and stir for about 5 minutes, or until the shallots are golden. Stir in the turmeric, coriander and chilli powder and continue stirring for about 30 seconds. Add the dissolved creamed coconut. Bring to the boil, then reduce the heat to medium and stir for about 2 minutes. Reduce the heat to low, add the fish and simmer for

1 minute, spooning the sauce over the fish and very gently stirring it around.

Add the prawns and continue to simmer for 4–5 minutes longer until the fish flesh flakes easily and the prawns turn pink and curl.

Add half the lime juice, then taste and add more lime juice and salt to taste. Sprinkle withthe lime rind and serve with lime wedges.

501 *Goan-style mustard seafood curry*

You can replace the mustard seeds with dry mustard powder if you like – add 2 teaspoons of mustard powder to the pan with the turmeric.

502 *Mixed seafood curry*

1 tbsp vegetable or peanut oil
3 shallots, finely chopped
2.5-cm/1-inch piece fresh galangal,
   peeled and thinly sliced
2 garlic cloves, finely chopped
400 ml/14 fl oz canned coconut milk
2 lemon grass stalks, snapped in half
4 tbsp fish sauce
2 tbsp chilli sauce
225 g/8 oz raw king prawns, peeled

225 g/8 oz baby squid, cleaned and
   thickly sliced
225 g/8 oz salmon fillet, skinned and
   cut into chunks
175 g/6 oz tuna steak, cut into chunks
225 g/8 oz fresh mussels, scrubbed and
   debearded
lime wedges, to garnish
boiled rice, to serve

Heat the oil in a large wok and stir-fry the shallots, galangal and garlic for 1–2 minutes, until they start to soften. Add the coconut milk, lemon grass, fish sauce and chilli sauce. Bring to the boil, reduce the heat, and simmer for 1–2 minutes.

Add the prepared prawns, squid, salmon and tuna, and simmer for 3–4 minutes, until the prawns have turned pink and the fish is cooked.

Add the mussels to the wok and cover with a lid. Simmer for 1–2 minutes, until they have opened. Discard any mussels that remain closed. Garnish with lime wedges and serve immediately with rice.

503 *Quick mixed seafood curry*

For a quicker curry, add ready-prepared shelled mussels with the squid. Replace the tuna (or the salmon) with monkfish or cod of a similar weight.

Prawn biryani

SERVES 8

1 tsp saffron strands
50 ml/2 fl oz tepid water
2 shallots, coarsely chopped
3 garlic cloves, crushed
1 tsp chopped fresh ginger
2 tsp coriander seeds
2 tsp black peppercorns
2 cloves
seeds from 2 green cardamom pods
2.5-cm/1-inch piece cinnamon stick
1 tsp ground turmeric
1 fresh green chilli, chopped
½ tsp salt

2 tbsp ghee
1 tsp whole black mustard seeds
500 g/1 lb 2 oz raw tiger prawns in their
    shells, or 400 g/14 oz raw and peeled
300 ml/½ pint coconut milk
300 ml/½ pint low-fat natural yogurt
freshly cooked basmati rice, to serve

TO GARNISH
flaked almonds, toasted
1 spring onion, sliced
sprigs of fresh coriander

Soak the saffron in the tepid water for 20 minutes. Put the shallots, garlic, spices and salt into a spice grinder or mortar and grind to a paste. Heat the ghee in a saucepan and add the mustard seeds. When they start to pop, add the prawns and stir over a high heat for 1 minute. Stir in the spice mix, then the coconut milk and yogurt. Simmer for 20 minutes.

Spoon the prawn mixture into serving bowls. Top with the freshly cooked basmati rice and drizzle over the saffron water. Serve, garnished with the flaked almonds, spring onion and sprigs of coriander.

505 *Prawn & pineapple curry*

SERVES 4

500 ml/18 fl oz coconut cream
½ fresh pineapple, peeled and
    chopped
2 tbsp Thai red curry paste
2 tbsp Thai fish sauce
2 tsp sugar
350 g/12 oz raw jumbo prawns
2 tbsp chopped fresh coriander
edible flower, to garnish
steamed jasmine rice, to serve

Place the coconut cream, pineapple, curry paste, fish sauce and sugar in a large frying pan. Heat gently over a medium heat until almost boiling. Shell and devein the prawns. Add the prawns and chopped coriander to the pan and simmer gently for 3 minutes, or until the prawns are cooked.

Garnish with a fresh, edible flower and serve with steamed jasmine rice.

506 *With white fish*

For a more substantial dish, if using this curry as a main course on its own, add 300 g/10½ oz cubed, firm white fish – e.g. monkfish – to the pan with the coconut cream etc., and simmer for 3–4 minutes until just cooked through before adding prawns.

Prawns with spring onions & straw mushrooms

2 tbsp vegetable or groundnut oil	2 tbsp fish sauce
bunch of spring onions, chopped	2 tbsp Thai soy sauce
2 garlic cloves, finely chopped	6 fresh Thai basil sprigs
175 g/6 oz creamed coconut, roughly chopped	400 g/14 oz canned straw mushrooms, drained
2 tbsp Thai red curry paste	350 g/12 oz large cooked peeled prawns
450 ml/16 fl oz fish stock	cooked jasmine rice, to serve

Heat the oil in a wok and stir-fry the spring onions and garlic for 2–3 minutes. Add the creamed coconut, curry paste and stock and heat gently until the coconut has dissolved. Stir in the fish sauce and soy sauce, then add the basil, mushrooms and prawns. Gradually bring to the boil and serve immediately with cooked jasmine rice.

508 *Prawns with shiitake mushrooms*

For a change, or if you can't find straw mushrooms, use 300 g/10½ oz fresh shiitake (or other oriental) mushrooms, sliced as necessary, and add them to the pan with the spring onions. Or you can use sliced button mushrooms.

509 *Fish curry with rice noodles*

2 tbsp vegetable or peanut oil	2 tbsp Thai red curry paste
1 large onion, chopped	400 g/14 oz canned coconut milk
2 garlic cloves, chopped	handful of fresh coriander, chopped
85 g/3 oz white mushrooms	1 tsp soft light brown sugar
225 g/8 oz monkfish, cut into cubes, each about 1 inch	1 tsp fish sauce
225 g/8 oz salmon fillets, cut into cubes, each about 1 inch	115 g/4 oz rice noodles
	3 spring onions, chopped
225 g/8 oz cod, cut into cubes, each about 1 inch	50 g/2 oz bean sprouts
	few Thai basil leaves

Heat the oil in a wok and gently sauté the onion, garlic and mushrooms until softened but not browned. Add the fish, curry paste and coconut milk and bring gently to the boil. Simmer for 2–3 minutes before adding half the coriander, the sugar and the fish sauce. Keep warm.

Meanwhile, soak the noodles until tender (check the packet instructions), and drain through a colander. Put the colander and noodles over a pan of simmering water. Add the spring onions, bean sprouts and most of the basil and steam for 1–2 minutes or until wilted.

Pile the noodles onto plates and top with the curry. Sprinkle the remaining coriander and basil over the top and serve immediately.

510 *Fish curry with rice noodles & broccoli*

Replace the white mushrooms with 100 g/3½ oz broccoli, divided into small florets and blanched for a minute. Add to the pan with the coconut milk. If you don't have Thai basil leaves, use some more fresh coriander leaves to steam with the noodles and garnish.

511　Prawn laksa

20–24 large raw unpeeled prawns
450 ml/16 fl oz fish stock
pinch of salt
1 tsp groundnut oil
450 ml/16 fl oz coconut milk
2 tsp nam pla (Thai fish sauce)
½ tbsp lime juice
115 g/4 oz dried medium rice noodles
55 g/2 oz beansprouts
sprigs of fresh coriander, to garnish

LAKSA PASTE
6 coriander stalks with leaves
3 large garlic cloves, crushed
1 fresh red chilli, deseeded and
chopped
1 lemon grass stalk, centre part only,
chopped
2.5-cm/1-inch piece fresh ginger,
peeled and chopped
1½ tbsp shrimp paste
½ tsp turmeric
2 tbsp groundnut oil

Peel and devein the prawns. Put the fish stock, salt and the prawn heads, shells and tails in a saucepan over a high heat and slowly bring to the boil. Lower the heat and simmer for 10 minutes.

Meanwhile, make the laksa paste. Put all the ingredients except the oil in a food processor and blend. With the motor running, slowly add up to 2 tablespoons of oil just until a paste forms. (If your food processor is too large to work efficiently with this small quantity, use a pestle and mortar.)

Heat the oil in a large saucepan over a high heat. Add the paste and stir-fry until it is fragrant. Strain the stock through a sieve lined with muslin. Stir the stock into the laksa paste, along with the coconut milk, nam pla and lime juice. Bring to the boil, then lower the heat, cover and simmer for 30 minutes.

Meanwhile, soak the noodles in a large bowl with enough lukewarm water to cover for 20 minutes, until soft. Or, cook according to the packet instructions. Drain and set aside.

Add the prawns and beansprouts to the stew and continue simmering just until the prawns turn opaque and curl. Divide the noodles between 4 bowls and ladle the stew over, making sure everyone gets an equal share of the prawns. Garnish with the coriander and serve.

512　Crab laksa

Use the same recipe but substitute 150 g/5½ oz dressed white crab meat (fresh if possible) for the prawns.

513　Thai fish curry

juice of 1 lime
4 tbsp fish sauce
2 tbsp Thai soy sauce
1 fresh red chilli, deseeded and chopped
350 g/12 oz monkfish fillet, cut into cubes
350 g/12 oz salmon fillets, skinned and
cut into cubes

400 ml/14 fl oz coconut milk
3 kaffir lime leaves
1 tbsp Thai red curry paste
1 lemon grass stalk (white part only),
finely chopped
cooked jasmine rice with chopped fresh
coriander, to serve

Combine the lime juice, half the fish sauce and all of the soy sauce in a shallow non-metallic dish. Add the chilli and the fish, stir to coat, cover with clingfilm and chill for 1–2 hours, or overnight.

Bring the coconut milk to the boil in a saucepan and add the lime leaves, curry paste, the remaining fish sauce and the lemon grass. Simmer gently for 10–15 minutes.

Add the fish with its marinade and simmer gently for 4–5 minutes, until the fish is cooked. Serve hot accompanied by cooked jasmine rice with chopped coriander stirred through it.

514　With sweet red peppers

Deseed and thinly slice 2 sweet red peppers and add to the saucepan with 1 tablespoon of groundnut oil – stir-fry for 5 minutes until soft but not coloured and add to the curry with the fish.

515 Thai prawn curry

450 g/1 lb raw tiger prawns
2 tbsp groundnut oil
2 tbsp Thai green curry paste
4 kaffir lime leaves, shredded
1 lemon grass stalk, chopped
225 ml/8 fl oz coconut milk

2 tbsp Thai fish sauce
½ cucumber, deseeded and cut into batons
12 fresh basil leaves, plus extra to garnish
2 fresh green chillies, sliced

Peel and devein the prawns. Heat the groundnut oil in a preheated wok or heavy-based frying pan. Add the curry paste and cook over a medium heat for 1 minute, or until it is bubbling. Add the prawns, lime leaves and lemon grass and stir-fry for 2 minutes, or until the prawns have turned pink. Stir in the coconut milk and bring to the boil, then reduce the heat and simmer, stirring occasionally, for 5 minutes. Stir in the fish sauce, cucumber and basil. Transfer to a warmed serving dish. Scatter over the chilli slices, garnish with fresh basil leaves and serve.

516 With baby corn

Add 150 g/5½ oz baby corn, each sliced on the diagonal into two, to the pan with the coconut milk for added crunch, colour and flavour.

517 Thai prawn noodle bowl

1 bunch spring onions
2 celery sticks
1 red pepper
200 g/7 oz rice vermicelli noodles
2 tbsp groundnut oil
55 g/2 oz unsalted peanuts
1 fresh bird's eye chilli, sliced

1 lemon grass stalk, crushed
400 ml/14 fl oz fish or chicken stock
200 ml/7 fl oz coconut milk
2 tsp Thai fish sauce
350 g/12 oz cooked peeled king prawns
salt and pepper
3 tbsp chopped fresh coriander, to garnish

Trim the spring onions and celery and thinly slice diagonally. Deseed and thinly slice the pepper. Place the noodles in a bowl, cover with boiling water and leave to stand for 4 minutes, or until tender. Drain. Heat the oil in a wok and stir-fry the peanuts for 1–2 minutes, until golden. Lift out with a slotted spoon. Add the sliced vegetables to the wok and stir-fry over a high heat for 1–2 minutes.

Add the chilli, lemon grass, stock, coconut milk and fish sauce and bring to the boil. Stir in the prawns and bring back to the boil, stirring. Season to taste with salt and pepper, then add the noodles. Serve in warmed bowls, sprinkled with fresh coriander.

518 Thai prawn noodle bowl with sweetcorn

You can replace the peanuts with unsalted cashew nuts or, if you prefer, omit the nuts altogether and instead stir in 85 g/3 oz sweetcorn with the other vegetables.

Seafood nabe

1 carrot, finely sliced
6 shiitake mushrooms, sliced
1 leek, finely sliced
225 g/8 oz skinless salmon fillet,
    cut into strips
12 raw prawns, peeled and deveined
250 g/9 oz live mussels, scrubbed and
    debearded
8 scallops, shelled and cleaned

STOCK
1.5 litres /2¾ pints dashi stock
6 tbsp sake
4 tbsp mirin
1 tbsp shoyu (Japanese soy sauce)

TO GARNISH
4-cm/1½-inch piece daikon
½ small fresh red chilli
4 spring onions, minced
1 lemon, cut into wedges
shoyu (Japanese soy sauce)

To prepare the garnishes, finely grate the daikon and chilli together to make a pink paste. Shape it into a mound in a small serving dish. Put the spring onions in a separate dish and the lemon wedges in another. Put all the stock ingredients in a large fondue pot or ovenproof casserole and bring to a simmer. Add the vegetables and cook for 1 minute, then add some of the salmon and prawns and cook for 1 minute.

Add some of the mussels and scallops and cook until the scallops have turned opaque and the mussels have opened. Discard any mussels that remain closed. To eat, mix some shoyu with a squeeze of lemon and some of the garnish. Lift the fish or shellfish out of the stock and dip in the sauce. Return the stock to the heat and add more ingredients when required.

520 *Seafood nabe with crayfish & clams*

Try replacing the prawns with crayfish and the mussels with clams for a change. Cook them in the same way.

521 *Ginger prawns with oyster mushrooms*

150 ml/5 fl oz chicken stock
2 tsp sesame seeds
1 tbsp grated fresh ginger
1 tbsp soy sauce
¼ tsp hot pepper sauce
1 tsp cornflour
3 tbsp vegetable oil
3 carrots, thinly sliced

350 g/12 oz oyster mushrooms, sliced
1 large red pepper, deseeded and thinly
    sliced
450g/1 lb raw king prawns, peeled and
    deveined
2 garlic cloves, crushed
freshly cooked rice, to serve
fresh coriander sprigs, to garnish

In a small bowl, stir together the stock, sesame seeds, ginger, soy sauce, hot pepper sauce and cornflour until well blended. Set aside. Add 2 tablespoons of the oil to a large wok and heat. Stir-fry the carrots for 3 minutes, remove from the wok and set aside. Add the remaining oil to the wok and stir-fry the mushrooms for 2 minutes.

Remove from the wok and set aside. Add the red pepper, prawns and garlic to the wok and stir-fry for 3 minutes, until the prawns turn pink and start to curl. Stir the sauce again and pour it into the wok. Cook until the mixture bubbles, then return the carrots and mushrooms to the wok. Cover and cook for a further 2 minutes, until heated through.

Serve over cooked rice and garnish with coriander sprigs.

522 *Ginger prawns with dried mushrooms*

If you can't find fresh oyster mushrooms you can use other fresh oriental mushrooms or reconstitute a 25 g pack of dried oyster mushrooms in a little hot water for 20 minutes. Drain and reserve the liquid (add this to the sauce mixture). Chop the mushrooms if necessary and add to the pan to stir-fry.

523 Fresh baked sardines

2 tbsp olive oil
2 large onions, sliced into rings
3 garlic cloves, chopped
2 large courgettes, cut into sticks
3 tbsp fresh thyme, stalks removed
8 large sardine fillets
115 g/4 oz grated Parmesan cheese
4 eggs, beaten
300 ml/10 fl oz milk
salt and pepper

Heat 1 tablespoon of the olive oil in a frying pan. Add the onion rings and chopped garlic and fry over a low heat, stirring occasionally, for 2–3 minutes, until soft and translucent. Add the courgettes to the pan and cook, stirring occasionally, for about 5 minutes, or until turning golden. Stir 2 tablespoons of the thyme leaves into the mixture and remove from the heat. Place half the onions and courgettes in the base of a large ovenproof dish. Top with the sardine fillets and half the grated Parmesan cheese. Place the remaining onions and courgettes on top and sprinkle with the remaining thyme. Mix the eggs and milk together in a bowl and season to taste with salt and pepper. Pour the mixture into the dish. Sprinkle the remaining Parmesan cheese over the top.

Bake in a preheated oven, 180°C/350°F/Gas Mark 4 for 20–25 minutes, or until golden and set. Serve the fresh baked sardines hot.

524 Fresh baked sardines with tomatoes

Omit the eggs and milk. Instead pour 400 g/14 oz canned chopped tomatoes over the sardines and vegetables in the dish. Top with the remaining grated cheese and bake for 20 minutes.

525 Monkfish parcels

4 tsp olive oil
2 courgettes, sliced
1 large red pepper, peeled, deseeded and cut into strips
2 monkfish fillets, about 125 g/4½ oz each, skin and membrane removed

6 smoked streaky bacon rashers
salt and pepper
freshly cooked pasta and slices of olive bread, to serve

Preheat the oven to 190°C/375°F/Gas Mark 5. Cut 4 large pieces of foil, each about 23 cm/9 inches square. Brush them lightly with a little of the oil, then divide the courgettes and pepper among them.

Rinse the fish fillets under cold water and pat dry with kitchen paper. Cut them in half, then put 1 piece on top of each pile of courgettes and pepper. Cut the bacon rashers in half and lay 3 pieces across each piece of fish. Season to taste with salt and pepper, drizzle over the remaining oil and seal up the parcels. Transfer to an ovenproof dish, bake for 25 minutes, then remove and serve with pasta and slices of olive bread.

526 With herbs & lemon

Add ½ teaspoon each of chopped rosemary, thyme and parsley, and the juice of ¼ lemon to each parcel before baking.

527 Moules marinière

300 ml/10 fl oz dry white wine
6 shallots, finely chopped
1 bouquet garni
2 kg/4 lb 8 oz live mussels
pepper
sprigs of fresh flat-leaf parsley,
to garnish
crusty bread, to serve

To prepare the mussels, cut off and discard any beards, then scrub any dirty shells. Discard any mussels with broken shells or open ones that do not instantly close when tapped.

Pour the wine into a large heavy-based saucepan, add the shallots and bouquet garni and season to taste with pepper.

Bring the wine to the boil over a medium heat.

Add the mussels, cover tightly and cook, shaking the saucepan occasionally, for 3–4 minutes, or until the mussels have opened. Remove from the saucepan and discard the bouquet garni and any mussels that remain closed.

Divide the mussels between 4 soup bowls, using a slotted spoon. Tilt the saucepan to let any sand settle, then spoon the cooking liquid over the mussels, garnish with the parsley and serve immediately with the bread.

528 Moules a la crème Normande

2 kg/4 lb 8 oz live mussels
4 tbsp sunflower oil
2 onions, finely chopped
1 large garlic clove, finely chopped
400 ml/14 fl oz dry cider, ideally
from Normandy
1 bay leaf
200 ml/7 fl oz double cream
salt and pepper
chopped fresh flat-leaf parsley,
to garnish
sliced French bread, to serve

To prepare the mussels, cut off and discard any beards, then scrub any dirty shells. Discard any mussels with broken shells or open ones that do not instantly close when tapped.

Heat the oil in a large heavy-based saucepan with a tight-fitting lid over a medium–high heat. Add the onions and sauté for 3 minutes, then add the garlic and continue sautéeing for a further 2 minutes, or until the onions are soft, but not coloured. Add the cider and bay leaf and bring to the boil. Continue boiling until the cider is reduced by half, then reduce the heat to very low.

Add the mussels to the saucepan, cover tightly and simmer for 4 minutes, shaking the pan frequently. When the mussels are all open, transfer them to a bowl, cover and keep warm. Discard any that do not open.

Line a large sieve with a piece of muslin or kitchen cloth and place over a large bowl. Strain the cooking juices into the bowl, then return them to the pan. Add the cream and boil until reduced by one third. Season to taste with salt and pepper, then pour over the mussels and sprinkle with parsley. Serve with French bread to mop up the juices.

529 *Omelette Arnold Bennett*

175 g/6 oz undyed smoked haddock, skinned
25 g/1 oz butter
4 eggs
1 tbsp olive oil
4 tbsp single cream
2 tbsp grated Cheddar or Parmesan cheese
salt and pepper

Place the fish in a large saucepan and cover with water. Bring the water to the boil, then turn down to a simmer and poach the fish for 8–10 minutes until it flakes easily. Remove from the heat and drain onto a plate. When cool enough to handle, flake the fish and remove any bones. Melt half the butter in a small saucepan and add the haddock, to warm. Beat the eggs together gently with a fork and season carefully with the salt and pepper, taking care not to add too much salt because the haddock will already be quite salty.

Melt the remaining butter with the oil in a 23-cm/9-inch frying pan over a medium heat. When the butter starts to froth, pour in the eggs and spread them around by tilting the frying pan.

Use a spatula or fork to move the egg around until it is cooked underneath but still liquid on top. Tip in the hot haddock and spread over the omelette. Pour over the cream and top with the cheese, then place the frying pan under a hot grill for 1 minute until the cheese is melted. Serve immediately on warmed plates.

530 *Smoked salmon omelette*

Omit the haddock and cut 100 g/3½ oz smoked salmon into thin strips. Cook the omelette as normal and add the salmon to the top of the omelette before folding over. Add 1 tablespoon of finely chopped fresh parsley, if wished.

531 *Fluffy prawn omelette*

115 g/4 oz cooked peeled prawns, thawed if frozen
4 spring onions, chopped
55 g/2 oz courgette, grated
4 eggs, separated
few dashes of Tabasco sauce, to taste
3 tbsp milk
1 tbsp corn or olive oil
25 g/1 oz mature Cheddar cheese, grated
salt and pepper

Pat the prawns dry with kitchen paper, then mix with the spring onions and courgette in a bowl and set aside. Using a fork, beat the egg yolks with the Tabasco, milk, salt and pepper in a separate bowl. Whisk the egg whites in a large bowl until stiff, then gently stir the egg yolk mixture into the egg whites, taking care not to overmix.

Heat the oil in a large, non-stick frying pan and when hot pour in the egg mixture. Cook over a low heat for 4–6 minutes, or until lightly set. Preheat the grill. Spoon the prawn mixture on top of the eggs and sprinkle with the cheese. Cook under the preheated grill for 2–3 minutes, or until set and the top is golden brown. Cut into wedges and serve immediately.

532 *Fluffy prawn omelette with mushroom*

Instead of the courgette, finely chop 85 g/3 oz button mushrooms and add to the prawn mixture.

533 *Fluffy prawn omelette with pepper*

Instead of the courgettes, finely chop half a deseeded red pepper and add to the prawn mixture.

Roasted seafood

600 g/1 lb 5 oz new potatoes
3 red onions, cut into wedges
2 courgettes, cut into chunks
8 garlic cloves, peeled but left whole
2 lemons, cut into wedges

4 fresh rosemary sprigs
4 tbsp olive oil
350 g/12 oz unpeeled raw prawns
2 small raw squid, cut into rings
4 tomatoes, quartered

Preheat the oven to 200°C/400°F/Gas Mark 6. Scrub the potatoes to remove any dirt. Cut any large potatoes in half. Parboil the potatoes in a saucepan of boiling water for 10–15 minutes.

Place the potatoes in a large roasting tin together with the onions, courgettes, garlic, lemons and rosemary sprigs. Pour over the oil and toss to coat all the vegetables in it. Roast in the oven for 30 minutes, turning occasionally, until the potatoes are tender.

Once the potatoes are tender, add the prawns, squid and tomatoes, tossing to coat them in the oil, and roast for 5 minutes. All the vegetables should be cooked through and slightly charred for full flavour. Transfer the roasted seafood and vegetables to warmed serving plates and serve hot.

535 *With smoked sweet paprika*

Stir 2 teaspoons of smoked sweet paprika into the pan for the last 15 minutes of cooking time – it will give the seafood a lovely colour and aroma.

536 *Seafood omelette*

2 tbsp unsalted butter
1 tbsp olive oil
1 onion, very finely chopped
175 g/6 oz courgette, halved lengthways
    and sliced
1 celery stick, very finely chopped
85 g/3 oz white mushrooms, sliced
55 g/2 oz French beans, cut into
    5-cm/2-inch lengths

4 eggs
85 g/3 oz mascarpone cheese
1 tbsp chopped fresh thyme
1 tbsp shredded fresh basil
200 g/7 oz canned tuna, drained and flaked
115 g/4 oz cooked peeled prawns
salt and pepper

Melt the butter with the olive oil in a heavy-based frying pan with a flameproof handle. If the pan has a wooden handle, protect it with foil because it needs to go under the grill. Add the onion and cook over a low heat, stirring occasionally, for 5 minutes, until softened.

Add the courgette, celery, mushrooms and beans and cook, stirring occasionally, for a further 8–10 minutes, until starting to brown. Beat the eggs with the mascarpone, thyme and basil, and season to taste with salt and pepper. Stir the tuna into the mixture, then add the prawns.

Pour the egg mixture into the pan and cook for 5 minutes, until it is just starting to set. Draw the egg from the sides of the pan towards the centre to let the uncooked egg run underneath. Put the pan under a preheated grill and cook until the egg is just set and the surface is starting to brown. Cut the omelette into wedges and serve.

537 *Seafood omelette with crab*

Replace three-quarters of the tuna with canned white crabmeat and the rest with brown crabmeat. Brown crabmeat is very rich so you don't need much.

538 *Sicilian tuna*

4 tuna steaks, about 140 g/5 oz each
2 fennel bulbs, thickly sliced
lengthways
2 red onions, sliced
2 tbsp extra virgin olive oil
crusty rolls, to serve

MARINADE
125 ml/4 fl oz extra virgin olive oil
4 garlic cloves, finely chopped
4 fresh red chillies, deseeded and
finely chopped
juice and finely grated rind of 2
lemons
4 tbsp finely chopped fresh flat-leaf
parsley
salt and pepper

Whisk all the marinade ingredients together in a small bowl. Put the tuna steaks in a large shallow dish and spoon over 4 tablespoons of the marinade, turning until well coated. Cover and leave to marinate in the refrigerator for 30 minutes. Reserve the remaining marinade.

Heat a ridged pan over a high heat. Add the oil, fennel and onions to the pan and cook for 5 minutes on each side until just beginning to colour.

Transfer to 4 warmed serving plates, drizzle with the reserved marinade and keep warm. Add the tuna steaks to the pan and cook, turning once, for 4–5 minutes until firm to the touch but still moist inside. Transfer the tuna to the serving plates and serve immediately with crusty rolls.

539 *Sicilian swordfish*

Meaty, tasty swordfish makes a good substitute for tuna in this recipe – choose 4 thick steaks.

---

540 *Herrings with orange tarragon stuffing*

1 orange
4 spring onions, chopped
50 g/1¾ oz fresh wholemeal
breadcrumbs
1 tbsp chopped fresh tarragon
4 herrings, cleaned and gutted
salt and pepper
green salad, to serve

TO GARNISH
2 oranges
1 tbsp light brown sugar
1 tbsp olive oil
sprigs of fresh tarragon

on a plate in order to catch all of the juice. Mix together the orange flesh, juice, rind, spring onions, breadcrumbs and tarragon in a bowl. Season to taste.

Divide the stuffing into 4 equal portions and use it to fill the body cavities of the fish. Place each fish on to a square of lightly greased kitchen foil and wrap the foil around the fish so that it is completely enclosed. Place on a baking sheet and cook in the preheated oven for 20–30 minutes until the fish are cooked

through – the flesh should be white and firm to the touch.

Meanwhile make the garnish. Peel and thickly slice the 2 oranges and sprinkle over the sugar. Just before the fish is cooked, drizzle a little oil over the orange slices and place them on the barbecue for about 5 minutes to heat through. Transfer the fish to serving plates and garnish with the barbecued orange slices and sprigs of fresh tarragon. Serve with a green salad.

Preheat the oven to 200°C/400°F/ Gas Mark 6.

To make the orange tarragon stuffing, grate the rind from half of the orange, using a zester. Peel and chop all of the orange flesh

541 *Herrings with lemon coriander stuffing*

For the stuffing, replace the orange with 1 lemon and the tarragon with 1 tablespoon of chopped fresh coriander leaf. Add 1 teaspoon of ground coriander seed to the stuffing. Replace the orange garnish with lemon.

Mediterranean swordfish

2 tbsp olive oil
1 onion, finely chopped
1 celery stick, finely chopped
115 g/4 oz green olives, stoned
450 g/1 lb tomatoes, chopped

3 tbsp bottled capers, drained
4 swordfish steaks, about 140 g/5 oz each
salt and pepper
fresh flat-leaf parsley sprigs, to garnish

Heat the oil in a large heavy-based frying pan. Add the onion and celery and cook over a low heat, stirring occasionally, for 5 minutes, or until softened. Meanwhile, roughly chop half the olives. Stir the chopped and whole olives into the saucepan with the tomatoes and capers and season to taste with salt and pepper.

Bring to the boil, then reduce the heat, cover and simmer gently, stirring occasionally, for

15 minutes. Add the swordfish steaks to the frying pan and return to the boil. Cover and simmer, turning the fish once, for 20 minutes, or until the fish is cooked and the flesh flakes easily. Transfer the fish to serving plates and spoon the sauce over them. Garnish with fresh parsley sprigs and serve immediately.

543 *Quick Mediterranean swordfish*

For a more simple sauce but with similar flavours, fry the seasoned swordfish steaks in half the oil until cooked through and golden, remove to warm serving plates then add rest of oil, 8 chopped spring onions and 1 finely chopped stick celery and fry for 3 minutes until soft. Add the olives and capers to the pan with 15 g/½ oz butter and the juice of 1 lemon, stir for 2 minutes, then garnish with parsley to serve.

544 *Mediterranean cod steaks with thyme & marjoram*

4 cod steaks, defrosted if frozen
2 tsp fresh lemon juice
2 tbsp extra virgin olive oil
1 onion, finely chopped
2 cloves of garlic, crushed
1 tbsp tomato purée
400 g/14 oz canned tomatoes
1 tbsp fresh thyme leaves or 2 tsp dried thyme

2 tsp fresh marjoram leaves or 1 tsp dried marjoram
2 tbsp green olives stuffed with pimento, halved
salt and pepper
freshly boiled plain rice, to serve
leafy green salad, to serve

545 *Cod steaks with rosemary & tomatoes*

Omit the tomato purée and canned tomatoes. Add 200 g/7 oz cherry tomatoes to the dish with the fish and pour over 250 ml/9 fl oz passata instead of the canned tomatoes. Continue with recipe, replacing the marjoram with 2 teaspoons of fresh chopped rosemary.

546 *Cod steaks with basil & mozzarella*

In the original recipe, replace the thyme and marjoram with 3 tablespoons of fresh chopped basil leaves. Use black, stoned chopped olives instead of the green olives and when baking, top the fish with 55 g/2 oz slices of mozzarella cheese for the last 3 minutes of cooking time until melted and golden – keep the lid off.

Preheat the oven to 375°F/190°C/Gas Mark 5.

Place the cod steaks in a flameproof casserole and sprinkle them with lemon juice.

In a large saucepan, heat the oil and fry the onion until soft, then add the garlic and tomato purée. Add the tomatoes, herbs and olives. Season to taste

with salt and pepper. Cook on a medium heat for about 10 minutes, then pour the sauce over the fish. Put a lid on the casserole and bake on a high shelf in the oven for 25–30 minutes.

Serve with freshly boiled plain rice and a green salad.

1 kg/2 lb 4 oz monkfish tail
4 tbsp lime juice
1 garlic clove, finely chopped
1 tsp ground cumin
1 tsp paprika
1 onion, sliced into rings

2 fresh red chillies, deseeded and finely
  chopped
1 tbsp chopped fresh coriander
2 tbsp olive oil
salt and pepper

Remove the grey membrane that covers the monkfish tail with a sharp knife, then cut along one side of the central bone to remove the fillet of flesh. Repeat on the other side to remove the other fillet from the bone, then tie the 2 fillets together with string. Transfer the tied fillets to a shallow, non-metallic, ovenproof dish. Place the lime juice, garlic, cumin and paprika in a bowl, stir to mix, and season to taste with salt and pepper.

Spoon the marinade over the monkfish, cover and leave to marinate in the refrigerator for 1 hour. Preheat the oven to 220°C/425°F/Gas Mark 7. Sprinkle the onion rings, chillies and the chopped coriander over the fish and drizzle with the oil. Roast in the preheated oven for 20 minutes, or until cooked through and the flesh flakes easily. Cut the fish into slices and serve.

548 *Stuffed baked monkfish*

Combine lime juice, garlic, cumin, paprika and finely chopped chillies in a bowl with chopped coriander. Add 6 finely chopped spring onions and 1 tablespoon of olive oil. Use this mix to stuff the two fillets of monkfish before you tie them. Drizzle the fish with oil and roast. Sprinkle with chopped coriander to serve.

549 *Roasted sea bass*   SERVES 4

1.3–1.8 kg/3–4 lb whole sea bass,
  gutted
1 small onion, finely chopped
2 garlic cloves, finely chopped
2 tbsp finely chopped fresh herbs, such
  as parsley, chervil and tarragon
25 g/1 oz anchovy fillets, finely
  chopped
25 g/1 oz butter
150 ml/¼ pint white wine
2 tbsp crème fraîche
salt and pepper

Preheat the oven to 200°C/400°F/ Gas Mark 6. Remove any scales from the fish and clean it thoroughly both inside and out. If desired, trim off the fins with a pair of scissors. Using a sharp knife, make 5–6 cuts diagonally into the flesh of the fish on both sides. Season well with salt and pepper, both inside and out. Mix together the onion, garlic, herbs and anchovies in a bowl.

Stuff the fish with half the mixture and spoon the remainder into a roasting tin. Place the bass on top. Spread the butter over the bass, pour over the wine and place in the oven.

Roast for 30–35 minutes until the fish is cooked through. Remove the fish from the tin to a warmed serving dish. Return the tin to the top of the stove and stir the onion mixture and juices together over a medium heat. Add the crème fraîche and pour into a warmed serving bowl.

Serve the sea bass whole and divide at the table. Spoon a little sauce on the side.

550 *Roasted red mullet*

Red mullet, weighing 280–350 g/10–12 oz each, take only 15–20 minutes to roast. Serve 1 per person. Brush well with butter and stuff simply with fresh herbs, lemon slices and some anchovy butter – finely chopped anchovy blended with butter at room temperature.

60 g/2¼ oz pak choi, shredded
40 g/1½ oz beansprouts
40 g/1½ oz shiitake mushrooms,
sliced
40 g/1½ oz oyster mushrooms, torn
20 g/¾ oz spring onions, finely sliced
1 tsp finely grated fresh ginger
1 tbsp finely sliced lemon grass
2 x 90-g/3¼-oz skinned and boned
sea bass fillets,
10 g/¼ oz sesame seeds, toasted

SWEET & SOUR SAUCE
90 ml/3 fl oz unsweetened pineapple
juice
1 tbsp sugar
1 tbsp red wine vinegar
2 star anise, crushed
6 tbsp tomato juice
1 tbsp cornflour, blended with a little
cold water

Cut 2 x 38-cm/15-inch squares of greaseproof paper and 2 x 38-cm/15-inch squares of foil.

To make the sauce, heat the pineapple juice, sugar, red wine vinegar, star anise and tomato juice. Simmer for 1–2 minutes, then thicken with the cornflour and water mixture, whisking continuously. Pass through a fine sieve into a small bowl to cool. In a separate large bowl mix together the pak choi, beansprouts, mushrooms and spring onions, then add the ginger and lemon grass. Toss all the ingredients together.

Put a square of greaseproof paper on top of a square of foil and fold into a triangle. Open up and place half the vegetable mix in the centre, pour half the sweet and sour sauce over the vegetables and place the sea bass on top. Sprinkle with a few sesame seeds. Close the triangle over the mixture and, starting at the top, fold the right corner and crumple the edges together to form an airtight triangular bag. Repeat to make another bag.

Place on a baking sheet and cook in a preheated oven, 200°C/400°F/ Gas Mark 6, for 10 minutes, until the foil bags puff with steam. To serve, place on individual plates and snip open at the table.

552 Chargrilled swordfish

MARINADE
3 tbsp rice wine or sherry
3 tbsp chilli oil
2 garlic cloves, finely chopped
juice of 1 lime
1 tbsp chopped fresh coriander

4 swordfish steaks, about 150 g/
5½ oz each
salt and pepper
chopped fresh coriander and lime
wedges, to garnish
fresh rocket leaves, to serve

To make the marinade, put all the ingredients into a bowl and mix well. Rinse the fish steaks under cold running water, then pat dry with kitchen paper. Arrange in a shallow, non-metallic dish which will not react with acid. Season with salt and pepper, then pour over the marinade and turn the fish until well coated. Cover with clingfilm and refrigerate for about 1½ hours. Meanwhile, place a ridged cast-iron frying pan over a high heat until you can feel the heat rising from the surface. When the fish is thoroughly marinated, place on the hot pan and chargrill for 4 minutes. Turn the fish over, brush with more marinade and chargrill on the other side for another 4 minutes, or until cooked through. Remove from the heat and garnish with coriander and lime. Serve with fresh rocket.

553 Traditional Greek baked fish

6 tbsp olive oil
2 garlic cloves
2 onions, thinly sliced
2 celery sticks
2 carrots, thinly sliced
1 large lemon
150 ml/5 fl oz dry white wine
400 g/14 oz canned chopped tomatoes
pinch of sugar
2 tbsp chopped fresh flat-leaf parsley
1 tsp chopped fresh marjoram
900g–1.3 kg/2–3 lb round whole fish
salt and pepper

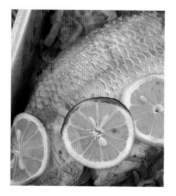

Preheat the oven to 180°C/350°F/ Gas Mark 4. Heat 4 tablespoons of the oil in a large saucepan. Finely chop the garlic and add to the pan with the onions. Fry for 5 minutes until softened. Finely slice the celery and add to the pan with the carrots. Fry for 5–10 minutes until they are slightly softened.

Thinly slice the lemon. Pour the white wine into the saucepan and bring to the boil. Add the tomatoes, the sugar, half the lemon, and salt and pepper. Simmer for 20 minutes, then add the chopped fresh flat-leaf parsley and marjoram to the pan.

Grease a shallow, ovenproof dish with half of the remaining oil. Meanwhile, scale and gut the fish if not done already, then place it in the prepared dish. Arrange the vegetables around the fish, placing some of the lemon slices on top. Sprinkle with the remaining oil and season to taste with salt and pepper. Bake the fish, uncovered, in the preheated oven for 45 minutes–1 hour, depending on the thickness of the fish, until tender.

Serve immediately, straight from the oven.

554 Quick Greek baked fish

For a quicker take on this Greek baked fish, simply place your whole fish in a shallow casserole dish and add slices of peeled lemon, sliced fresh tomatoes, crushed garlic, chopped parsley and marjoram and drizzle olive oil over. Bake, covered, for 30 minutes and remove cover to finish cooking (from 15 minutes depending on size). Add a little fish stock or water to the dish if it looks too dry. Baste with juices to serve.

555 Monkfish with a lemon & parsley crust

4 tbsp sunflower oil

4 tbsp fresh breadcrumbs

4 tbsp chopped fresh parsley, plus extra
    sprigs to garnish

finely grated rind of 1 large lemon

4 monkfish fillets, about 140–175 g/
    5–6 oz each

salt and pepper

Preheat the oven to 180°C/350°F/Gas Mark 4. Mix together the oil, breadcrumbs, parsley and lemon rind in a bowl until well combined. Season to taste with salt and pepper. Place the fish fillets in a large roasting tin. Divide the breadcrumb mixture between the fish and press it down with your fingers to ensure it covers the fillets.

Bake in the preheated oven for 7–8 minutes, or until the fish is cooked through. Garnish with parsley sprigs and serve.

556 Cod with a lemon & parsley crust

You can use various other types of white fish in this recipe – try cod steaks, plaice, haddock or sea bass fillets. Try adding a little finely chopped black olive to the crust for stronger-tasting fishes such as sea bass.

557 Fish roasted with lime

1 kg/2 lb 4 oz white fish fillets, such as
    bass, plaice or cod

1 lime, halved

3 tbsp extra virgin olive oil

1 large onion, finely chopped

3 garlic cloves, finely chopped

2–3 pickled jalapeño chillies (jalapeños
    en escabeche), chopped

6–8 tbsp chopped fresh coriander

salt and pepper

lemon and lime wedges, to serve

Preheat the oven to 180°C/350°F/Gas Mark 4. Place the fish fillets in a non-metallic bowl and season to taste with salt and pepper. Squeeze the juice from the lime halves over the fish.

Heat the oil in a frying pan. Add the onion and garlic and cook, stirring frequently, for 2 minutes, or until softened. Remove the frying pan from the heat. Place a third of the onion mixture and a little of the chillies and coriander in the base of a shallow ovenproof dish or roasting tin. Arrange the fish on top. Top with the remaining onion mixture, chillies and coriander.

Roast in the oven for 15–20 minutes, or until the fish has become slightly opaque and firm to the touch. Serve immediately, with lemon and lime wedges for squeezing over the fish.

175 ml/6 fl oz Spanish olive oil

12 small fresh sardines, cleaned and
   filleted, and heads and tails removed
   if wished

4 tbsp sherry vinegar

2 carrots, cut into julienne strips

1 onion, thinly sliced

1 garlic clove, crushed

1 bay leaf

4 tbsp chopped fresh flat-leaf parsley

salt and pepper

few sprigs of fresh dill, to garnish

lemon wedges, to serve

Heat 4 tablespoons of the olive oil in a large heavy-based frying pan. Add the sardines and cook for 10 minutes or until browned on both sides. Using a spatula, very carefully remove the sardines from the pan and transfer to a large, shallow non-metallic dish that will hold the sardines in a single layer.

Gently heat the remaining olive oil and the sherry vinegar in a large saucepan, add the carrot strips, onion, garlic and bay leaf and simmer gently for 5 minutes or until softened. Season the vegetables to taste with salt and pepper. Allow the mixture to cool slightly, then pour the marinade over the sardines.

Cover the dish and allow the sardines to cool before transferring to the refrigerator. Marinate for about 8 hours or overnight, spooning the marinade over the sardines occasionally.

Return the sardines to room temperature before serving. Sprinkle with parsley, garnish with dill sprigs and serve with lemon wedges.

559 *Salmon marinated in sherry vinegar*

Fresh salmon (or trout) fillets can be given the same treatment, but instead of pan-frying the fish, it is better to steam the fillets for 5 minutes, or until tender. When cooked, slice each fillet in half lengthwise. You will need 6 fish fillets for this recipe.

6 tbsp groundnut oil
280 g/10 oz salmon steak, skinned and
  cut into 2.5-cm/1-inch chunks
225 g/8 oz scallops
3 carrots, thinly sliced
2 celery sticks, cut into 2.5-cm/1-inch
  pieces
2 yellow peppers, thinly sliced
175 g/6 oz oyster mushrooms, thinly
  sliced
1 clove garlic, crushed
6 tbsp chopped fresh coriander
3 shallots, thinly sliced
2 limes, juiced
1 tsp lime zest
1 tsp dried red pepper flakes
3 tbsp dry sherry
3 tbsp soy sauce
cooked noodles, to serve

In a large wok or frying pan, heat the oil over a medium heat. Add the salmon and scallops, and stir-fry for 3 minutes. Remove from the wok, set aside and keep warm.

Add the carrots, celery, peppers, mushrooms and garlic to the wok and stir-fry for 3 minutes. Add the coriander and shallots and stir. Add the lime juice and zest, dried red pepper flakes, sherry and soy sauce and stir. Return the salmon and scallops to the wok and stir-fry carefully for another minute. Serve immediately on a bed of freshly cooked noodles.

561 *Salmon & scallops with mixed peppers*

Replace the carrot and celery with 1 red pepper and 1 orange pepper, deseeded and thinly sliced. Add them to the pan with the yellow pepper.

562 *Bouillabaisse* SERVES 4

200 g/7 oz live mussels
100 ml/3½ fl oz olive oil
3 garlic cloves, chopped
2 onions, chopped
2 tomatoes, deseeded and chopped
700 ml/1¼ pints fish stock
400 ml/14 fl oz white wine
1 bay leaf
pinch of saffron threads
2 tbsp chopped fresh basil
2 tbsp chopped fresh parsley
250 g/9 oz snapper or monkfish fillets
250 g/9 oz haddock fillets, skinned
200 g/7 oz prawns, peeled and
  deveined
100 g/3½ oz scallops
salt and pepper
fresh baguettes, to serve

Soak the mussels in lightly salted water for 10 minutes. Scrub the shells under cold running water and pull off any beards. Discard any with broken shells. Tap the remaining mussels and discard any that refuse to close. Put the rest into a large pan with a little water, bring to the boil and cook over high heat for 4 minutes.

Transfer the cooked mussels to a bowl, discarding any that remain closed, and reserve.

Wipe out the pan with kitchen paper. Heat the oil in the pan over a medium heat. Add the garlic and onions and cook, stirring, for 3 minutes. Stir in the tomatoes, stock, wine, bay leaf, saffron and herbs. Bring to the boil, reduce the heat, cover and simmer for 30 minutes.

When the tomato mixture is cooked, rinse the fish fillets, pat dry and cut into chunks. Add to the pan and simmer for 5 minutes. Add the mussels, prawns and scallops and season with salt and pepper. Cook for 3 minutes, until the fish is cooked through.

Remove from the heat, discard the bay leaf and ladle into serving bowls. Serve with fresh baguettes.

563 *Bouillabaisse with other fish*

This famous French chunky soup/stew is a bit of a moveable feast – you can use whatever mixed fish and seafood you have, For example, you could replace the scallops or prawns with lobster or crab; you could use turbot, bream, or mullet instead of snapper/monkfish. The meal is traditionally garnished with a garlic mayonnaise called rouille.

564 Roasted monkfish

675 g/1 lb 8 oz monkfish tail, skinned
4–5 large garlic cloves, peeled
3 tbsp olive oil
1 onion, cut into wedges
1 small aubergine, cut into chunks

1 red pepper and 1 yellow pepper,
  deseeded and cut into wedges
1 large courgette, cut into wedges
salt and pepper
1 tbsp shredded fresh basil, to garnish

Preheat the oven to 200°C/400°F/ Gas Mark 6. Remove the central bone from the fish if not already removed and make small slits down each fillet. Cut 2 of the garlic cloves into thin slivers and insert into the fish. Place the fish on a sheet of greaseproof paper, season to taste and drizzle over 1 tablespoon of the oil. Bring the top edges together. Form into a pleat and fold over, then fold the ends underneath, completely encasing the fish. Reserve.

Put the remaining garlic cloves and all the vegetables into a roasting tin and drizzle with the remaining oil, turning the vegetables so that they are well coated. Roast in the preheated oven for 20 minutes, turning occasionally. Put the fish parcel on top of the vegetables and cook for a further 15–20 minutes. Remove from the oven, cut the monkfish into thick slices and arrange on top of the vegetables. Sprinkle with the basil and serve.

565 Roasted monkfish with fennel

Replace the peppers with 1 large bulb of Florence fennel. Trim root end and snip off feathery tops, then thinly slice and blanch in boiling water to soften. Drain thoroughly then add to the pan with the other vegetables.

566 Cod in lemon & parsley sauce

2 onions
1 garlic clove
2 tbsp olive oil
4 tomatoes, peeled and quartered
grated rind and juice of ½ lemon
6 tbsp dry white wine

3 tbsp chopped fresh mixed herbs, such
  as parsley, thyme and chives
4 cod steaks, about 175 g/6 oz each
salt and pepper
fresh thyme sprigs, to garnish

Finely chop the onions and garlic. Heat the olive oil in a large, heavy-based frying pan. Add the onion and cook over a low heat, stirring occasionally, for 5 minutes, or until softened.

Add the garlic and tomatoes and cook for 3–4 minutes. Add the lemon rind and juice, white wine, chopped herbs and cod steaks, and season to taste with salt and pepper. Set the heat as low as possible, then cover the frying pan and simmer gently for 15 minutes, or until the fish is cooked through and flakes easily when tested with the point of a knife. Serve immediately, garnished with fresh thyme sprigs.

567 Cod in lemon cream & parsley sauce

This is a similar recipe, but replaces the tomatoes and onions with crème fraîche. First fry the fish steaks in a little butter rather than olive oil until almost cooked, then stir in some very finely chopped garlic for 1 minute, the juice of ½ lemon, 3 tablespoons of dry white wine, plenty of seasoning and fresh chopped parsley and chives. Allow to simmer for 2–3 minutes, then stir in 3 tablespoons of full fat crème fraîche and warm through before serving.

about 2 tbsp plain flour
4 hake fillets, about
    140 g/5 oz each
4 tbsp extra virgin olive oil
125 ml/4 fl oz dry white wine

2 large garlic cloves, very finely chopped
6 spring onions, finely sliced
25 g/1 oz fresh parsley, very finely chopped
salt and pepper

Turn the fish over and season with salt and pepper. Pour in the wine and add the garlic, spring onions and parsley. Transfer the casserole to the oven and bake, uncovered, for 5 minutes, or until the flesh flakes easily. Serve the fish straight from the casserole.

Preheat the oven to 230°C/450°F/Gas Mark 8. Spread the flour out on a large, flat plate and season well with salt and pepper. Coat the skin side of the hake fillets in the seasoned flour, then shake off any excess. Set aside.

Heat a shallow, ovenproof casserole over a high heat until you can feel the heat rising. Add the oil and heat until a cube of bread sizzles in 30 seconds. Add the hake fillets, skin-side down, and cook for 3 minutes until the skin is golden brown.

569 *Plaice in white wine*

You can replace the hake in this recipe with plaice – try to find thick fillets – or skate. If you use skate you will need to allow 7 minutes cooking in the oven.

173

570 *Italian fish stew*

SERVES 4

2 tbsp olive oil
2 red onions, finely chopped
1 garlic clove, crushed
2 courgettes, sliced
400 g/14 oz canned chopped tomatoes
850 ml/1¾ pints fish or vegetable stock
85 g/3 oz dried pasta shapes
350 g/12 oz firm white fish, such as hake
1 tbsp chopped fresh basil or oregano,
    plus extra to garnish
1 tsp grated lemon rind
1 tbsp cornflour
1 tbsp water
salt and pepper

Heat the oil in a large pan. Add the onions and garlic and cook over a low heat, stirring occasionally, for about 5 minutes, until softened. Add the courgettes and cook, stirring frequently, for 2–3 minutes. Add the tomatoes and stock to the pan and bring to the boil. Add the pasta, bring back to the boil, reduce the heat and cover. Simmer for 5 minutes.

Skin and bone the fish, then cut it into chunks. Add to the pan with the basil and lemon rind and simmer gently for 5 minutes, until the fish is opaque and flakes easily (take care not to overcook it) and the pasta is tender, but still firm to the bite.

Place the cornflour and water in a small bowl, mix to a smooth paste and stir into the stew. Cook gently for 2 minutes, stirring constantly, until thickened. Season to taste with salt and pepper. Ladle the stew into 4 warmed soup bowls. Garnish with basil and serve immediately.

571 *With French beans & broccoli*

Add 85 g/3 oz each French beans and broccoli to the stew with the tomatoes. For a thinner but very tasty broth you can omit the cornflour stage.

572 *Squid stew*

SERVES 4

750 g/1 lb 10 oz squid
3 tbsp olive oil
1 onion, chopped
3 garlic cloves, finely chopped
1 tsp fresh thyme leaves
400 g/14 oz canned chopped tomatoes
150 ml/5 fl oz red wine
300 ml/10 fl oz water
1 tbsp chopped fresh parsley
salt and pepper
crusty bread, to serve

Preheat the oven to 140°C/275°F/ Gas Mark 1.

To prepare whole squid, hold the body firmly and grasp the tentacles just inside the body. Pull firmly to remove the innards. Find the transparent quill and remove. Grasp the wings on the outside of the body and pull to remove the outer skin. Trim the tentacles just below the beak and reserve. Wash the body and tentacles under running water. Slice the body into rings. Drain well on kitchen paper. Heat the oil in a large flameproof casserole. Add the prepared squid and cook over a medium heat, stirring occasionally, until the squid is lightly browned.

Reduce the heat and add the onion, garlic and thyme. Cook, stirring occasionally, for a further 5 minutes until softened. Stir in the tomatoes, red wine and water. Bring to the boil, then transfer the casserole to the oven for 2 hours. Stir in the parsley and season to taste with salt and pepper. Serve with crusty bread.

573 *Squid stew with white wine*

Replace the red wine with dry white wine and try using fish stock instead of the water.

574 Fish stew with cider

2 tsp butter
1 large leek, thinly sliced
2 shallots, finely chopped
125 ml/4 fl oz dry cider
300 ml/10 fl oz fish stock
250 g/9 oz potatoes, diced
1 bay leaf

4 tbsp plain flour
200 ml/7 fl oz milk
200 ml/7 fl oz double cream
55 g/2 oz fresh sorrel leaves
350 g/12 oz skinless monkfish or cod fillet,
    cut into 2.5-cm/1-inch pieces
salt and pepper

Melt the butter in a large saucepan over a medium–low heat. Add the leek and shallots and cook for about 5 minutes, stirring frequently, until they start to soften. Add the cider and bring to the boil. Stir in the stock, potatoes and bay leaf with a large pinch of salt (unless the stock is salty) and bring back to the boil. Reduce the heat, cover and cook gently for 10 minutes. Put the flour in a small bowl and very slowly whisk in a few tablespoons of the milk to make a thick paste. Stir in a little more to make a smooth liquid.

Adjust the heat so the stew bubbles gently. Stir in the flour mixture and cook, stirring frequently, for 5 minutes. Add the remaining milk and half the cream. Continue cooking for about 10 minutes until the potatoes are tender. Finely chop the sorrel and combine with the remaining cream. Stir the sorrel cream into the stew and add the fish.

Continue cooking, stirring occasionally, for about 3 minutes, until the monkfish stiffens. Taste the stew and adjust the seasoning, if needed. Ladle into warmed bowls and serve.

575 Fish stew with white wine & spinach

You can make the same recipe using medium dry white wine instead of cider. If you can't get sorrel you can use spinach leaves or half spinach, half basil.

576 Brazilian seafood stew

2 tbsp olive oil
1 onion, finely chopped
2 garlic cloves, very finely chopped
400 g/14 oz canned chopped tomatoes
¼ tsp cayenne pepper
pinch of saffron threads
900 g/2 lb cod steaks, cut into chunks
450 g/1 lb mussels, scrubbed
    and debearded
225 g/8 oz raw tiger prawns,
    peeled and deveined
200 g/7 oz canned crabmeat, drained
200 g/7 oz bottled clams
salt and pepper
3 tbsp chopped fresh coriander,
    to garnish

Heat the oil in a large saucepan or flameproof casserole over a medium heat, add the onion and cook, stirring frequently, for 5 minutes, or until softened. Stir in the garlic, tomatoes, cayenne pepper and saffron. Season to taste and simmer, stirring occasionally, for 5 minutes.

Add the cod and mussels, then pour in enough water to just cover and bring to the boil. Reduce the heat to low, cover and simmer for 10 minutes, or until the mussels have opened. Discard any that remain closed. Add the prawns, crabmeat and clams with their juice. Simmer for a further 5 minutes, or until the prawns turn pink. Stir in the coriander just before serving.

577 Quick Brazilian seafood stew

For a quicker version you can replace the mussels, prawns and clams with a supermarket pack of ready-mixed seafood.

578 Marseille-style fish stew

SERVES 4–6

large pinch of saffron threads
900 g/2 lb fresh Mediterranean fish,
such as sea bass, monkfish, red
snapper or haddock
24 large raw prawns in their shells
1 raw squid
2 tbsp olive oil
1 large onion, finely chopped
1 fennel bulb, thinly sliced, feathery
fronds reserved
2 large garlic cloves, crushed
4 tbsp pastis, such as Pernod
1 litre/1¾ pints fish stock
2 large sun-ripened tomatoes, peeled,
deseeded and diced, or 400 g/14 oz
chopped canned tomatoes
1 tbsp tomato purée
1 bay leaf
pinch of sugar
pinch of chilli flakes (optional)
salt and pepper
French bread, to serve

Put the saffron threads in a small dry frying pan over a high heat and toast, stirring constantly for 1 minute, or until you can smell the aroma. Immediately tip out of the pan and set aside.

Prepare the fish as necessary, discarding all skin, bones and heads. Cut the flesh into large chunks. Peel and devein the prawns. Cover and refrigerate the fish and prawns until required.

To prepare the squid, use your fingers to rub off the thin membrane that covers the body. Pull the head and insides out of the body sac, then cut off and reserve the tentacles. Pull out the thin, clear quill that is inside the body. Rinse the squid inside and out, then cut the body into 5-mm/¼-inch rings. Cover and refrigerate the squid until required.

Heat the oil in a large flameproof casserole or heavy-based saucepan and cook the onion and sliced fennel for 3 minutes. Add the garlic and cook for a further 5 minutes, or until the onion and fennel are softened but not browned.

Remove the casserole from the heat. Warm the pastis in a ladle or small saucepan, ignite and pour over the onion and fennel to flambé. When the flames die down, return the casserole to the heat and stir in the stock, tomatoes, tomato purée, bay leaf, sugar, chilli flakes, if using,

and salt and pepper to taste. Slowly bring to the boil, then reduce the heat and simmer for 15 minutes. Taste, and adjust the seasoning if necessary.

Add the prawns and squid and simmer just until the prawns have turned pink and the squid is opaque. Using a slotted spoon, transfer the prawns and squid to warmed serving bowls.

Add the fish to the broth and simmer just until the flesh flakes easily – not longer than 5 minutes, depending on the type of fish. Transfer the fish and broth to the serving bowls, removing the smaller, thinner pieces first. Garnish with the reserved fennel fronds and serve with sliced French bread.

579 Marseille-style stew with fennel seeds

If you haven't got a bulb of fennel, add 2–3 teaspoons of crushed fennel seeds to the stew instead and add in 1–2 sticks celery, roughly chopped.

580 Moroccan fish tagine

2 tbsp olive oil
1 large onion, finely chopped
pinch of saffron threads
½ tsp ground cinnamon
1 tsp ground coriander
½ tsp ground cumin
½ tsp ground turmeric
200 g/7 oz canned chopped tomatoes
300 ml/10 fl oz fish stock
4 small red mullet, cleaned, boned
and heads and tails removed
55 g/2 oz stoned green olives
1 tbsp chopped preserved lemon
3 tbsp chopped fresh coriander
salt and pepper
couscous, to serve

Heat the oil in a large saucepan or flameproof casserole over a low heat. Add the onion and cook, stirring occasionally, for 10 minutes, or until softened but not coloured. Add the saffron, cinnamon, ground coriander, cumin and turmeric and cook for a further 30 seconds, stirring.

Add the tomatoes and stock and stir well. Bring to the boil, then reduce the heat, cover and simmer for 15 minutes. Uncover and allow the sauce to simmer for a further 20–35 minutes, or until thickened.

Cut each red mullet in half, then add the pieces to the pan, pushing them into the sauce. Simmer for a further 5–6 minutes, or until the fish is just cooked.

Carefully stir in the olives, preserved lemon and fresh coriander. Season to taste and serve with couscous.

581 Spicy Moroccan fish tagine

Use whole tilapia or bream instead of the mullet. Stir 1 tablespoon of rose harissa into the tagine with the fish to give a delicious heat to the dish.

582 Prawn gumbo

2 tbsp vegetable oil
2 tbsp butter
250 g/9 oz okra, trimmed and thickly
    sliced
1 onion, finely chopped
2 celery sticks, quartered lengthways
    and diced
1 green pepper, deseeded and diced
2 garlic cloves, very finely chopped

200 g/7 oz canned chopped tomatoes
½ tsp dried thyme or oregano
1 fresh bay leaf
850 ml/1½ pints chicken stock or water
450 g/1 lb fresh or frozen raw prawns,
    peeled and deveined
few drops of Tabasco sauce
salt and pepper
2 tbsp chopped fresh coriander, to garnish

Heat the oil and butter in a large saucepan over a medium heat. Add the okra and cook, uncovered, for about 15 minutes, or until it loses its gummy consistency.

Add the onion, celery, pepper, garlic, tomatoes, thyme and bay leaf. Season to taste with salt and pepper. Cover and cook over a medium–low heat for 10 minutes.

Pour in the stock. Bring to the boil, then cover and simmer over a medium–low heat for 15 minutes, or until the vegetables are al dente. Add the prawns and Tabasco sauce. Cook for 5 minutes, or until the prawns are pink.

Stir in the coriander to garnish just before serving.

583 Prawn gumbo with bacon

Add 4 rashers of lean bacon, sliced, to the pan with the okra for the last few minutes of its cooking time and before adding the onions.

Seafood chilli

115 g/4 oz raw prawns, peeled
250 g/9 oz prepared scallops, thawed if frozen
115 g/4 oz monkfish fillet, cut into chunks
1 tbsp chilli powder
1 tsp ground cumin
3 tbsp chopped fresh coriander
2 garlic cloves, finely chopped
1 fresh green chilli, deseeded and chopped
3 tbsp maize oil
1 onion, roughly chopped

1 red pepper, deseeded and roughly chopped
1 yellow pepper, deseeded and roughly chopped
¼ tsp ground cloves
pinch of ground cinnamon
pinch of cayenne pepper
350 ml/12 fl oz fish stock
400 g/14 oz canned chopped tomatoes
400 g/14 oz canned red kidney beans, drained and rinsed
salt

Place the prawns, scallops and monkfish chunks in a large non-metallic dish with ¼ teaspoon of the chilli powder, ¼ teaspoon of the ground cumin, 1 tablespoon of the chopped coriander, half the garlic, the fresh chilli and 1 tablespoon of the oil. Cover with clingfilm and leave to

marinate for up to 1 hour. Meanwhile, heat 1 tablespoon of the remaining oil in a flameproof casserole or large heavy-based saucepan. Add the onion, the remaining garlic and the red and yellow peppers and cook over a low heat, stirring occasionally, for 5 minutes, or until softened.

Add the remaining chilli powder, the remaining cumin, the cloves, cinnamon and cayenne pepper with the remaining oil, if necessary, and season to taste with salt. Cook, stirring, for 5 minutes, then gradually stir in the stock and the tomatoes.

Partially cover and simmer for 25 minutes. Add the beans to the tomato mixture and spoon the fish and shellfish on top. Cover and cook for 10 minutes, or until the fish and shellfish are cooked through. Sprinkle with the remaining coriander and serve.

585 # With smoked paprika

Use as many fresh chillies as you like in this dish – their heat will vary according to type. Try adding 2 teaspoons of smoked paprika.

586 # Seafood in saffron sauce

225 g/8 oz live mussels
225 g/8 oz live clams
2 tbsp olive oil
1 onion, sliced
pinch of saffron threads
1 tbsp chopped fresh thyme
2 garlic cloves, finely chopped
800 g/1 lb 12 oz canned tomatoes, drained and chopped
175 ml/6 fl oz dry white wine
2 litres/3½ pints fish stock
350 g/12 oz red mullet fillets, cut into bite-sized chunks
450 g/1 lb monkfish fillets, cut into bite-sized chunks
225 g/8 oz raw squid rings
2 tbsp fresh shredded basil leaves
salt and pepper
fresh bread, to serve

Heat the oil in a large flameproof casserole and cook the onion with the saffron, thyme and a pinch of salt over a low heat, stirring occasionally, for 5 minutes, or until softened. Add the garlic and cook, stirring, for 2 minutes. Add the tomatoes, wine and stock, season to taste with salt and pepper and stir well. Bring to the boil, then reduce the heat and simmer for 15 minutes.

Add the fish chunks and simmer for a further 3 minutes. Add the clams, mussels and squid

rings and simmer for a further 5 minutes, or until the mussels and clams have opened. Discard any that remain closed. Stir in the basil and serve immediately, accompanied by plenty of fresh bread to mop up the broth.

Clean the mussels and clams by scrubbing the shells and pulling out any beards that are attached to the mussels. Discard any with broken shells or any that refuse to close when tapped.

587 # Quick seafood in saffron sauce

If you don't want to use live mussels and clams then you can buy ready-prepared mussels in the shell from the supermarket and add to that a pack of mixed frozen seafood – defrost before using.

588 *South-western seafood stew*

SERVES 4

1 each of yellow, red and orange peppers, cored, deseeded and quartered
450 g/1 lb ripe tomatoes
2 large fresh mild green chillies, such as poblano
6 garlic cloves, peeled but left whole
2 tsp dried oregano or dried mixed herbs
2 tbsp olive oil, plus extra for drizzling
1 large onion, finely chopped
450 ml/16 fl oz fish, vegetable or chicken stock
finely grated rind and juice of 1 lime
2 tbsp chopped fresh coriander, plus extra to garnish
1 bay leaf
450 g/1 lb red snapper fillets, skinned and cut into chunks
225 g/8 oz raw prawns, peeled
225 g/8 oz cleaned squid, cut into rings
salt and pepper
warmed flour tortillas, to serve

Preheat the oven to 200°C/400°F/Gas Mark 6. Place the pepper quarters skin-side up in a roasting tin with the tomatoes, chillies and garlic. Sprinkle with the dried oregano and drizzle with oil. Roast in the oven for 30 minutes, or until the peppers are well browned and softened.

Remove the roasted vegetables from the oven and leave to stand until cool enough to handle. Peel off the skins from the peppers, tomatoes and chillies and chop the flesh. Finely chop the garlic.

Heat the oil in a large saucepan. Add the onion and cook for 5 minutes, or until softened. Add the peppers, tomatoes, chillies, garlic, stock, lime rind and juice, chopped coriander, bay leaf and salt and pepper to taste. Bring to the boil, then stir in the seafood.

Reduce the heat, cover and leave to simmer gently for 10 minutes, or until the seafood is just cooked through. Discard the bay leaf, then garnish with chopped coriander before serving with the warmed flour tortillas.

589 *Mixed south-western seafood stew*

You can use any other firm fish fillets or a mixture, if you prefer. Instead of the fresh tomatoes you can use a can of whole tomatoes, roughly chopped.

590 Wok-fried jumbo prawns in spicy sauce

3 tbsp vegetable or groundnut oil

450 g/1 lb raw king prawns, deveined
but unpeeled

2 tsp finely chopped fresh ginger

1 tsp finely chopped garlic

1 tbsp chopped spring onion

2 tbsp chilli bean sauce

1 tsp Shaoxing rice wine

1 tsp sugar

½ tsp light soy sauce

1–2 tbsp chicken stock

In a preheated wok, heat the oil, then add the prawns and stir-fry over
a high heat for about 4 minutes. Arrange the prawns on the sides of the
wok out of the oil, then add the fresh ginger and garlic and stir until
fragrant. Add the spring onion and chilli bean sauce. Stir the prawns
into this mixture.

Lower the heat slightly and add the Shaoxing, sugar, light soy sauce
and a little chicken stock. Cover and cook for a further minute, then
serve immediately.

591 Spicy Thai seafood stew

200 g/7 oz squid, cleaned and tentacles
discarded

500 g/1 lb 2 oz firm white fish fillet
(preferably monkfish or halibut)

1 tbsp corn oil

4 shallots, finely chopped

2 garlic cloves, finely chopped

2 tbsp Thai green curry paste

2 small lemon grass stems, finely chopped

1 tsp shrimp paste

500 ml/16 fl oz coconut milk

200 g/7 oz raw king prawns, peeled and
deveined

12 live clams in shells, cleaned

8 fresh basil leaves, finely shredded

fresh basil leaves, to garnish

cooked rice, to serve

Using a sharp knife, cut the squid into thick rings and cut the fish into
bite-sized chunks. Preheat a large wok, then add the oil and heat. Add
the shallots, garlic and curry paste and stir-fry for 1–2 minutes. Add the
lemon grass and shrimp paste, then stir in the coconut milk and bring
to the boil. Reduce the heat until the liquid is simmering gently, then
add the squid, fish and prawns and simmer for 2 minutes. Discard any
clams with broken shells and any that refuse to close when tapped. Add
the clams and simmer for a further minute, or until the clams have
opened. Discard any that remain closed.

Transfer the stew to serving plates, garnish with basil leaves and serve
immediately with freshly cooked rice.

592 Sweet & spicy Thai seafood stew

*Replace the squid with scallops and use crayfish instead of the prawns for
a delicious sweet curry. If you don't want to use the clams, garnish the stew
with whole cooked unpeeled prawns instead.*

Calamari with prawns & broad beans

SERVES 4–6

2 tbsp olive oil
4 spring onions, thinly sliced
2 garlic cloves, finely chopped
500 g/1 lb 2 oz cleaned squid bodies,
  thickly sliced
100 ml/3½ fl oz dry white wine
225 g/8 oz fresh or frozen baby
  broad beans

250 g/9 oz raw king prawns, peeled
  and deveined
4 tbsp chopped fresh flat-leaf parsley
salt and pepper
crusty bread, to serve

Heat the oil in a large frying pan with a lid, add the spring onions and cook over a medium heat, stirring occasionally, for 4–5 minutes, until soft. Add the garlic and cook, stirring, for 30 seconds, until soft. Add the squid and cook over a high heat, stirring occasionally, for 2 minutes, or until golden brown. Stir in the wine and bring to the boil. Add the beans, reduce the heat, cover and simmer for 5–8 minutes if using fresh beans, or 4–5 minutes if using frozen beans, until tender.

Add the prawns, re-cover and simmer for a further 2–3 minutes, until the prawns turn pink and start to curl. Stir in the parsley and season to taste with salt and pepper. Serve hot with crusty bread to mop up the juices.

594 Calamari with prawns & pasta

Omit the bread but instead cook 400 g/14 oz (dry weight) spaghetti and stir it lightly into the squid, prawns and beans to serve, garnished with parsley.

Garlic & herb Dublin Bay prawns

SERVES 2

12 raw Dublin Bay prawns in their shells
juice of ½ lemon
2 garlic cloves, crushed
3 tbsp chopped fresh parsley

1 tbsp chopped fresh dill
3 tbsp softened butter
salt and pepper
lemon wedges and crusty bread, to serve

Rinse the prawns. Devein, using a sharp knife to slice along the back from the head end to the tail and removing the thin black intestine. Mix the lemon juice with the garlic, herbs and butter to form a paste. Season well. Spread the paste over the prawns and marinate for 30 minutes. Meanwhile, preheat the grill to medium. Cook the prawns under the preheated grill for 5–6 minutes. Turn out onto plates and pour over the juices. Serve immediately with lemon wedges and crusty bread.

596 Garlic & chilli Dublin Bay prawns

Fry the prawns in 2 tablespoons of butter with 2 cloves chopped garlic, 1–2 very finely chopped red chillies and 2 tablespoons of chopped parsley. When cooked add the juice of a lime and plenty of black pepper.

large pinch of saffron threads
4 tbsp almost-boiling water
6 tbsp olive oil
1 large onion, chopped
2 garlic cloves, finely chopped
1½ tbsp chopped fresh thyme leaves
2 bay leaves
2 red peppers, deseeded and roughly
chopped
800 g/1 lb 12 oz canned chopped
tomatoes
1 tsp smoked paprika
250 ml/9 fl oz fish stock
140 g/5 oz blanched almonds, toasted
and finely ground
12–16 live mussels
12–16 live clams
600 g/1 lb 5 oz thick boned hake or
cod fillets, skinned and cut into
5-cm/2-inch chunks
12–16 raw prawns, peeled and
deveined
salt and pepper
thick crusty bread, to serve

Put the saffron threads in a heatproof jug with the water and leave for at least 10 minutes to infuse.

Heat the oil in a large heavy-based flameproof casserole over a medium–high heat. Reduce the heat to low and cook the onion, stirring occasionally, for 10 minutes, or until golden but not browned. Stir in the garlic, thyme, bay leaves and red peppers and cook, stirring frequently, for 5 minutes, or until the peppers are softened and the onions have softened further.

Add the tomatoes and paprika and simmer, stirring frequently, for a further 5 minutes. Stir in the stock, the saffron and its soaking liquid and the almonds and bring to the boil, stirring. Reduce the heat and simmer for 5–10 minutes, until the sauce reduces and thickens. Season to taste.

Meanwhile, clean the mussels and clams by scrubbing or scraping the shells and pulling out any beards that are attached to the mussels. Discard any with broken shells and any that refuse to close immediately when tapped.

Gently stir the hake into the stew so that it doesn't break up, then add the prawns, mussels and clams. Reduce the heat to very low, cover and simmer for 5 minutes, or until the hake is opaque, the mussels and clams have opened and the prawns have turned pink. Discard any mussels or clams that remain closed. Serve immediately with plenty of thick crusty bread for soaking up the juices.

598 Skate in black butter sauce

4 skate wings, about 175 g/6 oz each
600 ml/1 pint fish stock
225 ml/8 fl oz dry white wine
4 tbsp butter

2 tbsp lemon juice
2 tsp capers in brine, rinsed
2 tbsp chopped fresh parsley
salt and pepper

Put the fish in a large heavy-based frying pan or ovenproof casserole, pour in the stock and wine, and season with salt and pepper. Bring to the boil, then reduce the heat and simmer for 10–15 minutes until the fish is tender.

Meanwhile, melt the butter in a large heavy-based frying pan over a very low heat and cook until it turns brown but not black. Stir in the lemon juice, capers and parsley and heat for a further 1–2 minutes. Transfer the skate wings to warmed serving plates with a spatula, pour the black butter sauce over and serve immediately.

599 Pan-fried skate in black butter

Fry the skate wings in a pan with 1 tablespoon of olive oil and 1 tablespoon of butter until cooked through. Remove and keep warm. Add butter to pan to brown, then add lemon juice, capers and parsley, and heat. Pour over the skate.

600 Peppered tuna steaks

4 tuna steaks, about
175 g/6 oz each
4 tsp sunflower oil or olive oil
1 tsp salt
2 tbsp pink, green and black
peppercorns, roughly crushed
handful of fresh rocket leaves,
to garnish
lemon wedges, to serve

Brush the tuna steaks with the oil. Sprinkle with the salt. Coat the fish in the crushed peppercorns.

Heat a ridged griddle pan over a medium heat. Add the tuna and cook for 2–3 minutes on each side. Garnish with rocket and serve with lemon wedges for squeezing over.

601 Peppered salmon or swordfish steaks

Salmon steaks make a perfect substitute for the tuna in this recipe. You can use swordfish steaks too – cook these for a minute longer or until opaque all the way through.

602 *Spanish swordfish stew*

SERVES 4

4 tbsp olive oil
3 shallots, chopped
2 garlic cloves, chopped
225 g/8 oz canned chopped tomatoes
1 tbsp tomato purée
650 g/1 lb 7 oz potatoes, sliced
250 ml/9 fl oz vegetable stock
2 tbsp lemon juice

1 red pepper, deseeded and chopped
1 orange pepper, deseeded and chopped
20 black olives, pitted and halved
1 kg/2 lb 4 oz swordfish steak, skinned
    and cut into bite-sized pieces
salt and pepper
parsley sprigs and lemon slices,
    to garnish

Heat the oil in a saucepan over a low heat, add the shallots and cook, stirring frequently, for 4 minutes, or until softened. Add the garlic, tomatoes and tomato purée, cover and simmer gently for 20 minutes.

Meanwhile, put the potatoes in a flameproof casserole with the stock and lemon juice. Bring to the boil, then reduce the heat and add the peppers. Cover and cook

for 15 minutes. Add the olives, swordfish and the tomato mixture to the potatoes. Season with salt and pepper.

Stir well, then cover and simmer for 7–10 minutes, or until the swordfish is cooked to your taste. Remove from the heat and garnish with parsley sprigs and lemon slices.

603 *Spanish tuna stew*

Use the same recipe but replace the swordfish with 4 large tuna steaks, cut into chunks.

604 *Shellfish stew*

SERVES 4

24 live mussels
24 live clams
450 g/1 lb sea bream fillets
1.5 litres/2¾ pints fish stock
225 ml/8 fl oz dry white wine
2 shallots, finely chopped
24 raw prawns, peeled and deveined
700 g/1 lb 9 oz tomatoes, peeled,
    deseeded and roughly chopped
3 tbsp snipped fresh chives
grated rind of 1 lemon
pinch of saffron threads
3 tbsp finely chopped fresh parsley
salt and pepper

Clean the mussels and clams by scrubbing or scraping the shells and pulling out any beards that are attached to the mussels. Discard any with broken shells or any that refuse to close immediately when tapped. Cut the sea bream into bite-sized pieces.

Pour the stock and wine into a large heavy-based saucepan and bring to the boil. Add the mussels, clams and shallots, cover and cook over a medium heat for 4 minutes. Tip into a sieve, reserving the stock. Discard any mussels or clams that remain closed.

Rinse the saucepan and strain the stock back into it through a muslin-lined sieve. Return to the boil and add the prawns and sea bream. Stir in the tomatoes, chives, lemon rind, saffron and parsley and season to taste. Gently simmer for 10 minutes, or until the fish flakes easily when tested.

Remove the saucepan from the heat and add the mussels and clams. Cover and leave to stand for 5 minutes.

Divide the stew between 4 soup bowls and serve.

605 *Shellfish stew with basil & coriander*

Sea bream is not always available – you can use fillets of sea bass, tilapia or cod instead. Try adding chopped fresh basil and coriander to the dish instead of the parsley.

2 tsp sesame oil
450 g/1 lb monkfish steaks, cut into
2.5-cm/1-inch chunks
1 red onion, thinly sliced
3 garlic cloves, finely chopped
1 tsp grated fresh ginger

225 g/8 oz fine tip asparagus
175 g/6 oz mushrooms, thinly sliced
2 tbsp soy sauce
1 tbsp lemon juice
lemon wedges, to garnish
cooked noodles, to serve

Heat the oil in a wok over a medium–high heat. Add the fish, onion, garlic, ginger, asparagus and mushrooms. Stir-fry for 2–3 minutes. Stir in the soy sauce and lemon juice and cook for another minute. Remove from the heat and transfer to warm serving dishes.

Garnish with lemon wedges and serve immediately on a bed of cooked noodles.

607 *Monkfish stir-fry with broccoli*

Try using tenderstem broccoli instead of the asparagus and you can use baby corn to replace the mushrooms for a change.

608 *Monkfish stir-fry with chilli*

Replace 1 tablespoon of soy sauce with fish sauce (nam pla), use the juice of 1 lime instead of lemon juice and add 1 mild finely chopped green chilli to the pan with the garlic.

16 large scallops
1 tbsp butter
1 tbsp vegetable oil
1 tsp crushed garlic
1 tsp grated fresh ginger
1 bunch of spring onions, finely sliced

finely grated rind of 1 lime
1 small fresh red chilli, deseeded and
  very finely chopped
3 tbsp lime juice
lime wedges, to garnish
freshly cooked rice, to serve

stir-fry for 1 minute. Add the scallops and continue stir-frying over high heat for 4–5 minutes. Stir in the lime rind, chilli and lime juice and cook for a further 1 minute.

Transfer the scallops to serving plates, then spoon over the cooking juices and garnish with lime wedges. Serve hot with freshly cooked rice.

Using a sharp knife, trim the scallops to remove any black intestine, then wash and pat dry with kitchen paper. Separate the corals from the white parts, then slice each white part in half horizontally, making 2 circles.

Heat the butter and oil in a preheated wok. Add the garlic and ginger and stir-fry for 1 minute without browning. Add the spring onions and

610 *Spicy scallops with galangal*

Ginger is a familiar ingredient in Asian cooking. Galangal is another root also often used there, but little in the West. You can buy galangal in specialist stores – if you can find it, use in this recipe to replace the ginger – it has a delicious and unusual fragrance and taste.

Pad Thai

225 g/8 oz thick rice-stick noodles
2 tbsp vegetable or groundnut oil
2 garlic cloves, chopped
2 fresh red chillies, deseeded and chopped
175 g/6 oz pork fillet, thinly sliced
115 g/4 oz raw prawns, peeled and chopped
8 fresh Chinese chives, chopped
2 tbsp fish sauce
juice of 1 lime
2 tsp soft light brown sugar
2 eggs, beaten
115 g/4 oz beansprouts
4 tbsp chopped fresh coriander
115 g/4 oz unsalted peanuts, chopped, plus extra to serve
crispy fried onions, to serve

Soak the noodles in warm water for 10 minutes, drain well and set aside. Heat the oil in a wok and stir-fry the garlic, chillies and pork for 2–3 minutes. Add the prawns to the wok and stir-fry for a further 2–3 minutes.

Add the chives and noodles, then cover and cook for another 1–2 minutes. Add the fish sauce, lime juice, sugar and eggs. Cook, stirring and tossing constantly to mix in the eggs.

Stir in the beansprouts, coriander and peanuts, and serve with small dishes of crispy fried onions and extra chopped peanuts.

612 *With spring onions & tomato ketchup*

Add 6 spring onions, cut diagonally, to the pan with the garlic and chillies. Add 1 tablespoon of tomato ketchup with the fish sauce and, if you like, replace the pork with double the weight of prawns.

---

613 *Prawns with coconut rice*

115 g/4 oz dried Chinese mushrooms
2 tbsp vegetable or groundnut oil
6 spring onions, chopped
55 g/2 oz desiccated coconut
1 fresh green chilli, deseeded and chopped

225 g/8 oz jasmine rice
150 ml/5 fl oz fish stock
400 ml/14 fl oz coconut milk
350 g/12 oz cooked peeled prawns
6 sprigs fresh Thai basil

Place the mushrooms in a small bowl, cover with hot water and set aside to soak for 30 minutes. Drain, then cut off and discard the stalks and slice the caps.

Heat 1 tablespoon of the oil in a wok and stir-fry the spring onions, coconut and chilli for 2–3 minutes, until lightly browned. Add the mushrooms and stir-fry for 3–4 minutes. Add the rice and stir-fry for 2–3 minutes, then add the stock and bring to the boil. Reduce the heat and add the coconut milk. Simmer for 10–15 minutes, until the rice is tender. Stir in the prawns and basil, heat through and serve.

614 *Prawns with straw mushrooms*

Replace the dried mushrooms with a 400 g/14 oz can of straw mushrooms (drained) and use 2 shallots instead of the spring onions.

615 Stir-fried noodles with marinated fish

450 g/1 lb monkfish or cod, cubed
225 g/8 oz salmon fillets, cubed
115 g/4 oz wide rice noodles
2 tbsp vegetable or groundnut oil
2 shallots, sliced
2 garlic cloves, finely chopped
1 fresh red chilli, deseeded and
    chopped
2 tbsp Thai soy sauce

2 tbsp chilli sauce
chopped coriander, to garnish

MARINADE
2 tbsp vegetable or groundnut oil
2 fresh green chillies, deseeded and
    chopped
grated rind and juice of 1 lime
1 tbsp fish sauce

Place the fish in a shallow bowl. To make the marinade, mix the oil, green chillies, lime juice and rind and fish sauce together and pour over the fish. Cover and chill for 2 hours.

Put the noodles in a bowl and cover with boiling water. Leave for 8–10 minutes (check the packet instructions) and drain well.

Heat the oil in a wok and sauté the shallots, garlic and red chilli until lightly browned. Add the soy sauce and chilli sauce. Add the fish and the marinade to the wok and stir-fry gently for 2–3 minutes until cooked through.

Add the drained noodles and stir gently. Sprinkle with coriander and serve immediately.

616 Stir-fried marinated fish

Omit the rice noodles. Cook the dish as in the recipe above but serve with egg thread noodles or jasmine rice or soba noodles. Try different fish – trout instead of salmon or seabass instead of monkfish.

617 Stir-fried scallops with asparagus

225 g/8 oz scallops
2 tsp salt
225 g/8 oz asparagus
3 tbsp vegetable or groundnut oil
55 g/2 oz fresh or canned bamboo shoots,
    rinsed and thinly sliced (if using fresh,
    boil in water first for 30 minutes)

1 small carrot, finely sliced
4 thin slices of fresh ginger
pinch of white pepper
2 tbsp Shaoxing rice wine
2 tbsp chicken stock
1 tsp sesame oil

Sprinkle the scallops with 1 teaspoon of the salt and set aside for 20 minutes. Trim the asparagus, discarding the tough ends. Cut into 5-cm/2-inch pieces and blanch in a large pan of boiling water for 30 seconds. Drain and set aside.

In a preheated wok, heat 1 tablespoon of the oil and cook the scallops for 30 seconds. Drain and set aside.

In the clean wok, heat another tablespoon of the oil and stir-fry the asparagus, bamboo shoots and carrot for 2 minutes. Season with the remaining salt. Drain and set aside.

In the clean wok, heat the remaining oil, then add the ginger and stir-fry until fragrant. Return the scallops and vegetables to the wok and sprinkle with the pepper, Shaoxing and stock. Cover and continue cooking for 2 minutes, then add the sesame oil, toss and serve.

618 Stir-fried scallops with broccoli

When asparagus is not in season a good substitute is tenderstem broccoli with slim green tasty spears, which are quite similar and cook in the same time. You could also use French beans, which should be blanched for 1 minute.

Stir-fried squid with hot black bean sauce

- 750 g/1 lb 10 oz squid, cleaned and tentacles discarded
- 1 large red pepper, deseeded
- 115 g/4 oz mangetout
- 1 head of pak choi
- 3 tbsp black bean sauce
- 1 tbsp Thai fish sauce
- 1 tbsp rice wine or dry sherry
- 1 tbsp dark soy sauce
- 1 tsp brown sugar
- 1 tsp cornflour
- 1 tbsp water
- 1 tbsp maize oil
- 1 tsp sesame oil
- 1 small fresh red Thai chilli, chopped
- 1 garlic clove, finely chopped
- 1 tsp grated fresh ginger
- 2 spring onions, chopped

Cut the squid body cavities into quarters lengthways. Score a diamond pattern into the flesh, with the tip of a small, sharp knife. Pat dry with kitchen paper.

Cut the pepper into long, thin slices and cut the mangetout in half diagonally. Coarsely shred the pak choi.

Mix the black bean sauce, fish sauce, rice wine, soy sauce and sugar together in a bowl. Blend the cornflour with the water and stir into the other sauce ingredients. Reserve the mixture until required.

Heat the oils in a preheated wok. Add the chilli, garlic, ginger and spring onions and stir-fry for 1 minute. Add the pepper slices and stir-fry for 2 minutes.

Add the squid and stir-fry over high heat for a further 1 minute.

Stir in the mangetout and pak choi and stir for a further 1 minute, or until wilted.

Stir in the sauce ingredients and cook, stirring constantly, for 2 minutes, or until the sauce thickens and clears. Serve the stir-fry immediately.

620 *Stir-fried squid with sugar snap peas*

Sugar snap peas and shredded Chinese cabbage make good alternatives to mangetout and pak choi.

Stir-fried fresh crab with ginger

- 3 tbsp vegetable or groundnut oil
- 2 large fresh crabs, cleaned, broken into pieces and legs cracked with a cleaver
- 55 g/2 oz fresh ginger, julienned
- 100 g/3½ oz spring onions, chopped into 5-cm/2-inch lengths
- 2 tbsp light soy sauce
- 1 tsp sugar
- pinch of white pepper

In a preheated wok, heat 2 tablespoons of the oil and cook the crab over high heat for 3–4 minutes. Remove and set aside. Wipe the wok clean.

In the clean wok, heat the remaining oil, then add the ginger and stir until fragrant. Add the spring onions, then stir in the crab pieces. Add the light soy sauce, sugar and pepper. Cover and simmer for 1 minute and serve immediately.

622 *Stir-fried fresh crab with chilli*

Replace the ginger with 3–4 medium–hot fresh chillies, finely chopped.

Rice and Pasta

½ tsp saffron threads
2 tbsp hot water
3 tbsp olive oil
1 courgette, diced
150 g/5½ oz button mushrooms
2 spring onions, diced
2 garlic cloves, crushed
1 tsp paprika
¼ tsp cayenne pepper
250 g/9 oz canned red kidney beans
(drained weight)
225 g/8 oz tomatoes, peeled and
chopped
375 g/13 oz paella rice
1.2 litres/2 pints simmering
vegetable stock
125 g/4½ oz peas
1 tbsp chopped fresh flat-leaf parsley,
plus extra to garnish
4 large red peppers, tops cut off and
reserved and seeds removed
100 g/3½ oz Manchego or Parmesan
cheese, grated
salt and pepper
mixed salad and crusty bread,
to serve

Preheat the oven to 180°C/350°F/Gas Mark 4. Put the saffron threads and water in a bowl to infuse. Meanwhile, heat the oil in a paella pan over a medium heat and cook the courgette, stirring, for 3 minutes.

Add the mushrooms and spring onions and cook, stirring, until softened. Add the garlic, paprika, cayenne pepper, and saffron and its soaking liquid and cook, stirring, for 1 minute. Add the beans and tomatoes and cook, stirring, for 2 minutes.

Add the rice and cook, stirring, for 1 minute to coat. Add most of the stock and bring to the boil, then simmer, uncovered, for 10 minutes. Do not stir during cooking, but shake the pan once or twice. Add the peas and parsley, season, and shake the pan. Cook for 10–15 minutes, or until the rice grains are cooked, adding remaining stock if necessary. When all the liquid has been absorbed, remove from the heat.

Cover with foil and let stand for 5 minutes. Blanch the red peppers and their tops in a pan of boiling water for 2 minutes. Drain and pat dry with kitchen paper. Spoon a little cheese into each, then fill with paella and top with the remaining cheese.

Replace the tops. Wrap each pepper in foil, then stand in an ovenproof dish and bake in the oven for 25–30 minutes.

Garnish with chopped parsley and serve with a mixed salad and warm crusty bread.

624 *Paella-stuffed peppers with ham*

The recipe above is suitable for vegetarians and vegans. For meat eaters, cook 150 g/5½ oz diced Serrano ham, or prosciutto, in 1 tablespoon of olive oil for 5 minutes, then mix it with the paella just before stuffing the peppers.

½ tsp saffron threads
2 tbsp hot water
150 g/5½ oz cod fillet, skinned and
rinsed under cold running water
1.2 litres/2 pints simmering fish stock
12 large raw prawns, peeled
and deveined
450 g/1 lb raw squid, cleaned and cut
into rings or bite-sized pieces
(or use the same quantity
of shucked scallops)
3 tbsp olive oil
1 large red onion, chopped
2 garlic cloves, crushed
1 small fresh red chilli, deseeded
and minced
225 g/8 oz tomatoes, peeled and cut
into wedges
375 g/13 oz medium-grain paella rice
1 tbsp chopped fresh parsley
2 tsp chopped fresh dill
salt and pepper
1 lemon, cut into halves, to serve

Put the saffron threads and water in a small bowl and leave to infuse for a few minutes.

Add the cod to the saucepan of simmering stock and cook for 5 minutes, then transfer to a colander, rinse under cold running water and drain. Add the prawns and squid to the stock and cook for 2 minutes. Cut the cod into chunks, then transfer with the other seafood to a bowl and set aside. Let the stock simmer.

Heat the oil in a paella pan and stir in the onion over a medium heat until softened. Add the garlic, chilli and saffron and its soaking liquid and cook, stirring, for 1 minute. Add the tomato wedges and cook, stirring, for 2 minutes. Add the rice and herbs and cook, stirring, for 1 minute. Add most of the stock and bring to the boil. Simmer, uncovered, for 10 minutes. Do not stir during cooking, but shake the pan once or twice and also when adding ingredients. Season and cook for 10 minutes, until the rice is almost cooked. Add more stock if necessary. Add the seafood and cook for 2 minutes.

When all the liquid has been absorbed and you detect a faint toasty aroma coming from the rice, remove from the heat immediately.

Cover with foil and stand for 5 minutes. Serve with the lemon halves.

626 *Seafood paella with white fish*

Instead of the cod, try using other types of tasty white fish – for example, bream, tilapia, hake, megrim, lemon sole or red or grey mullet. Take care to remove all bones or ask your fishmonger to do this for you.

125 g/4½ oz butter
900 g/2 lb skinless, boneless
chicken breasts, thinly sliced
1 large onion, chopped
500 g/1 lb 2 oz risotto rice
150 ml/5 fl oz white wine
1 tsp crumbled saffron threads
1.2 litres/2 pints chicken stock,
simmering
55 g/2 oz freshly grated Parmesan
cheese
salt and pepper

Heat 55 g/2 oz of the butter in a deep saucepan. Add the chicken and onion and cook, stirring frequently, for 8 minutes, or until golden brown.

Add the rice and mix to coat in the butter. Cook, stirring constantly for 2–3 minutes, or until the grains are translucent. Add the wine and cook, stirring constantly, for 1 minute until reduced. Add the saffron and a quarter of the stock and cook, stirring constantly, until the liquid is absorbed. Gradually add the remaining hot stock, a ladleful at a time. Stir constantly and add more liquid as the rice absorbs each addition.

Cook for 20 minutes, or until all the liquid is absorbed and the rice is creamy. Season to taste with salt and pepper. Remove the risotto from the heat and add the remaining butter.

Mix well, then stir in the Parmesan until it melts. Spoon the risotto onto warmed plates and serve immediately.

628 *Golden chicken risotto*

SERVES 4

2 tbsp sunflower oil
1 tbsp butter
1 leek, thinly sliced
1 large yellow pepper, deseeded
and diced
3 skinless, boneless chicken breasts,
diced
350 g/12 oz arborio rice
few saffron threads
1.5 litres/2¾ pints chicken stock,
simmering
200 g/7 oz canned sweetcorn
55 g/2 oz toasted unsalted peanuts
55 g/2 oz freshly grated
Parmesan cheese
salt and pepper

Heat the oil and butter in a large heavy-based saucepan. Add the leek and pepper and fry for 1 minute, then stir in the chicken and cook, stirring constantly, until golden brown.

Stir in the rice and cook for 2–3 minutes. Stir in the saffron threads and add salt and pepper to taste. Add the stock, a ladleful at a time, then cover and cook over a low heat, stirring occasionally, for 20 minutes, or until the rice is tender and most of the liquid is absorbed. Do not let the risotto dry out – add more stock if necessary.

Stir in the sweetcorn, peanuts and Parmesan cheese, then taste and adjust the seasoning if necessary. Serve the risotto hot.

629 *Golden chicken risotto with squash*

For a pretty mix of yellow, gold and light orange, omit the leek but replace with 4 spring onions (white parts only), chopped, and add 175 g/6 oz orange-fleshed pumpkin or squash – chop it into 1-cm/⅓-inch cubes and add to the frying pan with the pepper.

125 g/4½ oz butter
900 g/2 lb skinless, boneless turkey
   breasts, thinly sliced
1 large onion, chopped
500 g/1 lb 2 oz arborio rice
1.2 litres/2 pints chicken or turkey stock
125 ml/4 fl oz white wine

25 ml/1 fl oz Marsala wine or dry sherry
1 tsp crumbled saffron threads
salt and pepper
fresh flat-leaf parsley sprigs, to garnish
55 g/2 oz freshly grated Parmesan cheese,
   to serve

Heat 55 g/2 oz of the butter in a deep frying pan. Add the turkey and onion and fry until golden brown. Add the rice, stir well and cook gently for 5 minutes.

Heat the stock in a separate saucepan until boiling, then gradually add to the rice a ladleful at a time. Reserve the last ladleful of stock. Add the wine, Marsala, saffron, salt and pepper to taste and mix well. Simmer gently for 20 minutes, stirring occasionally and adding extra stock if the risotto becomes too dry.

A risotto should have moist but separate grains. Stock should be added a little at a time and only when the previous addition has been completely absorbed. Remove the frying pan from the heat and leave to stand for a few minutes. Just before serving, add the reserved stock and simmer for a further 10 minutes. Transfer the risotto to 4 large serving plates and garnish with the parsley. Serve with the grated Parmesan cheese and remaining butter.

631 *With extra stock*

Although adding white wine to a risotto does make it taste even better, you can omit the wine and simply add more stock. You can also make the risotto using leftover cooked chicken or other poultry – simply add the meat pieces to the frying pan with the rice.

Prawn & chicken paella

16 live mussels
½ tsp saffron threads
2 tbsp hot water
350 g/12 oz paella rice
6 tbsp olive oil
6–8 boned chicken thighs
140 g/5 oz Spanish chorizo
sausage, sliced
100 g/3½ oz French beans, chopped
125 g/4½ oz frozen peas
1.3 litres/2¼ pints fish stock
16 raw prawns, peeled and deveined
2 red peppers, halved and
deseeded, then grilled, peeled
and sliced
salt and pepper
35 g/1¼ oz fresh chopped
parsley, to garnish

Soak the mussels in lightly salted water for 10 minutes. Put the saffron threads and water in a small bowl or cup and leave to infuse for a few minutes.

Meanwhile, put the rice in a sieve and rinse in cold water until the water runs clear. Set aside. Heat 3 tablespoons of the oil in a 30-cm/12-inch paella pan or ovenproof casserole. Cook the chicken thighs over a medium–high heat, turning frequently, for 5 minutes, or until golden and crispy. Using a slotted spoon, transfer to a bowl. Add the chorizo to the pan and cook, stirring, for 1 minute, or until beginning to crisp. Add to the chicken. Add the drained rice, beans and peas and stir until coated in oil. Return the chicken and chorizo and any accumulated juices to the pan. Stir in the stock, saffron and its soaking liquid, and salt and pepper to taste and bring to the boil, stirring constantly. Reduce the heat to low and let simmer, uncovered and without stirring, for 15 minutes, or until the rice is almost tender. Arrange the mussels, prawns and red peppers on top, then cover and simmer, without stirring, for a further 5 minutes, or until the prawns turn pink and the mussels open (discard any that remain closed). Taste and adjust the seasoning if necessary. Sprinkle with the parsley and serve.

633 *Prawn & chicken paella with crayfish*

You can omit the mussels and instead add 16 unpeeled crayfish to the ingredients. If raw, cook them with the chicken thighs for 2–3 minutes, then remove from the pan, reserve and use to garnish the dish.

Seafood paella with saffron rice

1 heaped tsp saffron threads
850 ml/1½ pints hot fish or vegetable
stock, plus extra if needed
3 tbsp olive oil
400 g/14 oz monkfish fillet, cut into
bite-sized pieces
1 large Spanish onion, roughly
chopped
2 red peppers, deseeded and roughly
chopped
1 tsp paprika
1 beef tomato, chopped
275 g/9¾ oz paella or white
long-grain rice
100 g/3½ oz frozen
petits pois, thawed
500 g/1 lb 2 oz live mussels, scrubbed
and debearded
150 g/5½ oz (prepared weight)
large raw prawns, peeled and tails
left intact

Soak the saffron threads in a little of the stock in a jug or small bowl for 15 minutes. Meanwhile, heat half the oil in a large frying pan or paella pan over a high heat, add the monkfish pieces and cook for 1 minute on each side until lightly browned. Remove with a fish slice and set aside.

Heat the remaining oil in the frying pan or paella pan over a medium–high heat, add the onion and red peppers and cook, stirring, for 5 minutes, or until softened. Add the paprika and tomato and cook, stirring, for 1–2 minutes, then add the rice and stir to coat well.

Add the saffron threads and their soaking liquid, the remaining stock and the petits pois, stir again and bring to a simmer. Cover and leave to simmer gently for 30 minutes.

Add the mussels and prawns with the monkfish, mixing in well. Cook for a further 10 minutes, or until the prawns are cooked and the mussels have opened, (discard any that do not open) adding a little more stock if needed.

Test a mouthful of rice to make sure that it is tender (cook for a little longer if not quite ready), then serve immediately.

635 *Seafood & chicken paella*

You can replace the monkfish with the same weight of chicken breast fillet, cut into bite-sized pieces, cooked in the same way – but brown the pieces in the pan for 3 minutes.

450 g/1 lb undyed smoked haddock,
  skinned
2 tbsp olive oil
1 onion, finely chopped
1 tsp mild curry paste

175 g/6 oz long-grain rice
55 g/2 oz butter
3 hard-boiled eggs
salt and pepper
2 tbsp chopped fresh parsley, to garnish

Place the smoked haddock in a large saucepan and cover with water.
Bring the water to the boil, then turn down to a simmer and poach the
fish for 8–10 minutes until it flakes easily.

Remove the fish and keep warm, reserving the water in a jug or
bowl. Add the oil to the saucepan and gently soften the onion for
about 4 minutes. Stir in the curry paste and add the rice.

Measure 600 ml/1 pint of the haddock water and return to the
saucepan. Bring to a simmer and cover. Cook for 10–12 minutes until
the rice is tender and the water has been absorbed. Season to taste with
salt and pepper. Flake the fish and add to the saucepan with the butter.
Stir very gently over a low heat until the butter has melted. Chop 2 of
the hard-boiled eggs and add to the saucepan.

Turn the kedgeree into a serving dish, slice the remaining egg and
use to garnish. Scatter the parsley over and serve immediately.

637 *With petits pois*

Peas are often included in kedgeree – add 100 g/3½ oz cooked petits pois
to the ingredients and stir into the rice with the fish.

638 *Kedgeree with individual spices*

You can use individual spices instead of the curry paste if you like – use
4 cardamom pods and ¼ teaspoon each of ground turmeric, coriander seed,
cumin and hot chilli powder plus 1 bay leaf. Stir into the oil when the onion
is nearly ready, until you smell the aromas. Remove bay leaf before serving.

639 *Kedgeree with salmon*

Replace the smoked haddock with 450 g/1 lb salmon.

Lobster risotto

SERVES 2

1 cooked lobster, about 400–450 g/
    14 oz–1 lb
1 tbsp olive oil
55 g/2 oz butter
½ onion, finely chopped
1 garlic clove, finely chopped
1 tsp chopped fresh thyme leaves

175 g/6 oz arborio rice
150 ml/5 fl oz sparkling white wine
600 ml/1 pint fish stock, simmering
1 tsp green or pink peppercorns in brine,
    drained and roughly chopped
1 tbsp chopped fresh parsley

To prepare the lobster, remove the claws by twisting them. Crack the claws using the back of a large knife and set aside. Split the body lengthways. Remove and discard the intestinal vein, the stomach sac and the spongy gills.

Remove the meat from the tail and roughly chop. Set aside with the claws.

Heat the oil with half the butter in a large saucepan over a medium heat. Add the onion and cook, stirring occasionally, for 5 minutes until softened. Add the garlic and cook for a further 30 seconds. Stir in the thyme. Reduce the heat, add the rice and mix to coat in butter and oil. Cook, stirring constantly, for 2–3 minutes, or until the grains are translucent.

Stir in the wine and cook, stirring constantly, for 1 minute until reduced. Gradually add the hot stock, a ladleful at a time. Stir constantly and add more liquid as the rice absorbs each addition.

Increase the heat to medium so that the liquid bubbles. Cook for 20 minutes, or until all the liquid is absorbed and the rice is creamy. Five minutes before the end of cooking time, add the lobster meat and claws.

Remove the saucepan from the heat and stir in the peppercorns, remaining butter and the parsley. Spoon onto warmed plates and serve immediately.

641 *King prawn risotto*

For a slightly less expensive version, you could substitute 450 g/1 lb King or tiger prawns for the lobster. If you peel them yourself, you can use the heads and shells to make a delicately flavoured shellfish stock.

642 *Risotto with sole & tomatoes*

SERVES 4

3 tbsp butter
3 tbsp olive oil
1 small onion, finely chopped
280 g/10 oz arborio rice
1.2 litres/2 pints fish or chicken
    stock, simmering
450 g/1 lb tomatoes, peeled, deseeded
    and cut into strips
6 sun-dried tomatoes in olive oil,
    drained and thinly sliced
3 tbsp tomato purée
50 ml/2 fl oz red wine
450 g/1 lb sole or flounder fillets,
    skinned
115 g/4 oz freshly grated Parmesan
    or Grana Padano cheese
salt and pepper
2 tbsp finely chopped fresh coriander,
    to garnish

Melt 2 tablespoons of the butter with 1 tablespoon of the oil in a deep saucepan over a medium heat. Stir in the onion and cook, stirring occasionally, for 5 minutes, or until soft and starting to turn golden.

Reduce the heat, add the rice and mix to coat in the oil and butter. Cook, stirring constantly, for 2–3 minutes, or until the grains are translucent. Add the hot stock, a ladleful at a time, stirring constantly, until all the liquid is absorbed and the rice is creamy. Season with salt and pepper.

Meanwhile, heat the remaining oil in a large, heavy-based frying pan. Add the fresh and dried tomatoes. Stir well and cook over a medium heat for 10–15 minutes, or until soft and slushy. Stir in the tomato purée and wine. Bring to the boil, then reduce the heat until it is just simmering. Cut the fish into strips and gently stir into the sauce. Cook for 5 minutes, or until the fish flakes when checked with a fork. Most of the liquid should be absorbed but, if it isn't, remove the fish and then increase the heat to reduce the sauce.

Remove the risotto from the heat when all the liquid has been absorbed and add the remaining butter. Mix well, then stir in the Parmesan until it melts. Place the risotto on serving plates and arrange the fish and sauce on top. Garnish with chopped fresh coriander and serve immediately.

643 *Light risotto with sole & tomatoes*

For a lighter risotto in colour and flavour, use a white wine such as Pinot Grigio instead of the red wine – you can also stir 50 g/2 oz buffalo mozzarella cheese, torn into small pieces, into the risotto with the Parmesan cheese.

3 tbsp olive oil
1 onion, finely chopped
1 red pepper, deseeded and thinly sliced
1 garlic clove, crushed
225 g/8 oz long-grain white rice
700 ml/1¼ pints fish, chicken or
    vegetable stock
1 bay leaf
400 g/14 oz peeled, cooked prawns,
    thawed and drained if frozen

salt and pepper
grated kefalotiri or pecorino cheese,
    to serve
cubes of Greek feta cheese, to serve

TO GARNISH
whole cooked prawns
lemon wedges
black Greek olives

taste. Bring to the boil, cover the pan with a tightly fitting lid and simmer for about 15 minutes or until the rice is tender and the liquid has been absorbed. Do not stir during cooking. When the rice is cooked, very gently stir in the prawns.

Remove the lid, cover the frying pan with a clean tea towel, replace the lid and stand in a warm place for 10 minutes to dry out. Stir with a fork to separate the grains. Serve garnished with whole prawns, lemon wedges and black olives. Accompany with kefalotiri or pecorino cheese for sprinkling on top, and a bowl of feta cubes.

645 *With courgette*

Try adding 1 thinly sliced courgette to the oiled pan before you add the onion and pepper. Cook it over medium–high heat, stirring, until golden, then turn the heat down to add the remainder of the vegetables.

Heat the oil in a large, lidded frying pan. Add the onion, red pepper and garlic and fry for 5 minutes or until softened.

Add the rice and cook for 2–3 minutes, stirring all the time, until the grains look transparent. Add the stock, bay leaf and salt and pepper to

8–12 raw baby squid, cleaned, rinsed
and patted dry
150 g/5½ oz butter
1 tbsp olive oil
1 small onion, finely chopped
280 g/10 oz arborio rice
1.2 litres/2 pints fish
or chicken stock, simmering
3 garlic cloves, crushed
85 g/3 oz freshly grated Parmesan
or Grana Padano cheese
salt and pepper
2 tbsp finely chopped fresh parsley,
to garnish

Cut the squid in half lengthways, then score with a sharp knife, making horizontal and vertical cuts. Dice the larger tentacles.

Melt 2 tablespoons of the butter with the oil in a deep saucepan over a medium heat. Cook the onion, stirring, until soft and starting to turn golden. Stir in the rice and cook, stirring, until the grains are translucent. Gradually add the hot stock, a ladleful at a time. Stir constantly and add more liquid as the rice absorbs each addition. Cook for 20 minutes, or until all the liquid is absorbed and the rice is creamy. Season to taste with salt and pepper. When the risotto is nearly cooked, melt 115 g/4 oz of the remaining butter in a heavy-based frying pan.

Add the garlic and cook over a low heat until soft. Increase the heat to high, add the squid and toss to cook for no more than 2–3 minutes or the squid will become tough. Remove the squid from the pan, draining carefully and reserving the garlic butter.

Remove the risotto from the heat and stir in the remaining butter, then stir in the Parmesan until it melts. Transfer to warmed serving plates and arrange the squid on top. Spoon some garlic butter over each portion. Serve immediately, sprinkled with chopped parsley.

647 *Risotto with octopus & herb butter*

Use octopus meat instead of the squid – 1 or 2 tentacles, weighing about 250 g/9 oz in total should be sufficient – cut into slices and use as above. Add 2 teaspoons of fresh chopped oregano to the pan with the garlic and butter.

Fish & rice with dark rum

SERVES 4

450 g/1 lb firm white fish fillets
(such as cod or monkfish), skinned
and cut into 2.5-cm/1-inch cubes
2 tsp ground cumin
2 tsp dried oregano
2 tbsp lime juice
150 ml/5 fl oz dark rum
1 tbsp dark muscovado sugar
3 garlic cloves, finely chopped
1 large onion, chopped
1 each of red pepper, green pepper,
yellow pepper, deseeded and sliced
into rings
1.2 litres/2 pints fish stock
350 g/12 oz long-grain rice
salt and pepper
fresh oregano leaves and lime wedges ,
to garnish
crusty bread, to serve

Place the cubes of fish in a bowl and add the cumin, oregano, lime juice, rum and sugar. Season to taste with salt and pepper. Mix thoroughly, cover with clingfilm and set aside to chill for 2 hours.

Meanwhile, place the garlic, onion and peppers in a large saucepan. Pour in the stock and stir in the rice. Bring to the boil, reduce the heat, then cover and simmer for 15 minutes.

Gently stir in the fish and the marinade juices. Bring back to the boil and simmer, uncovered, stirring occasionally but taking care not to break up the fish, for about 10 minutes, until the fish is cooked through and the rice is tender.

Season to taste with salt and pepper and transfer to a warmed serving plate. Garnish with fresh oregano and lime wedges and serve with crusty bread.

Tiger prawn & asparagus risotto

SERVES 4

1.2 litres/2 pints vegetable stock
350 g/12 oz fresh asparagus spears, cut
into 5-cm/2-inch lengths
2 tbsp olive oil
1 onion, finely chopped
1 garlic clove, finely chopped
325 g/11½ oz risotto rice

450 g/1 lb raw tiger prawns, shelled
and deveined
2 tbsp olive paste or tapenade
2 tbsp chopped fresh basil
salt and pepper
freshly grated Parmesan cheese, to garnish
fresh basil sprigs, to garnish

Bring the stock to the boil in a large pan. Add the asparagus and cook for 3 minutes until just tender. Strain, reserving the stock, and refresh the asparagus under cold running water. Drain and set aside. Return the stock to the pan and keep simmering gently over a low heat while you are cooking the risotto. Heat the olive oil in a large heavy-based pan. Add the onion and cook over medium heat, stirring occasionally, for 5 minutes until softened. Add the garlic and cook for an additional 30 seconds. Reduce the heat, add the rice, and mix to coat in oil. Cook, stirring constantly, for 2–3 minutes, or until the grains are translucent.

Gradually add the hot stock, a ladleful at a time. Stir constantly and add more liquid as the rice absorbs each addition. Increase the heat to medium so that the liquid bubbles. Cook for about 20 minutes, until all the liquid is absorbed and the rice is creamy. Add the prawns and asparagus with the last ladleful of stock and cook until the prawns are pink.

Remove the pan from the heat, stir in the olive paste and basil, and season to taste. Serve immediately, garnished with Parmesan cheese and basil sprigs.

Tiger prawn risotto with pesto

Replace the olive tapenade with 2 tablespoons of red pepper pesto for a nice change and a pretty colour.

651 Venetian seafood risotto

SERVES 4

225 g/8 oz prepared raw prawns, heads and shells reserved	1 tbsp olive oil
2 garlic cloves, halved	1 onion, finely chopped
1 lemon, sliced	2 tbsp chopped fresh flat-leaf parsley
225 g/8 oz live mussels, scrubbed and debearded	350 g/12 oz arborio rice
225 g/8 oz live clams, scrubbed	125 ml/4 fl oz dry white wine
600 ml/1 pint water	225 g/8 oz cleaned raw squid, cut into small pieces, or squid rings
115 g/4 oz butter	4 tbsp Marsala
	salt and pepper

Wrap the prawn heads and shells in a square of muslin and pound with a pestle. Put the wrapped shells and their liquid in a saucepan with the garlic, lemon, mussels and clams. Add the water, cover and bring to the boil over a high heat. Cook, shaking the pan frequently, for 5 minutes until the shellfish have opened. Discard any that remain closed. Cool, then shell the mussels and clams and set aside.

Strain the cooking liquid through a muslin-lined sieve and add water to make 1.2 litres/ 2 pints. Bring to the boil in a pan, then simmer over a low heat. Melt 2 tablespoons of butter with the olive oil. Cook the onion and half the parsley until softened. Reduce the heat, stir in the rice and cook, stirring, until the grains are translucent. Add the wine and cook, stirring, for 1 minute. Add the hot cooking liquid a ladleful at a time, stirring constantly, until all the liquid is absorbed.

Melt 55 g/2 oz of the remaining butter in a pan. Cook the squid, stirring frequently, for 3 minutes. Add the prawns and cook for 2–3 minutes, until the squid is opaque and the prawns have changed colour. Add the Marsala, bring to the boil, and cook until the liquid has evaporated. Stir the seafood into the rice, add the remaining butter and parsley, and season. Heat gently and serve immediately.

652 Venetian seafood risotto with sherry

Marsala is an Italian semi-sweet fortified wine – you can substitute it with medium sherry or Madeira if you like.

653 Spicy monkfish rice

SERVES 4

1 fresh hot red chilli, deseeded and chopped	375 g/12 oz monkfish fillet, cut into bite-sized pieces
1 tsp chilli flakes	1 onion, finely chopped
2 garlic cloves, chopped	225 g/8 oz long-grain rice
pinch of saffron	400 g/14 oz canned chopped tomatoes
3 tbsp roughly chopped fresh mint leaves	200 ml/7 fl oz coconut milk
4 tbsp olive oil	115 g/4 oz peas
2 tbsp lemon juice	salt and pepper
	2 tbsp chopped fresh mint, to garnish

Process the chilli, chilli flakes, garlic, saffron, mint, olive oil and lemon juice in a food processor or blender until combined, but not smooth. Put the monkfish into a non-metallic dish and pour over the spice paste, turning to coat. Cover and set aside for 20 minutes to marinate.

Heat a large pan until very hot. Using a slotted spoon, lift the monkfish from the marinade and add, in batches, to the hot pan. Cook for 3–4 minutes until browned and firm. Remove with a slotted spoon and set aside.

Add the onion and remaining marinade to the pan and cook for 5 minutes until softened and lightly browned. Add the rice and stir until well coated. Add the tomatoes and coconut milk.

Bring to the boil, cover and simmer gently for 15 minutes. Stir in the peas, season and arrange the fish over the top. Cover with foil and continue to cook over a very low heat for 5 minutes. Serve garnished with the chopped mint.

654 With aubergine

Try adding 1 small aubergine, thinly sliced, to the pan before the onion, and 1–2 tablespoons of extra oil. Cook until lightly golden then turn the heat down a little and proceed with the recipe.

Risotto with tuna & pine kernels

SERVES 4

3 tbsp butter
4 tbsp olive oil
1 small onion, finely chopped
280 g/10 oz arborio rice
1.2 litres/2 pints fish or chicken
stock, simmering
225 g/8 oz tuna, canned and drained,
or grilled fresh steaks
8–10 black olives, pitted and sliced
1 small pimiento, thinly sliced
1 tsp finely chopped fresh parsley
1 tsp finely chopped fresh marjoram
2 tbsp white wine vinegar
55 g/2 oz pine kernels
1 garlic clove, chopped
225 g/8 oz fresh tomatoes, peeled,
deseeded and diced
85 g/3 oz freshly grated Parmesan or
Grana Padano cheese, plus extra
to serve
salt and pepper

Melt 2 tablespoons of the butter with 1 tablespoon of the oil in a deep saucepan over a medium heat. Add the onion and cook, stirring occasionally, until softened. Reduce the heat, add the rice and mix to coat in oil and butter. Cook, stirring constantly, until the grains are translucent. Add the hot stock, a ladleful at a time, stirring constantly, until all the liquid is absorbed and the rice is creamy. Season to taste.

While the risotto is cooking, flake the tuna and mix with the olives, pimiento, parsley, marjoram, vinegar and seasoning in a bowl.

Heat the remaining oil in a small frying pan over a high heat. Add the pine kernels and garlic. Cook, stirring constantly, for

2 minutes. Add the tomatoes and mix well. Continue cooking over a medium heat for 3–4 minutes or until they are thoroughly warm. Pour the tomato mixture over the tuna mixture and mix. Fold into the risotto 5 minutes before the end of the cooking time.

Remove the risotto from the heat when all the liquid has been absorbed and add the remaining butter. Mix well, then stir in the Parmesan until it melts. Serve immediately with cheese to hand round separately.

656 Risotto with tuna & almonds

Use 85 g/3 oz toasted flaked almonds instead of the pine kernels and use sliced stoned green olives instead of the black ones.

Hot pepper lamb in red wine risotto

SERVES 4

4 tbsp plain flour
50 ml/2 fl oz olive oil
8 pieces neck of lamb or lamb cutlets
1 green pepper, deseeded and thinly
sliced
1–2 fresh green chillies, deseeded and
thinly sliced
1 small onion, thinly sliced
2 garlic cloves, thinly sliced

2 tbsp roughly torn fresh basil
125 ml/4 fl oz red wine
4 tbsp red wine vinegar
8 cherry tomatoes
125 ml/4 fl oz water
1 quantity Basic Risotto (see page 9)
made with beef stock and red wine
salt and pepper

Mix the flour with salt and pepper to taste on a plate. Heat the oil in a frying pan large enough to take all the lamb in a single layer over a high heat. Coat the lamb in the seasoned flour, shaking off any excess. Brown the lamb in the pan, remove with a slotted spoon and set aside. Toss the pepper, chillies, onion, garlic and basil in the oil left in the pan for 3 minutes, or until lightly browned. Add the wine and vinegar, bring to the boil and continue cooking over a high heat for 3–4 minutes, or until reduced to 2 tablespoons.

Add the tomatoes and water to the pan, stir and bring to the boil. Return the meat, cover and reduce the heat as low as possible.

Cook for 30 minutes, or until the meat is tender, turning occasionally. Check regularly and add 2–3 tablespoons of water if necessary. Meanwhile, prepare the Basic Risotto as on page 9. Arrange a scoop of risotto on each plate and sprinkle with some of the lamb, peppers and tomatoes and serve.

658 Hot pepper pork in red wine risotto

Pork fillet makes a good alternative to lamb in this recipe – cook it in the same way. You could even use chicken fillet or steak, both of which would not need so long simmering – they should be ready after 10 minutes.

Baked tomato rice

2 tbsp vegetable oil
1 onion, roughly chopped
1 red pepper, deseeded and chopped
2 garlic cloves, finely chopped
½ tsp dried thyme
300 g/10½ oz long-grain rice
1 litre/1¾ pints chicken or vegetable
stock
225 g/8 oz canned chopped tomatoes
1 bay leaf
2 tbsp shredded fresh basil
175 g/6 oz mature Cheddar cheese,
grated
2 tbsp snipped fresh chives
4 herbed pork sausages, cooked and
cut into 1-cm/½-inch pieces
2–3 tbsp freshly grated Parmesan
cheese

Preheat the oven to 180°C/350°F/Gas Mark 4. Heat the oil in a large flameproof casserole over a medium heat. Add the onion and pepper and cook, stirring frequently, for 5 minutes, or until soft. Stir in the garlic and thyme and cook for a further minute. Add the rice and cook, stirring frequently, for 2 minutes, or until the rice is translucent.

Stir in the stock, tomatoes and bay leaf. Bring to the boil, then simmer rapidly for 5 minutes, or until the stock is almost completely absorbed.

Stir in the basil, Cheddar cheese, chives and sausages and bake, covered, in the oven for 25 minutes. Sprinkle with the Parmesan cheese and return to the oven, uncovered, for 5 minutes, or until the top is golden. Serve hot.

660 *Vegetarian baked tomato rice*

For a vegetarian version, replace the pork sausages with 400 g/14 oz canned drained butter beans, kidney beans or sweetcorn. Alternatively, try a mixture of sautéed mushrooms and courgettes.

Mexican tomato rice

400 g/14 oz long-grain rice
1 large onion, chopped
2–3 garlic cloves, crushed
350 g/12 oz canned Italian plum
tomatoes
3–4 tbsp olive oil
1 litre/1¾ pints chicken stock
1 tbsp tomato purée
1 habanero or other hot chilli
175 g/6 oz frozen peas, thawed
4 tbsp chopped fresh coriander, plus
extra to serve
salt and pepper

TO SERVE
1 large avocado, peeled, stoned, sliced
and sprinkled with lime juice
lime wedges
4 spring onions, chopped

In a bowl, cover the rice with hot water and set aside to stand for 15 minutes. Drain, then rinse under cold running water and drain again.

Place the onion and garlic in a food processor or blender and process until a smooth purée forms. Scrape the purée into a small bowl and set aside. Put the tomatoes in the food processor and process until smooth, then press through a nylon sieve into another bowl, pushing through any solids with the back of a wooden spoon.

Heat the oil in a flameproof casserole over a medium heat. Add the rice and cook, stirring frequently, for 4 minutes until golden and translucent. Add the onion purée and cook, stirring frequently, for a further 2 minutes. Add the stock, processed tomatoes and tomato purée and bring to the boil.

Using a pin or long needle, carefully pierce the chilli in 2–3 places. Add to the rice, season to taste and reduce the heat to low. Cover and simmer for 25 minutes, or until the rice is tender and the liquid is just absorbed. Discard the chilli, stir in the peas and coriander and cook for a further 5 minutes to heat through.

To serve, fork the rice mixture into a large warmed, shallow serving bowl. Arrange the avocado slices and lime wedges on top. Sprinkle over the spring onions and coriander and serve immediately.

662 *Mexican tomato rice with sweetcorn*

For a change, use sweetcorn insead of the peas and/or use a finely chopped green pepper.

2 tbsp vegetable or groundnut oil
2 garlic cloves, finely chopped
2 fresh red chillies, deseeded and chopped
115 g/4 oz mushrooms, sliced
50 g/2 oz mangetout, halved
50 g/2 oz baby corn, halved
3 tbsp Thai soy sauce
1 tbsp palm sugar or soft, light
   brown sugar

a few Thai basil leaves
350 g/12 oz rice, cooked and cooled
2 eggs, beaten

CRISPY ONION TOPPING
2 tbsp vegetable or groundnut oil
2 onions, sliced

Heat the oil in a wok or large frying pan and fry the garlic and chillies for 2–3 minutes. Add the mushrooms, mangetout and baby corn and stir-fry for 2–3 minutes before adding the soy sauce, sugar and basil. Stir in the rice.

Push the mixture to one side of the wok and add the eggs to the base and stir until lightly set before combining into the rice mixture. Heat the oil in another frying pan and sauté the onions until crispy and brown. Serve the rice topped with the onions.

664 Egg-fried rice with spring onion

Omit the crispy onion topping and instead chop 8 spring onions and add to the stir-fry mixture for the last minute of stirring time.

665 Egg-fried rice with other vegetables

Replace the mushrooms with 1 chopped red pepper; replace mangetout with 50 g/2 oz sliced French beans, and use 50 g/2 oz sweetcorn instead of the baby corn.

Sausage & rosemary risotto

2 long fresh rosemary sprigs, plus
extra to garnish
2 tbsp olive oil
55 g/2 oz butter
1 large onion, finely chopped
1 celery stick, finely chopped
2 garlic cloves, finely chopped
½ tsp dried thyme leaves
450 g/1 lb pork sausage, such as
Cumberland, cut into 1-cm/½-inch
pieces
350 g/12 oz risotto rice
125 ml/4 fl oz fruity red wine
1.3 litres/2¼ pints chicken stock,
simmering
85 g/3 oz freshly grated
Parmesan cheese
salt and pepper

Strip the long thin leaves from the rosemary sprigs and chop finely, then set aside. Heat the oil and half the butter in a deep saucepan over a medium heat.

Add the onion and celery and cook, stirring occasionally, for 2 minutes. Stir in the garlic, thyme, sausage and rosemary. Cook, stirring frequently, for 5 minutes, or until the sausage starts to brown. Transfer the sausage to a plate.

Reduce the heat and stir in the rice. Cook, stirring constantly, for 2–3 minutes, or until the grains are translucent.

Add the wine and cook, stirring, for 1 minute until reduced. Gradually add the hot stock, a ladleful at a time.

Stir constantly and add more liquid as the rice absorbs each addition. Increase the heat to medium so that the liquid bubbles. Cook for 20 minutes, or until all the liquid is absorbed and the rice is creamy.

Towards the end of cooking, return the sausage pieces to the risotto and heat through. Season to taste. Remove from the heat and add the remaining butter. Mix well, then stir in the Parmesan until it melts. Spoon the risotto onto warmed plates, garnish with rosemary sprigs and serve.

667 # Sausage, bacon & rosemary risotto

Try replacing a quarter of the sausage with lean unsmoked bacon and add in 50 g/2 oz thinly sliced chorizo. Omit the red wine and increase the amount of stock accordingly, adding 1 tablespoon of sherry to the pan.

Rice & peas

1 litre/1¾ pints chicken or
vegetable stock
85 g/3 oz butter
3 shallots, finely chopped
115 g/4 oz pancetta or rindless streaky
bacon, diced
280 g/10 oz arborio rice
150 ml/¼ pint dry white wine
225 g/8 oz petits pois, thawed if
using frozen
salt and pepper
Parmesan cheese shavings,
to garnish

Pour the stock into a large saucepan and bring to the boil. Lower the heat and simmer gently.

Melt 55 g/2 oz of the butter in another large heavy-based saucepan. Add the shallots and pancetta or bacon and cook over a low heat, stirring occasionally, for 5 minutes, until the shallots are softened. Add the rice and cook, stirring constantly, for 2–3 minutes, until all the grains are thoroughly coated and glistening. Pour in the wine and cook, stirring constantly, until it has almost completely evaporated.

Add a ladleful of hot stock and cook, stirring constantly, until all the stock has been absorbed. Continue cooking and adding the stock, a ladleful at a time, for about 10 minutes. Add the peas, then continue adding the stock, a ladleful at a time, for a further 10 minutes, or until the rice is tender and the liquid has been absorbed.

Stir in the remaining butter and season to taste. Transfer the risotto to a warmed serving dish, garnish with Parmesan shavings and serve immediately.

Orange turkey with rice

1 tbsp olive oil
1 onion, chopped
450 g/1 lb skinless lean turkey
  (such as fillet), cut into thin strips
300 ml/10 fl oz unsweetened orange juice
1 bay leaf
225 g/8 oz small broccoli florets
1 large courgette, diced

1 large orange
350 g/12 oz cooked brown rice
salt and pepper
25 g/1 oz stoned black olives in brine,
  drained and quartered, to garnish
shredded basil leaves, to garnish
tomato and onion salad, to serve

Heat the oil in a large frying pan and fry the onion and turkey, stirring, for 4–5 minutes until lightly browned.

Pour in the orange juice and add the bay leaf and seasoning. Bring to the boil and simmer for 10 minutes.

Meanwhile, bring a large saucepan of water to the boil, add the broccoli florets and cook, covered, for 2 minutes. Add the diced courgette, bring back to the boil, cover and cook for 3 minutes (do not overcook). Drain and set aside.

Using a sharp knife, peel off the skin and white pith from the orange. Thinly slice across the orange to make round slices, then halve each slice.

Stir the broccoli, courgette, rice and orange slices into the turkey mixture. Gently mix together and season, then heat through for a further 3–4 minutes until piping hot. Transfer the turkey rice to warmed serving plates and garnish with black olives and shredded basil leaves. Serve with a tomato and onion salad.

670 Orange turkey with rice & pepper

Replace the courgette with 1 large orange pepper, deseeded and sliced. You could even use 1 small sweet potato, peeled, cut into small cubes and steamed until tender – stir it in with the broccoli.

Shredded spinach & ham risotto

225 g/8 oz fresh young spinach leaves
115 g/4 oz cooked ham
1 litre/1¾ pints chicken or vegetable
  stock, simmering
1 tbsp olive oil
40 g/1½ oz butter
1 small onion, finely chopped
280 g/10 oz arborio rice
150 ml/5 fl oz dry white wine
50 ml/2 fl oz single cream
85 g/3 oz freshly grated Parmesan
  or Grana Padano cheese
salt and pepper

Wash the spinach well and slice into thin shreds. Cut the ham into thin strips. Bring the stock to the boil in a saucepan, then reduce the heat and keep simmering gently over a low heat while you are cooking the risotto. Heat the oil with 25 g/1 oz of the butter in a deep saucepan over a medium heat until the butter has melted. Add the onion and cook, stirring occasionally, for 5 minutes, or until soft and starting to turn golden. Do not brown. Reduce the heat, add the rice and mix to coat in oil and butter. Cook, stirring constantly, for 2–3 minutes, or until the grains are translucent.

Add the wine and cook, stirring constantly, for 1 minute until reduced.

Gradually add the hot stock, a ladleful at a time. Stir constantly and add more liquid as the rice absorbs each addition. Increase the heat to medium so that the liquid bubbles. Cook for 20 minutes, or until all the liquid is absorbed and the rice is creamy. Add the spinach and ham with the last ladleful of stock.

Remove the risotto from the heat and add the remaining butter and the cream. Mix well, then stir in the Parmesan until it melts. Season to taste with salt and pepper and serve immediately.

672 Shredded spinach & mushroom risotto

Vegetarians and many other people will appreciate the taste of mushrooms in this risotto instead of the ham. Add 175 g/6 oz chestnut mushrooms, sliced, to the pan with the onion and cook until lightly golden and just soft.

½ tsp saffron threads
2 tbsp hot water
150 g/5½ oz pork tenderloin, cut into
bite-sized chunks
150 g/5½ oz skinless, boneless chicken
breast, cut into bite-sized chunks
1 tsp paprika
½ tsp cayenne pepper
3 tbsp olive oil
150 g/5½ oz Spanish chorizo sausage,
casing removed, cut into ½-inch/
1-cm slices
1 large red onion, chopped
2 garlic cloves, crushed
1 small fresh red chilli, deseeded
and minced
225 g/8 oz cherry tomatoes, halved
1 red and 1 green pepper, halved and
deseeded, then grilled, peeled, and
coarsely chopped
375 g /13 oz medium-grain
paella rice
1 tbsp chopped fresh thyme, plus extra
sprigs to garnish
2 tbsp sherry
90 ml/3 fl oz white wine
1.2 litres/2 pints beef or chicken stock
or water, simmering
12 black olives, pitted and halved
salt and pepper
1 lemon, cut into wedges, to serve

Put the saffron threads and water in a small bowl or cup and let infuse for a few minutes.

Meanwhile, season the pork and chicken with the paprika, cayenne pepper and salt and pepper to taste. Heat the oil in a paella pan or wide, shallow frying pan and cook the pork, chicken and chorizo over a medium heat, stirring, for 5 minutes. Add the onion and cook, stirring, for 2–3 minutes, or until softened. Add the garlic, chilli and saffron, and its soaking liquid, and cook, stirring constantly, for 1 minute. Add the tomatoes and peppers and cook, stirring, for an additional 2 minutes.

Add the rice and thyme and cook, stirring constantly, for 1 minute, or until the rice is glossy and coated. Pour in the sherry, wine and about 1 litre/1¾ pints of the hot stock and bring to a boil. Reduce the heat and leave to simmer, uncovered, for 10 minutes. Do not stir during cooking, but shake the pan once or twice.

Add the olives and season to taste with salt and pepper. Shake the pan and cook for an additional 10 minutes, or until the rice grains are plump and almost cooked. If the liquid is absorbed too quickly, pour in a little more hot stock, then shake the pan to spread the liquid through the paella. Do not stir it in. Taste and adjust the seasoning if necessary and cook for an additional 2 minutes.

When all the liquid has been absorbed and you detect a faint toasty aroma coming from the rice, remove from the heat immediately to prevent burning. Cover the pan with a clean dish towel or foil and leave to stand for 5 minutes. Garnish with thyme sprigs and serve direct from the pan with the lemon wedges for squeezing over the rice. Alternatively, divide the paella between warmed plates and garnish with the thyme, then serve with the lemon wedges.

674 Artichoke paella

SERVES 4–6

½ tsp saffron threads
2 tbsp hot water
3 tbsp olive oil
1 large onion, chopped
1 courgette, roughly chopped
2 garlic cloves, crushed
¼ tsp cayenne pepper
225 g/8 oz tomatoes, peeled and cut
into wedges
425 g/15 oz canned chickpeas,
drained
425 g/15 oz canned artichoke hearts,
drained and roughly sliced
350 g/12 oz medium-grain paella rice
1.3 litres/2¼ pints vegetable stock,
simmering
150 g/5½ oz French beans, blanched
salt and pepper
1 lemon, cut into wedges,
to serve

Put the saffron threads and water in a small bowl to infuse for a few minutes.

Meanwhile, heat the oil in a paella pan and cook the onion and courgette over a medium heat, stirring, for 2–3 minutes, or until softened. Add the garlic, cayenne pepper, and saffron and its soaking liquid and cook, stirring constantly, for 1 minute. Add the tomato wedges, chickpeas and artichokes and cook, stirring, for a further 2 minutes. Add the rice and cook, stirring constantly, for 1 minute, or until the rice is glossy and coated. Pour in most of the hot stock and bring to the boil, then simmer, uncovered, for 10 minutes. Do not stir during cooking, but shake the pan once or twice. Add the French beans and season. Shake the pan and cook for a further 10–15 minutes, or until the rice grains are plump and cooked. If the liquid is absorbed too quickly, pour in a little more hot stock, then shake the pan to spread the liquid through the paella.

When all the liquid has been absorbed and you detect a faint toasty aroma coming from the rice, remove from the heat immediately to prevent burning. Cover the pan with foil and let stand for 5 minutes. Serve direct from the pan with the lemon wedges to squeeze over the rice.

675 Artichoke paella with asparagus

Try adding asparagus tips instead of the French beans and 100 g/3½ oz petits pois instead of the courgette. Add the peas with the tomatoes.

676 Paella with mussels & white wine

SERVES 4–6

150 g/5½ oz cod fillet, skinned and
rinsed in cold water
1.3 litres/2¼ pints fish stock,
simmering
200 g/7 oz live mussels, prepared
3 tbsp olive oil
1 large red onion, chopped
2 garlic cloves, crushed
½ tsp cayenne pepper
½ tsp saffron threads infused in
2 tbsp hot water
225 g/8 oz tomatoes, peeled and
cut into wedges
1 red pepper, deseeded and sliced
1 green pepper, deseeded and sliced
375 g/13 oz medium-grain paella rice
100 ml/3½ fl oz white wine
150 g/5½ oz shelled peas
1 tbsp chopped fresh dill, plus extra
to garnish
salt and pepper
lemon wedges, to serve

Cook the cod in the saucepan of simmering stock for 5 minutes. Transfer the cod to a colander, rinse under cold running water and drain. Cut into chunks, then transfer to a bowl.

Cook the mussels in the stock for 5 minutes, or until opened, then transfer to the bowl with the cod, discarding any that remain closed.

Heat the oil in a paella pan and stir in the onion over a medium heat until softened. Add the garlic, cayenne pepper and saffron and its soaking liquid and cook, stirring constantly, for 1 minute. Add the tomatoes and peppers and cook, stirring, for 2 minutes.

Add the rice and cook, stirring, for 1 minute. Add the wine and most of the stock and bring to the boil, then simmer for 10 minutes. Do not stir during cooking, but shake the pan once or twice and when adding ingredients. Add the peas, dill, salt and pepper. Cook for 10 minutes, or until the rice is almost cooked, adding more stock if necessary. Add the cod and mussels and cook for 3 minutes. When all the liquid has been absorbed and you detect a faint toasty aroma coming from the rice, remove from the heat immediately. Cover with foil and stand for 5 minutes. Garnish with dill and serve with lemon wedges.

677 Paella with mussels & French beans

You can replace the shelled peas with 175 g/6 oz French beans, cut into 2.5-cm/1-inch chunks, if you like. Any firm white fish fillet such as bass or haddock can be used instead of the cod.

678 Minted green risotto

2 tbsp unsalted butter
450 g/1 lb fresh shelled peas or
thawed frozen peas
1 kg/2 lb 4 oz young spinach leaves
1 bunch of fresh mint, leaves stripped
from stalks
2 tbsp chopped fresh basil
2 tbsp chopped fresh oregano
pinch of freshly grated nutmeg
4 tbsp mascarpone cheese
2 tbsp vegetable oil
1 onion, finely chopped
4 celery sticks, including leaves,
finely chopped
2 garlic cloves, finely chopped
½ tsp dried thyme
300 g/10½ oz arborio or carnaroli rice
50 ml/2 fl oz dry white vermouth
1 litre/1¾ pints simmering chicken or
vegetable stock
85 g/3 oz freshly grated
Parmesan cheese
spring onions, finely sliced,
to garnish

Heat half the butter in a deep frying pan over a medium–high heat. Add the peas, spinach, herbs and nutmeg. Cook, stirring, for 3 minutes, or until the spinach is wilted. Transfer to a food processor and process for 15 seconds. Add the mascarpone cheese and process again for 1 minute. Set aside. Heat

the oil and remaining butter in a large heavy-based saucepan over a medium heat. Add the onion, celery, garlic and thyme and cook for 2 minutes, or until softened.

Add the rice and cook, stirring, for 2 minutes, or until translucent and well coated. Pour in the vermouth; it will bubble and steam rapidly. When it is almost absorbed, add a ladleful of the simmering stock. Cook, stirring constantly, until the stock is

completely absorbed.

Continue adding the stock, about half a ladleful at a time, allowing each addition to be absorbed before adding the next. This should take 20–25 minutes. The risotto should have a creamy consistency and the rice should be tender but still firm to the bite. Stir in the spinach-cream mixture and the Parmesan cheese. Serve the risotto immediately, garnished with spring onions.

679 Minted green risotto with chard

You can use chopped chard instead of the spinach if you like, removing any large stalks; and baby broad beans instead of the peas. Add the chard to the oiled pan and cook for 2 minutes before adding the peas/beans – continue with recipe. Chopped parsley is also a good replacement for the basil; it marries very well with mint.

680 Parmesan risotto with mushrooms

2 tbsp olive oil or vegetable oil
225 g/8 oz risotto rice
2 garlic cloves, crushed
1 onion, chopped
2 celery sticks, chopped
1 red or green pepper, deseeded
and chopped
225 g/8 oz mushrooms, thinly sliced
1 tbsp chopped fresh oregano or 1 tsp
dried oregano

1 litre/1¾ pints hot vegetable stock,
simmering
55 g/2 oz sun-dried tomatoes in olive oil,
drained and chopped (optional)
55 g/2 oz finely grated Parmesan cheese
salt and pepper
fresh flat-leaf parsley sprigs or bay leaves,
to garnish

Heat the oil in a deep saucepan. Add the rice and cook over a low heat, stirring constantly, for 2–3 minutes, until the grains are thoroughly coated in oil and translucent. Add the garlic, onion, celery and pepper and cook, stirring frequently, for 5 minutes.

Add the mushrooms and cook for 3–4 minutes. Stir in the oregano. Gradually add the hot stock, a ladleful at a time. Stir constantly and add more liquid as the rice absorbs each addition. Increase the heat to medium so that the liquid bubbles. Cook for

20 minutes, or until all the liquid is absorbed and the rice is creamy. Add the sun-dried tomatoes, if using, 5 minutes before the end of the cooking time and season to taste with salt and pepper.

Remove the risotto from the heat and stir in half the Parmesan cheese until it melts. Transfer the risotto to warmed bowls. Top with the remaining cheese, garnish with flat-leaf parsley and serve immediately.

681 Parmesan risotto with cherry tomatoes

Omit the peppers and instead add 175 g/6 oz cherry tomatoes to the pan with the mushrooms.

½ tsp saffron threads

2 tbsp hot water

3 tbsp olive oil

175 g/6 oz Serrano ham, diced

1 large carrot, diced

150 g/5½ oz button mushrooms

4 large spring onions, diced

2 garlic cloves, crushed

1 tsp paprika

¼ tsp cayenne pepper

225 g/8 oz tomatoes, peeled and cut
into wedges

1 red pepper, halved and deseeded,
then grilled, peeled and sliced

1 green pepper, halved and deseeded,
then grilled, peeled and sliced

350 g/12 oz medium-grain paella rice

2 tbsp chopped mixed fresh herbs,
plus extra to garnish

100 ml/3½ fl oz white wine

1.2 litres/2 pints chicken
stock, simmering

55 g/2 oz shelled peas

100 g/3½ oz asparagus
spears, blanched

salt and pepper

lemon wedges, to serve

Put the saffron threads and water in a small bowl and leave to infuse for a few minutes.

Heat 2 tablespoons of the oil in a paella pan and cook the ham over a medium heat, stirring, for 5 minutes. Transfer to a bowl. Heat the remaining oil in the pan and cook the carrot, stirring, for 3 minutes. Add the mushrooms and cook, stirring, for 2 minutes. Add the spring onions, garlic, paprika, cayenne pepper and saffron and its soaking liquid and cook, stirring, for 1 minute. Add the tomatoes and peppers and cook, stirring, for 2 minutes.

Add the rice and herbs and cook, stirring, for 1 minute, to coat the rice. Pour in the wine and most of the hot stock and bring to the boil, then simmer, uncovered, for 10 minutes. Do not stir during cooking, but shake the pan once or twice and when adding ingredients. Add the peas and season to taste with salt and pepper. Cook for 10 minutes, or until the rice is almost cooked, adding a little more stock if necessary. Return the ham and any juices to the pan. Arrange the asparagus around the paella in a wheel pattern and cook for 2 minutes.

When all the liquid has been absorbed and you detect a faint toasty aroma coming from the rice, remove from the heat. Cover with foil and let stand for 5 minutes. Sprinkle over chopped herbs to garnish and serve with lemon wedges.

683 *Paella primavera with baby carrots*

The Italian word primavera means 'spring' so if you can cook this recipe in springtime and use all baby, springtime vegetables it will be all the better. Replace the large carrot with a small bunch of tiny baby carrots with the base of the stalks still intact – halve them lengthways if they are thicker than a little finger. Continuing with this theme you could omit the sweet peppers and instead add 1 level tablespoon of sweet smoked paprika to the pan with the other spices.

225 g/8 oz canned artichoke hearts
1 tbsp olive oil
40 g/1½ oz butter
1 small onion, finely chopped
280 g/10 oz risotto rice
1.2 litres/2 pints simmering
vegetable stock
85 g/3 oz freshly grated Parmesan or
Grana Padano cheese
salt and pepper
fresh flat-leaf parsley sprigs,
to garnish

Drain the artichoke hearts, reserving the liquid, and cut them into quarters. Heat the oil with 25 g/1 oz of the butter in a deep saucepan over a medium heat until the butter has melted. Stir in the onion and cook gently, stirring occasionally, for 5 minutes, or until soft and starting to turn golden. Do not brown. Add the rice and mix to coat in oil and butter. Cook, stirring constantly, for 2–3 minutes, or until the grains are translucent. Gradually add the artichoke liquid and the hot stock, a ladleful at a time. Stir constantly and add more liquid as the rice absorbs each addition.

Increase the heat to medium so that the liquid bubbles. Cook for 15 minutes, then add the artichoke hearts. Cook for 5 minutes, or until all the liquid is absorbed and the rice is creamy. Season to taste with salt and pepper.

Remove the risotto from the heat and add the remaining butter. Mix well, then stir in the cheese until it melts. Season, if necessary. Spoon the risotto into warmed bowls, garnish with parsley and serve immediately.

685 *Risotto with artichoke hearts & ham*

This simple risotto made with luxurious artichoke hearts can also be made with Parma ham. Although this Italian ham can be eaten as it is, in this recipe you need to add 85 g/3 oz slices to a pan lightly brushed with oil and cook them until lightly crisp. Crumble using your fingers, and stir into the risotto to serve.

686 *Pumpkin & chestnut risotto* SERVES 4

1 litre/1¾ pints vegetable stock
1 tbsp olive oil
40 g/1½ oz butter
1 small onion, finely chopped
225 g/8 oz pumpkin, diced
225 g/8 oz chestnuts, cooked and peeled
280 g/10 oz risotto rice

150 ml/5 fl oz dry white wine
1 tsp crumbled saffron threads (optional)
85 g/3 oz Parmesan or Grana Padano
cheese, freshly grated, plus extra
shavings, to serve
salt and pepper

Bring the stock to the boil, then reduce the heat and keep it simmering gently over a low heat while you are cooking the risotto.

Heat the oil with 25 g/1 oz of the butter in a deep saucepan over a medium heat until the butter has melted.

Stir in the onion and pumpkin and cook, stirring occasionally, for 5 minutes, or until the onion is soft and starting to turn golden and the pumpkin begins to colour.

Roughly chop the chestnuts and add to the mixture. Stir thoroughly to coat. Reduce the heat, add the rice and mix to coat in oil and butter. Cook, stirring constantly, for 2–3 minutes, or until the grains are translucent. Add the wine and cook, stirring constantly, for 1 minute until it has reduced. If using the saffron threads, dissolve them in 4 tablespoons of the hot stock and add the liquid to the rice after the wine has been absorbed. Cook, stirring constantly, until the liquid has been absorbed.

Gradually add the hot stock, a ladleful at a time, stirring constantly. Add more liquid as the rice absorbs each addition. Increase the heat to medium so that the liquid bubbles. Cook for 20 minutes, or until all the liquid has been absorbed and the rice is creamy. Season to taste.

Remove the risotto from the heat and add the remaining butter. Mix well, then stir in the grated cheese until it melts. Adjust the seasoning, if necessary, spoon the risotto onto 4 warmed plates and serve immediately, sprinkled with the cheese shavings.

687 *Pumpkin & pine kernel risotto*

Omit the chestnuts, increase the amount of pumpkin to 300 g/11 oz and sprinkle 40 g/1½ oz toasted pine kernels over the risotto to serve.

688 *Risotto Milanese*

1 litre/1¾ pints chicken stock
1 litre/1¾ pints white wine
1 tsp saffron strands
1 tbsp olive oil
3 tbsp butter
1 small onion, finely chopped
400 g/14 oz arborio rice
55 g/2 oz Parmesan cheese, freshly grated, plus extra shavings to garnish
salt and pepper

Bring the stock and white wine to the boil, then reduce the heat and simmer. Infuse the saffron strands in the stock and continue to simmer while preparing the risotto. Heat the oil with 2 tablespoons of butter in a deep saucepan over a medium heat until the butter has melted. Stir in the onion and cook gently until soft and beginning to turn golden but not brown. Add the rice and mix to coat in oil and butter. Cook, stirring, for 2–3 minutes, or until the grains are translucent.

Gradually add the stock and saffron mixture, a ladleful at a time. Stir constantly, adding more liquid as the rice absorbs it. Increase the heat slightly so that the liquid bubbles. Cook for 20 minutes, or until all the liquid is absorbed.

Remove the risotto from the heat. Add the remaining butter, mix well, then stir in the grated Parmesan cheese. Season to taste with salt and pepper, garnish with Parmesan shavings and serve immediately.

689 *With sweetcorn or mushrooms*

Try adding 2 tablespoons of cooked sweetcorn or some chopped button mushrooms for about 5 minutes before the end of cooking time – or scatter over a handful of flaked almonds, or pine kernels.

690 *Risotto primavera*

225 g/8 oz fresh thin asparagus spears
4 tbsp olive oil
175 g/6 oz young French beans, cut into 2.5-cm/1-inch lengths
175 g/6 oz young courgettes, quartered and cut into 2.5-cm/1-inch lengths
225 g/8 oz shelled fresh peas
1 onion, finely chopped
1–2 garlic cloves, finely chopped
350 g/12 oz risotto rice
1.5 litres/2¾ pints chicken or vegetable stock, simmering
4 spring onions, cut into 2.5-cm/1-inch lengths
55 g/2 oz butter
115 g/4 oz freshly grated Parmesan cheese
2 tbsp snipped fresh chives
2 tbsp shredded fresh basil
salt and pepper

Trim the woody ends of the asparagus and cut off the tips. Cut the stems into 2.5-cm/1-inch pieces and set aside with the tips. Heat 2 tablespoons of the oil in a large frying pan over a high heat until very hot. Add the asparagus, beans, courgettes and peas and stir-fry for 3–4 minutes until they are bright green and just starting to soften. Set aside. Heat the remaining oil in a large heavy-based saucepan over a medium heat. Add the onion and cook, stirring occasionally, for 3 minutes, or until it starts to soften.

Stir in the garlic and cook, stirring, for 30 seconds. Reduce the heat, add the rice and mix to coat in oil.

Cook, stirring constantly, for 2–3 minutes, or until the grains are translucent. Gradually add the hot stock, a ladleful at a time, until all but 2 tablespoons of the liquid is absorbed and the rice is creamy.

Stir in the stir-fried vegetables, onion mixture and spring onions with the remaining stock. Cook for 2 minutes, stirring frequently, then season to taste with salt and pepper. Stir in the butter, Parmesan, chives and basil.

Remove the pan from the heat. Transfer the risotto to a warmed serving dish and serve immediately.

691 *Risotto primavera with white wine*

Why not add a little white wine to the risotto? Replace 150 ml/5 fl oz of the stock with an Italian dry white wine such as Frascati. Add the wine to the pan before the stock, and let it bubble for a few seconds.

1 tbsp olive oil

3 tbsp butter

1 small onion, finely chopped

280 g/10 oz risotto rice

1.2 litres/2 pints chicken or vegetable
  stock, simmering

225 g/8 oz roasted vegetables, such as
  peppers, courgettes and aubergines,
  cut into chunks

85 g/3 oz freshly grated Parmesan or
  Grana Padano cheese

salt and pepper

2 tbsp finely chopped fresh herbs, to garnish

Heat the oil with 2 tablespoons of the butter in a deep saucepan over
a medium heat until the butter has melted. Add the onion and cook,
stirring occasionally, for 5 minutes, until soft and starting to turn
golden. Do not brown.

Reduce the heat, add the rice and mix to coat in oil and butter. Cook,
stirring constantly, for 2–3 minutes, or until the grains are translucent.

Gradually add the hot stock, a ladleful at a time. Stir constantly and
add more liquid as the rice absorbs each addition. Increase the heat to
medium so that the liquid bubbles. Cook for 15 minutes, then add most
of the roasted vegetables, setting aside a few pieces to use as a garnish.

Cook for a further 5 minutes, or until all the liquid is absorbed and the
rice is creamy. Season to taste with salt and pepper.

Remove the risotto from the heat and add the remaining butter. Mix
well, then stir in the Parmesan until it melts. Spoon the risotto onto
warmed individual plates, arrange vegetables around it or on top to
garnish, then sprinkle with fresh herbs and serve immediately.

693 *Risotto with roasted fennel*

*Florence fennel bulbs are much used in Italian cooking and they become
delicious when roasted – with a mellow, lightly aniseed flavour. The frondy
leaves attached to the bulb can be snipped off and reserved as a garnish. First
slice your fennel (1 large or 2 smaller) into slices about ½ cm thick. Blanch
over a pan of boiling water for 3 minutes to soften, remove and pat dry.
Now toss in olive oil and seasoning and roast at 200°C/400°F/Gas Mark 6
for 40 minutes, turning once or twice, until cooked and golden. Follow the
recipe above, replacing the mixed roast vegetables with the fennel slices,
roughly broken up and stirred into the risotto. Garnish with the leaves.*

Sage & Gorgonzola risotto

50 g/2 oz unsalted butter
150 g/5½ oz pancetta, cubed
1 small onion, chopped
2 garlic cloves, crushed
300 g/10½ oz risotto rice
125 ml/4 fl oz white wine or vermouth

1 litre/1¾ pints stock, simmering
200 g/7 oz Gorgonzola cheese, crumbled
2 tbsp chopped fresh sage, plus extra
     leaves, to garnish
2 tbsp finely grated Parmesan cheese
salt and pepper

Heat half the butter in a large pan or frying pan and cook the pancetta over medium–high heat, stirring frequently, until the fat melts and the pancetta is beginning to brown. Add the onion and garlic and cook, stirring frequently, for 5 minutes, or until the onion is soft.

Add the rice and stir to coat in the pancetta mixture. Pour in the wine and cook, stirring constantly, until almost all the liquid has been absorbed. Start to add the hot stock, a ladleful at a time, stirring constantly and letting each addition be absorbed before adding the next. Continue adding the stock until it is all absorbed and the rice is creamy but still firm to the bite.

Remove from the heat, then add the Gorgonzola cheese and sage and stir until the cheese has melted. Season to taste with salt and pepper and add the remaining butter and the Parmesan cheese. Serve immediately garnished with sage.

695 ## Sage & Gorgonzola risotto cakes

To make risotto cakes, simply let the risotto cool completely, then add 2 tablespoons of plain flour and 1 egg yolk. Mix well, and form into flat cakes. Cook in hot oil until golden.

696 ## Sunshine risotto

about 12 sun-dried tomatoes
1.5 litres/2¾ pints chicken or
     vegetable stock
2 tbsp olive oil
1 large onion, finely chopped
4–6 garlic cloves, finely chopped
400 g/14 oz risotto rice
2 tbsp chopped fresh flat-leaf
     parsley
115 g/4 oz freshly grated aged
     pecorino cheese
extra virgin olive oil, for drizzling

15 seconds. Reduce the heat, add the rice and mix to coat in the oil. Cook, stirring constantly, for 2–3 minutes, or until the grains are translucent.

Gradually add the hot stock, a ladleful at a time. Stir constantly and add more liquid as the rice absorbs each addition. Increase the heat to medium so that the liquid bubbles. After about 15 minutes, stir in the sun-dried tomatoes. Continue adding the stock, stirring constantly, until the risotto has been cooking for 20 minutes, or until all the liquid is absorbed and the rice is creamy.

Remove the saucepan from the heat and stir in the chopped parsley and half the pecorino. Spoon the risotto onto plates. Drizzle with the olive oil and sprinkle the remaining pecorino on top. Serve immediately.

Place the sun-dried tomatoes in a heatproof bowl and pour over enough boiling water to cover. Set aside to soak for 30 minutes, or until soft and supple. Drain and pat dry with kitchen paper, then shred finely and set aside. Bring the stock to the boil in a saucepan, then reduce the heat and keep simmering gently over a low heat while you are cooking the risotto.

Heat the olive oil in a deep saucepan over a medium heat. Add the onion and cook, stirring occasionally, for about 2 minutes, or until beginning to soften. Add the garlic and cook for a further

697 ## Sunshine risotto with butternut squash

Squash is a really lovely addition to this simple risotto – peel 225 g/8 oz butternut squash and cut into 1.5-cm/½-inch dice. Blanch for 2 minutes in boiling water, drain and dry, then add to the frying pan with the oil before you put in the onion. Cook over medium–high heat, stirring occasionally, until cooked through and turning golden. Then turn the heat down and add the onion before proceeding with the recipe.

1.2 litres/2 pints chicken or
vegetable stock
2 leeks
115 g/4 oz butter
300 g/10½ oz risotto rice
4 tbsp dry white vermouth or
white wine
125 ml/4 fl oz double cream
freshly grated nutmeg
salt and ¼–½ tsp ground white pepper
115 g/4 oz freshly grated Parmesan
cheese
115–175 g/4–6 oz fresh black truffles,
brushed clean
50 ml–90 ml/2–3 fl oz truffle oil
(optional)

Bring the stock to the boil in a pan, reduce the heat and keep simmering gently over low heat while you are cooking the risotto. Slice the leeks in half lengthways, then shred thinly. Heat half the butter in a heavy-based pan over medium heat. Add the leeks and cook for 1 minute, or until just starting to soften.

Reduce the heat, add the rice and mix to coat in butter. Cook, stirring constantly, for 2–3 minutes, or until the grains are translucent. Add the vermouth and cook, stirring constantly, for 1 minute until reduced.

Gradually add the hot stock, a ladleful at a time. Stir constantly and add more liquid as the rice absorbs each addition. Increase the heat to medium so that the liquid bubbles. Cook for 20 minutes, or until all the liquid is absorbed and the rice is creamy.

Just before the end of the cooking time, stir in the cream. Season with a little nutmeg and the salt and white pepper. Continue cooking for 3–4 minutes until the liquid is absorbed.

Remove the risotto from the heat and add the remaining butter. Mix well, then stir in the Parmesan cheese until it melts. Spoon into serving dishes and shave equal amounts of truffle over each portion. Drizzle over the truffle oil, if using, and serve immediately.

699 *Risotto with truffle oil*

White truffles can also be used to make this dish. Bought fresh, both black and white truffles have an incomparable flavour, but are expensive and their season is short. An alternative is to use the preserved variety – you can buy them in oil, or use truffle oil to replace half the butter in the recipe, and instead add 125 g/4 oz chopped porcini mushrooms – a tasty Italian variety. Fry these in the butter before adding the leeks, remove with a slotted spoon and keep warm – return to the pan when the risotto is nearly cooked.

700 *Vegetarian paella*

½ tsp saffron threads
2 tbsp hot water
6 tbsp olive oil
1 Spanish onion, sliced
3 garlic cloves, crushed
1 red pepper, deseeded and sliced
1 orange pepper, deseeded and sliced
1 large aubergine, cubed

200 g/7 oz medium-grain paella rice
600 ml/1 pint vegetable stock
450 g/1 lb tomatoes, peeled and chopped
115 g/4 oz button mushrooms, sliced
115 g/4 oz French beans, halved
400 g/14 oz canned pinto beans
salt and pepper

Put the saffron threads and water in a small bowl or cup and let infuse for a few minutes. Meanwhile, heat the oil in a paella pan or wide, shallow frying pan and cook the onion over medium heat, stirring, for 2–3 minutes, or until softened. Add the garlic, peppers and aubergine and cook, stirring frequently, for 5 minutes. Add the rice and cook, stirring constantly, for 1 minute, or until glossy and coated.

Pour in the stock and add the tomatoes, saffron and its soaking water and salt and pepper to taste. Bring to the boil, then reduce the heat and let simmer, shaking the frying pan frequently and stirring occasionally, for 15 minutes.

Stir in the mushrooms, French beans and pinto beans with their can juices. Cook for a further 10 minutes, then serve immediately.

701 *Vegetarian paella with courgettes*

Replace the mushrooms with 2 small courgettes, sliced into rounds. Cook in the pan with the peppers and aubergines, adding another tablespoon of oil.

702 Wild mushroom risotto

55 g/2 oz dried porcini or morel
  mushrooms
about 500 g/1 lb 2 oz mixed fresh wild
  mushrooms, such as porcini, girolles,
  horse mushrooms and chanterelles,
  halved if large
4 tbsp olive oil
3–4 garlic cloves, finely chopped
4 tbsp unsalted butter
1 onion, finely chopped

350 g/12 oz arborio or carnaroli rice
50 ml/2 fl oz dry white vermouth
1.2 litres/2 pints simmering chicken stock
115 g/4 oz freshly grated Parmesan
  cheese
4 tbsp chopped fresh flat-leaf parsley
salt and pepper
6 fresh parsley sprigs, to garnish
crusty bread, to serve

Place the dried mushrooms in a heatproof bowl and pour over enough boiling water to cover. Leave to soak for 30 minutes, then carefully lift out and pat dry.

Strain the soaking liquid through a sieve lined with kitchen paper and reserve. Trim the wild mushrooms and gently brush clean.

Heat 3 tablespoons of the oil in a frying pan over a low heat. Add the fresh mushrooms and fry for 1–2 minutes. Add the garlic and soaked mushrooms and cook, stirring frequently, for 2 minutes. Transfer to a plate and reserve.

Heat the remaining oil and half the butter in a large saucepan over a low heat. Add the onion and cook, stirring occasionally, for 2 minutes, or until softened. Add the rice and cook, stirring, for 2 minutes, or until it is translucent and well coated. Add the vermouth.

When almost absorbed, add a ladleful (about 225 ml/8 fl oz) of the stock. Cook, stirring, until the stock is completely absorbed.

Continue adding the stock, about half a ladleful at a time, allowing each addition to be absorbed before adding the next. This should take 20–25 minutes. The risotto should have a creamy consistency and the rice should be tender but still firm to the bite.

Add half the reserved mushroom soaking liquid to the risotto and stir in the mushrooms. Season to taste with salt and pepper and add more mushroom liquid, if necessary. Remove from the heat and stir in the remaining butter, the Parmesan cheese and chopped parsley.

Transfer to 6 warmed serving dishes, garnish with parsley sprigs and serve with crusty bread.

703 Spiced basmati pilau

500 g/1 lb 2 oz basmati rice
175 g/6 oz broccoli, trimmed
6 tbsp vegetable oil
2 large onions, chopped
225 g/8 oz mushrooms, sliced
2 garlic cloves, crushed
6 cardamom pods, split
6 whole cloves
8 black peppercorns
1 cinnamon stick or piece of
  cassia bark
1 tsp turmeric
1.2 litres/2 pints vegetable stock or
  water
salt and pepper
60 g/2¼ oz seedless raisins
60 g/2¼ oz unsalted pistachios,
  roughly chopped

Place the rice in a sieve and wash well under cold running water. Drain. Trim off most of the broccoli stalk and cut the head into small florets, then quarter the stalk lengthways and cut diagonally into 1-cm/½-inch pieces. Heat the oil in a large saucepan. Add the onions and broccoli stalks and cook over a low heat, stirring frequently, for 3 minutes. Add the mushrooms, rice, garlic and spices and cook for 1 minute, stirring, until the rice is coated in oil.

Add the stock and season to taste. Stir in the broccoli florets and return the mixture to the boil. Cover, reduce the heat and cook over a low heat for 15 minutes without uncovering the pan.

Remove the pan from the heat and leave the pilau to stand for 5 minutes without uncovering. Remove the whole spices, add the raisins and pistachios and gently fork through to fluff up the grains. Serve the pilau hot.

704 Spiced basmati pilau with carrot

Replace the cloves and cinnamon with ½ teaspoon each of ground coriander and cumin seed. Omit the mushrooms and add 1 medium finely grated carrot. The pistachios can be replaced with flaked almonds or cashew nuts.

Baked pasta with spicy meat sauce   SERVES 4-6

2 tbsp olive oil
1 onion, finely chopped
2 garlic cloves, finely chopped
650 g/1 lb 7 oz lean lamb
or beef mince
400 g/14 oz canned chopped tomatoes
pinch of sugar
2 tbsp chopped fresh flat-leaf parsley
1 tbsp chopped fresh marjoram
1 tsp ground cinnamon
½ tsp grated nutmeg
¼ tsp ground cloves
225 g/8 oz long, dried macaroni
or other short pasta
2 eggs, beaten
300 ml/10 fl oz Greek yogurt
55 g/2 oz feta cheese, grated
25 g/1 oz kefalotiri or pecorino cheese,
grated
salt and pepper

frequently and breaking up the meat. Add the tomatoes to the saucepan, then the sugar, parsley, marjoram, cinnamon, nutmeg, cloves, and salt and pepper. Bring to the boil, then simmer, uncovered, for 30 minutes, stirring occasionally.

Meanwhile, bring a large saucepan of lightly salted water to the boil. Add the macaroni, bring back to the boil, and cook for 8–10 minutes or until tender but still firm to the bite. Drain well. Beat together the eggs, yogurt and

feta cheese. Season with salt and pepper. When the meat is cooked, transfer it to a large ovenproof dish. Add the macaroni in a layer to cover the meat, then pour over the sauce. Sprinkle over the kefalotiri cheese. Bake in the oven for 30–45 minutes, until golden brown. Serve hot or warm, cut into portions.

Preheat the oven to 190°C/375°F/ Gas Mark 5.

Heat the oil in a saucepan, add the onion and garlic and fry for 5 minutes, until softened. Add the lamb and fry for about 5 minutes, until browned all over, stirring

706 *Baked pasta with spicy chicken sauce*

Chop 4 skinless chicken breast fillets into small bite-sized pieces and add them to the sauce instead of the minced meat. Omit the cloves and cinnamon and instead add 1 teaspoon of ground paprika.

Pasta courgette sauce with lemon & rosemary   SERVES 4

6 tbsp olive oil
1 small onion, very thinly sliced
2 garlic cloves, very finely chopped
2 tbsp chopped fresh rosemary
1 tbsp chopped fresh flat-leaf parsley
450 g/1 lb small courgettes, cut into
4 cm x 5-mm/1½ x ¼-inch strips

finely grated rind of 1 lemon
450 g/1 lb dried fusilli
4 tbsp freshly grated Parmesan
salt and pepper

Heat the olive oil in a large frying pan over a medium–low heat. Add the onion and fry gently, stirring occasionally, for about 10 minutes until golden. Raise the heat to medium–high. Add the garlic and herbs. Cook for a few seconds, stirring. Add the courgettes and lemon rind. Cook for 5–7 minutes, stirring occasionally, until the courgettes are just tender. Season with salt and pepper. Remove from the heat. Cook the pasta in plenty of boiling salted water. Drain and transfer to a warm serving dish. Briefly reheat the courgettes. Pour over the pasta and toss well to mix. Sprinkle with the Parmesan and serve immediately.

708 *Pasta sauce with mint & coriander*

Replace the rosemary and parsley with the same amount of finely chopped fresh mint and coriander leaf.

709 *Aubergine pasta sauce with herbs*

Replace the courgettes with 1 large or 2 small aubergines, cut into 1-cm/ ½-inch rounds and then halved. Replace the rosemary and parsley with 4 tablespoons of fresh chopped basil – but just stir it in at the end of cooking.

Linguine with wild mushrooms

55 g/2 oz butter
1 onion, chopped
1 garlic clove, finely chopped
350 g/12 oz wild mushrooms, sliced
350 g/12 oz dried linguine
300 ml/10 fl oz crème fraîche
2 tbsp shredded fresh basil leaves, plus
    extra to garnish
4 tbsp freshly grated Parmesan cheese,
    plus extra to serve
salt and pepper

Melt the butter in a large heavy-based frying pan. Add the onion and garlic and cook over a low heat for 5 minutes, or until softened. Add the mushrooms and cook, stirring occasionally, for a further 10 minutes.

Meanwhile, bring a large, heavy-based saucepan of lightly salted water to the boil. Add the pasta, return to the boil and cook for 8–10 minutes, or until tender but still firm to the bite.

Stir the crème fraîche, basil and Parmesan cheese into the mushroom mixture and season to taste with salt and pepper.

Cover and heat through gently for 1–2 minutes. Drain the pasta and transfer to a warmed serving dish. Add the mushroom mixture and toss lightly. Garnish with extra basil and serve immediately with extra Parmesan cheese.

711 *Linguine with parsley & lemon*

Replace the basil leaves with 2 tablespoons of fresh chopped flat-leaf parsley and add the juice of ½ lemon to the sauce before heating.

712 *Creamy linguine with wild mushrooms*

Instead of crème fraîche, use 150 ml/5 fl oz mascarpone cheese beaten in a bowl with about 100 ml/3½ fl oz milk until you have a creamy sauce. Omit the basil and use 2 tablespoons each of chopped fresh chives and parsley.

713 *Linguine with anchovies, olives & capers*

3 tbsp olive oil
2 garlic cloves, finely chopped
10 anchovy fillets, drained and chopped
140 g/5 oz black olives, stoned and
    chopped
1 tbsp capers, rinsed
450 g/1 lb plum tomatoes, peeled,
    deseeded and chopped
pinch of cayenne pepper
400 g/14 oz dried linguine
salt
2 tbsp chopped fresh flat-leaf parsley,
    to garnish

Heat the olive oil in a heavy-based saucepan. Add the garlic and cook over a low heat, stirring frequently, for 2 minutes. Add the anchovies and mash them to a pulp with a fork. Add the olives, capers and tomatoes and season to taste with cayenne pepper. Cover and simmer for 25 minutes.

Meanwhile, bring a saucepan of lightly salted water to the boil. Add the pasta, bring back to the boil and cook for 8–10 minutes, until tender, but still firm to the bite.

Drain and transfer to a warmed serving dish. Spoon the anchovy sauce into the dish and toss the pasta, using 2 large forks. Garnish with the parsley and serve immediately.

714 *Linguine with sardines & pine kernels*

Ask your fishmonger to fillet 8–12 (depending on size) fresh sardines for you. Cook your pasta as above and keep warm. Heat 2 tablespoons of olive oil in a pan and add 2 garlic cloves, chopped, with the sardines – cook over medium heat for 2 minutes a side or until cooked through, then toss in 50 g/2 oz plump sultanas and 50 g/2 oz toasted pine kernels. Add the juice of ½ lemon and season. Serve tossed with the pasta, garnished with chopped parsley.

butter, for greasing
450 g/1 lb dried rigatoni
115 g/4 oz sun-dried tomatoes,
drained and sliced

FILLING
200 g/7 oz canned flaked tuna,
drained
225 g/8 oz ricotta cheese

SAUCE
125 ml/4 fl oz double cream
225 g/8 oz freshly grated Parmesan
cheese
salt and pepper

Preheat the oven to 200°C/400°F/ Gas Mark 6. Lightly grease a large ovenproof dish with butter. Bring a large saucepan of lightly salted water to the boil. Add the rigatoni, bring back to the boil and cook for 8–10 minutes, until just tender but still firm to the bite. Drain the pasta and leave until cool enough to handle.

Meanwhile, mix the tuna and ricotta cheese together in a bowl to form a soft paste. Spoon the mixture into a piping bag and use to fill the rigatoni. Arrange the filled pasta tubes side by side in the prepared dish.

Mix the cream and Parmesan cheese together in a bowl and season to taste. Spoon the sauce over the rigatoni and top with the sun-dried tomatoes, arranged in a criss-cross pattern. Bake in the preheated oven for 20 minutes. Serve hot straight from the dish.

716 *Walnut & ricotta rigatoni*

For a vegetarian alternative to this recipe, simply substitute a mixture of stoned and chopped black olives and chopped walnuts for the tuna. Follow exactly the same cooking method.

717 *Salmon & mascarpone rigatoni*

Replace the tuna and ricotta filling with 200 g/7 oz salmon fillet, poached and 225 g/8 oz mascarpone cheese and some black pepper. Beat together and use to fill the pasta.

718 *Lower-fat tuna & ricotta rigatoni*

For a lower-fat version of the sauce (which can also be used with either of the above variations), simply make 250 ml/9 fl oz standard béchamel (white) sauce using low-fat spread instead of butter, and add 85 g/3 oz grated Cheddar cheese. Sprinkle 25 g/1 oz grated Parmesan cheese on top to bake.

719 Hot chilli pasta

150 ml/5 fl oz dry white wine
1 tbsp sun-dried tomato purée
2 fresh red chillies
2 garlic cloves, finely chopped
350 g/12 oz dried tortiglioni
4 tbsp chopped fresh flat-leaf parsley
pecorino cheese shavings, to garnish

SUGOCASA
5 tbsp extra virgin olive oil
450 g/1 lb plum tomatoes, chopped
salt and pepper

First make the sugocasa. Heat the olive oil in a frying pan until it is almost smoking. Add the tomatoes and cook over a high heat for 2–3 minutes. Reduce the heat to low and cook gently for 20 minutes, or until very soft. Season with salt and pepper, then pass through a sieve or process in a blender and put into a clean saucepan. Add the wine, sun-dried tomato purée, whole chillies and garlic to the sugocasa and bring to the boil. Reduce the heat and simmer gently.

Meanwhile, bring a large saucepan of lightly salted water to the boil. Add the pasta, return to the boil and cook for 8–10 minutes, or until tender but still firm to the bite.

Meanwhile, remove the chillies and taste the sauce. If you prefer a hotter flavour, chop some or all of the chillies and return them to the saucepan. Check the seasoning at the same time, then stir in half the parsley.

Drain the pasta and tip it into a warmed serving bowl. Add the sauce and toss to coat. Sprinkle with the remaining parsley, garnish with the pecorino shavings and serve immediately.

If time is short, use ready-made sugocasa, available from most supermarkets and sometimes labelled crushed tomatoes. Failing that, you could use passata, but the sauce will be thinner.

720 With prawns

Stir 200 g/7 oz peeled cooked prawns into the sauce before tossing with the pasta. Garnish with a few unpeeled cooked prawns and the parsley.

721 Pepperoni pasta

3 tbsp olive oil
1 onion, chopped
1 red pepper, deseeded and diced
1 orange pepper, deseeded and diced
800 g/1 lb 12 oz canned chopped tomatoes
1 tbsp sun-dried tomato purée

1 tsp paprika
225 g/8 oz pepperoni sausage, sliced
2 tbsp chopped fresh flat-leaf parsley, plus extra to garnish
450 g/1 lb dried garganelli
salt and pepper
mixed salad leaves, to serve

Heat 2 tablespoons of the olive oil in a large heavy-based frying pan. Add the onion and cook over a low heat, stirring occasionally, for 5 minutes, or until softened. Add the red and orange peppers, tomatoes, sun-dried tomato purée and paprika and bring to the boil. Add the pepperoni and parsley and season to taste with salt and pepper. Stir well, bring to the boil, then reduce the heat and simmer for 10–15 minutes.

Meanwhile, bring a large heavy-based saucepan of lightly salted water to the boil. Add the pasta, return to the boil and cook for 8–10 minutes, or until tender but still firm to the bite. Drain well and transfer to a warmed serving dish. Add the remaining olive oil and toss. Add the sauce and toss again. Sprinkle with parsley and serve immediately with mixed salad leaves.

722 Spicy sausage pasta

You could substitute other spicy sausages, such as kabanos or chorizo, if you like. If you cannot find garganelli pasta, then use penne or another pasta shape, such as fusilli, bucati or farfalle.

723 Vegetable lasagne

SERVES 4

1 aubergine, sliced
3 tbsp olive oil
2 garlic cloves, crushed
1 red onion, halved and sliced
1 green pepper, deseeded and diced
1 red pepper, deseeded and diced
1 yellow pepper, deseeded and diced
225 g/8 oz mushrooms, sliced
2 celery sticks, sliced
1 courgette, diced
½ tsp chilli powder
½ tsp ground cumin
2 tomatoes, chopped
300 ml/10 fl oz passata

2 tbsp chopped fresh basil
8 no pre-cook lasagne verde sheets
salt and pepper

CHEESE SAUCE
2 tbsp butter or margarine
1 tbsp flour
150 ml/5 fl oz vegetable stock
300 ml/10 fl oz milk
75 g/2¾ oz Cheddar cheese, grated
1 tsp Dijon mustard
1 tbsp chopped fresh basil
1 egg, beaten
salt and pepper

Preheat the oven to 180°C/350°F/Gas Mark 4. Place the aubergine slices in a colander, sprinkle with salt and leave to stand for 20 minutes. Rinse under cold running water, drain and reserve.

Heat the oil in a large frying pan. Add the garlic and onion and sauté for 1–2 minutes. Add the peppers, mushrooms, celery and courgette and cook for 3–4 minutes, stirring. Stir in the spices and cook for 1 minute. Mix the tomatoes, passata and basil together, then season well with salt and pepper.

To make the sauce, melt the butter or margarine in a saucepan. Add the flour and cook for 1 minute. Remove from the heat and stir in the stock and milk. Return to the heat and add half the cheese and mustard. Boil, stirring, until thickened. Stir in the basil and season to taste with salt and pepper. Remove the saucepan from the heat and stir in the egg.

Place half the lasagne sheets in an ovenproof dish. Top with half the vegetables, then half the tomato sauce. Cover with half the aubergines. Repeat and spoon the cheese sauce on top. Sprinkle with the remaining cheese and cook in the oven for 40 minutes. Serve immediately.

724 Simple vegetable lasagne

The vegetable content of the lasagne can be varied according to what you have – for example, you can omit the mushrooms and peppers and simply increase the amount of aubergine, courgette and onion. Or you can use just 1 red pepper and add 225 g/8 oz cherry tomatoes to the mixture.

725 With mascarpone & spinach topping

Make the vegetable filling and layer in the dish with the pasta and passata but instead of the cheese sauce topping, combine 225 g/8 oz mascarpone cheese with enough milk to thin it down to a thick sauce consistency, then beat in 400 g/14 oz cooked, well-drained spinach and 50 g/2 oz grated Parmesan. Spoon over the top of the pasta, sprinkle on more Parmesan cheese and bake.

726 Spinach lasagne

SERVES 4

115 g/4 oz butter, plus extra for greasing
2 garlic cloves, finely chopped
115 g/4 oz shallots, finely chopped
225 g/8 oz wild mushrooms, such as
    chanterelles, sliced
450 g/1 lb spinach, cooked, drained and
    finely chopped
225 g/8 oz Cheddar cheese, grated

¼ tsp freshly grated nutmeg
1 tsp chopped fresh basil
6 tbsp plain flour
600 ml/1 pint hot milk
55 g/2 oz Cheshire cheese, grated
8 no pre-cook lasagne sheets
salt and pepper

Preheat the oven to 200°C/400°F/Gas Mark 6. Lightly grease a large, fairly deep, rectangular or square ovenproof dish with a little butter. Melt 55 g/2 oz of the butter in a large frying pan. Add the garlic, shallots and mushrooms and fry over a low heat, stirring occasionally, for 3 minutes.

Stir in the spinach, Cheddar cheese, nutmeg and basil. Season with salt and pepper to taste, remove from the heat and set aside. Melt the remaining butter in a saucepan over a low heat. Add the flour and cook over a low heat, stirring constantly, for 1 minute.

Gradually stir in the hot milk, whisking constantly until smooth and thick. Remove the pan from the heat, stir in 25 g/1 oz of the Cheshire cheese and season to taste with salt and pepper. Spread half the mushroom and spinach mixture over the base of the prepared dish.

Cover with half the lasagne sheets and then with half of the cheese sauce. Repeat the layers and then sprinkle the remaining grated Cheshire cheese over the top. Bake in the oven for 30 minutes, or until golden brown. Serve hot.

222

727 Baked lasagne

3 tbsp olive oil
1 onion, finely chopped
1 celery stick, finely chopped
1 carrot, finely chopped
100 g/3½ oz pancetta or rindless
streaky bacon, finely chopped
175 g/6 oz fresh beef mince
175 g/6 oz fresh pork mince
100 ml/3½ fl oz dry red wine
150 ml/5 fl oz beef stock
1 tbsp tomato purée
1 clove
1 bay leaf
150 ml/5 fl oz boiling milk
400 g/14 oz dried lasagne
55 g/2 oz unsalted butter, diced, plus
extra for greasing
300 ml/10 fl oz Béchamel Sauce
(see page 9)
140 g/5 oz mozzarella cheese, diced
140 g/5 oz freshly grated Parmesan
cheese
salt and pepper

Heat the olive oil in a large heavy-based saucepan. Add the onion, celery, carrot, pancetta, beef and pork and cook over a medium heat, stirring frequently and breaking up the meat with a wooden spoon, for 10 minutes, or until lightly browned. Add the wine, bring to the boil and cook until reduced. Add about two thirds of the stock, bring to the boil and cook until reduced. Combine the remaining stock and tomato purée and add to the saucepan. Season to taste with salt and pepper, add the clove and bay leaf and pour in the milk. Cover and leave to simmer over a low heat for 1½ hours.

Preheat the oven to 200°C/400°F/Gas Mark 6. Unless you are using lasagne that needs no precooking, bring a large heavy-based saucepan of lightly salted water to the boil. Add the lasagne sheets, in batches, return to the boil and cook for about 10 minutes, or until tender but still firm to the bite. Remove with tongs and spread out on a clean tea towel. Remove the meat sauce from the heat and discard the clove and bay leaf.

Lightly grease a large ovenproof dish with butter. Place a layer of lasagne in the base and cover it with a layer of meat sauce. Spoon a layer of béchamel sauce on top and sprinkle with one third of the mozzarella and Parmesan cheeses. Continue making layers until all the ingredients are used, ending with a topping of sauce and sprinkled cheese.

Dot the top of the lasagne with the diced butter and bake in the preheated oven for 30 minutes, or until golden and bubbling.

728 Baked fresh lasagne

This classic Italian dish can be made with fresh lasagne for a richer taste, as it usually contains eggs. Fresh sheets can be layered direct into the lasagne dish. You can also use verdi (spinach) lasagne sheets and all minced beef or all minced pork if wished.

729 Baked lasagne with mushrooms

You can replace 100 g/3½ oz of the meat with 100 g/3½ oz finely chopped dark-gilled mushrooms – add to the pan with the meat. You can also add 200 g/7 oz chopped canned tomatoes to the pan with the meat for a deeper tomato taste.

730 Linguine with clams

200 g/7 oz dried linguine
3 tbsp extra virgin olive oil
4 garlic cloves, finely chopped
2 shallots, finely chopped
½ fresh red chilli, finely chopped
125 ml/4 fl oz white wine

1 kg/2 lb 4 oz fresh clams, tellines
    or cockles, cleaned
handful of parsley, chopped
zest of 1 lemon
salt and pepper

Cook the linguine according to the packet instructions, drain and toss with a splash of olive oil. Cover and keep warm. Add half the olive oil to a saucepan with a lid and place over a high heat. Add the garlic, shallots and chilli and cook gently for 8–10 minutes until soft. Add the wine, bring to the boil and cook for 2 minutes. Add the clams, cover and cook for a further 2–5 minutes, or until all the clams have opened – discard any that haven't. Add the drained linguine, parsley, lemon zest, the remaining olive oil and salt and pepper to taste and mix through. Serve.

731 Linguine with mussels

Replace the clams with live cleaned and debearded mussels. Discard any that don't close when tapped. After cooking, discard any that stay closed.

732 Pasta with spiced leek

150 g/5½ oz baby leeks, cut into
    2-cm/¾-inch slices
175 g/6 oz butternut squash, deseeded
    and cut into 2-cm/¾-inch chunks
1½ tbsp medium ready-prepared
    curry paste

1 tsp rapeseed or vegetable oil
175 g/6 oz cherry tomatoes
250 g/9 oz dried pasta of your choice
300 ml/½ pint Béchamel Sauce (see page 9)
2 tbsp fresh coriander leaves, chopped,
    to garnish

Preheat the oven to 200°C/400°F/Gas Mark 6. Bring a large saucepan of water to the boil, add the leeks and cook for 2 minutes. Add the butternut squash and cook for a further 2 minutes. Drain in a colander.

Mix the curry paste with the oil in a large bowl. Toss the leeks and butternut squash in the mixture to coat thoroughly. Transfer the leeks and squash to a non-stick baking tray and roast in the oven for 10 minutes until golden brown. Add the tomatoes and roast for a further 5 minutes.

Meanwhile, bring a large saucepan of lightly salted water to the boil. Add the pasta, bring back to the boil and cook for 8–10 minutes, until just tender but still firm to the bite. Drain. Put the sauce into a large saucepan and warm over a low heat. Add the leeks, butternut squash, tomatoes and coriander and stir in the warm pasta. Mix thoroughly and serve.

733 Pasta with spiced red onion

Follow the recipe above but replace the leeks with 1 medium red onion, cut in half and then each half cut into 4 or 5 wedges, and 1 medium sweet potato, peeled and cut into small cubes.

734 Rigatoni with spicy bacon & tomato sauce

6 tbsp olive oil
3 garlic cloves, thinly sliced
75 g/2¾ oz streaky bacon, chopped
800 g/1 lb 12 oz canned chopped
 tomatoes

½ tsp dried chilli flakes
450 g/1 lb dried rigatoni
10 fresh basil leaves, shredded
2 tbsp freshly grated pecorino
salt and pepper

Heat the oil and garlic in a large frying pan over a medium–low heat. Cook until the garlic is just beginning to colour. Add the bacon and cook until browned.

Stir in the tomatoes and chilli flakes. Season with a little salt and pepper. Bring to the boil, then simmer over a medium–low heat for 30–40 minutes, until the oil separates from the tomatoes.

Bring a large saucepan of slightly salted water to the boil. Add the pasta, bring back to the boil and cook for 8–10 minutes, until tender but still firm to the bite. Drain and transfer to a warm serving dish. Pour the sauce over the pasta. Add the basil and pecorino, then toss well to mix. Serve at once.

735 Rigatoni with spicy beef

Replace the bacon with 125 g/4 oz beef steak (a tender cut such as fillet or rump). Thinly slice it then cut into bite-sized pieces and cook in the oil for 2–3 minutes over high heat before you turn down the heat and add the garlic and tomatoes. Remove from pan using a slotted spatula and keep warm until sauce is ready, then stir in to serve.

736 Pork & pasta bake

2 tbsp olive oil
1 onion, chopped
1 garlic clove, finely chopped
2 carrots, diced
55 g/2 oz pancetta, chopped
115 g/4 oz mushrooms, chopped
450 g/1 lb fresh pork mince
125 ml/4 fl oz dry white wine
4 tbsp passata

200 g/7 oz canned chopped tomatoes
2 tsp chopped fresh sage, plus extra sprigs
 to garnish
225 g/8 oz dried penne
140 g/5 oz mozzarella cheese, diced
4 tbsp freshly grated Parmesan
300 ml/10 fl oz Béchamel Sauce
 (see page 9)
salt and pepper

Preheat the oven to 200°C/400°F/Gas Mark 6. Heat the oil in a large heavy-based frying pan. Add the onion, garlic and carrots and cook over a low heat, stirring occasionally, for 5 minutes, or until the onion has softened.

Add the pancetta and cook for 5 minutes. Add the chopped mushrooms and cook, stirring occasionally, for a further 2 minutes. Add the pork and cook, breaking it up with a wooden spoon, until the meat is browned all over. Stir in the wine, passata, tomatoes and chopped fresh sage.

Season to taste with salt and pepper, bring to the boil, then cover and simmer over a low heat for 25–30 minutes.

Meanwhile, bring a large heavy-based saucepan of lightly salted water to the boil. Add the pasta, return to the boil and cook for 8–10 minutes, or until tender but still firm to the bite. Spoon

the pork mixture into a large ovenproof dish. Stir the mozzarella cheese and half the Parmesan cheese into the Béchamel sauce.

Drain the pasta and stir the sauce into it, then spoon it over the pork mixture. Sprinkle with the remaining Parmesan cheese and bake in the preheated oven for 25–30 minutes, or until golden brown. Serve immediately, garnished with sage sprigs.

737 Turkey & pasta bake

Try the recipe using turkey, chicken or lamb mince instead of pork. You could omit the pancetta if using lamb mince and use 2 teaspoons of fresh chopped oregano instead of the sage.

Traditional cannelloni

2 tbsp olive oil
2 onions, chopped
2 garlic cloves, finely chopped
1 tbsp shredded fresh basil
800 g/1 lb 12 oz canned chopped tomatoes
1 tbsp tomato purée
350 g/12 oz dried cannelloni tubes

butter, for greasing
225 g/8 oz ricotta cheese
115 g/4 oz cooked ham, diced
1 egg
50 g/2 oz freshly grated Pecorino
or Parmesan cheese
salt and pepper

Preheat the oven to 350°F/180°C/Gas Mark 4. Heat the olive oil in a large heavy-based frying pan. Add the onions and garlic and cook over low heat, stirring occasionally, for 5 minutes, or until the onion is softened. Add the basil, chopped tomatoes and tomato purée and season to taste with salt and pepper. Reduce the heat and leave to simmer for 30 minutes, or until thickened.

Meanwhile, bring a large heavy-based pan of lightly salted water to a boil. Add the cannelloni tubes, return to the boil, and cook for 8–10 minutes, or until tender but still firm to the bite. Using a slotted spoon, transfer the cannelloni tubes to a plate and pat dry with paper towels.

Grease a large, shallow ovenproof dish with butter. Mix the ricotta, ham and egg together in a bowl and season to taste with salt and pepper. Using a teaspoon, fill the cannelloni tubes with the ricotta mixture and place in a single layer in the dish. Pour the tomato sauce over the cannelloni and sprinkle with the grated Romano cheese. Bake in the preheated oven for 30 minutes, or until golden brown. Serve immediately.

739 *Traditional cannelloni with chicken*

You can replace the ham with the same amount of skinless cooked chicken or turkey breast.

740 *Spaghetti with tomato & basil sauce*

5 tbsp extra virgin olive oil
1 onion, finely chopped
800 g/1 lb 12 oz canned chopped
tomatoes
4 garlic cloves, cut into quarters

450 g/1 lb dried spaghetti
large handful fresh basil leaves, shredded
salt and pepper
freshly grated Parmesan cheese, to serve

Heat the oil in a large saucepan over a medium heat. Add the onion and cook gently for 5 minutes, until soft. Add the tomatoes and garlic.

Bring to the boil, then simmer over a medium–low heat for 25–30 minutes, or until the oil separates from the tomatoes. Season to taste with salt and pepper. Bring a large saucepan of lightly salted water to the boil. Add the pasta, bring back to the boil and cook for 8–10 minutes, or until tender but still firm to the bite. Drain and transfer to a warmed serving dish.

Pour the sauce over the pasta. Add the basil and toss well to mix. Serve with the Parmesan cheese.

741 *Spaghetti with fresh tomato sauce*

Heat 2 tablespoons of olive oil in a frying pan and add 500 g/1 lb 2 oz fresh ripe tomatoes, quartered (and skinned, if you prefer.) Fry for a few minutes over medium heat to soften and just tinge with gold, adding 2 cloves chopped garlic and 8 chopped spring onions towards the end of cooking time. Stir in 1 tablespoon of sun-dried tomato purée, then add 250 ml/9 fl oz passata and 2 tablespoons of chopped basil. Simmer for 5 minutes, season to taste. Serve with the spaghetti, garnished with fresh basil leaves and grated Parmesan.

Cannelloni with spinach & ricotta

12 dried cannelloni tubes, 7.5 cm/
3 inches long
butter, for greasing

FILLING
140 g/5 oz frozen spinach, thawed
and drained
115 g/4 oz ricotta cheese
1 egg
3 tbsp freshly grated pecorino cheese
pinch of freshly grated nutmeg
salt and pepper

CHEESE SAUCE
600 ml/1 pint milk
25 g/1 oz unsalted butter
2 tbsp plain flour
85 g/3 oz freshly grated Gruyère
cheese
salt and pepper

Bring a large saucepan of lightly salted water to the boil. Add the cannelloni tubes, return to the boil and cook for 6–7 minutes until almost tender. Drain, refresh under cold running water and drain again.

Spread out the tubes on a clean tea towel. Put the spinach and ricotta in a blender or food processor and process for a few seconds until combined. Add the egg and pecorino cheese and process again to a smooth paste. Scrape the filling into a bowl and season to taste with nutmeg and salt and pepper.

Preheat the oven to 180°C/350°F/Gas Mark 4. Grease an ovenproof dish. Spoon the filling into a piping bag fitted with a 1-cm/½-inch nozzle. Open a cannelloni tube, stand it upright

and pipe in the filling. Put the filled cannelloni tube in the prepared dish, then fill the remaining tubes. To make the cheese sauce, heat the milk in a saucepan to just below boiling point. Meanwhile, melt the butter in a separate saucepan over a low heat. Add the flour to the butter and cook, stirring constantly, for 1 minute. Remove from the heat and gradually stir in the hot milk. Return to the heat and bring to

the boil, stirring constantly.

Reduce the heat to the lowest possible setting and simmer, stirring frequently, for 10 minutes, or until thickened and smooth. Remove from the heat, stir in the Gruyère cheese and season to taste with salt and pepper. Spoon the cheese sauce over the cannelloni. Cover the dish with foil and bake in the preheated oven for 20–25 minutes. Serve immediately.

Beef cannelloni

Replace the spinach with 150 g/5 oz minced beef. Cook 1 small finely chopped onion in 1 tablespoon of olive oil until soft, push to the sides of the pan, add the beef and cook over medium heat until browned and cooked through. Season, cool and beat with the ricotta – or you could use a cream cheese – then continue with recipe.

Chicken with creamy penne

200 g/7 oz dried penne
1 tbsp olive oil
2 skinless, boneless chicken breasts
4 tbsp dry white wine
115 g/4 oz frozen peas
5 tbsp double cream
salt
4–5 tbsp chopped fresh parsley,
to garnish

Bring a large saucepan of lightly salted water to the boil. Add the pasta, bring back to the boil and cook for about 8–10 minutes, until tender but still firm to the bite.

Meanwhile, heat the oil in a frying pan, add the chicken and cook over a medium heat for about 4 minutes on each side.

Pour in the wine and cook over a high heat until it has almost evaporated. Drain the pasta. Add the peas, cream and pasta to the frying pan and stir well. Cover and simmer for 2 minutes. Garnish with fresh parsley and serve.

2 tsp olive oil
1 small red onion, finely chopped
1 tbsp lemon juice
1 garlic clove, crushed
2 celery sticks, finely chopped
150 ml/5 fl oz fish stock
150 ml/5 fl oz dry white wine
small bunch fresh tarragon
450 g/1 lb live mussels, scrubbed
and debearded
225 g/8 oz raw prawns, peeled
and deveined
225 g/8 oz baby squid, cleaned and
cut into rings
8 small cooked crab claws, cracked
225 g/8 oz dried spaghetti
salt and pepper
2 tbsp chopped fresh tarragon,
to garnish

Heat the oil in a large saucepan and fry the onion with the lemon juice, garlic and celery for 3–4 minutes, or until softened. Pour in the stock and wine. Bring to the boil and add the tarragon and mussels. Reduce the heat, cover and simmer for 5 minutes.

Add the prawns, squid and crab claws to the pan, mix together and cook for 3–4 minutes, or until the mussels have opened, the prawns are pink and the squid is opaque. Discard the tarragon and any mussels that have not opened.

Meanwhile, cook the spaghetti according to the packet instructions, and drain well. Add the spaghetti to the shellfish mixture and toss together. Season to taste with salt and pepper. Serve garnished with the tarragon.

746 *Quick seafood spaghetti*

You can replace the mussels, prawns and squid with a 500 g/1 lb 2 oz pack mixed seafood, which usually contains these three ingredients, from the freezer counter. Thaw thoroughly and add to the pan once the stock and wine have come to a simmer – cook for 5 minutes. You can also replace the tarragon with parsley.

747 *Pasta with smoked salmon & mustard sauce*

SERVES 4

450 g/1 lb dried conchiglie
300 ml/10 fl oz soured cream
2 tsp Dijon mustard
4 large spring onions,
finely sliced

225 g/8 oz smoked salmon, cut into
bite-sized pieces
finely grated rind of ½ lemon
salt and pepper
fresh chives, to garnish

Bring a large saucepan of lightly salted water to the boil. Add the pasta, bring back to the boil and cook for 8–10 minutes, until just tender but still firm to the bite. Drain and return to the pan. Add the soured cream, mustard, spring onions, smoked salmon and lemon rind to the pasta. Stir over a low heat until heated through. Season with pepper. Transfer to a serving dish. Sprinkle with the chives, and serve.

748 *Pasta with smoked salmon & rocket*

Soften 2 cloves of well-crushed garlic in 1 tablespoon of butter in a pan then add soured cream, lemon zest and Parmesan cheese. Toss with the smoked salmon, 50 g/2 oz rocket leaves and pasta.

3 tbsp olive oil
1 red onion, finely chopped
2 garlic cloves, finely chopped
350 g/12 oz fresh beef mince
1 tsp finely chopped fresh thyme
1 fresh rosemary sprig, finely chopped
1 bay leaf

1.7 litres/3 pints beef stock
2 quantities Basic Pasta Dough
   (see page 9)
plain flour, for dusting
1 egg, lightly beaten
salt and pepper

Heat the oil in a saucepan. Add the onion and garlic and cook over a low heat, stirring occasionally, for 5 minutes, until softened but not browned. Add the beef, increase the heat to medium and cook, stirring with a wooden spoon to break up the meat, for 8–10 minutes, until evenly browned.

Stir in the herbs, season to taste with salt and pepper, add 125 ml/ 4 fl oz of the stock and bring to the boil. Cover and simmer for 25 minutes, then remove the lid and cook until all the liquid has evaporated. Remove from the heat and discard the bay leaf.

Roll out the pasta dough on a lightly floured surface to 2–3 mm/ $^{1}/_{16}$–$^{1}/_{8}$ inch thick. Using a 2-cm/¾-inch plain biscuit cutter, stamp out rounds. Place about

¼ teaspoon of the meat mixture in the centre of each round. Brush the edges of each round with a little beaten egg, then fold them in half to make half moons and press the edges to seal. Wrap a half moon around the tip of your index finger until the corners meet and press together to seal. Repeat with the remaining pasta half moons. Place the filled tortellini on a floured tea towel and leave to dry for 30 minutes.

Bring the remaining stock to the boil in a large saucepan. Add the tortellini, bring back to the boil and cook for 3–4 minutes, until tender but still firm to the bite. Ladle the tortellini and broth into warmed soup bowls and serve immediately.

350 g/12 oz dried conchiglie
   or gnocchi
4 tbsp olive oil
4 tbsp butter
3 large garlic cloves, thinly sliced
200 g/7 oz canned tuna, drained and
   broken into chunks
2 tbsp lemon juice
1 tbsp capers, drained
10–12 black olives, pitted and sliced
2 tbsp chopped fresh
   flat-leaf parsley, to serve

Cook the pasta in plenty of boiling salted water until firm to the bite. Drain and return to the pan. Heat the olive oil and half the butter in a frying pan over a medium–low heat. Add the garlic and cook for a few seconds.

Reduce the heat to low. Add the tuna, lemon juice, capers and olives. Stir gently until all the ingredients are heated through. Transfer the pasta or gnocchi to a warm serving dish. Pour the tuna mixture over the pasta. Add the parsley and remaining butter. Toss well to mix. Serve immediately.

751 *Fresh tuna with garlic, lemon & olives*

Use fresh tuna instead of canned, cut into slices and cook with the garlic for 1–2 minutes. Add 6 halved cherry tomatoes to the pan with the lemon juice.

Spinach & anchovy pasta

900 g/2 lb fresh, young spinach leaves
400 g/14 oz dried fettuccine
5 tbsp olive oil
3 tbsp pine kernels
3 garlic cloves, crushed
8 canned anchovy fillets, drained and chopped
salt

Trim off any tough spinach stalks. Rinse the spinach leaves under cold running water and place them in a large saucepan with only the water that is clinging to them after washing. Cover and cook over a high heat, shaking the saucepan from time to time, until the spinach has wilted, but retains its colour. Drain well, reserve and keep warm.

Bring a large heavy-based saucepan of lightly salted water to the boil. Add the pasta, return to the boil and cook for 8–10 minutes, or until tender but still firm to the bite.

Heat 4 tablespoons of the oil in a separate saucepan. Add the pine kernels and cook until golden. Remove the pine kernels from the saucepan and reserve until required.

Add the garlic to the saucepan and cook until golden. Add the anchovies and stir in the spinach. Cook, stirring, for 2–3 minutes, until heated through. Return the pine kernels to the saucepan.

Drain the pasta, toss in the remaining oil and transfer to a warmed serving dish. Spoon the anchovy and spinach sauce over the pasta, toss lightly together and serve immediately.

753 Spinach & Parmesan pasta

Omit the anchovies and add 85 g/3 oz shaved Parmesan cheese to the pasta and serve immediately.

754 With mozzarella

Tear 1 x 125 g/4 oz ball of good quality fresh mozzarella (e.g. buffalo mozzarella) into small pieces. Omit the anchovies and stir the mozzarella into the pasta with the spinach so it starts to melt. Serve immediately.

755 Vegetable ravioli

2 large aubergines, cut into 2.5-cm/1-inch chunks
6 large tomatoes
125 ml/4 fl oz olive oil
3 garlic cloves, chopped
1 large onion, chopped
3 large courgettes cut into 2.5-cm/1-inch chunks
1 large green pepper and 1 large red pepper, deseeded and cut into 2.5-cm/1-inch chunks
4½ tsp tomato purée
½ tsp chopped fresh basil, plus extra sprigs to garnish
1 quantity Basic Pasta Dough (see page 9)
plain flour, for dusting
6 tbsp butter
150 ml/5 fl oz single cream
85 g/3 oz freshly grated Parmesan cheese
salt and pepper

To make the filling, place the aubergine pieces in a colander, sprinkle with salt and leave for 20 minutes. Rinse and drain, then pat dry on kitchen paper.

Blanch the tomatoes in boiling water for 2 minutes. Drain, peel and chop the flesh. Heat the oil in a large pan over a low heat. Add the garlic and onion and cook for 3 minutes. Stir in the aubergines, courgettes, tomatoes, peppers, tomato purée and chopped basil. Season to taste with salt and pepper, cover and simmer for 20 minutes.

Roll out the pasta dough on a lightly floured surface to a rectangle 2–3 mm/1/16–1/8 inch thick. Using a 5-cm/2-inch plain biscuit cutter, stamp out rounds.

Place small mounds, about 1 teaspoon each, of the filling on half of the rounds. Brush the edges with a little water, then cover with the remaining rounds, pressing the edges to seal. Place on a floured tea towel and leave to stand for 1 hour. Preheat the oven to 200°C/400°F/Gas Mark 6. Bring a large pan of lightly salted water to the boil over a medium heat. Add the ravioli and cook for about 3–4 minutes. Drain and transfer to a greased ovenproof dish, dotting each layer with butter. Pour over the cream and sprinkle over the Parmesan.

Bake in the preheated oven for 20 minutes. Garnish with basil and serve.

756 Vegetable ravioli with mushrooms

Use 250 g/9 oz mushrooms instead of the courgettes and peppers. Try adding some toasted pine kernels to the mixture before filling the ravioli.

757 Spaghettini with quick tuna sauce

3 tbsp olive oil

4 tomatoes, peeled, deseeded and roughly
    chopped

115 g/4 oz mushrooms, sliced

1 tbsp shredded fresh basil

400 g/14 oz canned tuna, drained

100 ml/3½ fl oz fish or chicken stock

1 garlic clove, finely chopped

2 tsp chopped fresh marjoram

350 g/12 oz dried spaghettini

salt and pepper

115 g/4 oz freshly grated Parmesan
    cheese, to serve

Heat the oil in a large frying pan. Add the tomatoes and cook over a low heat, stirring occasionally, for 15 minutes, or until pulpy. Add the mushrooms and cook, stirring occasionally, for a further 10 minutes. Stir in the basil, tuna, stock, garlic and marjoram and season to taste with salt and pepper. Cook over a low heat for 5 minutes, or until heated through. Meanwhile, bring a large heavy-based saucepan of lightly salted water to the boil. Add the pasta, return to the boil and cook for 8–10 minutes, or until tender but still firm to the bite.

Drain the pasta well, transfer to a warmed serving dish and spoon over the tuna mixture. Serve with grated Parmesan cheese.

758 Spaghettini with quick tuna & sweetcorn

Replace the canned tuna with tuna canned in tomato sauce and add 85 g/3 oz canned sweetcorn to the pan with the tuna.

759 Spaghettini with quick salmon sauce

Use canned pink salmon instead of the tuna or you could also use canned sardines or mackerel fillets.

760 Penne with creamy mushrooms

55 g/2 oz butter

1 tbsp olive oil

6 shallots, sliced

450 g/1 lb chestnut mushrooms, sliced

1 tsp plain flour

150 ml/5 fl oz double cream

2 tbsp port

115 g/4 oz sun-dried tomatoes in oil,
    drained and chopped

pinch of freshly grated nutmeg

350 g/12 oz dried penne

salt and pepper

2 tbsp chopped fresh flat-leaf parsley,
    to garnish

Melt the butter with the oil in a large heavy-based frying pan. Add the shallots and cook over a low heat, stirring occasionally, for 4–5 minutes, or until softened. Add the mushrooms and cook over a low heat for a further 2 minutes. Season to taste with salt and pepper, sprinkle in the flour and cook, stirring, for 1 minute. Remove the frying pan from the heat and gradually stir in the cream and port. Return to the heat, add the sun-dried tomatoes and grated nutmeg and cook over a low heat, stirring occasionally, for 8 minutes.

Meanwhile, bring a large saucepan of lightly salted water to the boil. Add the pasta, return to the boil and cook for 8–10 minutes, or until tender but still firm to the bite. Drain the pasta and add to the mushroom sauce. Cook for 3 minutes, then transfer to a warmed serving dish. Sprinkle with the chopped parsley and serve immediately.

761 Penne with creamy garlic mushrooms

Omit the sun-dried tomatoes and add 3 garlic cloves, well crushed, with the shallots, plus 1 teaspoon each of chopped fresh rosemary and oregano.

762 Spaghetti alla carbonara

450 g/1 lb dried spaghetti
1 tbsp olive oil
225 g/8 oz rindless pancetta or streaky
    bacon, chopped

4 eggs
5 tbsp single cream
2 tbsp freshly grated Parmesan cheese
salt and pepper

Bring a large heavy-based saucepan of lightly salted water to the boil. Add the pasta, return to the boil and cook for 8–10 minutes, or until tender but still firm to the bite. Meanwhile, heat the oil in a heavy-based frying pan. Add the pancetta and cook over a medium heat, stirring frequently, for 8–10 minutes. Beat the eggs with the cream in a small bowl and season to taste. Drain the pasta and return it to the saucepan. Tip in the contents of the frying pan, then add the egg mixture and half the Parmesan cheese. Stir well, then transfer to a warmed serving dish. Serve immediately, sprinkled with the remaining cheese.

763 Simple spaghetti alla carbonara

Cook your pasta and leave in the hot pan over a low heat. Stir in 225 g/8 oz chopped good quality ham, 225 g/8 oz crème fraîche, 4 tablespoons of Parmesan cheese and plenty of seasoning.

764 With petits pois & herbs

To either of the above recipes, add 85 g/3 oz cooked petits pois and 1 tablespoon of fresh chopped mint or parsley.

765 Spaghetti with meatballs

1 potato, diced
400 g/14 oz steak mince
1 onion, finely chopped
1 egg
4 tbsp chopped fresh flat-leaf parsley
plain flour, for dusting
5 tbsp extra virgin olive oil
400 ml/14 fl oz passata
2 tbsp tomato purée
400 g/14 oz dried spaghetti
6 fresh basil leaves, shredded,
    to garnish
salt and pepper
freshly grated Parmesan cheese,
    to garnish

Place the potato in a small saucepan, add cold water to cover and a pinch of salt, and bring to the boil. Cook for 10–15 minutes, until tender, then drain. Either mash thoroughly with a potato masher or fork or pass through a potato ricer. Combine the potato, steak, onion, egg and parsley in a bowl and season to taste with salt and pepper.

Spread out the flour on a plate. With dampened hands, shape the meat mixture into walnut-sized balls and roll in the flour. Shake off any excess.

Heat the oil in a heavy-based frying pan, add the meatballs and cook over a medium heat, stirring and turning frequently, for 8–10 minutes, until golden all over. Add the passata and tomato purée and cook for a further 10 minutes, until the sauce is reduced and thickened.

Meanwhile, bring a large saucepan of lightly salted water to the boil. Add the pasta, bring back to the boil and cook for 8–10 minutes, until tender but still firm to the bite.

Drain well and add to the meatball sauce, tossing well to coat. Transfer to a warmed serving dish, garnish with the basil leaves and freshly grated Parmesan and serve immediately.

766 Spaghetti with pork meatballs

For a softer meatball, replace the steak with 350 g/12 oz minced pork fillet and 50 g/2 oz fresh breadcrumbs.

Layered spaghetti with smoked salmon & prawns

70 g/2½ oz butter, plus extra for greasing
350 g/12 oz dried spaghetti
200 g/7 oz smoked salmon, cut into strips
280 g/10 oz large Mediterranean
    prawns or tiger prawns, cooked,
    peeled and deveined

300 ml/10 fl oz Béchamel Sauce
    (see page 9)
115 g/4 oz freshly grated Parmesan cheese
salt

Preheat the oven to 180°C/350°F/Gas Mark 4. Grease a large, ovenproof dish. Bring a large saucepan of water to the boil, add the pasta, and cook for 8–10 minutes, or until tender but still firm to the bite. Drain, return to the saucepan, add 55 g/2 oz of the butter and toss well.

Spoon half the spaghetti into the dish, cover with the smoked salmon, then top with the prawns. Pour over half the béchamel sauce and sprinkle with half the Parmesan. Add the remaining spaghetti, cover with the remaining sauce and sprinkle with the remaining Parmesan. Dice the remaining butter and dot it over the surface. Bake in the oven for 15 minutes, or until the top is golden. Serve immediately.

768 *Spaghetti with halibut & mussels*

This dish would also be delicious made with smoked halibut instead of the salmon and smoked mussels instead of the prawns.

769 *Smoked salmon & prawn lasagne*

Replace the spaghetti with lasagne sheets, thinning down the Béchamel sauce with milk until it is the consistency of double cream (about 125 ml/4 fl oz).

Spinach & ricotta ravioli

350 g/12 oz spinach leaves
225 g/8 oz ricotta cheese
85 g/3 oz freshly grated Parmesan cheese,
2 eggs
pinch of freshly grated nutmeg
pepper

SPINACH PASTA DOUGH
Blanch, drain and finely chop 225 g/8 oz
    spinach and add to one quantity of
    Basic Pasta Dough (see page 9)
plain flour, for dusting

To make the filling, place the spinach in a heavy-based saucepan with just the water clinging to the leaves after washing, then cover and cook over a low heat for 5 minutes, or until wilted. Drain well and squeeze out as much moisture as possible. Leave to cool, then chop finely.

Beat the ricotta cheese until smooth, then stir in the spinach, 55g/2 oz Parmesan cheese and 1 of the eggs and season to taste with nutmeg and pepper.

Divide the pasta dough in half and wrap 1 piece in clingfilm. Roll out the other piece on a lightly floured surface to a rectangle 2–3 mm/¹⁄₁₆–¹⁄₈ inch thick. Cover with a damp tea towel and roll out the other piece of dough to the same size. Place small mounds, about 1 teaspoon each, of the

spinach and ricotta filling in rows 4 cm/1½ inches apart on a sheet of pasta dough. In a small bowl, lightly beat the remaining egg and use it to brush the spaces between the mounds.

Lift the second sheet of dough on top of the first and press down firmly between the pockets of filling, pushing out any air bubbles. Using a pasta wheel or sharp knife cut into squares. Place on a floured tea towel and leave to stand for 1 hour.

Bring a large saucepan of lightly salted water to the boil, add the ravioli, in batches, return to the boil and cook for 5 minutes. Remove with a perforated spoon and drain on kitchen paper. Transfer to a warmed dish and serve immediately, sprinkled with the rest of the Parmesan cheese.

771 Creamy chicken ravioli

115 g/4 oz cooked skinless, boneless
chicken breast, coarsely chopped
55 g/2 oz cooked spinach
55 g/2 oz prosciutto,
coarsely chopped
1 shallot, coarsely chopped
6 tbsp freshly grated Pecorino cheese
pinch of freshly grated nutmeg
2 eggs, lightly beaten
1 quantity Basic Pasta Dough
(see page 9)
plain flour, for dusting
300 ml/10 fl oz double cream
2 garlic cloves, finely chopped
115 g/4 oz chestnut mushrooms,
thinly sliced
2 tbsp shredded fresh basil, plus fresh
basil sprigs, to garnish
salt and pepper

Process the chicken, spinach, prosciutto and shallot in a food processor until chopped and blended. Transfer to a bowl, stir in 2 tablespoons of the grated cheese, the nutmeg and half the beaten egg, and season.

Halve the pasta dough and thinly roll out each half on a lightly floured board. Place small mounds of the filling in rows 4 cm/1½ inches apart on one sheet of dough and brush in between with beaten egg. Cover with the other half of dough. Press down between the mounds of filling, pushing out any air. Cut into squares and let rest on a floured tea towel for 1 hour.

Bring a saucepan of salted water to the boil. Add the ravioli, in batches, return to the boil and cook for 5 minutes. Remove and drain on kitchen paper, then transfer to a warmed dish.

Meanwhile, bring the cream to the boil with the garlic in a frying pan. Simmer for 1 minute, then add the mushrooms and 2 tablespoons of the remaining cheese. Season, simmer for 3 minutes, then stir in the basil. Pour the sauce over the ravioli, sprinkle with the remaining cheese, garnish with basil sprigs and serve.

772 Creamy salmon ravioli

Use the recipe above but replace the chicken with 115 g/4 oz salmon fillet, lightly poached until just cooked. Do not overcook it or it will become dry.

773 Garlic mushroom ravioli

75 g/2¾ oz butter
50 g/1¾ oz shallots, finely chopped
3 garlic cloves, crushed
50 g/1¾ oz mushrooms, wiped and
finely chopped
½ celery stick, finely chopped
25 g/1 oz pecorino cheese, finely
grated, plus extra to garnish
½ quantity Basic Pasta Dough
(see page 9)
plain flour, for dusting
1 egg, lightly beaten
salt and pepper

Heat 25 g/1 oz of the butter in a frying pan. Add the shallots, 1 crushed garlic clove, the mushrooms and celery and cook for 4–5 minutes. Remove the frying pan from the heat, stir in the pecorino cheese and season to taste. Divide the pasta dough in half and wrap 1 piece in clingfilm.

Roll out the other piece on a lightly floured surface to a rectangle 2–3 mm/¹⁄₁₆–⅛ inch thick. Cover with a damp tea towel and roll out the other piece of dough to the same size. Place small mounds, about 1 teaspoon each, of the filling in rows 4 cm/1½ inches apart on a sheet of pasta dough. Brush the spaces between the mounds with the beaten egg. Lift the second sheet of dough on top of the first and press down firmly between the pockets of filling, pushing out any air bubbles. Using a pasta wheel or sharp knife, cut into squares. Place on a floured tea towel and leave to stand for 1 hour. Bring a heavy-based saucepan of water to the boil, add the ravioli and cook in batches for 2–3 minutes.

Remove with a slotted spoon and drain. Meanwhile, melt the remaining butter in a frying pan. Add the remaining garlic and plenty of pepper and cook for 1–2 minutes. Transfer ravioli to plates and pour over the garlic butter. Garnish with pecorino cheese and serve immediately.

774 With fresh herbs

Add fresh herbs such as 2 tablespoons of fresh, finely chopped parsley or leaf coriander or fresh oregano to the mushroom mix for the last minute of mushroom cooking time.

Macaroni cheese & tomato

1 tbsp butter or margarine, plus
    extra for greasing
225 g/8 oz dried macaroni
175 g/6 oz freshly grated Cheddar cheese
100 g/3½ oz freshly grated
    Parmesan cheese
4 tbsp fresh white breadcrumbs
1 tbsp chopped fresh basil
salt and pepper

TOMATO SAUCE
1 tbsp olive oil
1 shallot, finely chopped
2 garlic cloves, crushed
500 g/1 lb 2 oz canned chopped tomatoes
1 tbsp chopped fresh basil
salt and pepper

Preheat the oven to 190°C/375°F/ Gas Mark 5. Grease a deep ovenproof dish with a little butter. To make the tomato sauce, heat the oil in a pan over a medium heat. Add the shallot and garlic and cook, stirring constantly, for 1 minute. Add the tomatoes and basil and season to taste with salt and pepper. Cook, stirring, for 10 minutes. Meanwhile, bring a large pan of lightly salted water to the boil over a medium heat. Add the macaroni and cook for 8–10 minutes, or until tender but still firm to the bite. Drain well. Mix the grated Cheddar and Parmesan cheeses together in a small bowl.

Spoon one third of the tomato sauce into the base of the prepared dish, then cover with one third of the macaroni and top with one third of the mixed cheeses. Season to taste with salt and pepper. Repeat these layers twice, ending with a layer of the grated cheeses.

Mix the breadcrumbs and basil together and sprinkle evenly over the top. Dot the topping with the butter and cook in the preheated oven for about 25 minutes, or until the topping is golden brown and bubbling. Serve.

776 With olives

Add 8 stoned sliced black olives to the tomato sauce for added piquancy. You can also reserve one quarter of the mixed cheeses and instead of layering all the cheese with the macaroni and tomato sauce, mix it with the crumbs before sprinkling over the top. You should then not need to dot with butter as the cheese is high in fat and will help the crumbs to turn golden without burning.

777 Double cheese macaroni

225 g/8 oz dried macaroni
250 g/9 oz ricotta cheese
1½ tbsp wholegrain mustard
3 tbsp snipped fresh chives, plus extra to
    garnish
200 g/7 oz cherry tomatoes, halved

100 g/3½ oz sun-dried tomatoes in oil,
    drained and chopped
butter or oil, for greasing
100 g/3½ oz Cheddar cheese, grated
salt and pepper

Preheat the oven to 190°C/375°F/Gas Mark 5. Bring a saucepan of lightly salted water to the boil. Add the pasta and cook for 10–12 minutes, or until tender. Drain. Mix the ricotta with the mustard, chives and salt and pepper. Stir in the macaroni, cherry tomatoes and sun-dried tomatoes. Grease a 1.7-litre/3-pint ovenproof dish, spoon in the macaroni mixture and sprinkle with the cheese. Then bake for 20 minutes or until the top is golden.

778 Triple cheese macaroni

For a richer dish, tear 125g/4 oz buffalo mozzarella into small pieces and stir into the macaroni with the ricotta.

Vegetarian

Chickpea & vegetable casserole

1 tbsp olive oil
1 red onion, halved and sliced
3 garlic cloves, crushed
225 g/8 oz spinach leaves
1 fennel bulb, cut into eighths
1 red pepper, deseeded and diced
1 tbsp plain flour
450 ml/16 fl oz vegetable stock

85 ml/3 fl oz dry white wine
400 g/14 oz canned chickpeas, drained
1 bay leaf
1 tsp ground coriander
½ tsp paprika
salt and pepper
fennel fronds, to garnish

Heat the oil in a large flameproof casserole. Add the onion and garlic and sauté for 1 minute, stirring. Add the spinach and cook for 4 minutes, or until wilted. Add the fennel and pepper and cook for 2 minutes, stirring. Stir in the flour and cook for 1 minute.

Add the stock, wine, chickpeas, bay leaf, coriander and paprika, cover and cook for 30 minutes. Season to taste with salt and pepper, garnish with fennel fronds and serve immediately.

780 *Chickpea & peppers casserole*

Omit the fennel and spinach and instead add 1 yellow pepper and 1 green pepper. Replace the dry white wine with passata. You can also use fresh basil leaves instead of the ground coriander, if you like.

781 *Borlotti bean & vegetable casserole*

Use 400 g/14 oz canned drained borlotti beans instead of the chickpeas.

Cold weather vegetable casserole

40 g/1½ oz butter
2 leeks, sliced
2 carrots, sliced
2 potatoes, cut into bite-sized pieces
1 swede, cut into bite-sized pieces
2 courgettes, sliced
1 fennel bulb, halved and sliced
2 tbsp plain flour
425 g/15 oz canned butter beans
600 ml/1 pint vegetable stock
2 tbsp tomato purée
1 tsp dried thyme
2 bay leaves
salt and pepper

DUMPLINGS
115 g/4 oz self-raising flour
pinch of salt
55 g/2 oz vegetarian suet
2 tbsp chopped fresh parsley
about 4 tbsp water

Melt the butter in a large heavy-based saucepan over a low heat. Add the leeks, carrots, potatoes, swede, courgettes and fennel and cook, stirring occasionally, for 10 minutes. Stir in the flour and cook, stirring constantly, for 1 minute. Stir in the can juice from the beans, the stock, tomato purée, thyme and bay leaves and season to taste with salt and pepper. Bring to the boil, stirring constantly, then cover and simmer for 10 minutes.

Meanwhile, make the dumplings. Sift the flour and salt into a bowl. Stir in the suet and parsley, then add enough water to bind to a soft dough. Divide the dough into 8 pieces and roll into balls. Add the butter beans and dumplings to the saucepan, cover and simmer for a further 30 minutes. Remove and discard the bay leaves before serving.

783 *Cold weather vegetable crumble*

Omit the dumplings and instead use a savoury crumble – combine 50 g/2 oz wholemeal flour, 50 g/2 oz rolled oats, 25 g/1 oz chopped mixed nuts and 40 g/1½ oz butter plus seasoning. Reduce the amount of stock in the recipe to 300 ml/10 fl oz. Sprinkle crumble over the casserole for the last 20 minutes of cooking time (without lid). Tip – if there is too much liquid in the pot the crumble will simply disappear into the casserole so you need to make sure the vegetables are sitting approximately one third out of the liquid before adding the crumble topping.

Layered vegetable casserole

SERVES 4

1 tbsp olive oil, for brushing
680 g/1 lb 8 oz potatoes, peeled and
thinly sliced
2 leeks, trimmed and sliced
2 beef tomatoes, sliced
8 fresh basil leaves
1 garlic clove, finely chopped
150 ml/5 fl oz vegetable stock
salt and pepper

Preheat the oven to 180°C/350°F/ Gas Mark 4. Brush a large flameproof casserole with a little of the olive oil. Place a layer of potato slices in the bottom of the casserole and cover with a layer of leeks. Top with a layer of tomato slices and a few basil leaves. Repeat these layers until all the vegetables are used up, ending with a layer of potatoes. Stir the garlic into the stock and season to taste with salt and pepper. Pour the stock over the vegetables and brush the top with the remaining oil. Bake in the centre of the preheated oven for 1½ hours, or until the vegetables are tender and the topping is golden brown. Serve immediately.

785 *Layered casserole with sweet potato*

For a change try using sweet potatoes instead of the potatoes – peel and slice to 5 mm/¼ inch thick. They will cook slightly quicker than the ordinary potatoes – allow 1 hour and 15 minutes.

Lentil & rice casserole

SERVES 4

225 g/8 oz split red lentils, washed
50 g/1¾ oz long-grain rice
1 litre/1¾ pints vegetable stock
150 ml/5 fl oz dry white wine
1 leek, cut into chunks
3 garlic cloves, crushed
400 g/14 oz canned chopped tomatoes
1 tsp ground cumin
1 tsp chilli powder

1 tsp garam masala
1 red pepper, deseeded and sliced
100 g/3½ oz small broccoli florets
8 baby corn, halved lengthways
50 g/1¾ oz French beans, halved
1 tbsp shredded fresh basil, plus extra
sprigs to garnish
salt and pepper

Place the lentils, rice, stock and wine in a flameproof casserole over a low heat and cook for 20 minutes, stirring occasionally. Add the leek, garlic, tomatoes, cumin, chilli powder, garam masala, pepper, broccoli, baby corn and beans. Bring the mixture to the boil, then reduce the heat, cover and simmer for a further 10–15 minutes, or until the vegetables are tender. Add the shredded basil and season to taste with salt and pepper.

Garnish with basil sprigs and serve immediately.

787 *Lentil & brown rice casserole*

You can use brown rice instead of white if you prefer – some brands of brown rice will need longer cooking – allow up to 35 minutes of simmering in the stock, etc., before adding remaining ingredients.

788 *Green lentil & rice casserole*

You can use other types of lentil – green, brown, black or Puy – all of which are highly nutritious. These may take a little longer to cook through than the red lentils – allow an extra 5–10 minutes of simmering time.

Pasta & bean casserole

225 g/8 oz dried haricot beans, soaked
    overnight and drained
6 tbsp olive oil
2 large onions, sliced
2 garlic cloves, chopped
2 bay leaves
1 tsp dried oregano
1 tsp dried thyme
5 tbsp red wine
2 tbsp tomato purée
850 ml/1½ pints vegetable stock

225 g/8 oz dried penne, or other short
    pasta shapes
2 celery sticks, sliced
1 fennel bulb, sliced
125 g/4½ oz mushrooms, sliced
225 g/8 oz tomatoes, sliced
1 tsp dark muscovado sugar
50 g/1¾ oz dried white breadcrumbs
salt and pepper
salad leaves and crusty
    bread, to serve

Preheat the oven to 180°C/350°F/Gas Mark 4. Place the beans in a saucepan, cover with water and bring to the boil. Boil rapidly for 20 minutes, then drain. Place the beans in a large flameproof casserole, stir in 5 tablespoons of the olive oil, the onions, garlic, bay leaves, herbs, wine and tomato purée and pour in the vegetable stock. Bring to the boil, then cover the casserole and bake in the oven for 2 hours. Towards the end of the cooking time, bring a large saucepan of lightly salted water to the boil, add the pasta and the remaining oil, and cook for 3 minutes. Drain and set aside.

Remove the casserole from the oven and add the pasta, celery, fennel, mushrooms and tomatoes and season to taste with salt and pepper. Stir in the sugar and sprinkle over the breadcrumbs. Cover the casserole again, return to the oven and continue cooking for 1 hour. Serve hot with salad leaves and crusty bread.

Potato & lemon casserole

100 ml/3½ fl oz olive oil
2 red onions, cut into 8 wedges
3 garlic cloves, crushed
2 tsp ground cumin
2 tsp ground coriander
pinch of cayenne pepper
1 carrot, thickly sliced

2 small turnips, quartered
1 courgette, sliced
500 g/1 lb 2 oz potatoes, thickly sliced
juice and grated rind of 2 large lemons
300 ml/10 fl oz vegetable stock
2 tbsp chopped fresh coriander
salt and pepper

Heat the olive oil in a flameproof casserole. Add the onions and sauté over a medium heat, stirring frequently, for 3 minutes.

Add the garlic and cook for 30 seconds. Stir in the ground cumin, ground coriander and cayenne and cook, stirring constantly, for 1 minute. Add the carrot, turnips, courgette and potatoes and stir to coat in the oil. Add the lemon juice and rind and the vegetable stock. Season to taste with salt and pepper. Cover and cook over a medium heat, stirring occasionally, for 20–30 minutes until tender. Remove the lid, sprinkle in the chopped fresh coriander and stir well. Serve immediately.

791 *Potato, squash & lemon casserole*

Try swapping the turnips for a similar weight of butternut squash, peeled and cubed.

792 Red cabbage casserole

1 red cabbage, about 750 g/1 lb 10 oz
2 onions, peeled and finely sliced
1 garlic clove, peeled and chopped
2 small cooking apples, peeled, cored and sliced
2 tbsp muscovado sugar

½ tsp ground cinnamon
whole nutmeg, for grating
2 tbsp red wine vinegar
zest and juice of 1 orange
2 tbsp redcurrant jelly
salt and pepper

Preheat the oven to 150°C/300°F/Gas Mark 2. Cut the cabbage into quarters and remove the centre stalk. Shred finely.

In the casserole dish, layer up the red cabbage, onions, garlic and apples. Sprinkle over the sugar and cinnamon and grate a quarter of the nutmeg over the top. Pour over the wine vinegar and orange juice and scatter over the orange zest. Stir well and season. The dish will be quite full but the volume of the cabbage will reduce during cooking.

Cook in the centre of the preheated oven for 1–1½ hours, stirring from time to time. If you prefer, you can cook it more quickly in a flameproof casserole dish on the top of the stove over a medium heat for 8–10 minutes until the cabbage is just tender. The stove way leaves the cabbage more crunchy.

Stir in the redcurrant jelly, and adjust the seasoning if necessary. Serve the casserole hot.

793 Mixed bean & vegetable crumble

1 large onion, peeled and chopped
125 g/4½ oz canned red kidney beans (drained weight)
125 g/4½ oz canned butter beans (drained weight)
125 g/4½ oz canned chickpeas (drained weight)
2 courgettes, roughly chopped
2 large carrots, roughly chopped
4 tomatoes, peeled and roughly chopped
2 sticks celery, trimmed and chopped
300 ml/10 fl oz vegetable stock
2 tbsp tomato purée
salt and pepper

CRUMBLE TOPPING
85 g/3 oz wholemeal breadcrumbs
25 g/1 oz hazelnuts, very finely chopped
1 heaped tbsp chopped fresh parsley
115 g/4 oz Cheddar cheese, grated

Preheat the oven to 180°C/350°F/Gas Mark 4. Put the onion, kidney beans, butter beans, chickpeas, courgettes, carrots, tomatoes and celery in a large ovenproof dish. Mix together the stock and tomato purée and pour over the vegetables. Season to taste. Transfer to the preheated oven and bake for 15 minutes. Meanwhile, to make the topping, put the breadcrumbs in a large bowl, add the hazelnuts, chopped parsley and grated cheese and mix together well. Remove the vegetables from the oven and carefully sprinkle over the crumble topping. Do not press it down or it will sink into the vegetables and go mushy. Return the crumble to the oven and bake for 30 minutes, or until the crumble topping is golden brown. Remove from the oven and serve hot.

794 Quick mixed bean & vegetable crumble

You can replace the 3 different beans with 400 g/14 oz canned ready-mixed beans, drained. You can also try using 1 parsnip instead of 1 carrot.

795 Aloo gobi

SERVES 4

55 g/2 oz ghee or 4 tbsp vegetable or
groundnut oil
½ tbsp cumin seeds
1 onion, chopped
4-cm/1½-inch piece
fresh ginger, finely chopped
1 fresh green chilli, deseeded and
thinly sliced
450 g/1 lb cauliflower, cut into small
florets
450 g/1 lb large waxy potatoes, peeled
and cut into large chunks
½ tsp ground coriander
½ tsp garam masala
¼ tsp salt
fresh coriander sprigs, to garnish

Heat the ghee in a flameproof casserole or large frying pan with a tight-fitting lid over a medium–high heat. Add the cumin seeds and stir around for about 30 seconds until they crackle and start to brown. Immediately stir in the onion, ginger and chilli and stir for 5–8 minutes until the onion is golden.

Stir in the cauliflower and potato, followed by the ground coriander, garam masala and salt, and continue stirring for about 30 seconds longer.

Cover the pan, reduce the heat to the lowest setting and simmer, stirring occasionally, for 20–30 minutes until the vegetables are tender when pierced with the point of a knife. Check occasionally that they aren't sticking to the base of the pan and stir in a little water, if necessary.

Serve garnished with sprigs of fresh coriander.

796 Aloo gobi with pumpkin

Although it isn't traditional, you can make the aloo gobi using pumpkin or winter squash instead of the potatoes – peel and cut into chunks.

797 Aubergine & bean curry

SERVES 4

2 tbsp vegetable or peanut oil
1 onion, chopped
2 garlic cloves, crushed
2 fresh red chillies, deseeded and chopped
1 tbsp Thai red curry paste
1 large aubergine, cut into chunks
115 g/4 oz pea or small aubergines
115 g/4 oz baby broad beans

115 g/4 oz French beans
300 ml/10 fl oz vegetable stock
55 g/2 oz block creamed coconut,
chopped
3 tbsp Thai soy sauce
1 tsp soft light brown sugar
3 kaffir lime leaves, coarsely torn
4 tbsp chopped fresh coriander

Heat the oil in a wok and sauté the onion, garlic and chillies for 1–2 minutes. Stir in the curry paste and cook for 1–2 minutes.

Add the aubergines and cook for 3–4 minutes, until starting to soften. (You may need to add a little more oil as aubergines soak it up quickly.) Add all the beans and stir-fry for 2 minutes.

Pour in the stock and add the creamed coconut, soy sauce, sugar and lime leaves. Bring gently to the boil and cook until the coconut has dissolved. Stir in the coriander and serve hot.

798 Indian-style aubergine & bean curry

For an Indian-style curry, replace the red curry paste with 1 tablespoon of Madras or Balti curry paste, replace the coconut with 100 ml/3½ fl oz thick full-fat yogurt and omit the Thai soy sauce.

242

Cauliflower & sweet potato curry

SERVES 4

4 tbsp ghee or vegetable oil
2 onions, finely chopped
1 tsp Panch Phoran
1 cauliflower, broken into small florets
350 g/12 oz sweet potatoes, diced
2 fresh green chillies, deseeded and finely
    chopped
1 tsp ginger purée
2 tsp paprika
1¹/₂ tsp ground cumin
1 tsp ground turmeric
¹/₂ tsp chilli powder
3 tomatoes, quartered
225 g/8 oz fresh or frozen peas
3 tbsp natural yogurt
225 ml/8 fl oz vegetable stock or water
salt
1 tsp garam masala
fresh coriander sprigs, to garnish

Heat the ghee in a large heavy-based frying pan. Add the onions and Panch Phoran and cook over a low heat, stirring frequently, for 10 minutes, or until the onions are golden. Add the cauliflower, sweet potatoes and chillies and cook, stirring frequently, for 3 minutes.

Stir in the ginger purée, paprika, cumin, turmeric and chilli powder and cook, stirring constantly, for 3 minutes. Add the tomatoes and peas and stir in the yogurt and stock. Season with salt to taste, cover and simmer for 20 minutes, or until the vegetables are tender. Sprinkle the garam masala over the curry, transfer to a warmed serving dish and serve immediately, garnished with fresh coriander sprigs.

800 Cauliflower, bean & sweet potato curry

Panch Phoran is a Bengali five-spice mix. If you can't find it, you can use a pinch each of ground cumin, fennel, fenugreek and black mustard seed. You can also replace the peas with French beans, cut into 3-cm/1¼-inch slices.

801 Chickpea & potato curry

SERVES 6

225 g/8 oz dried chickpeas, soaked
3 tbsp vegetable oil
¹/₂ tsp cumin seeds
¹/₂ tsp mustard seeds
1 onion, finely chopped
2 garlic cloves, very finely chopped
2-cm/³/₄-inch piece fresh ginger, very
    finely chopped
1 tsp salt
2 tsp ground coriander
1 tsp turmeric
¹/₂ tsp cayenne pepper
2 tbsp tomato purée
400 g/14 oz canned chopped tomatoes
2 potatoes, cubed
3 tbsp chopped fresh coriander
1 tbsp lemon juice
250–300 ml/9–10 fl oz vegetable stock
thinly sliced white or red onion rings,
    to garnish
freshly cooked rice, to serve

Boil the chickpeas rapidly in plenty of water for 15 minutes. Reduce the heat and boil gently for 1 hour, or until tender. Drain and set aside.

Heat the oil in a large saucepan or high-sided frying pan. Stirring all the time, add the cumin and mustard seeds, cover and cook for a few seconds, or until the seeds pop. Add the onion, cover and cook for 3–5 minutes, or until just brown. Add the garlic and ginger and cook for a few seconds.

Stir in the salt, ground coriander, turmeric and cayenne, then the tomato purée and tomatoes. Simmer for a few minutes. Add the chickpeas, potatoes and 2 tablespoons of the fresh coriander.

Stir in the lemon juice and 250 ml/9 fl oz of the stock. Bring to the boil, then reduce the heat, cover and simmer the curry for 30–40 minutes, or until the potatoes are cooked. Add the extra stock if the mixture becomes too dry.

Serve on a bed of rice, garnished with onion rings and the remaining fresh coriander.

802 Chickpea & sweet potato curry

Replace the potatoes with 300 g/10½ oz sweet potato, peeled and cubed – or use half and half for an attractive dish.

Cumin-scented aubergine & potato curry

1 large aubergine, about 350 g/12 oz
225 g/8 oz potatoes, boiled in their
skins and cooled
3 tbsp sunflower or olive oil
½ tsp black mustard seeds
½ tsp nigella seeds
½ tsp fennel seeds
1 onion, finely chopped
2.5-cm/1-inch piece fresh ginger,
grated
2 fresh green chillies, chopped
(deseeded if you like)
½ tsp ground cumin
1 tsp ground coriander
1 tsp ground turmeric
½ tsp chilli powder
1 tbsp tomato purée
450 ml/15 fl oz warm water
1 tsp salt, or to taste
½ tsp garam masala
2 tbsp chopped fresh coriander leaves
Indian bread, to serve

Quarter the aubergine lengthways and cut the stem end of each quarter into 5-cm/2-inch pieces. Halve the remaining part of each quarter and cut into the same size as above. Soak the aubergine pieces in cold water.

Peel the potatoes and cut into 5-cm/2-inch cubes. Heat the oil in a large saucepan over a medium heat. When hot, add the mustard seeds and, as soon as they start popping, add the nigella seeds and fennel seeds.

Add the onion, ginger and chillies and cook for 7–8 minutes, until the mixture begins to brown. Add the cumin, coriander, turmeric and chilli powder.

Cook for about a minute, then add the tomato purée. Cook for a further minute, pour in the warm water, then add the salt and aubergine pieces.

Bring to the boil and cook over a medium heat for 8–10 minutes, stirring frequently to ensure that the aubergine cooks evenly. At the start of cooking, the aubergine will float, but once it soaks up the liquid it will sink quite quickly. As soon as the aubergine sinks, add the potatoes and cook for 2–3 minutes, stirring. Stir in the garam masala and chopped coriander and remove from the heat. Serve with Indian bread.

804 Aubergine & sweet potato curry

Use sweet potato instead of potato, and replace the water with vegetable stock for even greater depth of flavour.

805 Spicy chickpea and aubergine curry

1 tbsp cumin seeds
2 tbsp coriander seeds
2 tsp dried oregano or thyme
5 tbsp vegetable oil
2 onions, chopped
1 red pepper, deseeded and cut into
2-cm/¾-inch chunks
1 aubergine, cut into 2-cm/¾-inch
chunks
2 garlic cloves, chopped
1 fresh green chilli, chopped
400 g/14 oz canned chopped tomatoes
400 g/14 oz canned chickpeas,
drained and rinsed
225 g/8 oz green beans, cut into
2-cm/¾-inch lengths
600 ml/1 pint stock
3 tbsp chopped fresh coriander

Dry-fry the seeds in a heavy-based frying pan for a few seconds, until aromatic. Add the oregano and cook for a further few seconds. Remove from the heat, transfer to a mortar and crush with a pestle.

Heat the oil in a large heavy-based casserole dish. Cook the onions, red pepper and aubergine for 10 minutes, until soft. Add the ground seed mixture, garlic and chilli and cook for a further 2 minutes.

Add the tomatoes, chickpeas, green beans and stock. Bring to the boil, then cover and simmer gently for 1 hour. Stir in the coriander and serve immediately.

Spiced black-eyed beans & mushrooms

SERVES 4

1 onion, roughly chopped
4 large garlic cloves, roughly chopped
2.5-cm/1-inch piece fresh ginger, roughly chopped
4 tbsp sunflower or olive oil
1 tsp ground cumin
1 tsp ground coriander
1/2 tsp ground fennel
1 tsp ground turmeric
1/2–1 tsp chilli powder
175 g/6 oz canned chopped tomatoes
400 g/14 oz canned black-eyed beans, drained and rinsed
115 g/4 oz large flat mushrooms, wiped and cut into bite-sized pieces
1/2 tsp salt, or to taste
175 ml/6 fl oz warm water
1 tbsp chopped fresh mint
1 tbsp chopped fresh coriander leaves
Indian bread, to serve

Purée the onion, garlic and ginger in a food processor or blender. Heat the oil in a medium saucepan over a medium heat and add the puréed ingredients.

Cook for 4–5 minutes, then add the cumin, ground coriander, ground fennel, turmeric and chilli powder. Stir-fry for about a minute, then add the tomatoes. Cook until the tomatoes are pulpy and the juice has evaporated. Add the black-eyed beans, mushrooms and salt. Stir well and pour in the warm water, bring to the boil, cover the pan and reduce the heat to low. Simmer for 8–10 minutes, stirring halfway through.

Stir in the chopped herbs and remove from the heat. Transfer to a serving dish and serve with Indian bread.

807 Spiced black lentils & mushrooms

Omit the black-eyed beans and instead use 175 g/6 oz (dry weight) black Beluga lentils (or Puy lentils). Boil for 25 minutes then drain and add to the recipe instead of the beans.

Vegetable curry

SERVES 4

1 aubergine
225 g/8 oz turnips
350 g/12 oz new potatoes
225 g/8 oz cauliflower
225 g/8 oz button mushrooms
1 large onion
3 carrots
6 tbsp ghee
2 garlic cloves, crushed
4 tsp finely chopped fresh ginger
1–2 fresh green chillies, deseeded and chopped
1 tbsp paprika
2 tsp ground coriander
1 tbsp mild or medium curry powder
450 ml/16 fl oz vegetable stock
400 g/14 oz canned chopped tomatoes
1 green pepper, deseeded and sliced
1 tbsp cornflour
150 ml/5 fl oz coconut milk
2–3 tbsp ground almonds
fresh coriander sprigs, to garnish
freshly cooked rice, to serve
salt

Cut the aubergine, turnips and potatoes into 1-cm/1/2-inch cubes. Divide the cauliflower into small florets. Leave the button mushrooms whole or slice them thickly, if preferred. Slice the onion and carrots. Heat the ghee in a large heavy-based saucepan. Add the onion, turnips, potatoes and cauliflower and cook over a low heat, stirring frequently, for 3 minutes. Add the garlic, ginger, chillies, paprika, ground coriander and curry powder and cook, stirring, for 1 minute.

Add the stock, tomatoes, aubergine and mushrooms, and season to taste with salt. Cover and simmer, stirring occasionally, for 30 minutes, or until tender. Add the green pepper and carrots, cover and cook for a further 5 minutes. Place the cornflour and coconut milk in a bowl, mix into a smooth paste and stir into the vegetable mixture. Add the ground almonds and simmer, stirring constantly, for 2 minutes. Taste and adjust the seasoning, if necessary.

Transfer to warmed serving plates, garnish with coriander sprigs and serve immediately with freshly cooked rice.

809 Vegetable curry with swede & broccoli

The turnips can be replaced with swede or squash and the cauliflower can be omitted – use broccoli instead.

Spiced cashew nut curry

SERVES 4

250 g/9 oz unsalted cashew nuts
1 tsp coriander seeds
1 tsp cumin seeds
2 green cardamom pods, crushed
1 tbsp sunflower oil
1 onion, thinly sliced
1 garlic clove, crushed

1 small fresh green chilli, deseeded
  and chopped
1 cinnamon stick
½ tsp ground turmeric
4 tbsp coconut cream
300 ml/10 fl oz hot vegetable stock
3 kaffir lime leaves, finely shredded
boiled jasmine rice, to serve

Soak the cashew nuts in cold water overnight. Drain thoroughly.
Crush the coriander seeds, cumin seeds and cardamoms using a pestle
and mortar.

Heat the oil in a frying pan and stir-fry the onion and garlic for
2–3 minutes, or until softened but not browned. Add the chilli, crushed
spices, cinnamon stick and turmeric and stir-fry for a further minute.
Add the coconut cream and the hot stock to the pan. Bring to the
boil, then add the cashew nuts and lime leaves. Cover the pan, reduce
the heat and simmer for 20 minutes. Serve hot, accompanied by
jasmine rice.

811 Cashew nut & pea curry

*To add bulk to the curry and some fresh flavour and colour try mixing
200 g/7 oz cooked tender peas into the curry for the last 5 minutes of
cooking time. Sliced French beans would be another good addition.*

812 Tofu & green vegetable curry

SERVES 4

vegetable or peanut oil, for deep-frying
225 g/8 oz firm tofu, cut into cubes
2 tbsp vegetable or groundnut oil
1 tbsp chilli oil
2 fresh green chillies, deseeded and sliced
2 garlic cloves, crushed
6 spring onions, sliced
2 medium courgettes, cut into sticks
½ cucumber, peeled, deseeded and sliced
1 green pepper, deseeded and sliced

1 small head of broccoli, cut into florets
55 g/2 oz fine French beans, halved
55 g/2 oz frozen peas, thawed
300 ml/10 fl oz vegetable stock
55 g/2 oz block creamed coconut,
  chopped
2 tbsp Thai soy sauce
1 tsp soft light brown sugar
4 tbsp chopped fresh parsley, to garnish

Heat the oil for deep-frying in a wok and carefully lower in the tofu
cubes, in batches, and cook for 2–3 minutes, until golden brown.
Remove with a slotted spoon and drain on kitchen paper.

Heat the other oils in a wok and stir-fry the chillies, garlic and spring
onions for 2–3 minutes. Add the courgettes, cucumber, green pepper,
broccoli and French beans, and stir-fry for a further 2–3 minutes.

Add the peas, stock, coconut, soy sauce and sugar. Cover and simmer
for 2–3 minutes, until all the vegetables are tender and the coconut has
dissolved. Stir in the tofu and serve immediately, sprinkled with the
parsley to garnish.

2 lemon grass stalks

50 ml/2 fl oz vegetable oil

3 large garlic cloves, crushed

1 large shallot, thinly sliced

2 tbsp Indian curry powder

700 ml/1¼ pints coconut milk

500 ml/18 fl oz coconut water (not coconut milk) or vegetable stock

2 tbsp fish sauce

4 fresh red bird's eye chillies or dried red Chinese (tien sien) chillies

6 kaffir lime leaves

1 carrot, peeled and cut diagonally into 1-cm/½-inch thick pieces

1 small–medium Asian aubergine, cut into 2.5-cm/1-inch pieces

1 small–medium bamboo shoot, cut into thin wedges

115 g/4 oz sugar snap peas, trimmed

12 large shiitake mushrooms, stems discarded, caps halved

450 g/1 lb firm or extra-firm tofu, drained and cut into 2.5-cm/1-inch cubes

fresh chopped coriander and fried shallots, to garnish

shallot and stir-fry for 5 minutes, or until golden. Add the lemon grass and curry powder and stir-fry for 2 minutes, or until fragrant. Add the coconut milk, coconut water, fish sauce, chillies and lime leaves and bring to the boil. Reduce the heat to low, then add the carrot and aubergine, cover and cook for 10 minutes.

Add the bamboo shoot, sugar snap peas, mushrooms and tofu and cook for a further 5 minutes. Serve garnished with the coriander and fried shallots.

814 *Vietnamese curry with coconut milk*

Coconut water is the 'juice' from inside fresh coconuts – it is available canned in the shops or you can buy a fresh coconut and crack it open to obtain the water. If you can't get it, instead of using vegetable stock, thin down a can of reduced-fat coconut milk half and half with water and use that instead.

Discard the bruised leaves and root ends of the lemon grass stalks, then slice 15–20 cm/6–8 inches of the lower stalks paper thin.

Heat the oil in a large saucepan over a high heat, add the garlic and

815 Pumpkin curry

150 ml/5 fl oz vegetable oil
2 medium onions, sliced
½ tsp white cumin seeds
500 g/1 lb 2 oz pumpkin, cubed
1 tsp dried mango powder
1 tsp finely chopped fresh ginger
1 tsp crushed garlic
1 tsp crushed dried red chilli
½ tsp salt
300 ml/10 fl oz water
chapatis or naan bread, to serve

Heat the vegetable oil in a large heavy-based frying pan. Add the onions and cumin seeds and fry over a medium heat, stirring occasionally, for about 5 minutes until the onions are light golden brown and the seeds are giving off their aroma.

Add the cubed pumpkin to the pan and stir-fry over a low heat for 3–5 minutes. Combine the dried mango powder, ginger, garlic, chilli and salt. Add the spice mixture to the pan, stirring well to combine with the vegetables.

Add the water, cover and cook over a low heat, stirring occasionally, for 10–15 minutes. Transfer to serving plates and serve with chapatis or naan bread.

816 Courgette curry

Substitute the pumpkin for 500 g/1 lb chopped courgettes. This recipe also works well with winter melon or marrow.

817 Onion dhal

100 g/3½ oz masoor dhal
6 tbsp vegetable oil
1 small bunch of spring onions, chopped
1 tsp finely chopped fresh ginger
1 tsp crushed garlic
1½ tsp chilli powder
1½ tsp turmeric
300 ml/10 fl oz water
1 tsp salt
1 fresh green chilli, deseeded and finely chopped, and chopped fresh coriander leaves, to garnish

Rinse the masoor dhal (split red lentils) thoroughly and set aside until required. Heat the oil in a heavy-based saucepan. Add the spring onions to the pan and fry over a medium heat, stirring frequently, until lightly browned. Reduce the heat and add the ginger, garlic, chilli powder and turmeric. Briefly stir-fry the spring onions with the spices. Add the lentils and stir to blend. Add the water to the lentil mixture, reduce the heat to low and cook for 20–25 minutes.

When the lentils are thoroughly cooked and tender, add the salt and stir gently to mix well. Transfer the onion dhal to a serving dish. Garnish with the chopped green chilli and fresh coriander leaves and serve immediately.

818 Onion dhal with yellow split peas

Replace the masoor dhal with the same weight of yellow split peas, or, if you increase the cooking time to 45 minutes, whole green or brown lentils.

Leeks with yellow bean sauce

450 g/1 lb leeks
175 g/6 oz baby corn
6 spring onions
3 tbsp groundnut oil
225 g/8 oz Chinese leaves, shredded
4 tbsp yellow bean sauce

Using a sharp knife, slice the leeks, halve the baby corn and thinly slice the spring onions.

Heat the groundnut oil in a large, preheated wok or frying pan until it is smoking. Add the leeks, shredded Chinese leaves and baby corn to the wok.

Stir-fry the vegetables over a high heat for about 5 minutes, or until the edges of the vegetables are slightly brown.

Add the spring onions to the wok or frying pan, stirring to combine. Add the yellow bean sauce to the wok. Continue to stir-fry the mixture in the wok for a further 2 minutes, or until the yellow bean sauce is heated through and the vegetables are thoroughly coated in the sauce. Transfer the stir-fried vegetables and sauce to warmed serving dishes and serve immediately.

820 Leeks, yellow bean sauce & peppers

Try using sliced red peppers instead of the baby corn. You can also use shredded pak choi instead of the Chinese cabbage.

---

821 Cauliflower korma

85 g/3 oz cashew nuts
1½ tbsp garlic and ginger purée
200 ml/7 fl oz water
55 g/2 oz ghee or 4 tbsp vegetable
or groundnut oil
1 large onion, chopped
5 green cardamom pods,
lightly crushed
1 cinnamon stick,
broken in half
¼ tsp ground turmeric
250 ml/9 fl oz double cream
140 g/5 oz new potatoes, scrubbed
and chopped into 1-cm/½-inch pieces
140 g/5 oz cauliflower florets
½ tsp garam masala
140 g/5 oz aubergine, chopped into
chunks
140 g/5 oz French beans, chopped into
1-cm/½-inch pieces
salt and pepper
chopped fresh mint or coriander,
to garnish

Heat a large flameproof casserole or frying pan with a tight-fitting lid over a high heat. Add the cashew nuts and stir until they start to brown, then tip them out of the casserole.

Put the nuts in a spice blender with the garlic and ginger purée and 1 tablespoon of the water and whizz until a coarse paste forms.

Melt half the ghee in the casserole over a medium–high heat. Add the onion and fry for 5–8 minutes, or until golden brown. Add the nut paste and stir for 5 minutes.

Stir in the cardamom pods, cinnamon stick and turmeric. Add the cream and the remaining water and bring to the boil, stirring. Reduce the heat to the lowest level, cover the casserole

and simmer for 5 minutes. Add the potatoes, cauliflower and garam masala to the casserole and simmer, covered, for 5 minutes. Stir in the aubergine and French beans and continue simmering for a further 5 minutes, or until all the vegetables are tender.

Check the sauce occasionally to make sure it isn't sticking to the base of the casserole, and stir in extra water if needed.

Taste and add seasoning, if necessary. Sprinkle with the chopped mint and serve.

822 Cauliflower korma with peanuts

If you have no cashew nuts you can grind peanuts or almonds instead and use those.

4 tbsp olive oil

1 bunch spring onions, white parts only, thinly sliced

450 g/1 lb frozen broad beans

100 ml/3½ fl oz water

juice of 1 lemon

400 g/14 oz canned artichoke hearts, drained and halved

2 tbsp chopped fresh dill

salt and pepper

Heat the oil in a large saucepan. Add the spring onions and fry for 5 minutes or until softened. Add the broad beans and stir to coat in the oil. Pour in the water and lemon juice; bring to the boil and boil, uncovered, for 5 minutes.

Add the artichoke hearts to the pan and gently boil for 5 minutes or until the beans are tender and most of the liquid has evaporated. Add the dill and season to taste with salt and pepper. Serve hot.

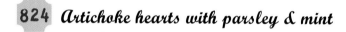

824 *Artichoke hearts with parsley & mint*

Follow the recipe as before, substituting the dill for 1 tablespoon fresh chopped parsley and 1 tablespoon fresh chopped mint.

825 *Cauliflower & beans with cashew nuts*

SERVES 4

1 tbsp vegetable or groundnut oil

1 tbsp chilli oil

1 onion, chopped

2 garlic cloves, chopped

2 tbsp Thai red curry paste

1 small cauliflower, cut into florets

175 g/6 oz runner beans, cut into 7.5-cm/3-inch lengths

150 ml/5 fl oz vegetable stock

2 tbsp Thai soy sauce

50 g/1¾ oz toasted cashew nuts, to garnish

Heat both the oils in a wok and stir-fry the onion and garlic until softened. Add the curry paste and stir-fry for 1–2 minutes.

Add the cauliflower and beans and stir-fry for 3–4 minutes, until softened. Pour in the stock and soy sauce and simmer for 1–2 minutes. Serve immediately, garnished with the cashew nuts.

Baked Mediterranean vegetables with feta SERVES 4

1 red onion, sliced into thick rings
1 small aubergine, thickly sliced
2 large mushrooms, halved
3 red peppers, halved and deseeded
3 tbsp olive oil, plus extra for brushing
3 plum tomatoes, peeled and diced
2 garlic cloves, very finely chopped
1 tbsp chopped fresh flat-leaf parsley
1 tsp chopped fresh rosemary
1 tsp dried thyme or oregano
finely grated zest of 1 lemon
75 g/2¾ oz stale, coarse breadcrumbs
6–8 black olives, stoned and sliced
25 g/1 oz feta cheese (drained weight),
    cut into 1-cm/½-inch cubes
salt and pepper

Put the onion, aubergine, mushrooms and peppers on a large baking tray, placing the peppers cut-side down. Grease lightly. Grill for 10–12 minutes, turning the onion, aubergine and mushroom halfway through, until beginning to blacken. Cut into even-sized chunks.

Place in a shallow ovenproof dish. Arrange the diced tomatoes on top. Season with salt and pepper. Preheat the oven to 220°C/425°F/Gas Mark 7. In a bowl, combine the garlic, parsley, rosemary, thyme and lemon zest with the breadcrumbs. Season with pepper. Add the 3 tablespoons of olive oil to bind the mixture together. Scatter the mixture over the vegetables. Add the olives and feta cheese. Bake in the preheated oven for 10–15 minutes, or until the vegetables are heated through and the topping is crisp. Serve straight from the dish.

827 *Mediterranean vegetables with fennel*

Omit the mushrooms and add 1 Florence fennel bulb, trimmed, 1 lemon, cut into 8 wedges, and 12 whole unpeeled cloves of garlic. Cut all vegetables into medium rather than thick slices. Toss with the garlic, lemon, seasoning, 3 teaspoons of Italian dried herbs and enough olive oil to coat well. Arrange in a roasting dish and roast at 190°C/375°F/Gas Mark 5 for 30 minutes, turning once or twice. Add 100 ml/3½ fl oz vegetable stock to the pan and baste everything – cook for another 20 minutes, adding olives and feta for the last 10 minutes.

828 *Broad beans with feta* SERVES 4–6

500 g/1 lb 2 oz shelled
    broad beans
4 tbsp extra virgin olive oil
1 tbsp lemon juice
1 tbsp finely chopped fresh
    dill, plus extra to garnish
55 g/2 oz feta cheese (drained weight),
    diced
salt and pepper

Bring a large saucepan of lightly salted water to the boil. Add the broad beans and cook for about 2 minutes, until tender. Drain thoroughly and set aside. When the beans are cool enough to handle, remove and discard the outer skins to reveal the bright green beans underneath. Put the peeled beans in a serving bowl. Combine the olive oil and lemon juice, then season to taste with salt and pepper. Pour the dressing over the warm beans, add the dill and stir gently.

If serving hot, add the cheese, toss gently and sprinkle with the extra dill, then serve immediately. Alternatively, set aside the beans in their dressing to cool and then chill until required. To serve cold, remove from the refrigerator 10 minutes before serving to bring to room temperature. Taste and adjust the seasoning, if necessary, then sprinkle with the cheese and extra dill.

Mixed herb omelette

2 large eggs
2 tbsp milk
40 g/1½ oz butter
leaves from 1 fresh flat-leaf
parsley sprig
1 fresh chervil sprig
2 fresh chives, chopped
salt and pepper
fresh salad leaves,
to serve

Break the eggs into a bowl. Add the milk and salt and pepper to taste, and quickly beat until just blended. Heat a 20-cm/8-inch omelette pan or frying pan over a medium–high heat until very hot and you can feel the heat rising from the surface. Add 25 g/1 oz of the butter and use a spatula to rub it over the base and around the side of the pan as it melts.

As soon as the butter stops sizzling, pour in the eggs. Shake the pan forwards and backwards over the heat and use the spatula to stir the eggs around the pan in a circular motion. Do not scrape the base of the pan. As the omelette begins to set, use the spatula to push the cooked egg from the edge towards the centre, so that the remaining uncooked egg comes in contact with the hot base of the pan. Continue doing this for 3 minutes, or until the omelette looks set on the bottom but is still slightly runny on top.

Put the herbs in the centre of the omelette. Tilt the pan away from the handle, so that the omelette slides towards the edge of the pan. Use the spatula to fold the top half of the omelette over the herbs. Slide the omelette onto a plate, then rub the remaining butter over the top. Serve immediately, accompanied by fresh salad leaves.

830 Sage omelette

Replace the chervil and chives with 2 teaspoons of fresh, finely chopped sage (use young tender leaves only) and 1 teaspoon of finely chopped marjoram.

831 Mushroom & garlic omelette

Replace the chervil and chives with 85 g/3 oz sliced button mushrooms, lightly fried for 2 minutes in 2 teaspoons of groundnut oil or butter with 1 finely chopped garlic clove. Add to the omelette when the egg is nearly cooked.

832 Tomato & potato tortilla

1 kg/2 lb 4 oz potatoes, peeled and cut
    into small cubes
2 tbsp olive oil
1 bunch spring onions, chopped
115 g/4 oz cherry tomatoes

6 eggs
3 tbsp water
2 tbsp chopped fresh parsley
salt and pepper

Cook the potatoes in a saucepan of lightly salted boiling water for 8–10 minutes, or until tender. Drain and reserve until required.

Preheat the grill to medium. Heat the oil in a large frying pan. Add the spring onions and fry until just soft. Add the potatoes and fry for 3–4 minutes, until coated with oil. Smooth the top and scatter over the tomatoes.

Mix the eggs, water, salt and pepper and parsley together in a bowl, then pour into the frying pan. Cook over a very gentle heat for 10–15 minutes, until the tortilla looks fairly set.

Place the frying pan under the hot grill and cook until the top is brown and set. Leave to cool for 10–15 minutes before sliding out of the frying pan on to a chopping board. Cut into wedges and serve the tortilla immediately.

833 Feta & spinach omelette

6 tbsp butter
1.3 kg/3 lb diced waxy potatoes
3 garlic cloves, crushed
1 tsp paprika
2 tomatoes, skinned, deseeded and diced
12 eggs
pepper

FILLING
225 g/8 oz baby spinach
1 tsp fennel seeds
125 g/4½ oz feta cheese (drained
  weight), diced
4 tbsp plain yogurt

Heat 2 tablespoons of the butter in a frying pan and cook the potatoes over low heat, stirring constantly, for 7–10 minutes, until golden. Transfer to a bowl. Add the garlic, paprika and tomatoes to the frying pan and cook for 2 minutes. Whisk the eggs together and season with pepper. Pour the eggs into the potatoes and mix well.

Cook the spinach for 1 minute in boiling water, until just wilted. Drain and refresh under cold running water. Pat dry with kitchen paper. Stir in the fennel seeds, feta cheese and yogurt. Heat a quarter of the remaining butter in a 15-cm/6-inch omelette pan. Ladle a quarter of the egg and potato mixture into the pan. Cook, turning once, for 2 minutes, until set. Transfer the omelette to a serving plate. Spoon a quarter of the spinach mixture onto one half of the omelette with some of the tomato mixture, then fold the omelette in half. Repeat 3 times, then serve.

834 Ricotta & spinach omelette

Replace the feta cheese and the yogurt with 175g/6 oz ricotta cheese – stir it in with the fennel seeds.

835 Pan haggerty

4 tbsp olive oil
55 g/2 oz butter
450 g/1 lb firm potatoes, Desirée or waxy
  salad potatoes

225 g/8 oz onions, halved and thinly
  sliced
115 g/4 oz Cheddar cheese, grated
salt and pepper

Heat half the olive oil and half the butter in a 23–25-cm/9–10-inch frying pan.

Peel the potatoes if necessary (you don't need to peel small salad potatoes). Slice thinly using a mandolin or food processor. Rinse the slices quickly in cold water and dry thoroughly using a tea towel or kitchen paper. Remove the oil and butter from the heat and arrange the sliced potato in the base of the pan. Build up layers of potato, onion and cheese, seasoning well with salt and pepper between each layer. Finish with a layer of potato and dot the remaining butter over the top.

Return to the heat and cook over a medium heat for 15–20 minutes. The base should become brown but not burn. Place a large plate over the frying pan and invert the potato onto the plate by tilting the frying pan. Add the remaining oil to the frying pan and slip the potato back in, cooking the other side for a further 15 minutes until the bottom is crusty. Remove from the heat and serve immediately on a warm plate.

836 Oven-baked haggerty

If preferred, the dish can be made in a shallow 25-cm/10-inch gratin dish and then cooked in the top of the oven at 180°C/350°F/Gas Mark 4 for 45–50 minutes until piping hot and golden brown.

837 Pepper & mushroom hash

675 g/1lb 8 oz potatoes, diced
1 tbsp olive oil
2 garlic cloves, crushed
1 green pepper, deseeded and diced
1 yellow pepper, deseeded and diced
3 tomatoes, diced

75 g/2¾ oz button mushrooms, halved
1 tbsp Worcestershire sauce
2 tbsp chopped fresh basil
salt and pepper
fresh basil leaves, to garnish

Cook the diced potatoes in a large saucepan of lightly salted boiling water for 7–8 minutes. Drain well and reserve.

Heat the olive oil in a large heavy-based frying pan. Add the potatoes and cook over a medium heat, stirring constantly, for about 8–10 minutes, until browned. Add the garlic and peppers and cook, stirring frequently, for 2–3 minutes.

Stir in the tomatoes and mushrooms and cook, stirring frequently, for 5–6 minutes.

Stir in the Worcestershire sauce and basil and season to taste with salt and pepper. Transfer to a warmed serving dish and garnish with basil sprigs.

838 Potato hash with shallots & spinach

Cook potatoes as above until lightly browned. Add 5 peeled and sliced shallots and 2 well-crushed garlic cloves to the pan with a little extra oil and stir for 5 minutes until soft and lightly golden. Season and stir 250 g/9 oz baby spinach leaves into the pan and continue stirring until they are wilted.

839 Potato & mushroom bake

2 tbsp butter
500 g/1 lb 2 oz waxy potatoes, thinly
    sliced and parboiled
150 g/5½ oz sliced mixed mushrooms
1 tbsp chopped fresh rosemary, plus extra
    to garnish

4 tbsp snipped chives, plus extra
    to garnish
2 garlic cloves, crushed
150 ml/5 fl oz double cream
salt and pepper

Preheat the oven to 190°C/375°F/ Gas Mark 5. Grease a shallow, round ovenproof dish with the butter. Layer a quarter of the potatoes in the base of the dish.

Arrange one third of the mushrooms on top of the potatoes and sprinkle with one third of the rosemary, chives and garlic. Continue making the layers in the same order, and finish with a layer of potatoes on top.

Pour the double cream evenly over the top of the potatoes.

Season to taste with salt and pepper. Place the dish in the preheated oven, and cook for about 45 minutes, or until the bake is golden brown and piping hot. Garnish with snipped chives and serve immediately straight from the dish.

840 Potato, cheese & mushroom bake

Grate 100 g/3½ oz Cheddar cheese and add one third to the dish each time you add mushrooms. Sprinkle 25 g/1 oz grated cheese over the top of the cream before baking.

841 *Potatoes in red wine*

125 g/4¹/₂ oz butter
450 g/1 lb new potatoes, halved
200 ml/7 fl oz red wine
6 tbsp vegetable stock
8 shallots, halved

125 g/4¹/₂ oz oyster mushrooms
1 tbsp chopped fresh sage or coriander
salt and pepper
fresh sage leaves or coriander sprigs,
* to garnish*

Melt the butter in a heavy-based frying pan and add the potatoes. Cook over a low heat for 5 minutes, stirring constantly. Add the red wine, vegetable stock and shallots. Season to taste with salt and pepper and simmer for 30 minutes. Stir in the mushrooms and chopped herbs and cook for 5 minutes. Turn the potatoes and mushrooms into a warm serving dish.

Garnish with fresh sage leaves and serve immediately.

842 *Ratatouille*

2 aubergines
4 courgettes
2 yellow peppers
2 red peppers
2 onions
2 garlic cloves
150 ml/5 fl oz olive oil
1 bouquet garni
3 large tomatoes, peeled, deseeded
* and roughly chopped*
salt and pepper

Roughly chop the aubergines and courgettes, and deseed and chop the peppers. Slice the onions and finely chop the garlic. Heat the oil in a large saucepan. Add the onions and cook over a low heat, stirring occasionally, for 5 minutes, or until softened. Add the garlic and cook, stirring frequently for a further 2 minutes. Add the aubergines, courgettes and peppers. Increase the heat to medium and cook, stirring occasionally, until the peppers begin to colour. Add the bouquet garni, reduce the heat, cover and simmer gently for 40 minutes.

Stir in the chopped tomatoes and season to taste with salt and pepper. Re-cover the saucepan and simmer for a further 10 minutes. Remove and discard the bouquet garni, and serve.

843 *Oven-baked ratatouille*

The ratatouille can be cooked in the oven – sauté the vegetables in a flameproof casserole then transfer the casserole to the oven at 180°C/350°F/ Gas Mark 4 for 45 minutes, stirring once or twice. Instead of using a bouquet garni you can use 1 tablespoon of fresh chopped oregano leaves, or stir in 2 tablespoons of chopped basil leaves at the end of cooking time.

Roast summer vegetables

1 fennel bulb
2 red onions
2 beef tomatoes
1 aubergine
2 courgettes
1 yellow pepper, deseeded
1 red pepper, deseeded

1 orange pepper, deseeded
2 tbsp olive oil
4 garlic cloves
4 fresh rosemary sprigs
pepper
crusty bread, to serve (optional)

Preheat the oven to 200°C/400°F/Gas Mark 6. Cut the fennel, onions and tomatoes into wedges. Thickly slice the aubergine and courgettes. Cut the peppers into chunks. Brush a large ovenproof dish with a little of the oil. Arrange the vegetables in the dish and tuck the garlic cloves and rosemary sprigs among them. Drizzle with the remaining oil and season to taste with plenty of freshly ground black pepper.

Roast the vegetables in the preheated oven for 20–25 minutes, turning once, until they are tender and beginning to turn golden brown. Serve the vegetables straight from the dish or transfer to a warmed serving platter. Serve immediately, with crusty bread, if you like, to mop up the juices.

845 *Other roast summer vegetables*

You can vary the vegetables you use according to what you have. A different tray, for example, would be chunks of summer squash, courgette, whole shallots, garlic and cauliflower florets.

846 Shallots à la Grecque

450 g/1 lb shallots
3 tbsp olive oil
3 tbsp clear honey
2 tbsp garlic wine vinegar
3 tbsp dry white wine

1 tbsp tomato purée
2 celery sticks, sliced
2 tomatoes, deseeded and chopped
salt and pepper
chopped celery leaves, to garnish

Peel the shallots. Heat the oil in a large saucepan, add the shallots and cook, stirring, for 3–5 minutes or until they begin to brown.

Add the honey and cook over high heat for a further 30 seconds, then add the garlic wine vinegar and white wine, stirring well.

Stir in the tomato purée, celery and tomatoes and bring the mixture to the boil. Cook over high heat for 5–6 minutes. Season to taste and set aside to cool slightly. Garnish with chopped celery leaves and serve warm. Alternatively, chill in the refrigerator before serving.

847 With garlic

If you don't have any garlic wine vinegar, add 2 cloves garlic, finely chopped, to the shallots for their last minute of cooking.

848 Sautéed garlic mushrooms

450 g/1 lb button mushrooms
5 tbsp olive oil
2 garlic cloves, finely chopped
squeeze of lemon juice

4 tbsp fresh flat-leaf parsley, chopped,
    plus extra sprigs to garnish
salt and pepper
crusty bread, to serve

Wipe or brush clean the mushrooms, then trim off the stalks close to the caps. Cut any large mushrooms in half or into quarters. Heat the olive oil in a large heavy-based frying pan, add the garlic and fry for 30 seconds–1 minute, or until lightly browned. Add the mushrooms and sauté over a high heat, stirring most of the time, until the mushrooms have absorbed all the oil in the pan. Reduce the heat to low. When the juices have come out of the mushrooms, increase the heat again and sauté for 4–5 minutes, stirring most of the time, until the juices have almost evaporated. Add a squeeze of lemon juice and season to taste with salt and pepper. Stir in the parsley and cook for a further minute.

Transfer the sautéed mushrooms to a warmed serving dish and serve piping hot or warm, garnished with the parsley sprigs. Accompany with chunks or slices of crusty bread for mopping up the garlic cooking juices.

849 Sautéed garlic & chilli mushrooms

Add 1 finely chopped red chilli to the pan with the garlic and use lime juice instead of the lemon juice – stir in fresh chopped coriander leaf instead of the parsley.

140 g/5 oz long-grain white
or brown rice
4 large red peppers
2 tbsp olive oil
1 garlic clove, chopped
4 shallots, chopped
1 celery stick, chopped
3 tbsp chopped toasted
walnuts
2 tomatoes, peeled and chopped
1 tbsp lemon juice
50 g/1¾ oz raisins
4 tbsp freshly grated Cheddar cheese
2 tbsp chopped fresh basil
salt and pepper
fresh basil sprigs, to garnish
lemon wedges, to serve

Preheat the oven to 180°C/350°F/Gas Mark 4. Cook the rice in a saucepan of lightly salted boiling water for 20 minutes if using white rice, or 35 minutes if using brown. Drain, rinse under cold running water, then drain again.

Meanwhile, using a sharp knife, cut the tops off the peppers and reserve. Remove the seeds and white cores, then blanch the peppers and reserved tops in boiling water for 2 minutes. Remove from the heat and drain well. Heat half the oil in a large frying pan. Add the garlic and shallots and cook, stirring, for 3 minutes. Add the celery, walnuts, tomatoes, lemon juice and raisins and cook for a further 5 minutes. Remove from the heat and stir in the rice, cheese, chopped basil and seasoning. Stuff the peppers with the rice mixture and arrange them in a baking dish.

Place the tops on the peppers, drizzle over the remaining oil, loosely cover with foil and bake in the preheated oven for 45 minutes. Remove from the oven. Garnish with basil sprigs and serve with lemon wedges.

851 *Stuffed red peppers with almonds*

You can use chopped toasted almonds, hazelnuts or toasted pine kernels instead of the walnuts. And you can use sultanas or currants instead of the raisins. Also, try soaking the dried fruit in water or orange juice for 15 minutes.

852 *Stuffed red peppers with pasta*

Replace the rice with the same weight of dry pasta – cook until tender and follow the recipe in the same way.

853 *Stuffed red peppers with couscous*

Replace the rice with 100 g/3½ oz couscous and re-constitute according to pack instructions. Replace the raisins with 50 g/2 oz ready-to-eat apricots, finely chopped.

Potatoes Dauphinois

SERVES 4–6

1 tbsp butter
675 g/1 lb 8 oz waxy potatoes, sliced
2 garlic cloves, crushed
1 red onion, sliced

85 g/3 oz Gruyère cheese, grated
300 ml/10 fl oz double cream
salt and pepper

Lightly grease a 1-litre/1¾-pint shallow ovenproof dish with the butter. Arrange a single layer of potato slices evenly in the base of the prepared dish. Top the potato slices with half the garlic, half the sliced red onion and one third of the grated Gruyère cheese. Season to taste with a little salt and some pepper. Repeat the layers in exactly the same order, finishing with a layer of potatoes topped with grated cheese.

Pour the cream over the top of the potatoes and cook in a preheated oven, 180°C/350°F/Gas Mark 4, for 1½ hours, or until the potatoes are cooked through and the top is browned and crispy. Serve immediately, straight from the dish.

855 *Tomato & aubergine layers*

SERVES 4

3 tbsp olive oil
2 aubergines, thinly sliced
4 tomatoes, peeled and sliced

3 tbsp chopped fresh flat-leaf parsley
salt and pepper

Preheat the oven to 190°C/375°F/Gas Mark 5. Heat the oil in a large frying pan, add the aubergine slices, in batches if necessary, and cook over a medium–low heat, turning once or twice, for 4 minutes. Remove with a fish slice or spatula. Make alternating layers of tomato slices, parsley and aubergine slices in a casserole dish, seasoning each layer with salt and pepper and ending with a layer of tomatoes. Cover and bake for 1 hour or until the vegetables are tender. Serve immediately.

856 *Tomato & aubergine layers with basil*

Add 50 ml/2 fl oz passata to each aubergine layer as you go for a moister finish. Replace the parsley with 4 tablespoons of chopped fresh basil.

Wild mushroom bruschetta

> 4 slices sourdough bread, such as Pugliese
> 3 garlic cloves, 1 halved and 2 crushed
> 2 tbsp extra virgin olive oil
> 225 g/8 oz mixed wild mushrooms, such as ceps, chanterelles and field mushrooms
> 1 tbsp olive oil
> 25 g/1 oz butter
> 1 small onion or 2 shallots, finely chopped
> 50 ml/2 fl oz dry white wine or Marsala
> salt and pepper
> 2 tbsp roughly chopped fresh flat-leaf parsley, to garnish

Preheat the oven to low. Toast the bread slices on both sides under a preheated grill or in a preheated ridged griddle pan, rub with the garlic halves and drizzle with the extra virgin olive oil. Transfer to a baking sheet and keep warm in the preheated oven.

Wipe the mushrooms thoroughly to remove any trace of soil and slice any large ones. Heat the olive oil with half the butter in a frying pan, add the mushrooms and cook over a medium heat, stirring frequently, for 3–4 minutes until soft. Remove with a slotted spoon and keep warm in the oven. Heat the remaining butter in the frying pan, add the onion and crushed garlic and cook over a medium heat, stirring frequently, for 3–4 minutes until soft. Add the wine, stir well and leave to bubble for 2–3 minutes until reduced and thickened. Return the

mushrooms to the frying pan and heat through. The sauce should be thick enough to glaze the mushrooms. Season to taste with salt and pepper. Pile the mushrooms on top of the warm bruschetta, scatter with the parsley and serve immediately.

Greek beans

> 400 g/14 oz canned cannellini beans, drained and rinsed
> 1 tbsp olive oil
> 3 garlic cloves, crushed
> 425 ml/15 fl oz vegetable stock
> 1 bay leaf
> 2 fresh oregano sprigs
> 1 tbsp tomato purée
> juice of 1 lemon
> 1 small red onion, chopped
> 25 g/1 oz black Greek olives, stoned and halved
> salt and pepper

Put the beans in an ovenproof casserole over a low heat, add the oil and garlic and cook, stirring frequently, for 4–5 minutes. Add the stock, bay leaf, oregano, tomato purée, lemon juice and onion and stir well to mix. Cover and simmer for 1 hour or until the sauce has thickened.

Stir in the olives, then season to taste with salt and pepper. This dish is delicious served either warm or cold.

859 *Greek beans with stuffed green olives*

You can use canned butterbeans instead of the cannellini beans if you like – and you can use green olives stuffed with red pepper, sliced, instead of the plain black olives.

860 Aubergine gratin

4 tbsp olive oil
2 onions, finely chopped
2 garlic cloves, very finely chopped
2 aubergines, thickly sliced
3 tbsp chopped fresh flat-leaf parsley
½ tsp dried thyme

400 g/14 oz canned chopped tomatoes
175 g/6 oz mozzarella cheese, coarsely grated
6 tbsp freshly grated Parmesan cheese
salt and pepper

Preheat the oven to 200°C/400°F/ Gas Mark 6. Heat the oil in a frying pan over a medium heat. Add the onion and cook for 5 minutes, or until softened. Add the garlic and cook for a few seconds, or until just beginning to colour. Using a slotted spoon, transfer the onion mixture to a plate. Cook the aubergine slices in batches in the same frying pan until they are just lightly browned.

Arrange a layer of aubergine slices in a shallow ovenproof dish. Sprinkle with some of the parsley, thyme, salt and pepper. Add a layer of onion, tomatoes and mozzarella and a sprinkling of parsley, thyme, salt and pepper. Continue layering, sprinkling parsley, thyme, salt and pepper over each layer and finishing with a layer of aubergine slices. Sprinkle with the Parmesan cheese. Bake, uncovered, in the oven for 20–30 minutes, or until the top is golden and the aubergines are tender. Serve hot.

861 With crunchy topping

For a crunchy topping, combine 50 g/2 oz slightly stale breadcrumbs and ¼ teaspoon of ground cumin with the Parmesan cheese and sprinkle over the top.

862 Aubergine & potato gratin

For a more substantial dish, peel and boil 350 g/12 oz potatoes and cut into rounds approximately ½ cm/¼ inch thick. Layer these with the aubergines, adding 200 g/7 oz extra chopped tomatoes.

863 Creamed mushrooms

juice of 1 small lemon
450 g/1 lb small button mushrooms
25 g/1 oz butter
1 tbsp sunflower or olive oil
1 small onion, finely chopped

125 ml/4 fl oz whipping or double cream
salt and pepper
1 tbsp chopped fresh parsley, plus
4 sprigs, to garnish

Sprinkle a little of the lemon juice over the mushrooms. Heat the butter and oil in a frying pan, add the onion and cook for 1 minute. Add the mushrooms, shaking the pan so they do not stick.

Season to taste with salt and pepper, then stir in the cream, chopped parsley and remaining lemon juice. Heat until hot but do not allow to boil, then transfer to a serving plate and garnish with the parsley sprigs. Serve immediately.

864 Borscht

1 onion
55 g/2 oz butter
350 g/12 oz raw beetroot, cut into thin batons, and 1 raw beetroot, grated
1 carrot, cut into thin batons
3 celery sticks, thinly sliced
2 tomatoes, peeled, deseeded and chopped
1.4 litres/2½ pints vegetable stock
1 tbsp white wine vinegar
1 tbsp sugar
2 tbsp snipped fresh dill
115 g/4 oz white cabbage, shredded
salt and pepper
150 ml/5 fl oz soured cream, to garnish
crusty bread, to serve (optional)

Slice the onion into rings. Melt the butter in a large heavy-based saucepan. Add the onion and cook over a low heat, stirring occasionally, for 3–5 minutes, or until softened. Add the beetroot batons, carrot, celery and chopped tomatoes and cook, stirring frequently, for 4–5 minutes.

Add the stock, vinegar, sugar and 1 tablespoon of the snipped dill into the saucepan. Season to taste with salt and pepper. Bring to the boil, reduce the heat and simmer for 35–40 minutes, or until the vegetables are tender.

Stir in the cabbage, cover and simmer for 10 minutes. Stir in the grated beetroot, with any juices, and cook for a further 10 minutes. Ladle into warmed bowls. Garnish with a spoonful of soured cream and the other tablespoon of snipped dill and serve with crusty bread, if liked.

865 Borscht with red cabbage

There are several versions of this beetroot dish made throughout Eastern Europe. Here is another one – simmer 1.2 litres/2 pints vegetable stock with 2 tablespoons of red wine vinegar, 225 g/8 oz grated beetroot, 1 large finely chopped onion and 400 g/14 oz potatoes, peeled and diced small, for 15 minutes. Add 500 g/1 lb 2 oz shredded red cabbage, 2 large peeled, deseeded and chopped tomatoes and 1 teaspoon of sugar. Cook for another 15 minutes, season to taste and stir in 150 ml/5 fl oz sour cream to serve.

866 Vegetable & lentil casserole

10 cloves
1 onion, peeled but kept whole
225 g/8 oz Puy or green lentils
1 bay leaf
1.5 litres/2¾ pints vegetable stock
2 leeks, sliced
2 potatoes, diced
2 carrots, chopped
3 courgettes, sliced
1 celery stick, chopped
1 red pepper, deseeded and chopped
1 tbsp lemon juice
salt and pepper

Preheat the oven to 180°C/350°F/Gas Mark 4. Press the cloves into the onion. Put the lentils into a large casserole, add the onion and bay leaf and pour in the stock. Cover and cook in the preheated oven for 1 hour.

Remove the onion and discard the cloves. Slice the onion and return it to the casserole with the vegetables. Stir thoroughly and season to taste with salt and pepper. Cover and return to the oven for 1 hour.

Discard the bay leaf. Stir in the lemon juice and serve straight from the casserole.

867 Black bean casserole

SERVES 4

6 Chinese dried mushrooms
275 g/9¾ oz firm tofu
3 tbsp vegetable oil
1 carrot, cut into thin strips
125 g/4½ oz mangetout
125 g/4½ oz baby corn, halved
    lengthways
225 g/8 oz canned sliced bamboo shoots,
    drained

1 red pepper, deseeded and cut into
    chunks
125 g/4½ oz Chinese leaves, shredded
1 tbsp soy sauce
1 tbsp black bean sauce
1 tsp sugar
1 tsp cornflour
vegetable oil, for deep-frying
250 g/9 oz Chinese rice noodles
salt and pepper

2–3 minutes. Add the Chinese leaves and tofu, and stir-fry for a further 2 minutes.

Stir in the soy and black bean sauces and the sugar, and season with a little salt. Add 6 tablespoons of the reserved mushroom liquid mixed with the cornflour. Bring to the boil, reduce the heat, cover and cook for about 2–3 minutes, until the sauce thickens slightly.

Heat the oil for deep-frying in a large pan. Deep-fry the noodles, in batches, until puffed up and lightly golden. Drain and serve with the casserole.

Soak the dried mushrooms in a bowl of warm water for 20–25 minutes. Drain and squeeze out the excess water, reserving the liquid. Remove the tough centres and slice the mushrooms thinly.

Cut the tofu into cubes, then boil in lightly salted water for 2–3 minutes to firm up, and drain.

Heat half the vegetable oil in a saucepan. Add the tofu and fry until lightly browned. Remove and drain on kitchen paper.

Add the remaining vegetable oil and stir-fry the mushrooms, carrot, mangetout, baby corn, bamboo shoots and pepper for

868 Mushroom & cauliflower cheese crumble

SERVES 4

1 medium cauliflower
55 g/2 oz butter, plus 2 tbsp
115 g/4 oz button mushrooms, sliced
salt and pepper

TOPPING
115 g/4 oz dry breadcrumbs
2 tbsp freshly grated Parmesan cheese
1 tsp dried oregano
1 tsp dried parsley

Preheat the oven to 230°C/450°F/Gas Mark 8. Bring a large saucepan of salted water to the boil. Break the cauliflower into small florets and cook in the boiling water for 3 minutes. Remove from the heat, drain well and transfer to a large shallow, ovenproof dish.

Melt the 55 g/2 oz butter in a frying pan over a medium heat. Add the mushrooms, stir to coat and cook for 3 minutes. Remove from the heat and add to the cauliflower. Season to taste with salt and pepper.

Combine the breadcrumbs, cheese and herbs in a small mixing bowl, then sprinkle the crumbs over the vegetables. Dice the remaining butter and dot over the crumbs.

Place the dish in the oven and bake for 15 minutes, or until the crumbs are golden brown and crisp. Serve straight from the dish.

869 Spicy roast cauliflower & mushrooms

Divide cauliflower into fairly large florets then blanch for 3 minutes and drain thoroughly. In a bowl, combine 2 tablespoons of olive oil, 1 tablespoon of melted butter, ½ teaspoon each of ground cumin and coriander and seasoning, then add florets and toss until coated. Stir in the sliced mushrooms. Put the florets into a roasting dish with the mushrooms tucked in between, and roast at 190°C/375°F/Gas Mark 5 for 20 minutes or until golden.

55 g/2 oz wholemeal flour
1/2 tsp ground coriander
1/2 tsp cumin seeds
1/4 tsp chilli powder
1/2 tsp turmeric
1/4 tsp salt
1 egg
3 tbsp milk
350 g/12 oz potatoes, peeled
1–2 garlic cloves, crushed
4 spring onions, chopped
55 g/2 oz sweetcorn
vegetable oil, for shallow frying

Place the flour in a bowl, stir in the spices and salt and make a well in the centre. Add the egg and milk and mix to form a fairly thick batter.

Coarsely grate the potatoes, place them in a sieve and rinse well under cold running water. Drain and squeeze dry, then stir them into the batter with the garlic, spring onions and sweetcorn and mix to combine thoroughly. Heat about 5 mm/1/4 inch of vegetable oil in a large frying pan and add a few separate tablespoons of the mixture at a time, flattening each one to form a thin cake. Fry over a low heat, turning frequently, for 2–3 minutes, or until golden brown and cooked through.

Drain the fritters on absorbent kitchen paper and keep them hot while frying the remaining mixture in the same way.

871 *Potato & carrot fritters*

Make the batter as above then stir in 350 g/12 oz grated carrot and 4 chopped spring onions. Omit the sweetcorn and garlic.

872 *Potato & parsnip fritters*

Replace half the potato with peeled cored parsnips, grated.

873 *Courgette fritters*

Replace the potatoes with 350 g/12 oz chopped courgettes. Omit the turmeric and chilli and instead add 2 teaspoons of very finely chopped fresh mint.

Ribollita

3 tbsp olive oil
2 medium red onions, roughly chopped
3 carrots, sliced
3 celery sticks, roughly chopped
3 garlic cloves, chopped
1 tbsp chopped fresh thyme
400 g/14 oz canned cannellini beans, drained and rinsed
400 g/14 oz canned chopped tomatoes

600 ml/1 pint water or vegetable stock
2 tbsp chopped fresh parsley
500 g/1 lb 2 oz cavolo nero or Savoy cabbage, trimmed and sliced
1 small day-old ciabatta loaf, torn into small pieces
salt and pepper
extra virgin olive oil, to serve

Heat the oil in a large saucepan and cook the onions, carrots and celery for 10–15 minutes, stirring frequently. Add the garlic, thyme, and salt and pepper to taste. Continue to cook for a further 1–2 minutes, until the vegetables are golden and caramelized. Add the cannellini beans to the pan and pour in the tomatoes. Add enough of the water to cover the vegetables. Bring to the boil and simmer for 20 minutes. Add the parsley and cavolo nero and cook for a further 5 minutes. Stir in the bread and add a little more water, if needed. The consistency should be thick.

Taste and adjust the seasoning, if needed. Ladle into warmed serving bowls and serve hot, drizzled with extra virgin olive oil.

Bubble & squeak

450 g/1 lb green cabbage
1 onion, thinly sliced
4 tbsp olive oil
salt and pepper

MASHED POTATO
450 g/1 lb floury potatoes, such as King Edwards, Maris Piper or Desirée, peeled and cut into chunks
55 g/2 oz butter
3 tbsp hot milk
salt and pepper

To make the mashed potato, cook the potatoes in a large saucepan of boiling salted water for 15–20 minutes. Drain well and mash with a potato masher until smooth. Season with salt and pepper, add the butter and milk and stir well.

Cut the cabbage into quarters, remove the centre stalk and shred finely. In a large frying pan, fry the onion in half the oil until soft.

Add the cabbage to the pan and stir-fry for 2–3 minutes until softened. Season with salt and pepper, add the mashed potato and mix together well. Press the mixture firmly into the frying pan and allow to cook over a high heat for 4–5 minutes so that the base is crispy. Place a plate over the frying pan and invert the pan so that the potato cake falls onto the plate. Add the remaining oil to the pan, reheat and slip the cake back into the pan with the uncooked side down. Continue to cook for a further 5 minutes until the bottom is crispy. Turn out onto a hot plate and cut into wedges for serving. Serve immediately.

Bubble & squeak cakes

This dish can be made with curly kale or Brussels sprouts instead of the cabbage. The potato and cabbage mix can also be formed into small cakes and fried separately like fish cakes.

Roasted vegetable moussaka

1 large aubergine
2 medium courgettes, thickly sliced
2 onions, cut into small wedges
2 red peppers, deseeded and roughly chopped
2 garlic cloves, roughly chopped
5 tbsp olive oil
1 tbsp chopped fresh thyme
2 eggs, beaten
300 ml/10 fl oz Greek-style yogurt
400 g/14 oz canned chopped tomatoes
55 g/2 oz feta cheese (drained weight)
salt and pepper

Preheat the oven to 220°C/425°F/Gas Mark 7. Cut the aubergine into slices, about 5 mm/¼ inch thick. Put in a colander, standing over a large plate, and sprinkle each layer with salt.

Cover with a plate and place a heavy weight on top. Leave for 30 minutes to degorge. Rinse the aubergine slices under cold running water, then pat dry with kitchen paper. Put the aubergine, courgettes, onions, peppers and garlic in a roasting tin. Drizzle over the oil, toss together and then sprinkle over the thyme and season with salt and pepper. Roast in the oven for 30–35 minutes, turning halfway through the cooking, until golden brown and tender.

Meanwhile, beat together the eggs, yogurt, salt and pepper. When the vegetables are cooked, reduce the oven temperature to 180°C/350°F/Gas Mark 4. Put half the vegetables in a layer in a large ovenproof dish. Spoon over the tomatoes then add the remaining vegetables. Pour over the yogurt mixture and crumble over the feta cheese. Bake in the oven for 45 minutes–1 hour, until golden brown. Serve hot, warm or cold.

878 *With Béchamel & cheese topping*

For a different topping, make up 500 ml/18 fl oz Béchamel sauce and add 85 g/3 oz grated Cheddar cheese and 1 beaten egg, then combine well. Pour over the vegetables and bake at 180°C/350°F/Gas Mark 4 for 45 minutes.

879 *Ratatouille moussaka*

Use the same vegetables but brown them in 3 tablespoons of olive oil in a large frying pan then simmer with the tomatoes, garlic, herbs and seasoning, covered, for 45 minutes or until soft, stirring occasionally. Transfer to the baking dish, spoon over the topping and bake for 20 minutes at 200°C/400°F/Gas Mark 6 to brown the topping.

880 *Ratatouille moussaka with lentils*

For a heartier dish, add 175 g/6 oz (dry weight) brown or green lentils to the pan with the vegetables and add 300 ml/10 fl oz water – the lentils will absorb the extra moisture as they cook. Check they are cooked through before transferring the mix to the baking dish.

Courgette, carrot & tomato frittata

1 tbsp olive oil
1 onion, cut into small wedges
1–2 garlic cloves, crushed
2 eggs
2 egg whites
1 courgette, about 85 g/3 oz, trimmed
and grated
2 carrots, about 115 g/4 oz, peeled
and grated
2 tomatoes, chopped
pepper
1 tbsp shredded fresh basil,
for sprinkling

Heat the oil in a large non-stick frying pan, add the onion and garlic and sauté for 5 minutes, stirring frequently. Beat the eggs and egg whites together in a bowl then pour into the pan. Using a spatula or fork, pull the egg mixture from the sides of the pan into the centre.

Once the base has set lightly, add the grated courgette and carrots with the tomatoes. Add pepper to taste and continue to cook over a low heat until the eggs are set to personal preference.

Sprinkle with the shredded basil, cut into quarters and serve.

882 *Courgette, broccoli & lemon frittata*

Omit the carrots and tomatoes and add 150 g/5½ oz broccoli, broken into small florets and blanched in boiling water for 3 minutes. Stir into the onion/ courgette mixture in the pan with 1 teaspoon of finely grated lemon zest.

883 *Baked celery with cream*

1 head of celery
½ tsp ground cumin
½ tsp ground coriander
1 garlic clove, crushed
1 red onion, thinly sliced
50 g/1¾ oz pecan nuts, halved

150 ml/5 fl oz vegetable stock
150 ml/5 fl oz single cream
50 g/1¾ oz fresh wholemeal
breadcrumbs
25 g/1 oz freshly grated Parmesan cheese
salt and pepper

Preheat the oven to 200°C/400°F/Gas Mark 6. Trim the celery and cut into matchsticks. Place the celery in an ovenproof dish with the cumin, coriander, garlic, red onion and pecan nuts.

Mix the stock and cream together in a jug and pour over the vegetables. Season to taste with salt and pepper. Mix the breadcrumbs and cheese together in a small bowl and sprinkle over the top to cover the vegetables.

Cook in the preheated oven for 40 minutes, or until the vegetables are tender and the top is crispy. Serve immediately.

884 *Baked celery with cream & walnuts*

Lightly chopped walnuts make a great alternative to the pecans in this recipe.

1 butternut squash, about 450 g/1 lb
1 onion, chopped
2–3 garlic cloves, crushed
4 small tomatoes, chopped
85 g/3 oz chestnut mushrooms,
chopped
85 g/3 oz canned butter beans,
drained, rinsed and roughly chopped
1 courgette, about 115 g/4 oz,
trimmed and grated
1 tbsp chopped fresh oregano,
plus extra to garnish
2 tbsp tomato purée
300 ml/10 fl oz water
4 spring onions, trimmed and
chopped
1 tbsp Worcestershire or hot pepper
sauce, or to taste
pepper

Preheat the oven to 190°C/375°F/Gas Mark 5. Prick the squash all over with a metal skewer then roast for 40 minutes, or until tender. Remove from the oven and leave until cool enough to handle.

Cut the squash in half, scoop out and discard the seeds then scoop out some of the flesh, making hollows in both halves. Chop the scooped out flesh and put in a bowl. Place the two halves side by side in a large roasting tin.

Add the onion, garlic, chopped tomatoes and mushrooms to the squash flesh in the bowl. Add the roughly chopped butter beans, grated courgette, chopped oregano and pepper to taste and mix well. Spoon the filling into the 2 halves of the squash, packing it down as firmly as possible.

Mix the tomato purée with the water, spring onions and Worcestershire sauce in a small bowl and pour around the squash.

Cover loosely with a large sheet of foil and bake for 30 minutes, or until piping hot. Serve on warmed plates, garnished with fresh chopped oregano.

886 *Roasted stuffed squash with rice*

Replace the butter beans with 100 g/3½ oz cooked brown rice and stir 50 g/2 oz grated Parmesan cheese into the mixture before stuffing the squash.

887 *Roasted stuffed marrow*

Use a small marrow instead of the squash – follow the recipe above but roast the marrows for only 30 minutes.

888 *Stuffed aubergines*

SERVES 4

225 g/8 oz dried penne or other short pasta shapes
4 tbsp olive oil, plus extra for brushing
2 aubergines
1 large onion, chopped
2 garlic cloves, crushed
400 g/14 oz canned chopped tomatoes
2 tsp dried oregano
55 g/2 oz mozzarella cheese, thinly sliced
25 g/1 oz Parmesan cheese, freshly grated
5 tbsp dry breadcrumbs
salt and pepper

Preheat the oven to 200°C/400°C/ Gas Mark 6. Bring a large saucepan of lightly salted water to the boil. Add the pasta and 1 tablespoon of the olive oil, bring back to the boil and cook for 8–10 minutes, or until the pasta is just tender, but still firm to the bite. Drain, return to the pan, cover and keep warm.

Cut the aubergines in half lengthways and score around the inside with a sharp knife, being careful not to pierce the shells. Scoop out the flesh with a spoon. Brush the insides of the shells with olive oil. Chop the flesh and set aside. Heat the remaining oil in a frying pan. Fry the onion over a low heat for 5 minutes, until soft. Add the garlic and fry for 1 minute. Add the chopped aubergine and fry, stirring frequently, for 5 minutes. Add the tomatoes and oregano and season to taste with salt and pepper. Bring to the boil and simmer for 10 minutes until thickened. Remove the pan from the heat and stir in the pasta.

Brush a baking tray with oil and arrange the aubergine shells in a single layer. Divide half of the tomato and pasta mixture between them. Scatter over the slices of mozzarella cheese, then pile the remaining tomato and pasta mixture on top. Mix the Parmesan cheese and breadcrumbs and sprinkle over the top, patting lightly into the mixture. Bake in the preheated oven for about 25 minutes, or until the topping is golden brown. Serve hot.

889 *Stuffed aubergines with rice*

Replace the pasta with the same weight of long-grain rice and boil or steam until tender.

890 *Stuffed aubergines with mushrooms*

Add 225 g/8 oz chestnut mushrooms, finely chopped, to the pan with the chopped aubergine.

891 *Italian vegetable stew*

SERVES 4

4 garlic cloves
1 small acorn squash, deseeded and peeled
1 red onion, sliced
2 leeks, sliced
1 aubergine, sliced
1 small celeriac, diced
2 turnips, sliced
2 plum tomatoes, chopped
1 carrot, sliced
1 courgette, sliced
2 red peppers, deseeded and chopped
1 fennel bulb, sliced
175 g/6 oz chard, chopped
2 bay leaves
½ tsp fennel seeds
½ tsp chilli powder
pinch each of dried thyme, dried oregano and sugar
125 ml/4 fl oz extra virgin olive oil
225 ml/8 fl oz vegetable stock
25 g/1 oz fresh basil leaves, torn
4 tbsp chopped fresh parsley
salt and pepper
2 tbsp freshly grated Parmesan cheese, to garnish

Finely chop the garlic and dice the squash. Put them in a large heavy-based saucepan with a tight-fitting lid. Add the onion, leeks, aubergine, celeriac, turnips, tomatoes, carrot, courgette, red peppers, fennel, chard, bay leaves, fennel seeds, chilli powder, thyme, oregano, sugar, oil, stock and half the basil.

Mix together well, then bring to the boil. Reduce the heat, cover and simmer for 30 minutes, or until all the vegetables are tender.

Sprinkle in the remaining basil and the parsley and season to taste with salt and pepper. Serve immediately, sprinkled with the cheese.

892 *Simple Italian vegetable stew*

While a large selection of different vegetables can be tasty, you can make a great Italian stew using fewer ingredients. You could omit the turnip and carrot, for example, and use a slightly larger squash. Or you could omit the acorn squash and turnip and instead use 2 aubergines and 2 carrots.

269

893 Aubergine tagine with polenta

1 aubergine, cut into 1-cm/½-inch cubes
3 tbsp olive oil
1 large onion, thinly sliced
1 carrot, diced
2 garlic cloves, chopped
115 g/4 oz mushrooms, sliced
2 tsp ground coriander
2 tsp cumin seeds
1 tsp chilli powder
1 tsp ground turmeric
600 ml/1 pint canned chopped tomatoes

300 ml/10 fl oz vegetable stock
1 tbsp tomato purée
75 g/2¼ oz ready-to-eat dried apricots, roughly chopped
400 g/14 oz canned chickpeas, drained
2 tbsp fresh coriander, to garnish

POLENTA
1.2 litres/2 pints hot vegetable stock
200 g/7 oz instant polenta

Toss the aubergine in 1 tablespoon of the oil and arrange in a grill pan. Cook under a grill preheated to medium for 20 minutes, turning occasionally, until softened and starting to blacken around the edges. Brush with more oil if the aubergine becomes too dry.

Heat the remaining oil in a large heavy-based saucepan over a medium heat. Add the onion and cook, stirring occasionally, for 8 minutes, or until soft and golden. Add the carrot, garlic and mushrooms and cook for 5 minutes. Add the spices and cook, stirring constantly, for a further minute. Add the tomatoes and stock, stir well, then add the tomato purée. Bring to the boil, then reduce the heat and simmer for

10 minutes, or until the sauce starts to thicken and reduce. Add the aubergine, apricots and chickpeas, partially cover, and cook for a further 10 minutes, stirring occasionally.

Meanwhile, to make the polenta, pour the hot stock into a saucepan and bring to the boil. Pour in the polenta in a steady stream, stirring constantly with a wooden spoon. Reduce the heat to low and cook for 1–2 minutes, or until the polenta thickens. Serve the tagine with the polenta, sprinkled with the fresh coriander.

894 Chickpea hotpot

225 g/8 oz dried chickpeas, soaked in cold water overnight
3 tbsp olive oil
1 large onion, sliced
2 garlic cloves, finely chopped
2 leeks, sliced
175 g/6 oz carrots, sliced

4 turnips, sliced
4 celery sticks, sliced
115 g/4 oz bulgur wheat
400 g/14 oz canned chopped tomatoes
2 tbsp snipped fresh chives, plus extra to garnish
salt and pepper

Drain the chickpeas and place in a heavy-based saucepan. Add enough water to cover and bring to the boil. Boil for 15 minutes, then simmer for 1½ hours. Meanwhile, heat the oil in a large saucepan. Add the onion and cook, stirring occasionally, for 5 minutes, until soft. Add the garlic, leeks, carrots, turnips and celery and cook, stirring occasionally, for 5 minutes. Stir in the bulgur, tomatoes and chives, season to taste with salt and pepper and bring to the boil. Spoon the mixture into a heatproof pudding basin and cover with a lid or circle of foil.

When the chickpeas have been cooking for 1½ hours, set a steamer over the saucepan. Place the basin in the steamer, cover tightly and cook for 40 minutes. Remove the basin from the steamer, drain the chickpeas, then stir them into the vegetable and bulgur mixture. Transfer to a warmed serving dish and serve immediately, garnished with chives.

895 Chickpea hotpot with celeriac

Replace the celery and turnips with 1 celeriac – peeled and cut into bite-sized cubes. Add to the pan with the leeks and carrots.

896 Provençal bean stew

350 g/12 oz dried pinto beans, soaked
    overnight in water to cover
2 tbsp olive oil
2 onions, sliced
2 garlic cloves, finely chopped
1 red pepper, deseeded and sliced
1 yellow pepper, deseeded and sliced
400 g/14 oz canned chopped tomatoes
2 tbsp tomato purée
1 tbsp torn fresh basil leaves
2 tsp chopped fresh thyme
2 tsp chopped fresh rosemary
1 bay leaf
55 g/2 oz black olives, stoned and halved
salt and pepper
2 tbsp chopped fresh parsley, to garnish

Drain the beans. Place in a large saucepan, add enough cold water to cover and bring to the boil. Reduce the heat, then cover and simmer for 1¼–1½ hours until almost tender. Drain, reserving 300 ml/10 fl oz of the cooking liquid.

Heat the oil in a heavy-based saucepan over a medium heat. Add the onions and cook, stirring, for 5 minutes, or until softened. Add the garlic and peppers and cook, stirring occasionally, for 10 minutes. Add the tomatoes, the reserved cooking liquid, tomato purée, basil, thyme, rosemary, bay leaf and beans. Season to taste with salt and pepper. Cover and simmer for 40 minutes. Add the olives and simmer for a further 5 minutes. Transfer to a warmed serving dish, sprinkle with the parsley and serve immediately.

897 Spicy Provençal bean stew

Instead of the pinto beans, use cannellini beans or flageolets. For a hint of heat, add a dash of chilli sauce to the pot.

898 Beans & greens stew

250 g/9 oz dried haricot or cannellini
    beans
1 tbsp olive oil
2 onions, finely chopped
4 garlic cloves, finely chopped
1 celery stick, thinly sliced
2 carrots, halved and thinly sliced
1.2 litres/2 pints water
¼ tsp dried thyme
¼ tsp dried marjoram
1 bay leaf
125 g/4½ oz leafy greens, such as chard,
    mustard, spinach and kale, washed
salt and pepper

Allow the stew to cool slightly, then transfer 450 ml/16 fl oz to a food processor or blender. Process until smooth and stir back into the stew in the pan. A handful at a time, cut the greens crossways into thin ribbons, keeping tender leaves like spinach separate. Add the thicker leaves to the pan and cook gently, uncovered, for 10 minutes. Stir in any remaining greens and continue cooking for 5–10 minutes, until all the greens are tender. Taste and adjust the seasoning, if necessary. Ladle the stew into warmed bowls and serve.

Pick over the beans, cover generously with cold water and leave to soak for 6 hours or overnight. Drain the beans, put in a saucepan and add enough cold water to cover by 5 cm/2 inches. Bring to the boil and boil for 10 minutes. Drain and rinse well. Heat the oil in a large saucepan over a medium heat. Add the onions and cook, covered, for 3–4 minutes, stirring occasionally, until the onions are just softened. Add the garlic, celery and carrots, and continue cooking for 2 minutes.

Add the water, drained beans, thyme, marjoram and bay leaf. When the mixture begins to bubble, reduce the heat to low. Cover and simmer gently, stirring occasionally, for about 1¼ hours until the beans are tender; the cooking time will vary depending on the type of bean. Season with salt and pepper.

Moroccan stew

2 tbsp olive oil
1 Spanish onion, finely chopped
2–4 garlic cloves, crushed
1 fresh red chilli, deseeded and sliced
1 aubergine, about 225 g/8 oz, cut into small chunks
1 tsp ground cumin
1 tsp ground coriander
pinch of saffron threads
1–2 cinnamon sticks
1/2–1 butternut squash, about 450 g/ 1 lb, peeled, deseeded and cut into small chunks
225 g/8 oz sweet potatoes, cut into small chunks
85 g/3 oz ready-to-eat dried prunes
450–600 ml/16 fl oz–1 pint vegetable stock
4 tomatoes, chopped
400 g/14 oz canned chickpeas, drained and rinsed
1 tbsp chopped fresh coriander, to garnish

Heat the oil in a large heavy-based saucepan with a tight-fitting lid and cook the onion, garlic, chilli and aubergine, stirring frequently, for 5–8 minutes until softened.

Add the cumin, coriander and saffron and cook, stirring constantly, for 2 minutes. Bruise the cinnamon stick.

Add the cinnamon, squash, sweet potatoes, prunes, 450 ml/ 16 fl oz stock and the tomatoes to the saucepan and bring to the boil. Reduce the heat, cover and simmer, stirring occasionally, for 20 minutes. Add the chickpeas to the saucepan and cook for a further 10 minutes, adding more stock if necessary. Discard the cinnamon and serve garnished with the fresh coriander.

900 *Moroccan stew with sultanas*

You can omit the sweet potato and instead use a slightly larger butternut squash. You can also replace the prunes with 85 g/3 oz sultanas or ready-to-eat chopped apricots.

Chinese vegetables

2 tbsp groundnut oil	6 spring onions, quartered
350 g/12 oz broccoli florets	2 garlic cloves, crushed
1 tbsp chopped fresh ginger	2 tbsp light soy sauce
2 onions, cut into 8 pieces	2 tsp caster sugar
3 celery sticks, sliced	2 tbsp dry sherry
175 g/6 oz baby spinach	1 tbsp hoisin sauce
125 g/4 1/2 oz mangetout	150 ml/5 fl oz vegetable stock

Heat the groundnut oil in a preheated wok until it is almost smoking. Add the broccoli florets, chopped ginger, onions and celery to the wok and stir-fry for 1 minute. Add the spinach, mangetout, spring onions and garlic and stir-fry for 3–4 minutes.

Mix together the soy sauce, caster sugar, sherry, hoisin sauce and vegetable stock. Pour the stock mixture into the wok, mixing well to coat the vegetables.

Cover the wok and cook over a medium heat for 2–3 minutes, or until the vegetables are cooked through, but still crisp. Transfer the vegetables to a warmed serving dish and serve immediately.

902 Vegetable goulash

SERVES 4

15 g/½ oz sun-dried tomatoes,
chopped
2 tbsp olive oil
½–1 tsp crushed dried chillies
2–3 garlic cloves, chopped
1 large onion, cut into small wedges
1 small celeriac, cut into small chunks
225 g/8 oz carrots, sliced
225 g/8 oz new potatoes, scrubbed
and cut into chunks
1 small acorn squash, deseeded,
peeled and cut into small chunks,
about 225 g/8 oz prepared weight
2 tbsp tomato purée
300 ml/10 fl oz vegetable stock
450 g/1 lb canned Puy or
green lentils, drained and rinsed
1–2 tsp hot paprika
a few sprigs fresh thyme
450 g/1 lb ripe tomatoes, chopped
soured cream, to garnish
crusty bread, to serve

Put the sun-dried tomatoes in a small heatproof bowl, cover with almost boiling water and leave to soak for 15–20 minutes. Drain, reserving the soaking liquid. Heat the oil in a heavy-based saucepan with a tight-fitting lid, and cook the chillies, garlic and vegetables, stirring, for 5–8 minutes until softened. Blend the tomato purée with a little of the stock in a jug and pour over the vegetable mixture, then add the remaining stock, lentils, the sun-dried tomatoes and their soaking liquid, and the paprika and thyme. Bring to the boil, then reduce the heat, cover and simmer for 15 minutes.

Add the tomatoes and simmer for 15 minutes. Serve topped with spoonfuls of soured cream, and crusty bread.

903 Vegetable goulash with courgettes

Try using 2 courgettes instead of the celeriac. You could also replace the lentils with 400 g/14 oz canned mixed beans.

904 Spring stew

SERVES 4

2 tbsp olive oil
4–8 baby onions, halved
2 celery sticks, cut into 5-mm/
¼-inch slices
225 g/8 oz baby carrots, scrubbed
and halved if large
300 g/10½ oz new potatoes, scrubbed
and halved, or quartered if large
850 ml–1.2 litres/1½–2 pints
vegetable stock
400 g/14 oz canned haricot beans,
drained and rinsed
1 fresh bouquet garni
1½–2 tbsp light soy sauce
85 g/3 oz baby corn
115 g/4 oz frozen or shelled fresh
broad beans, thawed if frozen
½–1 Savoy or spring cabbage,
about 225 g/8 oz
1½ tbsp cornflour
2 tbsp cold water
salt and pepper
55–85 g/2–3 oz Parmesan or mature
Cheddar cheese, grated, to serve

Heat the oil in a large heavy-based saucepan, with a tight-fitting lid. Add the onions, celery, carrots and potatoes and cook, stirring frequently, for 5 minutes, or until softened. Add the stock, drained beans, bouquet garni and soy sauce, then bring to the boil.

Reduce the heat, cover and simmer for 12 minutes. Add the baby corn and broad beans and season to taste. Simmer for a further 3 minutes. Meanwhile, discard the outer leaves and core from the cabbage and shred the leaves. Add to the pan and simmer for 3–5 minutes, or until the vegetables are tender.

Blend the cornflour with the water, stir into the saucepan and cook, stirring, for 4–6 minutes, or until the liquid has thickened. Serve with grated cheese.

905 Spring stew with baby leaf beet

Try replacing the spring cabbage with baby leaf beet (perpetual spinach) or shredded Brussels sprout tops. Chopped asparagus spears are also a great addition.

906 Tuscan bean stew

1 large fennel bulb
2 tbsp olive oil
1 red onion, cut into small wedges
2–4 garlic cloves, sliced
1 fresh green chilli, deseeded
    and chopped
1 small aubergine, about 225 g/8 oz, cut
    into chunks
2 tbsp tomato purée
450–600 ml/16 fl oz–1 pint
    vegetable stock
450 g/1 lb ripe tomatoes

1 tbsp balsamic vinegar
a few sprigs fresh oregano
400 g/14 oz canned borlotti beans
400 g/14 oz canned flageolet beans
1 yellow pepper, deseeded and cut into
    small strips
1 courgette, sliced into half moons
55 g/2 oz stoned black olives
25 g/1 oz Parmesan cheese,
    freshly shaved
salt and pepper
crusty bread or polenta wedges, to serve

Trim the fennel and reserve any feathery fronds, then cut the bulb into small strips.

Heat the oil in a large heavy-based saucepan with a tight-fitting lid, and cook the onion, garlic, chilli and fennel strips, stirring frequently, for 5–8 minutes, or until softened.

Add the aubergine and cook, stirring frequently, for 5 minutes. Blend the tomato purée with a little of the stock in a jug and pour over the fennel mixture, then add the remaining stock, and the tomatoes, vinegar and oregano. Bring to the boil, then reduce the heat, cover and simmer for

15 minutes, or until the tomatoes have begun to collapse.

Drain and rinse the beans, then drain again. Add them to the pan with the yellow pepper, courgette and olives. Simmer for a further 15 minutes, or until all the vegetables are tender. Taste and adjust the seasoning. Scatter with the Parmesan cheese shavings and serve garnished with the reserved fennel fronds, accompanied by crusty bread.

907 Tuscan bean stew with pasta

Omit the bread or polenta and instead add 200 g/7 oz wholewheat pasta shapes to the stew for the last 20 minutes of cooking time, adding another 200 ml/7 fl oz stock to the pan. If towards the end of cooking time the stew looks too dry, add a little more stock.

908 Vegetable chilli

1 aubergine, peeled (optional) and cut
    into 2.5-cm/1-inch slices
1 tbsp olive oil, plus extra for brushing
1 large red or yellow onion, finely chopped
2 red or yellow peppers, deseeded and
    finely chopped
3–4 garlic cloves, finely chopped or
    crushed
800 g/1 lb 12 oz canned chopped tomatoes
1 tbsp mild chilli powder
1/2 tsp ground cumin
1/2 tsp dried oregano

2 small courgettes, quartered lengthways
    and sliced
400 g/14 oz canned kidney beans, rinsed
    and drained
450 ml/16 fl oz water
1 tbsp tomato purée
salt and pepper
6 spring onions, finely chopped,
    to garnish
115 g/4 oz grated Cheddar cheese,
    to garnish

Brush the aubergine slices on one side with oil. Heat half the oil in a large heavy-based frying pan over a medium–high heat. Add the aubergine slices, oiled-side up, and cook for 5–6 minutes, or until browned underneath. Turn over and brown the other side.

Remove and cut into bite-sized

pieces. Heat the remaining oil in a large saucepan over a medium heat. Add the onion and peppers and cook, stirring occasionally, for 3–4 minutes, or until the onion is just softened but not browned. Add the garlic and cook for a further 2–3 minutes, or until the onion is just beginning to colour. Add the tomatoes, chilli powder, cumin and oregano. Season to taste with salt and pepper. Bring just to the boil, then reduce the heat, cover and simmer gently for

15 minutes. Add the courgettes, aubergine pieces and beans. Stir in the water and the tomato purée. Return to the boil, then reduce the heat, cover and simmer for 45 minutes, or until the vegetables are tender. Taste the chilli and adjust the seasoning if necessary.

If you prefer a hotter dish, stir in a little more chilli powder. Ladle into warmed bowls, top with spring onions and cheese and serve.

909 Vegetable chilli with taco shells

Use the chilli mixture to fill taco shells, topped with a little sour cream, or serve it on pasta or rice. You can also layer it in a baking dish with cooked sliced potatoes and top with grated cheese before baking for 25 minutes at 190°C/375°F/Gas Mark 5.

Vegetable hotpot with parsley dumplings

SERVES 6

½ swede, cut into chunks
2 onions, sliced
2 potatoes, cut into chunks
2 carrots, cut into chunks
2 celery sticks, sliced
2 courgettes, sliced
2 tbsp tomato purée
600 ml/1 pint hot vegetable stock
1 bay leaf
1 tsp ground coriander
½ tsp dried thyme
400 g/14 oz canned sweetcorn, drained
salt and pepper

PARSLEY DUMPLINGS
200 g/7 oz self-raising flour
115 g/4 oz vegetable suet
2 tbsp chopped fresh parsley
125 ml/4 fl oz milk

Put the swede, onions, potatoes, carrots, celery and courgettes into a slow cooker.

Stir the tomato purée into the stock and pour it over the vegetables. Add the bay leaf, coriander and thyme and season with salt and pepper. Cover and cook on low for 6 hours.

To make the dumplings, sift the flour with a pinch of salt into a bowl and stir in the suet and parsley. Add just enough milk to make a firm but light dough. Knead lightly and shape into 12 small balls.

Stir the sweetcorn into the vegetable casserole and place the dumplings on top. Cook on high for 30 minutes. Serve immediately.

911 Vegetable hotpot with parsnip mash

Omit the dumplings. Cook 400 g/14 oz potatoes with 200 g/7 oz peeled and diced parsnips and mash them together with 1 tablespoon of butter, 50 ml/2 fl oz milk and seasoning. Spoon the mash evenly over the vegetables in the ovenproof dish and sprinkle with cheese. Bake for 25 minutes or until golden.

912 Vegetable hotpot with puff pastry

Omit the dumplings and the potatoes and instead roll out 350 g/12 oz ready-made puff pastry to fit the dish. Brush with milk or beaten egg and bake at 200°C/400°C/Gas Mark 6 for 25 minutes or until golden.

913 Vegetable stew with green lentils

SERVES 6

1 tbsp olive oil
1 onion, finely chopped
1 garlic clove, finely chopped
1 carrot, halved and thinly sliced
450 g/1 lb young green cabbage, cored, quartered and thinly sliced
400 g/14 oz canned chopped tomatoes
½ tsp dried thyme

2 bay leaves
1.5 litres/2¾ pints vegetable stock
200 g/7 oz Puy lentils
450 ml/16 fl oz water
salt and pepper
chopped fresh parsley, to garnish

Heat the oil in a large saucepan over a medium heat, add the onion, garlic and carrot and cook for 3–4 minutes, stirring frequently, until the onion starts to soften. Add the cabbage and cook for a further 2 minutes.

Add the tomatoes, thyme and 1 bay leaf, then pour in the stock. Bring to the boil, reduce the heat to low and cook gently, partially covered, for about 45 minutes until the vegetables are tender.

Meanwhile, put the lentils in another saucepan with the remaining bay leaf and the water. Bring just to the boil, reduce the heat and simmer for about 25 minutes until tender. Drain off any remaining water, and set aside. Allow the stew to cool, then transfer to a food processor or blender and process until smooth, working in batches, if necessary. (If using a food processor, strain off the cooking liquid and reserve. Purée the solids with enough cooking liquid to moisten them, then combine with the remaining liquid.)

Return the stew to the saucepan and add the cooked lentils. Taste and adjust the seasoning, and cook for about 10 minutes to heat through. Ladle into warmed bowls and garnish with parsley.

914 Vegetable jambalaya

75 g/2¾ oz brown rice
2 tbsp olive oil
2 garlic cloves, crushed
1 red onion, cut into 8 wedges
1 aubergine, diced
1 green pepper, deseeded and diced
50 g/1¾ oz baby corn, halved
lengthways
50 g/1¾ oz frozen peas
100 g/3½ oz small broccoli florets
150 ml/5 fl oz vegetable stock
225 g/8 oz canned chopped tomatoes
1 tbsp tomato purée
1 tsp Creole seasoning
½ tsp dried chilli flakes
salt and pepper

Cook the rice in a large saucepan of boiling water for 20 minutes, or until cooked through. Drain and reserve until required.

Heat the oil in a heavy-based frying pan. Add the garlic and onion and cook, stirring constantly, for 2–3 minutes.

Add the aubergine, pepper, baby corn, peas and broccoli to the frying pan and cook the mixture, stirring occasionally, for 2–3 minutes.

Stir in the stock, tomatoes, tomato purée, Creole seasoning and chilli flakes. Season to taste with salt and pepper and cook over a low heat for 15–20 minutes, or until the vegetables are tender.

915 Jambalaya with courgettes

Replace the aubergine with 2 diced courgettes and if you haven't any baby corn use canned sweetcorn instead. Creole seasoning can be replaced with 1 teaspoon each of sweet paprika, cayenne pepper and mixed dried herbs.

916 Vegetable stew with pesto

1 tbsp olive oil
1 onion, finely chopped
1 large leek, thinly sliced
1 celery stick, thinly sliced
1 carrot, quartered and thinly sliced
1 garlic clove, finely chopped
1.4 litres/2½ pints water
1 potato, diced
1 parsnip, finely diced
1 small kohlrabi or turnip, diced
150 g/5½ oz French beans, cut into
small pieces
150 g/5½ oz fresh or frozen peas
2 small courgettes, quartered
lengthways and sliced
400 g/14 oz canned flageolet beans,
drained and rinsed
100 g/3½ oz spinach leaves, cut into
thin ribbons
1–2 tbsp ready-made basil pesto
salt and pepper

Heat the olive oil in a large saucepan over a medium–low heat. Add the onion and leek and cook for 5 minutes, stirring occasionally, until the onion softens. Add the celery, carrot and garlic and cook, covered, for a further 5 minutes, stirring frequently.

Add the water, potato, parsnip, kohlrabi and French beans. Bring to the boil, reduce the heat to low and simmer, covered, for about 5 minutes. Add the peas, courgettes and flageolet beans, and season generously with salt and pepper. Cover again and simmer for about 25 minutes, until all the vegetables are tender.

Add the spinach and simmer for a further 5 minutes. Taste and adjust the seasoning and stir in about a tablespoon of the pesto.

Ladle into warmed bowls and serve with the remaining pesto.

917 Vegetable stew with coriander pesto

Omit the ready-made basil pesto. Using a pestle and mortar, combine 2 peeled garlic cloves with 2 teaspoons of sea salt until creamy. Strip the leaves off 25 g/1 oz bunch fresh coriander leaves and add to the mortar, then pound thoroughly with a little olive oil until you have a rough paste. Add 25 g/1 oz pine kernels and black pepper and a little more oil and pound again. Use the coriander pesto in the stew.

Warm vegetable medley

SERVES 4

4 tbsp olive oil
2 celery sticks, sliced
2 red onions, sliced
450 g/1 lb aubergine, diced
1 garlic clove, finely chopped
5 plum tomatoes, chopped
3 tbsp red wine vinegar
1 tbsp sugar
3 tbsp green olives, stoned
2 tbsp capers
4 tbsp chopped fresh flat-leaf parsley
salt and pepper
ciabatta or panini, to serve

Heat half the olive oil in a large heavy-based saucepan. Add the celery and onions and cook over a low heat, stirring occasionally, for 5 minutes, until softened but not coloured. Add the remaining oil and the aubergine. Cook, stirring frequently, for about 5 minutes, until the aubergine starts to colour.

Add the garlic, tomatoes, vinegar and sugar, and mix well. Cover the mixture with a circle of waxed paper and simmer gently for about 10 minutes.

Remove the waxed paper, stir in the olives and capers and season to taste with salt and pepper. Pour the vegetables into a serving dish and set aside to cool to room temperature. Sprinkle the parsley over the vegetables and serve with fresh ciabatta or panini.

919 *Warm vegetable medley with cheese*

Once you have poured the vegetables into a warmed serving dish, gently stir 1 x 125-g/4-oz ball of fresh mozzarella into the medley and set aside to cool a little, by which time the mozzarella will have just melted. Eat warm.

Chilli bean stew

SERVES 4–6

2 tbsp olive oil
1 onion, chopped
2–4 garlic cloves, chopped
2 fresh red chillies, deseeded and sliced
225 g/8 oz canned kidney beans, drained and rinsed
225 g/8 oz canned cannellini beans, drained and rinsed
225 g/8 oz canned chickpeas, drained and rinsed
1 tbsp tomato purée
700–850 ml/1¼–1½ pints vegetable stock
1 red pepper, deseeded and chopped
4 tomatoes, roughly chopped
175 g/6 oz frozen or shelled fresh broad beans, thawed if frozen
1 tbsp chopped fresh coriander, plus extra to garnish
pepper
paprika, to garnish
soured cream, to serve

Heat the oil in a large heavy-based saucepan with a tight-fitting lid and cook the onion, garlic and chillies, stirring frequently, for 5 minutes, or until softened. Add the kidney and cannellini beans and the chickpeas. Blend the tomato purée with a little of the stock in a jug and pour over the bean mixture, then add the remaining stock. Bring to the boil, then reduce the heat and simmer for 10–15 minutes.

Add the red pepper, tomatoes, broad beans, and pepper to taste and simmer for a further 15–20 minutes, or until the vegetables are tender. Stir in the chopped coriander. Serve topped with spoonfuls of soured cream and garnished with chopped coriander and a pinch of paprika.

921 *Chilli bean stew with chocolate*

Try replacing 100 ml/3½ fl oz of the stock with red wine – and add a small piece of dark chocolate to the stew with the vegetables.

922 *Broccoli & mangetout stir-fry*

SERVES 4

2 tbsp vegetable or groundnut oil
dash of sesame oil
1 garlic clove, finely chopped
225 g/8 oz broccoli florets
115 g/4 oz mangetout, trimmed
225 g/8 oz Chinese leaves, chopped into
    1-cm/½-inch slices

5–6 spring onions, finely chopped
½ tsp salt
2 tbsp light soy sauce
1 tbsp Shaoxing rice wine
1 tsp sesame seeds, lightly toasted

In a preheated wok, heat the oils, then add the garlic and stir-fry vigorously. Add all the vegetables and salt and stir-fry over a high heat, tossing rapidly, for about 3 minutes. Pour in the light soy sauce and Shaoxing and cook for a further 2 minutes. Sprinkle with the sesame seeds and serve hot.

923 *Cauliflower & mangetout stir-fry*

Use half a cauliflower, divided into small florets, instead of the broccoli.

924 *Broccoli, French bean & peanut stir-fry*

Omit the mangetout and use sliced French beans instead. Add 100 g/3½ oz shelled peanuts to the pan with the vegetables so that they colour lightly.

925 *Broccoli & black bean stir-fry*

Omit the rice wine and instead stir 2 tablespoons of black bean sauce into the pan with 50 ml/2 fl oz vegetable stock.

926 *Butternut squash stir-fry*

SERVES 4

1 kg/2 lb 4 oz butternut squash, peeled
3 tbsp groundnut oil
1 onion, sliced
2 garlic cloves, crushed
1 tsp coriander seeds
1 tsp cumin seeds

2 tbsp chopped fresh coriander, plus
    extra to garnish
150 ml/5 fl oz coconut milk
100 ml/3½ fl oz water
100 g/3½ oz salted cashew nuts
lime wedges, to serve

Slice the squash into bite-sized cubes, using a sharp knife. Heat the oil in a large preheated wok. Add the squash, onion and garlic to the wok and stir-fry for 5 minutes. Stir in the coriander seeds, cumin seeds and chopped coriander, and stir-fry for 1 minute.

Add the coconut milk and water to the wok and bring to the boil. Cover the wok and leave to simmer for 10–15 minutes, or until the squash is tender. Add the cashew nuts and stir to combine thoroughly.

Transfer to warmed serving dishes and garnish with chopped coriander. Serve with lime wedges for squeezing over.

927 *Butternut squash chilli stir-fry*

Add 2 fresh red finely chopped chillies to the stir-fry with the onion and garlic.

Potato stir-fry

SERVES 4

900 g/2 lb waxy potatoes
2 tbsp vegetable oil
1 yellow pepper, deseeded and diced
1 red pepper, deseeded and diced
1 carrot, cut into matchsticks
1 courgette, cut into matchsticks
2 garlic cloves, crushed
1 fresh red chilli, deseeded and sliced

1 bunch spring onions, halved
  lengthways
125 ml/4 fl oz coconut milk
1 tsp chopped lemon grass
2 tsp lime juice
finely grated rind of 1 lime
1 tbsp chopped fresh coriander

Using a sharp knife, cut the potatoes into small cubes. Bring a large saucepan of water to the boil over a medium heat, add the diced potatoes and cook for 5 minutes. Drain thoroughly. Heat a wok or large heavy-based frying pan, add the vegetable oil and heat, swirling the oil around the base of the wok or pan until it is really hot. Add the potatoes, yellow and red peppers, carrot, courgette, garlic and chilli to the wok or pan and stir-fry over a medium heat for 2–3 minutes. Stir in the spring onions, coconut milk, lemon grass and lime juice and stir-fry the mixture for a further 5 minutes. Add the lime rind and chopped fresh coriander and stir-fry for 1 minute. Serve immediately, while hot.

929 Sweet potato stir-fry

Replace the potato with peeled, diced sweet potato, boiled for 3 minutes then drained. Add 50 g/2 oz flaked almonds to the pan with the coriander.

930 With water chestnuts

Add 125 g/4 oz canned, drained, sliced water chestnuts to the pan for the last few minutes of cooking time.

931 Stir-fried French beans with red pepper

SERVES 4–6

280 g/10 oz French beans, cut into
  6-cm/2½-inch lengths
1 tbsp vegetable or groundnut oil

1 red pepper, deseeded and thinly sliced
pinch of salt
pinch of sugar

Blanch the beans in a large pan of boiling water for 30 seconds. Drain and set aside.

In a preheated wok, heat the oil and stir-fry the beans for 1 minute over high heat. Add the red pepper and stir-fry for 1 more minute. Sprinkle the salt and sugar on top and serve.

932 Stir-fried French beans with carrots

Replace the red pepper with 1 large carrot, peeled and very thinly sliced, and 55 g/2 oz fresh beansprouts. Add 1 teaspoon of soy sauce with the sugar and omit the salt.

933 Stir-fried French beans with asparagus

Replace the red pepper with 100 g/3½ oz tender asparagus tips (if not small and tender, steam for 3 minutes before adding to the pan) and 8 baby corn, sliced on the diagonal.

MARINADE
75 ml/2½ fl oz vegetable stock
2 tsp cornflour
2 tbsp soy sauce
1 tbsp caster sugar
pinch of chilli flakes

STIR-FRY
4 tbsp groundnut oil
250 g/9 oz firm tofu, rinsed and
drained thoroughly and cut into
1-cm/½-inch cubes
1 tbsp grated fresh ginger
3 garlic cloves, crushed
4 spring onions, thinly sliced
1 head of broccoli, cut into florets
1 carrot, cut into thin strips
1 yellow pepper, deseeded and
thinly sliced
250 g/9 oz shiitake mushrooms,
thinly sliced
steamed rice, to serve

To make the marinade, blend the vegetable stock, cornflour, soy sauce, sugar and chilli flakes together in a large bowl. Add the tofu and toss well to cover in the marinade. Set aside to marinate for 20 minutes.

In a large wok, heat 2 tablespoons of the groundnut oil and stir-fry the tofu with its marinade until brown and crispy. Remove from the wok and set aside.

Heat the remaining 2 tablespoons of groundnut oil in the wok and stir-fry the ginger, garlic and spring onions for 30 seconds. Add the broccoli, carrot, yellow pepper and mushrooms to the wok and cook for 5–6 minutes. Return the tofu to the wok and stir-fry to reheat. Serve immediately over freshly steamed rice.

935 *Spicy tofu with lime & honey*

Make a different marinade – combine stock, cornflour, soy sauce, the juice of 1 lime, 1 tablespoon of runny honey, 1 fresh finely chopped chilli and ½ teaspoon of Chinese five spice. Continue with the recipe.

936 *Spicy tofu with mushroom ketchup*

Add ½ tablespoon of mushroom ketchup to the soy sauce/chilli marinade. Omit the broccoli and instead use 2 medium courgettes, thinly sliced.

937 Sweet & sour vegetables with cashew nuts

1 tbsp vegetable or groundnut oil
1 tsp chilli oil
2 onions, sliced
2 carrots, thinly sliced
2 courgettes, thinly sliced
115 g/4 oz head of broccoli, cut into florets

115 g/4 oz white mushrooms, sliced
115 g/4 oz small pak choi, halved
2 tbsp soft light brown sugar
2 tbsp Thai soy sauce
1 tbsp rice vinegar
55 g/2 oz cashew nuts

Heat the oils in a wok and stir-fry the onions for 1–2 minutes until they start to soften.

Add the carrots, courgettes and broccoli and stir-fry for 2–3 minutes.

Add the mushrooms, pak choi, sugar, soy sauce and rice vinegar and stir-fry the vegetables for 1–2 minutes.

Meanwhile, dry-fry or toast the cashew nuts. Sprinkle the cashews over the stir-fry and serve immediately.

938 Sweet & sour vegetables with peppers

Replace the carrots with 1 large or 2 small yellow or green peppers.

939 Sweet & sour vegetables with tofu

Follow the recipe as above but replace the pak choi with 125 g/4 oz silken tofu stirred into the pan for the last 1 minute of cooking time and garnish the dish with 1 tablespoon of sesame seeds. Omit the cashew nuts.

940 Cabbage & walnut stir-fry

350 g/12 oz white cabbage
350 g/12 oz red cabbage
4 tbsp groundnut oil
1 tbsp walnut oil
2 garlic cloves, crushed
8 spring onions, trimmed

225 g/8 oz firm tofu, cubed
2 tbsp lemon juice
100 g/3½ oz walnut halves
2 tsp Dijon mustard
salt and pepper
2 tsp poppy seeds, to garnish

Using a sharp knife, thinly shred the white and red cabbages and set aside until required.

Heat the groundnut and walnut oils in a preheated wok. Add the garlic, cabbage, spring onions and tofu and cook for 5 minutes, stirring.

Add the lemon juice, walnuts and mustard to the wok and stir to combine thoroughly.

Season the mixture to taste with salt and pepper and cook for a further 5 minutes, or until the cabbage is tender.

Transfer the stir-fry to a warmed serving bowl, sprinkle with poppy seeds and serve immediately.

941 Cauliflower & walnut stir-fry

Omit the two types of cabbage and instead use the same weights of cauliflower and broccoli.

942 Vegetable fajitas

2 tbsp corn oil
2 onions, thinly sliced
2 garlic cloves, finely chopped
2 green peppers, deseeded and sliced
2 red peppers, deseeded and sliced

4 fresh green chillies, deseeded and sliced
2 tsp chopped fresh coriander
12 wheat tortillas
225 g/8 oz mushrooms, sliced
salt and pepper

Heat the oil in a heavy-based frying pan over a low heat. Add the onions and garlic and cook, stirring occasionally, for 5 minutes, or until softened. Stir in the peppers, chillies and coriander and cook, stirring occasionally, for 10 minutes. Meanwhile, heat a separate, dry frying pan over a medium–high heat, add a tortilla and heat for 30 seconds on each side. Remove from the pan and keep warm in a low oven while you heat the remaining tortillas. Add the mushrooms to the vegetable mixture and cook, stirring constantly, for 1 minute. Season to taste. Divide the vegetables between the tortillas, roll up and serve immediately.

943 Vegetable fajitas with courgette

Omit the mushrooms and instead add 1 large courgette, thinly sliced – cook it with the peppers and an extra tablespoon of oil.

944 Leek & goat's cheese crêpes

SERVES 8

25 g/1 oz unsalted butter
½ tbsp sunflower oil
200 g/7 oz leeks, halved, rinsed and finely shredded
freshly grated nutmeg, to taste

1 tbsp finely snipped fresh chives
8 ready-made savoury crêpes
85 g/3 oz soft goat's cheese, rind removed if necessary, chopped
salt and pepper

Preheat the oven to 200°C/400°F/Gas Mark 6. Melt the butter with the oil in a heavy-based saucepan with a lid over a medium–high heat. Add the leeks and stir around so that they are well coated. Stir in salt and pepper to taste. Add a few gratings of nutmeg, then cover the leeks with a sheet of wet greaseproof paper and cover the pan.

Reduce the heat to very low and leave the leeks to sweat for 5–7 minutes until very tender, but not brown. Stir in the chives, then taste and adjust the seasoning if necessary.

Put 1 crêpe on the work surface and put one eighth of the leeks on the crêpe, top with one eighth of the cheese, then fold the crêpe into a square parcel or simply roll it around the filling. Place the stuffed crêpe on a baking tray, then continue to fill and fold or roll the remaining crêpes. Put the baking tray in the oven and bake for 5 minutes, or until the crêpes are hot and the cheese starts to melt. Serve hot.

945 Saucy borlotti beans

600 g/1 lb 5 oz fresh
borlotti beans
4 large fresh sage leaves, torn
1 tbsp olive oil
1 large onion, thinly sliced
300 ml/10 fl oz Basic Tomato Sauce
recipe (see page 9)
salt and pepper

Shell the beans. Bring a large saucepan of water to the boil, add the beans and torn sage leaves, bring back to the boil and simmer for 12 minutes or until the beans are tender. Drain and set aside.

Heat the olive oil in a large heavy-based frying pan over a medium heat. Add the onion and cook, stirring occasionally, for about 5 minutes until softened and translucent, but not browned.

Stir the tomato sauce into the frying pan with the cooked beans and sage. Increase the heat and bring to the boil, stirring. Reduce the heat, partially cover and simmer for about 10 minutes, or until the sauce has reduced. Adjust the seasoning, transfer to a serving bowl and serve hot.

946 With chilli

For a bit of spice, add one medium hot red chilli, finely diced and deseeded, at the same time as the onion.

947 Colcannon

225 g/8 oz green or white cabbage
6 spring onions, cut into 5-mm/¼-inch
pieces
salt and pepper
butter, to serve

MASHED POTATO
450 g/1 lb floury potatoes, such as King
Edwards, Maris Piper or Desirée,
peeled and cut into chunks
55 g/2 oz butter
150 ml/5 fl oz single cream
salt and pepper

To make the mashed potato, cook the potatoes in a large saucepan of boiling salted water for 15–20 minutes. Drain well and mash with a potato masher until smooth. Season with salt and pepper, add the butter and cream and stir well. The potato should be very soft.

Cut the cabbage into quarters, remove the centre stalk and shred finely. Cook the cabbage in a large saucepan of boiling salted water for just 1–2 minutes until it is soft. Drain thoroughly.

Mix the potato and cabbage together and stir in the spring onion. Season well with salt and pepper. Serve in individual bowls and top with a good piece of butter.

948 Colcannon with leftover greens

You can use shredded leftover cooked greens, in which case omit cooking stage. You can use Brussels sprouts or kale instead of the cabbage. Add some crisply fried lardons of bacon to the colcannon before serving to give even more flavour.

Desserts

Apple & blackberry crumble

900 g/2 lb cooking apples
300 g/10½ oz blackberries, fresh or frozen
55 g/2 oz light muscovado sugar
1 tsp ground cinnamon
single or double cream, to serve

CRUMBLE TOPPING
85 g/3 oz self-raising flour
85 g/3 oz plain wholemeal flour
115 g/4 oz unsalted butter
55 g/2 oz demerara sugar

Preheat the oven to 190°C/375°F/Gas Mark 5. Peel and core the apples and cut into chunks. Place in a bowl with the blackberries, muscovado sugar and cinnamon and mix together, then transfer to an ovenproof baking dish.

To make the crumble topping, sift the self-raising flour into a bowl and stir in the wholemeal flour. Add the unsalted butter and rub in with your fingers until the mixture resembles fine breadcrumbs. Stir in the demerara sugar. Spread the crumble over the apples and bake in the preheated oven for 40–45 minutes, or until the apples are soft and the crumble is golden brown and crisp. Serve hot with cream.

950 Apple & raspberry crumble

Replace the blackberries with 300 g/10½ oz fresh or frozen, thawed, raspberries.

951 Pear & blueberry crumble

Replace the apples with 1 kg/2 lb 4 oz peeled, cored, sliced pears and replace the blackberries with 150 g/5½ oz fresh blueberries.

Gooseberry & pistachio nut dessert

400 g/14 oz gooseberries
1 tbsp honey
85 g/3 oz caster sugar
1 tbsp orange juice
1 tbsp grated orange zest
6 tbsp water
thin strips of orange rind, to decorate

vanilla ice cream, to serve

CRUMBLE TOPPING
115 g/4 oz self-raising flour
100 g/3½ oz unsalted butter, diced
5 tbsp demerara sugar
50 g/1¾ oz pistachio nuts, finely chopped

Preheat the oven to 200°C/400°F/Gas Mark 6. Top and tail the gooseberries. Put them in an ovenproof pie dish, pour over the honey and cook in the preheated oven for 5–10 minutes until heated through.

Put the caster sugar, orange juice and zest, and water in a small saucepan and bring to the boil, stirring, over a medium heat. Reduce the heat and simmer for 5 minutes, then remove from the heat and leave to cool. Meanwhile, to make the crumble topping, put the flour in a bowl, then use your fingertips to rub in the butter until crumbly. Stir in 4 tablespoons of the demerara sugar and the pistachio nuts. Pour the cooled orange syrup over the gooseberries, then lightly sprinkle over the crumble mixture in an even layer. Sprinkle over the remaining demerara sugar. Bake in the preheated oven for 25–30 minutes or until the crumble topping is golden brown. Remove from the oven, decorate with strips of orange rind and serve with vanilla ice cream.

Apricot crumble

70 g/2¹/₂ oz unsalted butter, plus extra for
    greasing
100 g/3¹/₂ oz brown sugar
500 g/1 lb 2 oz fresh apricots, stoned and
    sliced
1 tsp ground cinnamon
fresh clotted cream, to serve

CRUMBLE TOPPING
175 g/6 oz wholemeal flour
50 g/1³/₄ oz unsalted butter
70 g/2¹/₂ oz brown sugar
50 g/1³/₄ oz hazelnuts, toasted and finely
    chopped

Preheat the oven to 200°C/400°F/Gas Mark 6. Grease a 1.2-litre/2-pint ovenproof dish with a little unsalted butter. Put the unsalted butter and the sugar in a saucepan and melt together, stirring, over a low heat. Add the apricots and cinnamon, cover the saucepan and simmer for 5 minutes. To make the crumble topping, put the flour in a bowl and rub in the unsalted butter. Stir in the sugar and then the hazelnuts.

Remove the fruit from the heat and arrange in the bottom of the prepared dish. Sprinkle the crumble topping evenly over the fruit until it is covered all over. Transfer to the preheated oven and bake for about 25 minutes until golden. Serve hot with fresh clotted cream.

954 *Apricot & almond crumble*

Omit the hazelnuts from the topping and instead add 50 g/2 oz ground almonds. Add 50 g/2 oz toasted flaked almonds to the apricot filling.

955 *Blueberry clafoutis*

2 tbsp butter, plus extra for greasing
125 g/4¹/₂ oz caster sugar
3 eggs
60 g/2¹/₄ oz plain flour
250 ml/9 fl oz single cream

¹/₂ tsp ground cinnamon
450 g/1 lb blueberries
icing sugar, to decorate
single cream, to serve

Preheat the oven to 180°C/350°F/Gas Mark 4. Grease a 1-litre/1³/₄-pint ovenproof dish with butter. Put the remaining butter in a bowl with the sugar and whisk together until fluffy. Add the eggs and beat together well. Mix in the flour, then gradually stir in the cream followed by the cinnamon. Continue to stir until smooth.

Arrange the blueberries in the bottom of the prepared dish, then pour over the cream batter. Transfer to the preheated oven and bake for about 30 minutes or until puffed and golden. Remove from the oven, dust lightly with icing sugar and serve with single cream.

956 *Cherry clafoutis*

Replace the blueberries with 450 g/1 lb stoned sweet cherries, lightly poached in a little water with 1 tablespoon of sugar added, or with fresh raspberries.

957 Chocolate fondue

selection of fresh fruit, such as apples, bananas, pears, seedless grapes, peaches and oranges
juice of 1 lemon
small sponge or Madeira cake

225 g/8 oz plain chocolate, broken into pieces
6 tbsp double cream
2 tbsp dark rum
55 g/2 oz icing sugar

Prepare the fruit according to type, cutting it into bite-sized pieces. Brush apples, pears and bananas with a little lemon juice to prevent them from discolouring. Cut the sponge cake into cubes. Arrange the fruit and cake on several serving plates. Place the chocolate and cream in the top of a double boiler and heat gently, stirring constantly, until melted and smooth. Alternatively, melt the chocolate and cream in a heatproof bowl set over a saucepan of barely simmering water. Remove the saucepan or bowl from the heat. Stir in the rum and sugar. Pour the mixture into a ceramic fondue pot set over a burner and hand round the fruit and cake separately. Each guest can then spear their chosen morsel and dip it in the hot chocolate mixture.

958 Exotic fruit parcels

1 papaya
1 mango
1 star fruit
1 tbsp grenadine
3 tbsp orange juice
single cream or natural yogurt, to serve

Preheat the oven to 180°C/350°F/ Gas Mark 4. Cut the papaya in half, scoop out the seeds and discard them. Peel the papaya and cut the flesh into thick slices. Prepare the mango by cutting it lengthways in half either side of the central stone. Score each mango half in a criss-cross pattern, then push each half inside out to separate the cubes and cut them away from the peel. Thickly slice the star fruit.

Place all of the fruit in a bowl. Mix the grenadine and orange juice together and pour over the fruit. Leave to marinate for at least 30 minutes. Divide the fruit among 4 double-thickness squares of kitchen foil and gather up the edges to form a parcel that completely encloses the fruit. Place the foil parcel on a baking tray in the oven and cook for 15–20 minutes. Serve the fruit in the parcel, with the yogurt.

959 Other exotic fruit parcels

Replace the fruits with 200 g/7 oz each of prepared pineapple chunks, peeled and sliced kiwi fruit and peeled and chunked banana. Halve 4 passion fruit and scoop the seeds and juice from inside over the fruit in each parcel before cooking as above.

sunflower oil, for deep-frying
1 large egg
pinch of salt
175 ml/6 fl oz water

55 g/2 oz plain flour
2 tsp ground cinnamon
55 g/2 oz caster sugar
4 eating apples, peeled and cored

Pour the sunflower oil into a deep fryer or large heavy-based saucepan and heat to 180°C/350°F, or until a cube of bread browns in 30 seconds.

Meanwhile, using an electric mixer, beat the egg and salt together until frothy, then quickly whisk in the water and flour. Do not overbeat the batter – it doesn't matter if it isn't completely smooth. Mix the cinnamon and sugar together in a shallow dish and reserve.

Slice the apples into 5-mm/¼-inch thick rings. Spear with a fork, 1 slice at a time, and dip in the batter to coat. Add to the hot oil, in batches, and cook for 1 minute on each side, or until golden and puffed up. Remove with a slotted spoon and drain on kitchen paper. Keep warm while you cook the remaining batches. Transfer to a large serving plate, sprinkle with the cinnamon sugar and serve.

961 *Pineapple fritters*

Replace the apples with 1 small fresh pineapple. Top, tail, peel and core it and cut into 1-cm/½-inch thick rings, then cut each ring into 4. Pat dry on kitchen paper then coat in the batter and fry.

962 *Blueberry fritters*

Replace the apples with 200 g/7 oz fresh blueberries. Stir the blueberries into the batter. Heat a large non-stick frying pan brushed with ½ tablespoon of groundnut oil until hot then add the fritter batter to the pan in individual tablespoonfuls to make small fritters – you should get 4 tablespoonfuls in the pan in one go. Cook for 1 minute, then turn each fritter with a spatula and brown the other side for another minute. Put on a warm plate while you continue until all the mixture is used up.

85 g/3 oz butter, softened
6 slices of thick white bread
55 g/2 oz mixed dried fruit (sultanas, currants and raisins)
25 g/1 oz candied peel
3 large eggs

300 ml/10 fl oz milk
150 ml/5 fl oz double cream
55 g/2 oz caster sugar
whole nutmeg, for grating
1 tbsp demerara sugar
cream, to serve

Preheat the oven to 180°C/350°F/Gas Mark 4. Use a little of the butter to grease a 20 x 25-cm/8 x 10-inch baking dish and butter the slices of bread. Cut the bread into quarters and arrange half overlapping in the dish. Scatter half the dried fruit and the candied peel over the bread, cover with the remaining bread slices and add the remaining fruit and peel. In a mixing jug, whisk the eggs well and mix in the milk, cream and sugar. Pour this over the pudding and leave to stand for 15 minutes to allow the bread to soak up some of the egg mixture. Tuck in most of the fruit as you don't want it to burn in the oven. Grate the nutmeg over the top of the pudding, according to taste, and sprinkle over the demerara sugar. Place the pudding on a baking tray and bake at the top of the oven for 30–40 minutes until just set and golden brown. Remove from the oven and serve warm with a little pouring cream.

964 *With brandy & vanilla*

Soak the dried fruit and peel in brandy for half an hour before using to increase their moisture and flavour. Add 1 teaspoon of vanilla extract to the custard mixture before pouring over the bread.

965 *Bread & butter orange pudding*

Soak dried fruit and peel in orange juice for half an hour before using. Add a dash of orange oil or 1 teaspoon of finely grated orange zest to the custard mixture, and brush 2 tablespoons of sweet fine-cut orange marmalade over the pudding once it is cooked – return to the oven for 5 minutes before serving.

966 *Panettone bread & butter pudding*

Replace the white bread with 300 g/10½ oz of thickly sliced panettone – the fruited Italian bread-like cake. Because it contains dried fruit and peel, you can omit the additional fruit and peel from the recipe, if you like.

Chocolate pancakes

325 g/11½ oz ricotta cheese
175 ml/6 fl oz milk
4 eggs, separated
125 g/4½ oz flour
1 tsp baking powder
pinch of salt
55 g/2 oz milk chocolate, grated
4 tbsp unsalted butter

TOFFEE ORANGE SAUCE
2 tbsp butter
85 g/3 oz soft light brown sugar
150 ml/5 fl oz double cream
2–3 tbsp orange juice or Cointreau

To make the toffee orange sauce, melt the butter with the sugar in a saucepan over a low heat until the sugar has melted, stir in the cream and bring to the boil. Simmer for 3–4 minutes. Remove from the heat and stir in the orange juice. Set aside.

To make the pancakes, put the ricotta cheese, milk and egg yolks in a mixing bowl and stir well. Sift in the flour, baking powder and salt, add the chocolate and mix well.

Whisk the egg whites until stiff, then fold into the ricotta mixture.

Heat a non-stick frying pan and wipe with a little of the butter. Spoon in 2 tablespoons of the batter and cook for 2–3 minutes, until bubbles appear, then flip the pancake over and cook for an additional 2–3 minutes. Repeat with a little more butter each time until you have 8 pancakes. Serve topped with the sauce.

968 Chocolate pancakes with coffee sauce

Omit the orange sauce and instead make a coffee sauce. Combine 50 g/2 oz caster sugar, 1 tablespoon of instant coffee, 3 tablespoons of golden syrup, 50 ml/2 fl oz water and 125 ml /4 fl oz evaporated milk in a pan over low heat until the sugar is dissolved. Serve warm.

Fried banana dumplings

vegetable oil, for deep-frying
140 g/5 oz plain flour
2 tbsp palm sugar or granulated sugar
½ tsp salt
2 tsp baking powder
2 large eggs
350 ml/12 fl oz canned unsweetened coconut milk
12 small, ripe Asian bananas, peeled
6 tbsp 100%-proof rice alcohol or rum (optional)
icing sugar, to decorate
toasted sesame seeds, to decorate

Half-fill a small to medium saucepan with oil and heat over a medium–high heat to 180°C/350°F, or until a cube of bread browns in 30 seconds.

Meanwhile, put the flour, granulated sugar, salt and baking powder in a medium-large bowl. Whisk to combine the ingredients.

Make a well in the centre and add the eggs and coconut milk. Whisk, gradually incorporating the dry ingredients into the wet ingredients, until the batter is smooth. Add the bananas to the batter, making sure they are coated evenly all over. Working in batches if necessary, lower the bananas into the hot oil and deep-fry for 5–7 minutes, or until golden and crisp all over. Drain on a plate lined with kitchen paper. Arrange 2 bananas on each individual dessert plate. To flambé, fill a tablespoon with rice alcohol and set alight with a match. Scatter the burning alcohol across a serving of bananas.

Repeat for each serving, letting the alcohol burn off while the flames dissipate. Decorate with a light sprinkling of icing sugar and sesame seeds before serving.

One-roll fruit pie

PASTRY
85 g/3 oz butter, cut into small pieces,
plus extra for greasing
175 g/6 oz plain flour
1 tbsp water
1 egg, separated
sugar lumps, crushed, for sprinkling
single or double cream, to serve

FILLING
600 g/1 lb 5 oz prepared plums,
rhubarb or gooseberries
60 g/2¼ oz soft light brown sugar
1 tbsp ground ginger

Grease a large baking sheet with a little butter and set aside until required. To make the pastry, place the butter and flour in a mixing bowl and rub in the butter with the fingertips until the mixture resembles fine breadcrumbs. Add the water and work the mixture together until a soft dough has formed. Form into a ball. Wrap the dough and chill in the refrigerator for 30 minutes.

Preheat the oven to 200°C/400°F/Gas Mark 6. Roll out the chilled pastry to a round about 35 cm/14 inches in diameter. Transfer the pastry circle to the centre of the prepared baking sheet. Lightly beat the egg yolk, then brush the pastry with it.

To make the filling, mix the plums with the sugar and ginger. Pile it into the centre of the pastry. Turn in the edges of the circle of pastry all the way around. Lightly beat the egg white, then brush the surface of the pastry with it and sprinkle with the crushed sugar lumps.

Bake in the preheated oven for 35 minutes, or until golden brown. Serve warm with cream.

971 Quick one-roll fruit pie

If you are in a hurry you can make the same pie using 300 g/10½ oz ready-made puff pastry. Roll into a circle and proceed with the recipe as above. You can also make the filling using peeled and sliced cooking apples (you may need a little more sugar) or dessert pears.

972 Chocolate marshmallow fingers

350 g/12 oz digestive biscuits
125 g/4½ oz plain chocolate, broken into
pieces
225 g/8 oz butter
25 g/1 oz caster sugar
2 tbsp cocoa powder
2 tbsp honey
55 g/2 oz mini marshmallows
100 g/3½ oz white chocolate chips

Put the digestive biscuits in a polythene bag and, using a rolling pin, crush into small pieces.

Put the chocolate, butter, sugar, cocoa and honey in a saucepan and heat gently until melted. Remove from the heat and leave to cool slightly. Stir the crushed biscuits into the chocolate mixture until well mixed. Add the marshmallows and mix well, then finally stir in the chocolate chips.

Turn the mixture into a 20-cm/8-inch square baking tin and lightly smooth the top. Put in the refrigerator and leave to chill for 2–3 hours, until set. Cut into fingers before serving.

973 Fruity chocolate marshmallow fingers

Replace half the white chocolate chips with dried cranberries.

974 Syrupy chocolate marshmallow fingers

Use golden syrup instead of the honey and replace the caster sugar with soft light brown sugar.

975 Fruity stuffed nectarines

4 ripe but firm nectarines or peaches
140 g/5 oz blueberries
115 g/4 oz fresh raspberries
150 ml/5 fl oz freshly squeezed orange juice
1–2 tsp clear honey, or to taste
1 tbsp brandy (optional)
200 ml/7 fl oz low fat Greek-style yogurt
1 tbsp finely grated orange rind

Preheat the oven to 180°C/350°F/ Gas Mark 4. Cut the nectarines in half, remove the stones then place in a shallow ovenproof dish. Mix the blueberries and raspberries together in a bowl and use to fill the hollows left by the removal of the nectarine stones. Spoon any extra berries around. Mix together the orange juice and honey, and brandy if using, in a small bowl and pour over the fruit. Blend the yogurt with the grated orange rind in another bowl and leave to chill in the refrigerator until required. Bake the berry-filled nectarines for 10 minutes, or until the fruit is hot. Serve with the orange-flavoured yogurt.

976 Fruity stuffed nectarines & hazelnuts

Replace the raspberries with strawberries, sliced as necessary, and add 1 tablespoon of chopped hazelnuts.

977 Golden baked apple pudding

450 g/1 lb cooking apples
1 tsp ground cinnamon
2 tbsp sultanas
115 g/4 oz wholemeal bread

125 g/4½ oz low-fat cottage cheese
4 tbsp soft light brown sugar
250 ml/9 fl oz semi-skimmed milk

Preheat the oven to 220°C/425°F/Gas Mark 7. Peel and core the apples and chop the flesh into 1-cm/½-inch pieces. Place in a bowl and toss with the cinnamon and sultanas. Remove the crusts and cut the bread into 1-cm/½-inch cubes. Add to the apples with the cottage cheese and 3 tablespoons of the brown sugar, then mix together. Stir in the milk. Turn into an ovenproof dish and sprinkle with the remaining sugar. Bake in the oven for 30–35 minutes, or until golden brown. Serve hot.

978 Golden baked pear pudding

You can make a similar pudding using peeled, cored and sliced pears. Drop the peeled slices into cold water containing the juice of ½ lemon, so that the slices don't discolour. Drain off the water and add to the dish.

FILLING
6 peaches, peeled and sliced
4 tbsp caster sugar
½ tbsp lemon juice
1½ tsp cornflour
½ tsp almond or vanilla essence

COBBLER TOPPING
175 g/6 oz plain flour
115 g/4 oz caster sugar
1½ tsp baking powder
½ tsp salt
85 g/3 oz butter, diced
1 egg
5–6 tbsp milk
vanilla or butter pecan ice cream,
to serve

Preheat the oven to 220°C/425°F/ Gas Mark 7. Put the peaches into a 23-cm/9-inch square ovenproof serving dish. Add the sugar, lemon juice, cornflour and almond essence and toss together. Bake the peaches in the preheated oven for 20 minutes.

Meanwhile, to make the cobbler topping, sift the flour, all but 2 tablespoons of the sugar, the baking powder and salt into a bowl. Rub in the butter with the fingertips until fine crumbs form. Combine the egg and 5 tablespoons of the milk in a jug and mix into the dry ingredients with a fork until a soft, sticky dough forms. If the dough seems dry, stir in the extra tablespoon of milk.

Reduce the oven temperature to 200°C/400°F/Gas Mark 6. Remove the peaches from the oven and drop spoonfuls of the topping over the surface, without smoothing. Sprinkle with the remaining sugar, return to the oven and bake for a further 15 minutes, or until the topping is golden brown and firm – the topping will spread as it cooks.

Serve either hot or at room temperature with ice cream on the side.

980 *Fruit cobbler*

You can replace the peaches with the same weight of a variety of fruits – try a mixture of apples and raspberries, or pears and blueberries, or nectarines and strawberries, or rhubarb and strawberries.

TOFFEE APPLE TOPPING
85 g/3 oz light muscovado sugar
55 g/2 oz unsalted butter
1 dessert apple, cored and
thinly sliced

BROWNIES
115 g/4 oz unsalted butter,
plus extra for greasing
175 g/6 oz light muscovado sugar
2 eggs, beaten
200 g/7 oz plain flour
1 tsp baking powder
½ tsp bicarbonate of soda
1½ tsp ground mixed spice
2 eating apples, peeled and
coarsely grated
85 g/3 oz hazelnuts, chopped

Preheat the oven to 180°C/350°F/ Gas Mark 4. Grease a 23-cm/ 9-inch square shallow baking tin.

For the topping, gently heat the sugar and butter in a small pan, stirring, until melted. Pour into the prepared tin. Arrange the apple slices over the mixture.

For the brownies, beat the butter and sugar in a bowl until pale and fluffy. Beat in the eggs gradually. Sift together the flour, baking powder, bicarbonate of soda and mixed spice, and fold into the mixture. Stir in the apples and nuts. Pour into the prepared tin and bake for 35–40 minutes, until firm and golden. Cool in the tin for 10 minutes, then turn out and cut into squares.

982 *Upside down toffee pear brownies*

The brownies are delicious made with sliced ripe dessert pears – such as William, Rocha or Comice – instead of the apples.

983 Pear & toffee crumble

CRUMBLE TOPPING
115 g/4 oz self-raising flour
100 g/3½ oz unsalted butter, diced
5 tbsp demerara sugar
2 tbsp finely chopped hazelnuts

TOFFEE
3 tbsp golden syrup
3 tbsp demerara sugar
1 tbsp unsalted butter
2 tbsp single cream
½ tsp vanilla extract
1 tbsp unsalted butter
4 large pears
vanilla ice cream, to serve

Preheat the oven to 200°C/400°F/Gas Mark 6. To make the crumble, put the flour in a large mixing bowl and rub in the unsalted butter until crumbly. Stir in 4 tablespoons of the sugar and the chopped hazelnuts, then cook in the preheated oven for 5–10 minutes until heated through.

For the toffee, put the golden syrup into a pan over a low heat. Add the rest of the ingredients, except the butter and pears, and bring gently to the boil.

Simmer for 3 minutes, stirring constantly, then remove from the heat and set aside. Put the unsalted butter in a frying pan and melt over a low heat. Peel and chop the pears, add them to the pan and cook for 3 minutes. Stir in the toffee and continue to cook, stirring, over a low heat for another 3 minutes. Transfer to an ovenproof pie dish. Spread the crumble over the top, then sprinkle with the remaining sugar. Bake for 25–30 minutes, or until golden brown. Serve hot with vanilla ice cream.

984 Poached pears with Marsala

6 Comice or other dessert pears, peeled but left whole with stalks attached
500 ml/18 fl oz Marsala
125 ml/4 fl oz water
1 tbsp soft brown sugar
1 piece of lemon rind or mandarin rind
1 vanilla pod
350 ml/12 fl oz double cream
1 tbsp icing sugar

Put the pears in a large saucepan with the Marsala, water, brown sugar and lemon rind and bring gently to the boil, stirring to make sure that the sugar has dissolved. Reduce the heat, cover and simmer for 30 minutes until the pears are tender. Leave the pears to cool in the liquid.

Remove the pears from the liquid, cover and chill in the refrigerator.

Discard the lemon rind and leave the liquid to bubble for 15–20 minutes, or until syrupy. Leave to cool.

Cut a thin sliver of flesh from the base of each pear so that they will stand upright. Slit the vanilla pod open and scrape out the seeds into a bowl. Whisk the cream, vanilla seeds and icing sugar together in a bowl until thick. Put each pear on a dessert plate and pour over a little syrup. Serve with the vanilla cream.

985 Poached pears with red wine

Prepare pears as above and put into a saucepan with 1 bottle of red wine (or enough to completely cover the pears), 225 g/8 oz caster sugar and 1 cinnamon stick. Poach until tender then remove the cinnamon and pears from the pan and boil the liquid until reduced by half. Pour back over the pears to serve.

986 Poached pears with white wine

Prepare pears as above and put into a saucepan with 400 ml/14 fl oz medium sweet white wine (e.g. Sauternes), the juice of 1 orange and 1 lemon, 200 g/7 oz caster sugar, 1 whole vanilla pod and 1 stick of cinnamon, with enough water so that the pears are completely covered in liquid. Poach until tender then remove the vanilla and cinnamon and reduce sauce as usual.

Rhubarb crumble

900 g/2 lb rhubarb
115 g/4 oz caster sugar
grated rind and juice of 1 orange
cream, yogurt or custard, to serve

CRUMBLE TOPPING
225 g/8 oz plain or wholemeal flour
115 g/4 oz unsalted butter
115 g/4 oz soft brown sugar
1 tsp ground ginger

Preheat the oven to 190°C/375°F/Gas Mark 5. Cut the rhubarb into 2.5-cm/1-inch lengths and place in a 1.7-litre/3-pint ovenproof dish with the sugar and the orange rind and juice. Make the crumble topping by placing the flour in a mixing bowl and rubbing in the unsalted butter until the mixture resembles breadcrumbs. Stir in the sugar and the ginger. Spread the crumble over the fruit and press down lightly. Bake in the centre of the oven on a baking tray for 25–30 minutes until the crumble is golden brown. Serve warm with cream, yogurt or custard.

988 Rhubarb & strawberry crumble

Use 750 g/1 lb 10 oz rhubarb and add 200 g/7 oz strawberries, sliced as necessary. Omit the ginger and instead add 1 teaspoon of vanilla extract.

989 Sherried nectarine crumble

6 nectarines
25 g/1 oz demerara sugar
2 tbsp sweet sherry
crème fraîche, to serve

CRUMBLE TOPPING
185 g/6½ oz plain flour
55 g/2 oz demerara sugar, plus extra for
  sprinkling
100 g/3½ oz unsalted butter, melted

Preheat the oven to 200°C/400°F/Gas Mark 6. Using a sharp knife, halve the nectarines, remove and discard the stones, then cut the flesh into fairly thick slices. Put the nectarine slices into an ovenproof pie dish, sprinkle over the sugar and sweet sherry, and cook in the preheated oven for 5–10 minutes until heated through.

To make the crumble topping, put the flour and sugar in a large bowl, then quickly mix in the melted butter until crumbly. Carefully arrange the crumble over the nectarines in an even layer. Scatter a little more sugar over the top, then transfer to the preheated oven and bake for 25–30 minutes, or until the crumble topping is golden brown. Serve hot with generous spoonfuls of crème fraîche.

990 Three-fruit crumble

You can use a mixture of orange coloured fruits in this crumble – try a mixture of nectarine, apricot and peach. You can also use orange juice instead of the sherry if you like.

1 large orange
1 lemon
1 litre/1¾ pints milk
250 g/9 oz Spanish short-grain rice
100 g/3½ oz caster sugar

1 vanilla pod, split
pinch of salt
125 ml/4 fl oz double cream
brown sugar, to serve (optional)

Finely grate the rinds from the orange and lemon and set aside. Rinse a heavy-based saucepan with cold water and do not dry it.

Put the milk and rice in the pan over a medium–high heat and bring to the boil. Reduce the heat and stir in the caster sugar, vanilla pod, orange and lemon rinds and salt and simmer, stirring frequently, until the pudding is thick and creamy and the rice grains are tender: this can take up to 30 minutes, depending on how wide the pan is.

Remove the vanilla pod and stir in the cream. Serve at once, sprinkled with brown sugar, if desired, or cool completely, cover and chill until required. The pudding will thicken as it cools, so stir in a little extra milk if necessary.

992 *With brûlée topping*

Make the rice pudding as above and spoon into individual ovenproof soufflé dishes; allow to cool. Top each with a thick layer of demerara sugar and heat the grill to high. Flash the puddings under the grill until the sugar melts. Leave to cool when the sugar will form a hard caramel topping.

993 *Chocolate brownies*   MAKES 15

225 g/8 oz butter, diced, plus extra
for greasing
150 g/5½ oz plain chocolate,
chopped
225 g/8 oz self-raising flour
125 g/4½ oz dark muscovado sugar
4 eggs, beaten
60 g/2¼ oz blanched
hazelnuts, chopped
60 g/2¼ oz sultanas
100 g/3½ oz plain
chocolate chips
115 g/4 oz white chocolate, melted,
to decorate

Preheat the oven to 180°C/350°F/Gas Mark 4. Grease and line a 28 x 18-cm/11 x 7-inch rectangular baking tin.

Put the butter and plain chocolate into a heatproof bowl set over a saucepan of gently simmering water until melted. Remove from the heat. Sift the flour into a large bowl, add the sugar and mix well. Stir the eggs into the chocolate mixture, then beat into the flour mixture. Add the nuts, sultanas and chocolate chips and mix well. Spoon into the prepared tin and level the top.

Bake in the oven for 30 minutes, or until firm. To check whether the mixture is cooked through, insert a skewer into the centre – it should come out clean. If not, return the tin to the oven for a few minutes.

Remove from the oven and leave to cool for 15 minutes. Turn out onto a wire rack to cool completely. To decorate, drizzle the melted white chocolate over the top, then cut into squares. Leave to set before serving.

994 *Chocolate & prune brownies*

For an even moister brownie, replace the nuts and sultanas with prunes – simmer 125 g/4 oz stoned ready-to-eat prunes in a little water for 3 minutes, drain, chop and add to the mixture just before the chocolate chips.

800 g/1 lb 12 oz strawberries,
hulled and halved
50 g/1¾ oz caster sugar
clotted cream, to serve

COBBLER TOPPING
200 g/7 oz self-raising flour,
plus extra for dusting
pinch of salt
3 tbsp butter
2 tbsp caster sugar
1 egg, beaten
25 g/1 oz sultanas
25 g/1 oz currants
about 5 tbsp milk, plus extra
for glazing

Preheat the oven to 200°C/400°F/ Gas Mark 6. Place the strawberries in the bottom of an ovenproof dish, then sprinkle over the sugar and cook in the preheated oven for 5–10 minutes until heated through. Meanwhile, to make the cobbler topping, sift the flour and salt into a large mixing bowl. Rub in the butter until the mixture resembles fine breadcrumbs, then stir in the sugar. Add the beaten egg, then the sultanas and currants, and mix lightly until incorporated. Stir in enough of the milk to make a smooth dough.

Transfer to a clean, lightly floured board, knead lightly, then roll out to a thickness of about 1 cm/½ inch. Cut out rounds using a 5-cm/2-inch biscuit cutter.

Arrange the dough rounds over the strawberries, then brush the tops with a little milk. Bake in the preheated oven for 25–30 minutes, or until the topping has risen and is lightly golden. Serve hot with clotted cream.

996 *Strawberry cream & blueberry cobbler*

Replace the sultanas and currants in the cobbler topping mixture with 50 g/2 oz fresh blueberries.

675 g/1 lb 8 oz mixed soft fruits, such as redcurrants, blackcurrants, raspberries and blackberries
140 g/5 oz caster sugar

2 tbsp crème de framboise liqueur (optional)
6–8 slices of good day-old white bread, crusts removed
double cream, to serve

You will need an 850-ml/1½-pint pudding basin. Place the fruits in a large saucepan with the sugar. Over a low heat, very slowly bring to the boil, stirring carefully to ensure that the sugar has dissolved. Cook over a low heat for only 2–3 minutes until the juices run but the fruit still holds its shape. Add the liqueur if using.

Line the pudding basin with some of the slices of bread (cut them to shape so that the bread fits well). Spoon in the cooked fruit and juices, reserving a little of the juice for later. Cover the surface of the fruit with the remaining bread. Place a saucer on top of the pudding and weight it down for at least 8 hours or overnight in the refrigerator. Turn out the pudding and pour over the reserved juices to colour any white bits of bread that may be showing. Serve with the thick cream.

998 *Summer pudding with loganberries*

Replace the raspberries with loganberries and use blueberries instead of blackcurrants. If you do use blueberries you can reduce the total amount of sugar to around 100 g/3½ oz or even less – taste the fruit liquid after you have poached it to see if it is sweet enough.

Winter rice pudding with dried fruits

1 tbsp peanuts
1 tbsp pine kernels
1 tbsp lotus seeds
225 g/8 oz mixed dried fruits (raisins, kumquats, prunes, dates, etc.)

2 litres/3½ pints water
115 g/4 oz sugar
225 g/8 oz glutinous rice, soaked in cold water for at least 2 hours

Soak the peanuts, pine kernels and lotus seeds in a bowl of cold water for at least 1 hour. Soak the dried fruits as necessary. Chop all larger fruits into small pieces. Bring the water to the boil in a saucepan, then add the sugar and stir until dissolved. Add the drained rice, nuts, lotus seeds and mixed dried fruits. Bring back to the boil. Cover and simmer over a very low heat for 1 hour, stirring frequently.

1000 **Winter rice pudding with apricots**

Omit the peanuts, pine kernels and lotus seeds and instead use 2 tablespoons of toasted flaked almonds and 1 tablespoon of sunflower seeds. Omit the mixed dried fruits and instead use 225 g/8 oz semi-dried chopped apricots or peaches.

1001 **Spiced mango & blueberry cobbler**

2 ripe mangoes, stoned and cut into fairly thick slices
250 g/9 oz blueberries
½ tsp nutmeg
1 tbsp lime juice
50 g/1¾ oz caster sugar, or to taste
warm custard, to serve

COBBLER TOPPING
200 g/7 oz self-raising flour, plus extra for dusting
pinch of salt
½ tsp cinnamon
3 tbsp unsalted butter
2 tbsp caster sugar
3 tbsp dried blueberries (optional)
1 egg, beaten
about 5 tbsp milk, plus extra for glazing

Preheat the oven to 200°C/400°F/Gas Mark 6. Put the fruit in the bottom of an ovenproof dish, then sprinkle over the nutmeg, lime juice and caster sugar. Cook for 5–10 minutes until heated through. To make the cobbler topping, sift the flour, salt and cinnamon into a large mixing bowl. Rub in the unsalted butter until the mixture resembles fine breadcrumbs, then mix in the sugar and the dried blueberries, if using. Add the beaten egg, then stir in enough of the milk to make a smooth dough. Transfer to a clean, lightly floured board, knead lightly, then roll out to a thickness of about 1 cm/½ inch. Cut out rounds using a 5-cm/2-inch biscuit cutter. Arrange the dough rounds over the fruit, then brush the tops with a little milk. Bake in the preheated oven for 25–30 minutes, or until the cobbler topping has risen and is lightly golden. Serve hot with custard.

Index

A

Aloo gobi 242
Aloo gobi with pumpkin 242
Apple & blackberry crumble 286
Apple & raspberry crumble 286
Apple fritters 289
Apricot & almond crumble 287
Apricot crumble 287
Artichoke hearts with broad beans 250
Artichoke hearts with parsley & mint 250
Artichoke paella 209
Artichoke paella with asparagus 209
Asian beef soup 25
Asian lamb 143
Asian lamb soup 25
Asian pork 143
Asparagus soup 34
Aubergine & bean curry 242
Aubergine & potato gratin 261
Aubergine & sweet potato curry 244
Aubergine gratin 261
    With crunchy topping 261
Aubergine pasta sauce with herbs 218
Aubergine tagine with polenta 270
Azerbaijani lamb pilau 76

B

Baby broad beans & chorizo 139
Baby broad beans, artichoke & chorizo 139
Baked celery with cream 267
Baked celery with cream & walnuts 267
Baked fresh lasagne 223
Baked lasagne 223
Baked lasagne with mushrooms 223
Baked Mediterranean vegetables with feta 251
Baked pasta with spicy chicken sauce 218
Baked pasta with spicy meat sauce 218
Baked tomato rice 204
Baked tuna & ricotta rigatoni 220
Balti beef curry 68
Balti beef curry with aubergine 68
Balti chicken 71
Balti chicken with broccoli & peas 71
Balti chicken with spinach & baby corn 71
Basque pork & beans 131
Basque pork sausages & beans 131
Bean & potato soup with bacon 15
Beans & greens stew 271
Beef & bean soup 12
Beef & red lentil soup 12
Beef & red wine pot roast 91
Beef & tomato gratin 83
    With mascarpone cheese topping 83

Beef & vegetable stew with corn cobs 100
Beef & vegetable stew with courgette 100
Beef & vegetable stew with squash 100
Beef bourguignon 101
Beef bourguignon with red onions 101
Beef broth with herbs & vegetables 13
Beef cannelloni 227
Beef chilli soup 31
Beef chop suey 141
    With beansprouts & noodles 141
Beef chop suey with cabbage & carrot 141
Beef cobbler with chilli 108
Beef fajitas 85
Beef goulash 101
Beef in beer with a crumb crust 102
Beef in beer with herb dumplings 102
Beef in the pot with potatoes & dill 92
Beef korma with almonds 69
Beef pot roast with potatoes & dill 92
Beef stew with garlic & shallots 102
Beef stew with olives 103
Beef stew with olives & bacon 103
Beef stir-fry with garlic & shallots 102
Beef vindaloo 80
Beef with onions & broccoli 141
Beef with peppers 144
Black bean casserole 263
Blueberry clafoutis 287
Blueberry fritters 289
Blue cheese & bacon soup 29
Borlotti bean & vegetable casserole 238
Borscht 262
Borscht with red cabbage 262
Bouillabaisse 171
Bouillabaisse with other fish 171
Braised Asian duck 87
Braised Asian guinea fowl 87
Braised chicken & parsley dumplings 109
Braised chicken & rosemary dumplings 109
Braised chicken with swede & celeriac 109
Braised lamb with cannellini beans 61
Braised lamb shanks with cannellini beans 61
Braised pork chops with garlic & herbs 65
Braised pork in red wine 54
Braised pork with garlic & herbs 65
Braised veal in red wine 54
Brazilian seafood stew 175
Bread & butter orange pudding 290
Bread & butter pudding 290
    With brandy & vanilla 290

Breton fish soup with cider & sorrel 19
Brittany chicken casserole 55
Brittany chicken casserole with leeks 55
Broad beans with feta 251
Broad beans with ham & potato 90
Broad beans with Serrano ham 90
Broccoli & black bean stir-fry 278
Broccoli & cheese soup 50
Broccoli & mangetout stir-fry 278
Broccoli & Stilton soup 34
Broccoli, French bean & peanut stir-fry 278
Brunswick stew 107
    With pasta 107
Brunswick stew with cannellini beans 107
Bubble & squeak 265
Bubble & squeak cakes 265
Burmese chicken curry 80
Burmese pork curry 80
Butternut squash chilli stir-fry 278
Butternut squash stir-fry 278

C

Cabbage & walnut stir-fry 281
Calamari with prawns & broad beans 181
Calamari with prawns & pasta 181
Cannellini, pumpkin & tomato soup 40
Cannelloni with spinach & ricotta 227
Caribbean beef stew 105
Caribbean fish chowder 20
Caribbean lamb stew 105
Caribbean red fish chowder 20
Cashew nut & pea curry 246
Catalan fish stew 182
Cauliflower & beans with cashew nuts 250
Cauliflower & sugar snap stir-fry 278
Cauliflower & sweet potato curry 243
Cauliflower & walnut stir-fry 281
Cauliflower, bean & sweet potato curry 243
Cauliflower korma 249
Cauliflower korma with peanuts 249
Celery & salt cod casserole 150
Celery & Stilton soup 34
Celery & tuna casserole 150
Chargrilled swordfish 168
Cheese & bacon soup 29
Cheese, sweet potato & bacon soup 29
Cheesy courgette & bacon gratin 147
Cheesy courgette & chicken gratin 147
Cheesy courgette & ham gratin 147
Cherry clafoutis 287
Chicken & apple pot 110
    With Calvados 110

Chicken & barley soup 16
Chicken & chestnut casserole 61
Chicken & potato soup with bacon 15
Chicken & potato soup with croûtons 15
Chicken & vegetable broth 30
Chicken Basquaise 111
Chicken Basquaise with green olives 111
Chicken, beans & chard with olives 56
Chicken, beans & spinach with olives 56
Chicken cacciatore 111
    With red pepper pesto 111
Chicken casserole with a herb crust 55
Chicken chow mein 142
    With Chinese five spice 142
Chicken Cobbler with chilli 108
Chicken dopiaza 71
Chicken fajitas 85
Chicken fricassee 113
Chicken fricassee with French beans 113
Chicken gumbo 112
    With prawns 112
Chicken gumbo with chorizo 112
Chicken hash with fried eggs 85
Chicken in a piquant sauce 138
Chicken in basil & coriander sauce 72
Chicken in mint & coriander sauce 72
Chicken in white wine 114
Chicken jalfrezi 73
Chicken korma with almonds 69
Chicken legs with olives 147
Chicken Madeira French-style 113
    With herbs 113
Chicken Marsala Italian-style 113
Chicken noodle soup 15
Chicken pasanda 73
Chicken, pepper & chorizo casserole 56
Chicken, pumpkin & chorizo casserole 56
Chicken risotto á la Milanese 194
Chicken soup 16
Chicken, squash & broccoli soup 16
Chicken, squash & spinach soup 16
Chicken stew with chickpeas 126
Chicken, sweet potato & spinach soup 16
Chicken tagine 115
    With harissa 115
Chicken tagine with flaked almonds 115
Chicken tagine with sultanas & dates 115
Chicken, tomato & aubergine casserole 57
Chicken, tomato & onion casserole 57

Chicken with 40 garlic cloves 95
Chicken with broccoli & coriander rice 125
Chicken with creamy penne 227
Chicken with fennel 138
Chicken with garlic 57
    With mushrooms 57
Chicken with peppers & sweetcorn 89
Chicken with red pepper & chilli pesto 93
Chicken with spring onion soup 19
Chicken with tomato & olive pesto 93
Chicken with vegetables & coriander rice 125
Chicken wonton soup 33
Chickpea & peppers casserole 238
Chickpea & potato curry 243
Chickpea & sweet potato curry 243
Chickpea & vegetable casserole 238
Chickpea hotpot 270
Chickpea hotpot with celeriac 270
Chilled garlic soup 48
Chilled garlic soup with dry sherry 48
Chilli bean stew 277
Chilli bean stew with chocolate 277
Chilli con carne 104
    With green peppers 104
    With extra chillies 104
Chinese vegetables 272
Chocolate & prune brownies 297
Chocolate brownies 297
Chocolate fondue 288
Chocolate marshmallow fingers 292
Chocolate pancakes 291
    with coffee sauce 291
Chorizo & kidney bean soup 30
Chorizo & mussel stew 125
Chorizo & seafood stew 125
Chorizo, chilli & chickpea casserole 65
Chorizo, chilli & potato casserole 65
Chorizo, pepper & prawn soup 24
Chorizo, sweetcorn & kidney bean soup 30
Chunky minestrone 35
Cinnamon lamb casserole 62
Clam & sweetcorn chowder 20
Classic lamb, chickpea & lentil soup 25
Classic poule au pot 94
    With extra sausage meat 94
Cock-a-leekie soup 17
    With rice 17
Coconut beef curry 69
Cod in lemon & parsley sauce 172
Cod in lemon cream & parsley sauce 172
Cod steaks with basil & mozzarella 165

Cod steaks with rosemary & tomatoes 165
Cod with a lemon & parsley crust 169
Colcannon 283
Colcannon with leftover greens 283
Cold weather vegetable casserole 238
Cold weather vegetable crumble 238
Coq au vin 116
Coq au vin with extra red wine 116
Country chicken bake 116
Country chicken bake with lentils 116
Country pork with onions 132
Country roast belly of pork 132
Courgette, broccoli & lemon frittata 267
Courgette, carrot & tomato frittata 267
Courgette fritters 264
Crab & leek soup 23
Crab laksa 157
Crab wonton soup 33
Cream of chicken soup 17
Creamed mushrooms 261
Creamy chicken fricassee 113
Creamy chicken ravioli 234
Creamy chicken tikka 74
Creamy Italian-style roast chicken 118
Creamy linguine with wild mushrooms 219
Creamy potato, onion & cheese soup 35
Creamy salmon ravioli 234
Creamy watercress soup 51
Cumin-scented aubergine & potato curry 244
    With sweet potato 244
Curried parsnip soup 43

D
Double cheese macaroni 235
Duck & red wine stew 124
Duck & white wine stew 124
Duck jambalaya-style stew 123
Duck legs with olives 147
Duck legs with olives & squash 147
Duck with lentils 60
Duck with lentils & orange juice 60
Duck with spring onion soup 19

E
Easy gazpacho 36
Easy herbed chicken 122
Easy Peshawar-style lamb curry 78
Egg-fried rice with other vegetables 205
Egg-fried rice with spring onion 205
Egg-fried rice with vegetables 205
English onion soup 37
Exotic fruit parcels 288

F
Feta & spinach omelette 253
Fiery chicken vindaloo 74
Fiery chilli & chorizo paella 208
Fish & rice with dark rum 201
Fish curry with rice noodles 156
Fish curry with rice noodles & broccoli 156
Fish roasted with lime 169
Fish stew with cider 175
Fish stew with wine & spinach 175
Fishermen's soup 21
Fishermen's soup with mixed seafood 21
Florida chicken 117
Florida lamb 117
Florida pork 117
Fluffy prawn omelette 162
Fluffy prawn omelette with mushroom 162
Fluffy prawn omelette with pepper 162
Fragrant coconut beef curry 69
French bean, mangetout & noodle soup 48
French country casserole 82
French casserole with squash 82
French onion soup 37
Fresh baked sardines 160
Fresh baked sardines with tomatoes 160
Fresh tuna with garlic, lemon & olives 229
Fried banana dumplings 291
Fruit cobbler 294
Fruity chocolate marshmallow fingers 292
Fruity lamb casserole 62
    With fresh mint 62
Fruity stuffed nectarines 293
Fruity stuffed nectarines & hazelnuts 293

G
Game with prunes 135
Gammon cooked in cider 133
Garlic & chickpea soup 37
Garlic & chilli Dublin Bay prawns 181
Garlic & herb Dublin Bay prawns 181
Garlic, chickpea & red pepper soup 37
Garlic mushroom ravioli 234
    With fresh herbs 234
Genoese fish soup 21
Genoese seafood soup 21
Ginger prawns with dried mushrooms 159
Ginger prawns with oyster mushrooms 159

Goan-style mustard seafood curry 154
Goan-style seafood curry 154
Golden baked apple pudding 293
Golden baked pear pudding 293
Golden chicken cobbler 59
Golden chicken crumble 59
Golden chicken risotto 194
Golden chicken risotto with squash 194
Golden chicken with 40 garlic cloves 95
Gooseberry & pistachio nut dessert 286
Greek beans 260
Greek beans with stuffed green olives 260
Green bean, mangetout & noodle soup 48
Green chunky minestrone 35
Green lentil & rice casserole 239
Green pumpkin curry 248
Green vegetable soup with basil pesto 38
Guinea fowl with cabbage 96

H
Hake in white wine 173
Ham hash with peas & fried eggs 85
Ham with black-eyed beans 137
Ham with red lentils 137
Hearty bean & pasta soup 39
Hearty French bean & pasta soup 39
Hearty lentil & butternut squash soup 39
Hearty lentil & vegetable soup 39
Herby lamb or chicken casserole 66
Herrings with lemon coriander stuffing 164
Herrings with orange tarragon stuffing 164
Hoisin pork with garlic noodles 144
    With cashew nuts or peanuts 144
Honeyed apricot lamb with lemon couscous 64
    With preserved lemon 64
Hot & sour soup with chicken 40
Hot & sour soup with tofu 40
Hot Azerbaijani lamb pilau 76
Hot chicken vindaloo 74
Hot chilli pasta 221
    With prawns 221
Hot pepper lamb in red wine risotto 203
Hot pepper pork in red wine risotto 203
Hunter's chicken 118
Hunter's game 118

I

Indian potato & pea soup 38
  With cauliflower 38
Indian-style aubergine & bean
  curry 242
Irish stew 129
Irish stew with lamb chops 129
Italian fish stew 174
  With French beans & broccoli 174
Italian-style roast chicken 118
Italian turkey steaks 140
Italian turkey steaks with courgette 140
Italian vegetable stew 269

J

Jamaican hotpot 119
Jamaican hotpot with allspice 119
Jamaican hotpot with chicken
  thighs 119
Jambalaya 119
Jambalaya with chorizo or ham 119
Jambalaya with courgettes 276

K

Kedgeree 197
  With petits pois 197
Kedgeree with individual spices 197
Kedgeree with salmon 197
Kidney bean, pumpkin & tomato
  soup 40
  Kidneys in mustard sauce 82
Kidneys in mustard sherry sauce 82
King prawn risotto 198

L

Lamb & aubergine moussaka 88
Lamb, barley & turnip soup 27
Lamb & orzo soup 27
Lamb & potato moussaka 88
Lamb & red wine pot roast 91
Lamb dhansak 77
Lamb, garlic & bean casserole 63
  With zesty breadcrumb topping 63
Lamb in mint & coriander sauce 72
Lamb jalfrezi 73
Lamb pasanda 78
Lamb pasanda with curry powder 78
Lamb roasted in a lemon & thyme
  crust 98
Lamb shanks 96
Lamb shanks with red wine 96
Lamb stew with chickpeas 126
Lamb stew with red peppers 126
Lamb with cinnamon & fenugreek 134
Lamb with courgettes & potatoes 127
Lamb with courgettes & tomatoes 127
Lamb with mint 127
Lamb with mint & leeks 127
Lamb with pears 128
Lamb with pineapple 128
Lamb with tomatoes, artichokes &
  olives 128
Lamb with tomatoes, beans &
  capers 128
Lancashire hotpot 129
  With Worcestershire sauce 129

Layered casserole with sweet
  potato 239
Layered spaghetti with smoked
  salmon & prawns 233
Layered vegetable casserole 239
Leek & goat's cheese crêpes 282
Leek & potato soup 41
Leek & sausage tortilla 88
Leeks with yellow bean sauce 249
Leeks, yellow bean sauce &
  peppers 249
Lemon & tarragon poussins 93
Lentil & brown rice casserole 239
Lentil & rice casserole 239
Light cinnamon lamb casserole 62
Light risotto with sole & tomatoes 198
Lime & basil poussins 92
Linguine with anchovies, olives &
  capers 219
Linguine with clams 224
Linguine with mussels 224
Linguine with parsley & lemon 219
Linguine with sardines & pine
  kernels 219
Linguine with wild mushrooms 219
Lobster bisque 22
Lobster risotto 198
Louisiana chicken 120
  With rice 120
Lower-fat cream of chicken soup 17
Lower-fat creamy chicken tikka 74
Lower-fat potato, onion & cheese
  soup 35
Lower-fat tuna & ricotta rigatoni 220

M

Macaroni cheese & tomato 235
  With olives 235
Maltese rabbit with fennel 138
Marseille-style fish stew 176
Marseille-style stew with fennel
  seeds 176
Meatball toad in the hole 90
Meatballs in creamy cashew nut
  sauce 70
Mediterranean cod steaks with thyme
  & marjoram 165
Mediterranean fish casserole 151
Mediterranean lamb with apricots &
  pistachios 63
Mediterranean lamb with aubergine 63
Mediterranean swordfish 165
Mediterranean vegetables with
  fennel 251
Mexican beef 140
Mexican chicken, chilli & potato
  pot 120
  With sweetcorn & coriander 120
Mexican-style beef & bean soup 14
Mexican-style beef & rice soup 14
Mexican-style chicken soup 14
Mexican tomato rice 204
Mexican tomato rice with
  sweetcorn 204

Mexican turkey 140
Middle Eastern soup with harissa 26
Minted green risotto 210
Minted green risotto with chard 210
Miso soup 41
  With asparagus 41
Miso soup with chicken and
  noodles 41
Mixed bean & vegetable crumble 241
Mixed Breton soup with wine 19
Mixed fish cobbler with dill 152
Mixed fish cobbler with fennel 152
Mixed herb omelette 252
Mixed seafood curry 154
Mixed south-western seafood stew 179
Monkfish parcels 160
  With herbs & lemon 160
Monkfish ragout 153
Monkfish ragout with squash 153
Monkfish stir-fry 185
Monkfish stir-fry with broccoli 185
Monkfish stir-fry with chilli 185
Monkfish with a lemon & parsley
  crust 169
Monkfish with onions & coriander 166
Moroccan fish tagine 177
Moroccan stew 272
Moroccan stew with sultanas 272
Moules à la crème Normande 161
Moules marinière 161
Mulligatawny soup 36
Mushroom & cauliflower cheese
  crumble 263
Mushroom & garlic omelette 252
Mushroom & ginger soup 42
  With bamboo shoots & water
  chestnuts 42
Mushroom & noodle soup 42
Mushroom & sherry soup 51
  With croûtons 51
Mushroom & vegetable soup 42

N

Nutty chicken 110

O

Omelette Arnold Bennett 162
One-roll fruit pie 292
Onion & potato soup 41
Onion dhal 248
Onion dhal with yellow split peas 248
Orange & rosemary poussins 92
Orange turkey with rice 207
Orange turkey with rice & pepper 207
Osso bucco 105
Other exotic fruit parcels 288
Other roast summer vegetables 256
Oven-baked haggerty 253
Oven-baked ratatouille 255

P

Pad Thai 187
  With spring onions & tomato
  ketchup 187
Paella primavera 211
  with baby carrots 211

Paella-stuffed Mediterranean
  peppers 192
Paella-stuffed peppers with ham 192
Paella with mussels & French
  beans 209
Paella with mussels & white wine 209
Panettone bread & butter pudding 290
Pan-fried skate in black butter 183
Pan haggerty 253
Paprika pork 133
Paprika pork with red pepper 133
Parmesan risotto with cherry
  tomatoes 210
Parmesan risotto with
  mushrooms 210
Parsnip soup with ginger & orange 43
Pasta & bean casserole 240
Pasta courgette sauce with lemon &
  rosemary 218
Pasta sauce with mint & coriander 218
Pasta with smoked salmon & mustard
  sauce 228
Pasta with smoked salmon &
  rocket 228
Pasta with spiced leek 224
Pasta with spiced red onion 224
Pasta with tuna, lemon, capers &
  olives 229
Peach cobbler 294
Pear & blueberry crumble 286
Pear & toffee crumble 295
Penne with creamy garlic
  mushrooms 231
Penne with creamy mushrooms 231
Pepper & mushroom hash 254
Pepper pot-style stew 106
Pepper pot-style stew & sweet
  potatoes 106
Peppered salmon or swordfish
  steaks 183
Peppered tuna steaks 183
Pepperoni pasta 221
Peshawar-style lamb curry 78
Pheasant & chestnut casserole 61
Pheasant with cabbage 96
Pheasant with mushrooms 139
Pheasant with mushrooms &
  chestnuts 139
Pineapple fritters 289
Plaice in white wine 173
Poached pears with Marsala 295
Poached pears with red wine 295
Poached pears with white wine 295
Pork & apple pot 110
Pork & paprika bake 89
Pork & pasta bake 225
Pork & prawn chop suey 141
Pork & red wine pot-roast 91
Pork & sausage bake 89
Pork & sweet potato ragout 135
Pork & vegetable broth 30
Pork & vegetable ragout 135
Pork casserole 66

Pork chilli soup 31
Pork chops with peppers &
    sweetcorn 89
Pork goulash 101
Pork noodle soup 15
Pork roasted in an orange & thyme
    crust 98
Pork stroganoff 134
    With brandy & hot paprika 134
Pork vindaloo 80
Pork with beans & carrots 81
Pork with cinnamon & fenugreek 134
Pork with mixed green beans 81
Pork with peppers 144
Pork with plum sauce 87
Pork with plum sauce & cucumber 87
Pork with prunes 135
Pork with red cabbage 98
Pork with red cabbage & vinegar 98
Pot-roast pork 99
Pot-roast venison 99
Potato & carrot fritters 264
Potato & lemon casserole 240
Potato & mushroom bake 254
Potato & parsnip fritters 264
Potato & pesto soup   12
Potato & sausage pan-fry 66
Potato, butterbean & sausage
    pan-fry 66
Potato, cheese & mushroom bake 254
Potato, chicken & red pesto soup 12
Potato fritters 264
Potato hash with shallots &
    spinach 254
Potato, squash & lemon casserole 240
Potato stir-fry 279
    With water chestnuts 279
Potatoes Dauphinois 259
Potatoes in red wine 255
Poulet Marengo with French beans
    121
Poulet Marengo-style 121
    With a herby breadcrumb
    topping 121
Poussins with herbs & wine 95
Prawn & chicken paella 196
Prawn & chicken paella with crayfish
    196
Prawn & pineapple curry 155
    With white fish 155
Prawn biryani 155
Prawn gumbo 177
Prawn gumbo with bacon 177
Prawn laksa 157
Prawn pilaf 199
    With courgette 199
Prawns with coconut rice 187
Prawns with shiitake mushrooms 156
Prawns with spring onions & straw
    mushrooms 156
Prawns with straw mushrooms 187
Provençal bean stew 271
Pumpkin & chestnut risotto 212

Pumpkin & pine kernel risotto 212
Pumpkin curry 248
Purple sprouting broccoli soup 34

Q
Quick & creamy fish pie 153
Quick & creamy fish pie with
    potato 153
Quick Brazilian seafood stew 175
Quick chicken in white wine 114
Quick gammon cooked in cider 133
Quick Greek baked fish 168
Quick lamb dhansak 77
Quick Mediterranean swordfish 165
Quick Middle Eastern soup 26
Quick mixed bean & vegetable
    crumble 241
Quick mixed seafood curry 154
Quick nutty chicken 110
Quick one-roll fruit pie 292
Quick red hot chilli chicken 122
Quick seafood in saffron sauce 178
Quick seafood spaghetti 228

R
Rabbit casserole with a herb crust 55
Railway lamb & vegetables 81
Railway pork & vegetables 81
Ratatouille 255
Ratatouille moussaka 266
Ratatouille moussaka with lentils 266
Red cabbage casserole 241
Red curry pork with courgette 79
Red curry pork with peppers 79
Red duck or beef curry 79
Red hot chilli chicken 122
Red lamb curry 79
Red pepper, cabbage & noodle
    soup 48
Rhubarb crumble 296
Rhubarb & strawberry crumble 296
Ribollita 265
Rice & peas 206
Rich beef stew 106
Rich beef stew & sun-dried
    tomatoes 106
Rich beef stew with fresh
    mushrooms 106
Rich Mediterranean chicken
    casserole 58
    With a herb mix 58
Ricotta & spinach omelette 253
Rigatoni with spicy bacon & tomato
    sauce 225
Rigatoni with spicy beef 225
Risotto Milanese 213
    With sweetcorn or mushrooms 213
Risotto primavera 213
Risotto primavera with white
    wine 213
Risotto with artichoke hearts 212
Risotto with artichoke hearts &
    ham 212
Risotto with octopus & herb
    butter 200

Risotto with roasted fennel 214
Risotto with roasted vegetables 214
Risotto with sole & tomatoes 198
Risotto with squid & garlic butter 200
Risotto with tuna & almonds 203
Risotto with tuna & pine kernels 203
Risotto with truffle oil 216
Roast lamb with orzo 97
Roast summer vegetables 256
Roast tomato soup 49
Roasted chicken with sun-dried
    tomato pesto 93
Roasted garlic & potato soup 44
Roasted garlic & sweet potato soup 44
Roasted Mediterranean vegetable
    soup 44
    With fennel & cheese garnish 44
Roasted monkfish 172
    With fennel 172
Roasted red mullet 166
Roasted sea bass 166
Roasted seafood 163
    With smoked sweet paprika 163
Roasted squash, sweet potato & garlic
    soup 45
    With herbs 45
Roasted stuffed butternut squash 268
Roasted stuffed marrow 268
Roasted stuffed squash with rice 268
Roasted vegetable moussaka 266
    With Béchamel & cheese
    topping 266
Rogan josh 76
Rogan josh with yogurt 76

S
Sage & Gorgonzola risotto 215
Sage & Gorgonzola risotto cakes 215
Sage omelette 252
Salmon & leek soup 23
Salmon & mascarpone rigatoni 220
Salmon & scallops with coriander &
    lime 171
Salmon & scallops with mixed
    peppers 171
Salmon marinated in sherry
    vinegar 170
Sardines marinated in sherry
    vinegar 170
Sardines with parsley & pine
    kernels 150
Saucy borlotti beans 283
    With chilli 283
Sausage & bean casserole 67
Sausage & courgette tortilla 88
Sausage & onion tortilla 88
Sausage & red cabbage soup 27
Sausage & rosemary risotto 206
Sausage & tomato hotpot 136
Sausage, bacon & rosemary risotto 206
Sausage, bean & pasta bake 67
Sausage, tomato & bean hotpot 136
Sausage with borlotti beans 137
    with cannellini beans 137

Sautéed garlic & chilli mushrooms 257
Sautéed garlic mushrooms 257
Sautéed veal with gremolata 105
Scotch broth 28
Seafood & chicken paella 196
Seafood chilli 178
    With smoked paprika 178
Seafood hotpot with red wine &
    bacon 151
Seafood hotpot with red wine &
    tomatoes 151
Seafood in saffron sauce 178
Seafood nabe 159
Seafood nabe with crayfish &
    clams 159
Seafood omelette 163
Seafood omelette with crab 163
Seafood paella with lemon &
    herbs 193
Seafood paella with saffron rice 196
Seafood paella with white fish 193
Seafood spaghetti 228
Seared monkfish in garlic broth 23
Seared scallops in garlic broth 23
Shallots à la Grecque 257
Shallots à la Grecque with garlic 257
Shellfish stew 184
Shellfish stew with basil &
    coriander 184
Shepherd's pie 100
    With celery & leek 100
Sherried nectarine crumble 296
Shredded spinach & ham risotto 207
Shredded spinach & mushroom
    risotto 207
Sicilian tuna 164
Sicilian swordfish 164
Simple Italian vegetable stew 269
Simple spaghetti alla carbonara 232
Simple vegetable lasagne 222
Skate in black butter sauce 183
Slow-cooked lamb with celeriac 97
Slow-cooked lamb with potatoes 97
Slow-roasted pork 99
Slow-roasted pork with rosemary 99
Smoked cod chowder 20
Smoked salmon & prawn lasagne 233
Smoked salmon omelette 162
Sour & spicy pork 145
Sour & spicy pork with sweetcorn 145
South-western seafood stew 179
Spaghetti alla carbonara 232
    With petits pois & herbs 232
Spaghetti with fresh tomato sauce 226
Spaghetti with halibut & mussels 233
Spaghetti with meatballs 232
Spaghetti with pork meatballs 232
Spaghetti with tomato & basil
    sauce 226
Spaghettini with quick salmon
    sauce 231
Spaghettini with quick tuna &
    sweetcorn 231

Spaghettini with quick tuna sauce 231
Spanish rice pudding 297
    With brûlée topping 297
Spanish swordfish stew 184
Spanish tuna stew 184
Spiced basmati pilau 217
Spiced basmati pilau with carrot 217
Spiced black-eyed beans &
    mushrooms 245
Spiced black lentils & mushrooms 245
Spiced carrot & swede soup 46
Spiced cashew nut curry 246
Spiced mango & blueberry cobbler 299
Spiced meatball & red cabbage
    soup 27
Spiced pumpkin soup 46
Spicy beef & noodle soup 14
Spicy beef with potato 142
Spicy beef with potato & chard 142
Spicy borlotti beans 283
Spicy chickpea & aubergine curry 244
Spicy courgette soup with rice &
    lime 46
Spicy lamb soup with cannellini
    beans 28
Spicy lamb soup with chickpeas 28
Spicy lamb stew with red peppers 126
Spicy meat & chipotle hash 84
    With sweet peppers 84
Spicy monkfish rice 202
    With aubergine 202
Spicy Moroccan fish tagine 177
Spicy pork & peppers hotpot 136
Spicy pork & vegetable hotpot 136
Spicy Provençal bean stew 271
Spicy roast cauliflower &
    mushrooms 263
Spicy sausage pasta 221
Spicy scallops with galangal 186
Spicy scallops with lime & chilli 186
Spicy squash & pinto bean soup 46
Spicy Thai seafood stew 180
Spicy tofu 280
Spicy tofu with lime & honey 280
Spicy tofu with mushroom
    ketchup 280
Spicy turkey & noodle soup 14
Spinach & anchovy pasta 230
    With mozzarella 230
Spinach & Parmesan pasta 230
Spinach & ricotta ravioli 233
Spinach lasagne 222
Spinach soup with basil pesto 38
Split pea & ham soup 32
Spring lamb stew 130
Spring stew 273
Spring stew with baby leaf beet 273
Springtime chicken cobbler 123
Springtime chicken pie 123
Squid, chorizo & tomato soup 24
Squid stew 174
Squid stew with white wine 174
Squid with parsley & pine kernels 150

Steak & kidney pudding 84
Steak & onion pudding 84
Stir-fried chicken with cranberry
    glaze 145
Stir-fried French beans with
    asparagus 279
Stir-fried French beans with carrots
    279
Stir-fried French beans with red
    pepper 279
Stir-fried fresh crab with chilli 189
Stir-fried fresh crab with ginger 189
Stir-fried marinated fish 188
Stir-fried noodles with marinated
    fish 188
Stir-fried scallops with asparagus 188
Stir-fried scallops with broccoli 188
Stir-fried squid with hot black bean
    sauce 189
Stir-fried squid with sugar snap
    peas 189
Stir-fried turkey with cranberry
    glaze 145
Strawberry cream & blueberry
    cobbler 298
Strawberry cream cobbler 298
Stuffed aubergines 269
Stuffed aubergines with rice 269
Stuffed aubergines with
    mushrooms 269
Stuffed baked monkfish 166
Stuffed chicken with herbs & wine 95
Stuffed red peppers with almonds 258
Stuffed red peppers with pasta 258
Stuffed red peppers with couscous 258
Summer pudding 298
Summer pudding with
    loganberries 298
Sunshine risotto 215
Sunshine risotto with butternut
    squash 215
Sweet & sour sea bass 167
Sweet & sour vegetables with cashew
    nuts 281
Sweet & sour vegetables with
    peppers 281
Sweet & sour vegetables with tofu 281
Sweet & spicy Thai seafood stew 180
Sweet potato stir-fry 279
Syrupy chocolate marshmallow
    fingers 292

T
Tagine of lamb with apricots, prunes
    & honey 131
Tagine of lamb with dates &
    squash 131
Tagine of lamb with figs &
    peaches 131
Tarragon chicken 122
Teriyaki steaks 108
Teriyaki pork 108
Thai chicken-coconut soup 18
Thai fish curry 157

With sweet red peppers 157
Thai green chicken curry 75
Thai green chicken curry with
    peppers 75
Thai prawn curry 158
    With baby corn 158
Thai prawn noodle bowl 158
Thai prawn noodle bowl with
    sweetcorn 158
Thai spiced chicken with
    courgettes 143
Thai-style seafood soup 24
Thai-style seafood soup with
    tilapia 24
Thick beef & pearl onion casserole 54
Thick lamb & pearl onion casserole 54
Thick Scotch broth 28
Three-fruit crumble 296
Tiger prawn & asparagus risotto 201
Tiger prawn risotto with pesto 201
Toad in the hole 90
Tofu & green vegetable curry 246
Tomato & aubergine layers 259
Tomato & aubergine layers with
    basil 259
Tomato & potato tortilla 252
Tomato broth with angel hair pasta 49
Tomato broth with rose harissa 49
Tomato soup 49
Tortellini in broth 229
Traditional cannelloni 226
Traditional cannelloni with
    chicken 226
Traditional Greek baked fish 168
Triple cheese macaroni 235
Truffle risotto 216
Tuna & noodle casserole 152
Tuna & noodle casserole with
    beans 152
Tuna & noodle casserole with
    celery 152
Turkey & cabbage stir-fry 146
Turkey & lentil soup 32
Turkey & pasta bake 225
Turkey, broccoli & pak choi
    stir-fry 146
Turkey in a piquant sauce 138
Turkey, leek & cheese gratin 83
Turkey risotto with Marsala 195
    With extra stock 195
Turkey with bamboo shoots &
    carrot 146
Turkey with bamboo shoots & water
    chestnuts 146
Tuscan bean stew 274
Tuscan bean stew with pasta 274
Tuscan chicken 86
Tuscan chicken with red peppers 86
U
Upside down toffee apple brownies 294
    Upside down toffee pear brownies
    294

V
Vegetable & lentil casserole 262
Vegetable & noodle soup 48
Vegetable chilli 274
Vegetable chilli with taco shells 274
Vegetable curry 245
Vegetable curry with swede &
    broccoli 245
Vegetable fajitas 282
Vegetable fajitas with courgette 282
Vegetable goulash 273
Vegetable goulash with courgettes 273
Vegetable hotpot with parsley
    dumplings 275
Vegetable hotpot with parsnip
    mash 275
Vegetable hotpot with puff pastry 275
Vegetable jambalaya 276
Vegetable lasagne 222
    With mascarpone & spinach
    topping 222
Vegetable ravioli 230
Vegetable ravioli with mushrooms 230
Vegetable stew with coriander
    pesto 276
Vegetable stew with green lentils 275
Vegetable stew with pesto 276
Vegetarian baked tomato rice 204
Vegetarian mulligatawny soup 36
Vegetarian paella 216
Vegetarian paella with courgettes 216
Venetian seafood risotto 202
Venetian seafood risotto with
    sherry 202
Venison & mushroom casserole 67
Venison casserole 67
Vietnamese vegetable curry 247
Vietnamese curry with coconut
    milk 247
W
Walnut & ricotta rigatoni 220
Warm vegetable medley 277
Warm vegetable medley with
    cheese 277
Watercress soup 51
White bean soup with olive
    tapenade 47
White bean soup with red pepper
    pesto 47
Whole chicken & mushroom soup 18
Whole chicken soup 18
Wild mushroom bruschetta 260
Wild mushroom risotto 217
Winter rice pudding with apricots 299
Winter rice pudding with dried
    fruits 299
Wok-fried jumbo prawns in a spicy
    sauce 180
Wonton soup 33
X
Xinjiang lamb casserole 58
Xinjiang lamb with lemon grass 58